# In The Shadow of
# the Enlightenment

The Publication of this work has been aided by a grant
from the Andrew W. Mellon Foundation

# In the Shadow of
# the Enlightenment

*Occultism and Renaissance Science in
Eighteenth-Century America*

HERBERT  LEVENTHAL

New York: New York University Press  •  1976

Permission to quote from the Diaries Miscellaneous Collection of Yale University Library has been granted for passages from Peter Pratt, *Diary;* John Tyler, *Book of Forensic Disputes,* Daniel N. Brinsmade, *Book of Disputes.*

Permission to quote from the Beinecke Rare Book and Manuscript Library of Yale University Library has been granted for excerpts from Manasseh Cutler, *Common-Place Book;* Ezra Stiles, *Literary Diary;* Peter Oliver letter to Jared Eliot; illustration for Ezra Stiles, *Literary Diary,* "The Universe or Intellectual World."

Permission to quote from the collection of the Queens Public Library has been granted for passages from Nathaniel Dominy, *Commonplace Book.*

Permission to quote from letters in the possession of the American Philosophical Society has been granted for passages from that of John Bastram to Peter Collison; Joseph Breintnall to Peter Collison; Christopher Witt to Peter Collison.

Permission to quote from the collection of the Historical Society of Pennsylvania has been granted for passages from John Paschall, *Commonplace Book;* Ebenezer Kinnersley, *A Course of Experiments on the Newly Discover'd Electrical Fire;* Joseph Black, "Lectures on Chemistry," MS notes by C. Dilloyes.

Permission to quote from the library of the College of Physicians of Philadelphia has been granted for passages from Benjamin Rush, *A Course of Lectures on the Theory and Practice of Chemistry;* William Shippen, *Anatomical Lectures.*

Permission to quote from the collection of the Massachusetts Historical Society has been granted for passages from Henry Flynt, *Common Place Book.*

Permission to quote from the collection of the Harvard University Archives has been granted for passages from J. Varney, *Manuscript Exercises.*

Permission to quote from the collection of the Houghton Library of Harvard University has been granted for passages from William Gerard De Brahm, *Survey of East Florida, Carolina, Georgia, & c.*

Permission to quote from the collection of the N.Y. Westchester Co.—Witchcraft, Manuscripts and Archives Division, The New York Public Library, Astor, Lenox and Tilden Foundations, has been granted for passages from William Hooker Smith, manuscript material.

Permission to excerpt from the Rare Book Division, the New York Public Library, Astor, Lenox and Tilden Foundations, is granted for the illustration "The Anatomy of Man's Body as governed by the 121 Constellations," from John Tobler, *Pennsilvania Town and Country-Man's Almanac . . . 1764.*

*Library of Congress Cataloging in Publication Data*

Leventhal, Herbert, 1941-

Bibliography: p.
1.  Occult sciences—United States.  2.  United
States—Intellectual life—18th century.  I.  Title.
BF1434.U6L38          133'.0973          75–13762
ISBN 0-8147-4965-8

Manufactured in the United States of America

*To my parents*

# ACKNOWLEDGMENTS

I wish to thank Professor Robert A. East for his advice and criticism throughout the research and writing of this work. I wish to thank Professor Brooke Hindle for his recommendations concerning the structure and scope of this study, and I also wish to thank professors Hans Trefousse, Harold C. Syrett, and Helene Zahler for their reading and corrections of an earlier version of this text. Of course, any remaining errors are my responsibility. I also gratefully acknowledge the financial support given me by the National Society of Colonial Dames.

I of course owe a debt of gratitude to all the libraries where I have worked, but special mention must be made of the Graduate Center Library of the City University of New York, especially for my use of their interlibrary loan facilities, and of the Rare Book Room of the New York Public Library, whose personnel brought me innumerable microcards of Early American imprints.

# CONTENTS

# 1

## Introduction

*Historians, like journalists, are apt to concentrate on news and to forget that there is a complex and broad situation which remained unaffected by the events of the moment.*

—Paul Oskar Kristeller, *Renaissance Thought*

### I

The tendency to ignore the continuation of the old in the development of the new is as much of a problem for the history of eighteenth-century America as it is for the history of the Renaissance. We tend to concentrate on the adoption of Enlightenment thought and the ideas of modern science, emphasizing only Newtonian physics, Linnaean natural history, and Lockian psychology. There is an almost total neglect of the continuation of ideas and concepts first articulated centuries earlier. Such neglect is sometimes apparently not so much the result of ignorance as of the exigencies of writing history. A scholar has recently noted that in both the Old World and the New, learned men "subscribed in varying degrees to many fundamental scientific notions which had been widely accepted since ancient times"; yet most works dealing with the thought of the eighteenth century pay little attention to old ideas still current in the period.[1]

This work is a study of such ideas. It examines those aspects of

1. Raymond Phineas Stearns, *Science in the British Colonies of America* (Urbana, Ill.: University of Illinois Press, 1970), p. 7.

eighteenth-century colonial thought which were not new, not the product of the Enlightenment, but rather, continuations of what E. M. W. Tillyard has called "the Elizabethan world picture." [2] This is a study in the continuity of Renaissance, sometimes even of Scholastic, thought in Enlightenment America.

The subject matter of this work is determined by two factors. The first is the Renaissance view of the nature of the universe, particularly its physical and occult characteristics. The second is a gap in our own understanding of eighteenth-century colonial thought. This gap, large but rather clearly defined, includes those aspects of the colonial inheritance from the Renaissance which are not seen as "Enlightened," and which were not to be incorporated into modern science. Thus the continuing influence into the eighteenth century (and, in some instances, even beyond) of such once respected beliefs as the "four elements," the "four humors," astrology, witchcraft, and alchemy have been too largely ignored. This is particularly apparent in the treatment of the old concept of the "chain of being." Although largely shorn of its one-time political and occult implications, it remained an important factor in both popular and scientific thought in the eighteenth century. This concept is well known to literary and cultural historians of the period, if only through the popularity of Alexander Pope's *Essay on Man;* yet studies of eighteenth-century colonial thought pay little attention to it.

Such a study, Janus-like, faces two ways. On the one hand, it illuminates otherwise neglected but nevertheless important areas of eighteenth-century thought. For example, it shows how new theories in medicine and chemistry were influenced by the continued existence of the hoary doctrines of the four elements and the four humors.

On the other hand, this study also looks back to the seventeenth century. What had happened to the Elizabethan world picture so prevalent then? Had it simply been erased around the turn of the century? Of course not. Some of it was to remain unabated, continuing to play a role in the thought of the new era—an important fact often missed by studies which concentrate too strongly upon only the development of the new. The various component parts of the Elizabethan world picture separated in the eighteenth century, each suffering different fates and having

2. E[ustace] M[andeville] W[entenhall] Tillyard, *The Elizabethan World Picture* (New York: Random House, n.d.).

different histories. The Ptolemaic universe had already died; astrology and witchcraft continued, although with a lower status; but the concept of chain-of-being and the element fire continued with perhaps as much significance and influence as they had ever had before. The persistence and influence of such old Renaissance concepts is a major aspect of this study.

## II

What is the time period of this work? It is difficult, not to say undesirable, to attempt to place any study of ideas into a strict chronological straitjacket, but our primary focus will be on the period from 1714 through the American Revolution. The date 1714 is a traditional starting point for any study of eighteenth-century America. The end of the first series of wars with France marked by the Treaty of Utrecht, the arrival at Yale of the so-called New Learning in the form of Jeremiah Dummer's gift of books, and perhaps also the succession of the Hanoverian dynasty have all combined to make 1714 a convenient date.[3] The arrival of the New Learning at Yale was, of course, the most significant of these events for our purposes.

The American Revolution is the obvious terminal date, and has the advantage of avoiding the subsequent impact both of the chemical revolution of Priestley and Lavoisier and also the impact of later Romanticism upon scientific and philosophical thought.

No date can be strictly adhered to, however. Earlier material will be found to be indispensable in explaining and illustrating concepts which survived, sometimes only in fragmentary form, into the eighteenth century. A number of earlier works, such as the science textbook used at Harvard, Morton's *Compendium Physicae,* are necessary where it can be

3. See Charles M. Andrews, *Colonial Folkways* (New Haven: Yale University Press, 1919), p. 3; James Truslow Adams, *Provincial Society, 1690-1763* (New York: The Macmillan Co., 1927), chaps. V and VI, p. 258; Edmund S. Morgan, "Ezra Stiles: The Education of a Yale Man, 1742-1746," *Huntington Library Quarterly,* XVII (May 1954): 268; Wesley Frank Craven, *The Colonies in Transition, 1660-1713* (New York: Harper & Row, 1968), p. 286; Henry F. May, "The Problem of the American Enlightenment," *New Literary History,* I (Winter 1970): 209; Edmund S. Morgan, *The Gentle Puritan: A Life of Ezra Stiles, 1727-1795* (New Haven: Yale University Press, 1962), p. 56.

proved that they remained influential after 1714.[4] Even works from the *post*-Revolutionary period must sometimes be used if they clearly illustrate themes and concepts developed *before* the Revolution.

Serious questions can be raised about the terms "Enlightenment" and "Renaissance." One distinguished authority has spoken of the American Enlightenment as consisting of the half-century from 1765 to 1815, but has modified this position by stating that the first waves of the Enlightenment had reached the colonies early in the eighteenth century.[5] Another authority has similarly spoken of the "efflorescence" of the American Enlightenment as occurring in the 1760s, presumably after it had already established itself in the colonies.[6] A fuller chronology (which I find most useful) has been offered by still another scholar, who distinguished three phases of the American Enlightenment. The first, from 1714 through the Revolution, witnessed the spread of the moderate English Enlightenment through the colonies. The second phase, from 1784 to 1800, saw the impact of the more radical French Enlightenment and the resulting counterattack from conservative elements in America. The third phase, 1800-15, saw the subsequent defeat of the Enlightenment, along, however, with the absorption into the general culture of many of its ideas.[7]

One reason for arguing that the period of the American Revolution was *the* period of the American Enlightenment is the great emphasis often placed upon its political aspects. The disputes between the colonies and Great Britain, and then between the Americans themselves, concerning the role and structure of government are sometimes seen as the true flowering of the American Enlightenment. This is too narrow a view. It is quite clear that the reception, spread, and acceptance of the Enlightenment in its broadest sense occurred earlier in America, and is in fact the same as the period being discussed here.

Another problem concerns the propriety of using the term "Enlightenment" when discussing eighteenth-century scientific thought.

4. Charles Morton, *Compendium Physicae. Collections of the Publications of the Colonial Society of Massachusetts,* XXXIII (1940).

5. Adrienne Koch, *The American Enlightenment: The Shaping of the American Experiment and a Free Society* (New York: George Braziller, 1965), pp. 19, 38-39.

6. Peter Gay, *The Science of Freedom,* Vol. II of *The Enlightenment: An Interpretation* (New York: Alfred A. Knopf, 1969), p. 558.

7. May, "The Problem of the American Enlightenment," pp. 201-14.

It is true that the *philosophes* were usually men of letters or of politics, the latter especially in America. Yet *philosophes* were everywhere deeply interested in the development of science, and considered the Enlightenment to be, at least in part, the replacement of medieval Scholasticism and superstition by "modern" science and scientific method.

What is meant by the term "Renaissance"? I have no intention of entering into the dispute over the nature of the Renaissance, and the related question as to whether or not there really was a Renaissance. I am merely using the term to denote beliefs about nature and the universe which had become current in late sixteenth- and early seventeenth-century England. These were the beliefs of Elizabethan England, well studied because they are the intellectual background for Shakespeare and the other Elizabethan playwrights, not to mention later writers such as Milton and the metaphysical poets. Such Elizabethan beliefs were the common beliefs of the first settlers in America, as Moses Coit Tyler long ago observed.

Many Elizabethan beliefs were more than a product of Renaissance teaching. Many had been developed in the medieval period, or even earlier. I am not, however, interested in a genetic history of such ideas. For our purposes, for the purposes of studying colonial culture, it suffices to say that the doctrine of astrology, for example, entered colonial thought simply as part of its general heritage from Elizabethan England. There is no need here for a detailed study of the origins and transmission of astrology from ancient Mesopotamia.

The seventeenth century, of course, contained much more than the continuation of Renaissance thought. It was also the century of Descartes, Newton, and Locke. It was the century when England accepted the Copernican universe. It was a creative century in its own right, much of it to be of great importance in the years to follow, and much to serve as the basis of the subsequent Enlightenment. I am not, however, interested in this creative aspect of the seventeenth century, and will deal with it only as it comes into conflict with aspects of America's Renaissance heritage.

### III

What was the Elizabethan world picture? Before discussing the survivals of the "old science" in Enlightenment America, it is necessary to have at least a summary knowledge of its contents.

The physical substance of terrestrial matter was held to consist of the four elements and their constituent qualities. They were fire, which was hot and dry; air, which was hot and moist; water, which was cold and moist; and earth, which was cold and dry. All matter on earth consisted of these four elements in varying proportions. Each element had its proper place in our sublunary sphere. Earth was the grossest element and therefore sought the lowest level, while fire was the purest and therefore sought the highest. Water and air ranged between. There was no such thing as a "force of gravity." There was merely the natural tendency of gross matter containing the element earth to seek its proper level at the bottom of things.

Earthly matter was not held to be representative of the entire universe, for the universe was still Ptolemaic, composed of the immutable fifth element, or quintessence. The sun and planets rotated about the earth in complex but predictable patterns, each on its own crystalline sphere. Closest to the earth was the moon, then came Mercury, Venus, the sun, Mars, Jupiter, and Saturn. After Saturn came the sphere of the fixed stars, the *stellatum*, and beyond that the final sphere, the *primum mobile*, which transmitted motion to all the other spheres.

Throughout the Renaissance, astrology had been extremely popular, although its limits were in dispute. Astrology was generally held to determine general events in the natural world—the weather or the general state of health in a region. This form of astrology, known as natural astrology, had no substantial opposition in the early seventeenth century. Many persons, however, also believed in what was known as judicial astrology. They held that heavenly bodies controlled the actions and decisions of individuals. This had met with strong opposition, however, threatening, as it did, both man's free will and the providence of God.

Despite a dispute over whether man could be influenced by the stars, there was no disputing the fact that he was influenced by his physical makeup. Most important were the four humors. The humors, analogous to the four elements, were themselves composed of the four qualities: choler, or yellow bile, was hot and dry; blood was hot and moist; melancholy, or black bile, was cold and dry; and phlegm was cold and moist.

Just as no substance on earth was composed of only one element, so no man was of only one humor. In traditional Renaissance theory, each humor was necessary for the proper functioning of the human body. Blood nourished and strengthened the entiry body; phlegm acted as a lubricant for its moving parts; choler helped maintain the body's heat and was needed for the proper functioning of the senses; and melancholy helped control the two hot humors, blood and choler, "preserving them in the blood, and nourishing the bones." [8] The most common cause of disease in medieval and Renaissance medical theory had been a disorder of these necessary fluids—either their corruption or an imbalance among them. The appropriate treatment for such illnesses thus required the elimination of the corrupt or excess humor. Bleeding, blistering, and purging were among the most common medical treatments. Each had been a means of restoring the proper balance among the humors, so as to restore the body to its proper health.

Even in healthy people, according to this venerable theory, there were a number of possible combinations of humors, and for each person a dominant humor was thought to determine temperament and personality. A person whose predominant humor was blood would be sanguine: ruddy in coloration, cheerful, and happy.

> Of such as to the sanguine are inclined,
> They're liberal, pleasant, kind, and courteous
> And like the liver all benignious
> For arts and sciences they are the fittest;
> And maugre Choler still they are the wittiest:
> With an ingenious working phantasy,
> A most voluminous large memory,
> And nothing wanting but solidity. [9]

So, too, a predominance of choler would result in an "angry choleric" temperament, phlegm in the "dull phlegmatic" temperament, and melancholy in the often morose and "neurotic melancholy" temperament.

Man had not only a material body, but also an immortal or rational soul. The Renaissance distinguished among three types of souls. The *vegetative soul* was found in plants and controlled the faculties of nutrition, growth,

8. Robert Burton, *The Anatomy of Melancholy*, pt. 1, sec. 1, memb. 2, subs. 2.

9. Anne Bradstreet, "Of the Four Humours in Man's Constitution," *The Works of Anne Bradstreet*, ed. by Jeannine Hensley (Cambridge: Harvard University Press, 1967), 11: 336-43. Unless otherwise noted, future citations of Bradstreet's poems are to this edition.

and propagation. The *sensitive soul* was found in beasts and included all the powers of the vegetative soul as well as the powers of sensation and motion. The *rational soul,* found only in men among mortal beings, contained all the powers of the other two as well as those of reason and intellect.

Linking the elemental body and the immaterial soul were the spirits. These were tenuous, barely material substances which served a number of critical functions. The natural spirits, which were generated in the liver from the blood, flowed through the veins carrying out the vegetative functions of life and growth. In the heart, some of these were transformed into the vital spirits which traveled in the arteries and maintained the body's heat. In the head, some of these in turn were themselves transformed into animal spirits. These linked body to soul, and traveling through the nerves carried the impulses of the rational soul to the material body.

> As our blood labours to beget
>   Spirits, as like soules as it can,
> Because such fingers need to knit
>   That subtile knot, which makes us man: . . .[10]

This Renaissance universe was bound and knitted together by various means, and ordered by the concept of the chain of being. God, by the very nature of His being, of His goodness, had created the universe as full of beings as possible. Everything that could be created was created, and there were no unfilled gaps or intervals in the chain of being. Moreover, all creation was ordered in a hierarchy, or, more accurately, a series of hierarchies, which ranked the entire universe. They ranged from inanimate objects to plants, animals, man, and above man the celestial hierarchy.[11]

Associated with the concept of the chain of being in the Renaissance,

10. John Donne, "The Extasie," ll: 61-64.

11. The classical work on this subject is Arthur O. Lovejoy, *The Great Chain of Being: A Study of the History of an Idea* (New York: Harper & Row, 1960). For its political implications see W. H. Greenleaf, *Order, Empiricism and Politics: Two Traditions of English Political Thought, 1500-1700* (New York: Published for the University of Hull by the Oxford University Press, 1964).

although not necessarily an essential component of it, was a complicated interlocking web of correspondences and relationships. There were special relationships, and often occult influences, between different but corresponding levels of the chain of being. The planets had rulership over specific humors and metals. Kings, the rulers of men, corresponded to lions, the rulers of the beasts, and the entire hierarchical society of man corresponded to the entire hierarchical universe. This interrelationship is well illustrated by some of the poems of Anne Bradstreet, the seventeenth-century American Puritan poetess, which linked corresponding elements, humors, seasons, and ages of man.

> When Spring had done, the Summer did begin,
> With melted tawny face, and garments thin,
> Resembling Fire, Choler, and Middle Age,
> As Spring did Air, Blood, and Youth in's equipage.[12]

## IV

As already indicated, this study is divided into two main parts. The first is concerned with the influence of Renaissance occultism in eighteenth-century America. Individual chapters treat of astrology, witchcraft, and alchemy. The final chapter on occultism discusses rattlesnake fascination, a belief that developed in the late seventeenth and the eighteenth centuries rather than in the Renaissance proper, but whose roots included important elements of Renaissance occultism as well as of American Indian mythology. Rattlesnake fascination is perhaps best understood as an occult belief which was at least partly "naturalized" by eighteenth-century natural historians.

Part Two of the study is concerned with the influence of "obsolete" sciences in eighteenth-century America. It has individual chapters on the "old heavens," including the Ptolemaic system and pre-Newtonian gravity, as well as a discussion of eighteenth-century alternatives to Newton

---

12. Bradstreet, "The Four Seasons of the Year," ll: 89-92. Two of the best discussions of the Renaissance world view can be found in Tillyard, *The Elizabethan World Picture* and C. S. Lewis, *The Discarded Image: An Introduction to Medieval and Renaissance Literature* (Cambridge: Cambridge University Press, 1964).

(including Hutchinsonianism); on the "old earth," including the four elements, the four humors, and the three spirits; and on the concept of the chain of being, with the discussion ranging all the way from growing minerals to Ezra Stiles's analysis of the angelic hierarchy.

Such separate treatment of the science of the heavens and the science of the earth is in accord with Renaissance (indeed, even Aristotelian) beliefs, which long held that the celestial and the earthly spheres not only were composed of different substances but were subject to different laws. The distinction between the occult and the scientific, on the other hand, is more in accord with eighteenth-century (and modern) viewpoints than with that of the Renaissance. In the European and English Renaissance, and even in the latter half of the seventeenth century, occultism and science were not yet necessarily separate and distinct. Joseph Glanvill could be a member of the Royal Society even while studying and defending the reality of witchcraft; Sir Isaac Newton could devote much of his time and energy to the mysteries of alchemy; the evil eye could have a scientific explanation; astrology and astral magic could influence both kings and popes; Giordano Bruno could promulgate Copernican ideas along with a belief in Hermetism; and well-educated physicians were prepared to cast horoscopes.

Those things were no longer true in the eighteenth century. Despite the presence of such men as Christopher Witt (who was both a Renaissance magus and an Enlightenment natural historian) and William Gerard De Brahm (who was not only an able surveyor, geographer, and cartographer, but also an alchemist), the occult and the natural had come to be seen as separate and distinct.[13]

13. Science and theology, however, were not unrelated topics for most Americans even in the eighteenth century. See George Edwards Bates, "The Emergence of a Modern Mind in Colonial America, 1700-1760" (unpublished Ph.D. dissertation, University of Illinois at Urbana-Champaign, 1970). For more about Witt and De Brahm see especially chapts. 3 and 4 below.

Part One

The Occult World

# 2

## Astrology

*You Starry Choristers at Boe peep Play,*
*When in your Chrystall socket down do dart*
*Your Influence on my Cask of clay.*
                              —Edward Taylor, *Valedictory Poems,* 1720s

## I

Astrology, the oldest of the Renaissance "sciences," retained considerable vitality in eighteenth-century America. During the Renaissance it had been almost universally accepted as a true and useful science. Virtually everyone believed that the planets influenced events on earth. Kings and popes consulted astrologers while learned scholars accepted the science's validity. Literary figures used astrological concepts and, on a lower level, almanacs full of prognostications catered to the lower classes, "the superstitious and the untutored." [1] Astrology was also an integral part of Renaissance medicine. It was used in diagnosing diseases, determining treatments, and making prognoses. Medicinal herbs often had specific astrological relationships, and there were elaborate astrological rules governing the use of some of the most common curative procedures such as purging, blistering, and bleeding.

There was opposition to astrology even at that time, but this opposition was mainly directed at astrology's excesses. Much of the dispute centered

1. Don Cameron Allen, *The Star-Crossed Renaissance: The Quarrel about Astrology and Its Influence in England* (New York: Octagon Books, Inc., 1966), p. 190.

upon the distinction between "natural" and "judicial" astrology. Natural astrology dealt with the influences of the planets and signs of the zodiac on material objects: the elements, the weather, the human body. Judicial astrology, on the other hand, dealt with their influences on the human will and on events which were contingent upon individual decisions and actions. It was judicial astrology which had been so often attacked; and its extreme position, that the planets fully determined the actions of individuals, had been largely abandoned in Renaissance England. [2]

Although it has been argued that belief in astrology had died out among the educated in the seventeenth century,[3] the American colonists were still being exposed to astrology in their early eighteenth-century formal education. In early eighteenth-century Harvard this exposure came from Charles Morton's *Compendium Physicae*. Morton had been educated at Wadham College, Oxford, during the English Civil War, when it was both a Puritan stronghold and a center of experimental science. After spending some time as a Presbyterian minister, Morton had opened a dissenting academy, Newington Green, which was considered to be one of the best in England (its most famous student was Daniel Defoe). Faced with Anglican harassment, Morton left England in

2. A good overall history of astrology can be found in Mark Graubard, *Astrology and Alchemy: Two Fossil Sciences* (New York: Philosophical Library, 1953). A detailed study of Renaissance astrology, with an emphasis on Elizabethan and Jacobean England is Allen, *The Star-Crossed Renaissance*. However, its first chapter dealing with Marsilio Ficino and Pico della Mirandola should be compared with Frances A. Yates, *Giordano Bruno and the Hermetic Tradition* (Chicago: University of Chicago Press, 1964). For the dispute over astrology see Paul H. Kocher, *Science and Religion in Elizabethan England* (New York: Octagon Books, 1969). Also useful are the appropriate sections in Tillyard, *The Elizabethan World Picture*, and C. S. Lewis, *The Discarded Image*.

The role of astrology in medicine is discussed in W. S. C. Copeman, *Doctors and Disease in Tudor Time* (London: Dawson's of Pall Mall, 1960); Carroll Camden, Jr., "Elizbethan Astrological Medicine," *Annals of Medical History*, n.s., II (March 1930): 217-26; and Charles Arthur Mercier, *Astrology in Medicine* (London: Macmillan & Co., Limited, 1914). I have also drawn upon *The Kalendar & Compost of Shepherds*, ed. by G. C. Haseltine (London: Peter Davies, 1931) and the various works of Nicholas Culpeper discussed in more detail below.

3. Graubard, *Astrology and Alchemy*, p. 231. See also Mark Graubard, "Astrology's Demise and Its Bearing on the Decline and Death of Beliefs," *Osiris*, XIII (1958): 210-61 and Mercier, *Astrology in Medicine*, pp. 2-3.

1686 and became a minister in Charlestown, Massachusetts. On leaving England he had taken with him his manuscript science text. This, the *Compendium Physicae,* was quickly adopted by Harvard, giving it an up-to-date science curriculum which only gradually became obsolete, and which apparently was not replaced until the late 1720s.[4]

Morton made the traditional distinction between natural and judicial astrology. He attempted to explain how the planetary aspects controlled the weather, although he noted that more study was needed to make astrological weather-predicting accurate. He accepted the influences of the planets on the human body and even went so far as to accept their indirect influences on the human mind. He therefore approvingly quoted from Robert Burton's *Anatomy of Melancholy,* "Thus much I find / Sick bodies bread Sick passions in the mind." However, he attacked fortune-telling as being either a fraud, or, far worse, trafficking with the devil. His considered judgment of astrology was:

> On the Whole matter I judge, that as to weathers, and temperatures of our bodyes with relations to health or Sickness by Good observations of prudent, and Philosophycal minds, a Usefull knowledge might be framed; but for all the rest that is pretended the books written about them might make a curious bonfire according to the primitive pattern *(Acts.* [19.] 19.) . . . .

> Nativities horary Quest[ion]s are Evill
> Stars ruling [countries] are all from the Divill [5]

The 1720s versions of the *Compendium,* by sharply abridging the discussion of astrology, were more ambiguous. They repeated Morton's com-

---

4. Morton, *Compendium Physicae,* pp. vii-xxix. This modern printed edition was taken primarily from a 1697 manuscript copy. I have, however, checked it against three manuscript copies made by students in the 1720s, and found them similar in substance although somewhat abbreviated. See Marston Cabot, "Commonplace Book (1723-1724)," MS, Harvard University Archives; J. Varney, "Manuscript Exercises, 1722-23," MS, Harvard University Archives; and [Charles] Morton, "Morton's Physics," MS, ca. 1729, Houghton Library, Harvard University.

5. Morton, *Compendium Physicae,* pp. 27-30.

ments on the planets having a direct influence on man's body and an
indirect one on his mind and then repeated his preliminary conclusion that
astrology "for want of Sufficient Observations, to make Rational Induc-
tions, Is very Imperfect & Uncertain in its rules." [6] This conclusion casts
doubt upon the validity of any prediction but not upon the basic assumptions of astrology and, by omitting Morton's sharp attack on judicial
astrology, remains ambiguous about it. There is, however, no reason to
assume that the earlier opposition to it had altered in any way. The
abridged text was simply inferior in clarity to its seventeenth-century
original.

Additional exposure to astrological concepts may well have reached
Harvard students of this period from two of the school's chief officials,
Samuel Willard and John Leverett. Willard, who graduated from Har-
vard in 1659, served as its vice president from 1701 to 1707 (during
which period Harvard had no president). After his death in 1707, his
sermons were collected and eventually published in 1726 as *A Compleat
Body of Divinity*. In this massive work, recently described as the *summa* of
New England theology,[7] astrology was discussed in passing. A biblical
passage often cited by supporters of astrology was Genesis 1:14: "And
God said, Let there be lights in the firmament of the heaven to divide the
day from the night; and let them be for signs, and for seasons, and for
days, and years: . . ." Willard's exegesis of this passage argued: "To be
for *Signs & Seasons, Days & Years:* For *Signs,* Prognosticating several
Natural Effects, likely to ensue. *Seasons* i.e. several Times of the Year,
made by the Motion of the Sun especially, . . ." [8]

Thus on the one hand, Willard distinguished the signs from judicial
astrology by limiting them to "natural effects," and on the other hand, he
distinguished them from mere timekeepers by giving that function to
other terms in the passage. Thus he accepted far more of the astrological
interpretation of this verse than had Calvin, who stated the signs were
only of seasons, months, years, and olympiads, or than had the Geneva

6. Varney, "Manuscript Exercises," chap. 4. They did, however, repeat
Morton's attack upon divination from comets. Morton, *Compendium Physicae,*
p. 93.

7. Perry Miller, *The New England Mind: From Colony to Province* (Boston:
Beacon Press, 1961), pp. 30, 213-14.

8. Samuel Willard, *A Compleat Body of Divinity* (Boston: B. Green and S.
Kneeland, 1726), p. 119.

Bible, which apparently followed Calvin in its marginalia on this verse, "Of things appertaining to naturall and political orders and seasons." [9]

In addition, while speaking of secondary causes, Willard explained that "The *Husbandman* must first Manure his Ground, and then cast in the Seed, the *Heavens* must then Distill their Showers, and assist with their Influences; . . ." [10] As we shall see, heavenly influences on plants included much more than rain and sunshine. Earlier, speaking of the possibility of predicting events without divine aid, Willard noted that *"Astrologers* have had their Predictions, that do sometimes fall out right," although he ominously coupled this with the fact that Satan, "who is a great Naturallist," can fortell many things. [11] These statements did not indicate a great interest in astrology (if anything, their casualness indicates the opposite), nor even approval of it, although the interpretation of Genesis 1:14 gave it a divine warrant; but they do indicate acceptance of astrology as something real and possible.

Willard was succeeded by John Leverett. Leverett was a Harvard graduate of the class of 1680, a tutor at Harvard from 1685 to 1697, Harvard's president from 1708 to 1724, a Fellow of the Royal Society, and a religious "liberal" bitterly opposed by Increase and Cotton Mather. In one of his "Expositions of Scripture" to the Harvard students, Leverett explained that God had told Noah that the flood would be caused by His supernatural providence and "not by any famous conjunction or conspiration of the Stars, or by any natural means." [12] What he was probably alluding to is stated more clearly in Cotton Mather's warning against the belief "that if there were a *Conjunction of all the Planets* in *Pisces*, it would portend that the World should be *Drowned.*" [13] While

9. John Calvin, *Commentaries on the First Book of Moses Called Genesis* (Grand Rapids, Mich.: Wm. B. Eerdmans Publishing Company, n.d.), I: 84-85.

10. Willard, *A Compleat Body of Divinity*, p. 137.

11. *Ibid.*, p. 17.

12. Arthur Daniel Kaledin, "The Mind of John Leverett" (unpublished Ph.D dissertation, Harvard University, 1965), pp. 44-45; John Leverett, "President Leverett's Exposition of Scripture, 1708-1724," MSS, Harvard University Archives, bk. 18, p. 6r.

13. Cotton Mather, *Manuductio Ad Ministerium: Directions for a Candidate of the Ministry* (New York: Columbia University Press for Facsimile Text Society, 1938), p. 54. See Kocher, *Science and Religion in Elizabethan England*, pp. 221-22; Raleigh, *History of the World*, in *The Works of Sir Walter Raleigh* [sic] *Kt.* (New York: Burt Franklin, n.d.), II: 202-3.

Mather denied the belief, Willard merely denied that it caused Noah's flood and appeared to link it with "any natural means" as a reasonable explanation for a flood.

In 1728 Morton's *Compendium Physicae*, by now obsolete, was abandoned with the arrival of Isaac Greenwood, Harvard's first Hollis Professor of Mathematics and Natural Philosophy. Isaac Greenwood was a Harvard graduate who had gone to London to study science. There he had convinced the English Baptist Thomas Hollis to endow Harvard with money for this chair. Although there were doubts about Greenwood's moral character, he had left London £300 in debt, Harvard quickly selected him when faced with the horrible possibility that Hollis might select a fellow Baptist for the chair. Greenwood was a success as a teacher and popularizer of science, and he published a number of papers in the *Philosophical Transactions* of the Royal Society and elsewhere, but in 1738, after repeated warnings, he was discharged for drunkenness.[14]

It seems likely that during his tenure students at Harvard were still exposed to some of the basic concepts of astrology. In 1731, in his *Philosophical Discourse concerning the Mutability and Changes of the Natural World,* Greenwood noted:

> In short, Tides are produced in the Ocean, Winds in the Atmosphere, many Changes in Inanimate and Animate Bodies, and in the Humane OEconomy itself. *Astrology* seems to have a Philosophical Foundation, and we know not how may Wonders & Mysteries may be the Genuine Effects of this great *Alterative in Nature.*[15]

He too opposed judicial astrology, and in a series of lectures on the mechanical philosophy included "A General Conclusion, concerning *Judicial Astrology;* wherein is shown, how contrary the *Principles* of that pretended *Science* are, to the Establish'd *Laws of Nature,* and how vain and absurd all such *Conclusions,* and *Calculations* are, that are made from them."[16] It should be noted that an attack on judicial astrology, by the

14. Samuel Eliot Morison, *Three Centuries of Harvard, 1636-1936* (Cambridge: Harvard University Press, 1936), pp. 79-81.

15. Isaac Greenwood, *A Philosophical Discourse Concerning the Mutability and Changes of the Material World;* . . . (Boston: S. Gerrich, 1731), p. 5.

16. Isaac Greenwood, *An Experimental Course of Mechanical Philosophy* (Boston, 1726), p. 9.

very act of specifying *judicial,* often implies a distinction between it and the valid and licit *natural* astrology.

Indeed, even as late as 1762 the basic belief of astrology, that the planets can influence events on earth, was upheld in a Harvard master's thesis [17] which answered in the affirmative the question: "Do the heavenly bodies produce certain changes in the bodies of animals?" [18]

If one can accept a 1699 student oration at face value, the College of William and Mary, as yet no more than a grammer school, had high hopes for its astrological studies. "Methinks we see already that happy time when we shall surpass the Asiaticans in civility, the Jews in religion, the Greeks in philosophy, the Egyptians in geometry, the Phoenicians in arithmetic, and Chaldeans in astrology. O happy Virginia!" [19]

With somewhat greater assurance we can observe that students at Yale were also exposed to astrology. Our best source of information for what was being taught at Yale in the second decade of the eighteenth century is Samuel Johnson, who graduated from Yale in 1714 and was a tutor there for several years. He became a Congregationalist minister, but in 1722 he was one of a group of Yale men who shocked New England by proclaiming doubts about the validity of Congregational ordination and then

17. It should be noted that both the master's thesis and the thesis of the graduating class were public statements of belief which the students, at least in theory, were committed to uphold if challenged. A thesis may not necessarily be the "official" position of the school but it is certainly one which the candidates or graduates believe they can uphold and which is at least acceptable to the school. Thus its value as evidence is very different from that of classroom disputations in which students were given both sides of an issue or proposition to defend as an exercise in logic and argumentation. In such disputations students found themselves arguing for propositions which neither they nor anyone else at school believed in or even found acceptable. Such disputations can be a useful source of information, especially of arguments and analogies used, and at times the tutor's decision as to the "correct" position is recorded but, nevertheless, such disputations must be treated much more gingerly than the relatively straightforward thesis.

18. Edward J. Young, "Subjects for Master's Degree in Harvard College from 1655-1791," *Proceedings of the Massachusetts Historical Society,* XVIII (June 1880): 131. (Hereinafter referred to as "Master's Degree in Harvard College.")

19. Louis B. Wright, *The First Gentlemen of Virginia: Intellectual Qualities of the Early Colonial Ruling Class* (San Marino, Calif.: The Huntington Library, 1940), p. 109.

by going to England to be ordained as an Anglican minister. After a long career as one of the foremost Anglicans in New England, Johnson became president of King's College (later to become Columbia University). He is a significant figure in colonial intellectual history not only for his Anglican polemics and presidency of King's College but also as the foremost disciple of the English idealist philosopher George Berkeley. His support for Berkeley and also his acceptance of the anti-Newtonian theories of John Hutchinson will be discussed later but, oddly enough, his major importance for us throughout most of this study will not be as a mature thinker but, rather, as a somewhat callow youth. From 1714 to 1716 he wrote a number of summaries, or encyclopedias, of knowledge (probably to fulfill the Yale requirement for a master's degree) which furnish us with an extensive and varied body of information about what was taught and believed at Yale in the second decade of the eighteenth century.[20]

In his 1716 "Revised Encyclopedia," as a topic under physics, Johnson included "The starry heavens and their power and influences for the subject of astrology."[21] Somewhat more informative about what was taught concerning the subject of astrology was a 1718 Yale thesis which argued, "All the predictions of the astrologers with regard to future contingent events are fallacious and vain."[22] The key phrase here is "contingent events." Contingent events are those occurrences that depend upon the will and action of an individual. Thus the thesis denies the validity of judicial astrology but implicitly accepts that of natural astrology.[23]

20. *Dictionary of American Biography.* For the requirements for the master's degree see Richard Warch, *School of the Prophets: Yale College, 1701-1740* (New Haven: Yale University Press, 1973), p. 196.

21. Samuel Johnson, *Samuel Johnson, President of King's College: His Career and Writings,* ed. by Herbert and Carol Schneider (New York: Columbia University Press, 1929), II: 213. (Hereinafter referred to as *Works.)*

22. James J. Walsh, *Education of the Founding Fathers of the Republic: Scholasticism in the Colonial Colleges* (New York: Fordham University Press, 1935), p. 20.

23. A similar treatment is found in the seventeenth-century text by I. B. Ricciolus, S.J., *Almagestum Novum Bonomiae,* which routinely accepted astrology but warned, "beware of the errors condemned by pontifical decree generally involving significations of future contingencies; . . ." Graubard, "Astrology's Demise," p. 212.

A similar pattern is found in a popular eighteenth-century English reference work, Chambers's *Cyclopedia: or an Universal Dictionary of Arts and Sciences.* This work was frequently used in the colonies throughout the eighteenth century. Samuel Keimer had printed an article from the *Cyclopedia* in each issue of his Philadelphia newspaper, the *Universal Instructor in All Arts and Sciences.* This practice ceased when the paper was sold to Benjamin Franklin, who also changed its name to the *Pennsylvania Gazette.* Franklin had earlier penned some mock protests when Keimer, innocently proceeding through the As, had printed Chambers's article on abortion. Nevertheless, Franklin too made use of the *Cyclopedia.* In 1737 he copied from it almost verbatim an essay about earthquakes, and he used it as an authority to identify "Gin seng." In 1749 he sent an order to London for "Chambers's Dictionary, the Best Edition." [24] The *Cyclopedia* was also used frequently by Jonathan Edwards. [25] William Johnson, the influential superintendent of Indian Affairs in the northern colonies, ordered it in 1749/50; [26] James Bowdoin, governor of Massachusetts in the 1780s, used it in his late eighteenth-century essay "Observations on Light"; [27] and it is found in numerous eighteenth-century Virginia and North Carolina estate inventories, auction listings, and advertisements. [28]

Chambers's *Cyclopidia* article "Astrology" made the traditional distinction between natural and judicial astrology. It attacked the latter as

24. Benjamin Franklin, *The Papers of Benjamin Franklin,* ed. by Leonard W. Labaree (New Haven: Yale University Press, 1959–), I: 111-13, 157-58; II: 184, 214; III: 379. (Hereinafter referred to as *Papers.)*

25. Thomas H. Johnson, "Jonathan Edwards' Background of Reading," *Publications of the Colonial Society of Massachusetts. Transactions,* XXVIII (1930-33): 213.

26. William Johnson, *The Papers of Sir William Johnson* (Albany, N.Y.: University of the State of New York, 1921-65), I: 264.

27. James Bowdoin, "Observations on Light, and the Waste of Matter in the Sun and fixt Stars . . . ," *Memoirs of the American Academy of Arts and Sciences,* I (1785): 207.

28. *William and Mary Quarterly,* 1st Series, X (April 1902): 232; VIII (January 1900): 145; *Virginia Gazette,* May 24, 1751, p. 3, July 20, 1769, p. 2, (Rind); Aug. 29, 1771, p. 3, (Purdie and Dixon); Nov. 25, 1775, p. 1; Stephen B. Weeks, "Libraries and Literature in North Carolina in the Eighteenth Century," *Annual Report of the American Historical Association for the Year 1895* (Washington, D.C.: GPO, 1896), p. 204; George K. Smart, "Private Libraries in Colonial Virginia," *American Literature,* X (1938-39): 43.

"superstition." The former, however, although warning was given that it "was only to be deduced, a posteriori, from phaenomena and observations," was not attacked, and the support of Chambers's favorite scientist, Robert Boyle, was adduced on its behalf.[29]

If the educated could learn something about astrology at the colonial colleges, and the self-educated could learn of it from encyclopedias and from still popular seventeenth-century works such as Sir Walter Raleigh's *History of the World*,[30] the less educated could learn of it from almanacs. The significance of almanacs for the less educated has been often recognized but perhaps never fully exploited. Chester Noyes Greenough has argued that people who rarely read anything else at least read the almanac.[31] Charles M. Andrews has said that "except for the Bible, probably no book was held in greater esteem or more widely read in the colonies in the eighteenth century than the almanacs.[32] Moses Coit Tyler told us that

> No one who would penetrate to the core of early American literature, and would read in it the secret history of the people in whose minds it took root and from whose minds it grew, may by any means turn away, in lofty literary scorn, from the almanac,—most despised, most prolific, most indispensable of books, which every man uses,

29. Ephraim Chambers, *Cyclopedia: or an Universal Dictionary of Arts and Sciences*, "Astrology," 7th ed., 1751; Arthur Hughes, "Science in English Encyclopedias, 1704-1875," *Annals of Science*, VII (Dec. 28, 1951): 354; Philip Shorr, *Science and Superstition in the Eighteenth Century* (New York: Columbia University Press, 1932), pp. 16-17.

30. For Raleigh and astrology see Walter Raleigh, *The History of the World*, II, 27-33; Allen, *The Star-Crossed Renaissance*, p. 153, and Tillyard, *The Elizabethan World Picture*, pp. 56-57. For the popularity of Raleigh in the colonies see H. Trevor Colbourn, *The Lamp of Experience: Whig History and the Intellectual Origins of the American Revolution* (Chapel Hill: University of North Carolina Press, 1965), pp. 202, 204, 207, 209, 210, 213, 214, 216, 218, 220, 222, 226, and Smart, "Private Libraries in Colonial Virginia," p. 40.

31. Chester Noyes Greenough, "New England Almanacs, 1766-1775 and the American Revolution," *Proceedings of the American Antiquarian Society*, VL (October 1935): 289.

32. Charles M. Andrews, *Colonial Folkways* (New Haven: Yale University Press, 1919), p. 151.

and no man praises; the very quack, clown, pack-horse, and pariah of modern literature, yet the one universal book of modern literature; the supreme and only literary necessity even in households where the Bible and newspaper are still undesired or unattainable luxuries.[33]

The role of the almanac in both natural and judical astrology will be discussed below, but it should be noted here that almanacs also played a purely educational role in presenting astrological concepts and terminology to their public. This terminology will indeed be more familiar to us than that of most areas of eighteenth-century thought, for it is essentially the same as that found in many newspapers and bookstores today. Thus, most almanacs included the twelve signs of the zodiac. These are the still familiar Aries, Leo, Taurus, Aquarius, etc. They are not the constellations but, rather, are an area of 30 degrees of the ecliptic, that is, a 30-degree segment of the sun's apparent orbit about the earth. Most almanacs also included the symbols and names of the traditional seven planets, namely the moon, the sun, Mercury, Venus, Mars, Jupiter, and Saturn. (The outer planets which are sometimes given a role in present-day astrology—Uranus, Neptune, and Pluto—were of course not yet discovered.) Each planet had its still traditional character, that is, Mars was associated with war and strife and was an unfortunate planet, while Venus was associated with love and was a fortunate one. (The tendency found in some current astrologers to deny that planets are unfortunate in themselves rather than in the uses man makes of their influences was not found in eighteenth-century astrology.) In many colonial almanacs were two terms which will be less familiar to today's readers of astrology columns: dragon's head and dragon's tail. These terms refer to the moon's nodes, that is, to the points on the moon where the orbit of the moon intersects the ecliptic, the apparent path of the sun about the earth. The point where the moon passes from south of the ecliptic to north of it is called the ascending, or northern, node or the dragon's head, and is considered lucky, while the opposite is called the southern, or descending, node or the dragon's tail, and is considered unlucky. To return to more familiar terminology, the almanacs usually listed the aspects. These are

33. Moses Coit Tyler, *A History of American Literature* (2 vols. in 1; New York: G. P. Putnam's Sons, 1881), II: 120.

geometric relationships formed between the planets, as viewed from earth, and are well explained by one of several almanacs which went beyond mere lists and attempted to explain the fundamentals of astrology to its readers.

| | | |
|---|---|---|
| ♂ | Conjunction, | Is when two Planets are both in the same Sign, Degree and Minute. |
| ss | Semisextile. | Two planets are said to bear a Semisextile Aspect with each other when they are one Sign or 30 Deg. distant. |
| ✡ | Sextile. | Two Planets are said to be in a Sexti'e Aspect with each other when they are 2 Digns [Signs], or 60 Deg. distant. |
| □ | Quartile. | Two Planets are said to be in a Quartile Aspect when they are 3 Signs or 90 Degrees distant from each other. |
| △ | Trine. | Two Planets are said to be in a Trine Aspect when they are 4 Signs or 120 Degrees distant. |
| Vc | Quincunx, | Is when two Planets are 5 Signs or 150 Deg. distant from each other. |
| ☍ | Opposition. | Two Planets are at Opposition when they are 6 Signs or 180 Deg distant. |

Note.    Astrologers are of the Opinion that the ss and the Vc Aspects are not so forcible in producing Changes on terrestrial Bodies and Affairs, as any one of the other Five.[34]

Indeed, most almanacs included only the five traditional aspects and omitted the semisextile and quincunx, although some used them, and at least one almanac listed no less than eight new aspects.[35]

A 1742 Virginia almanac gave a short course in astrological terminology. It defined the aspects, gave variant names for the planets—Saturn

34. Nathaniel Low, *An Astronomical Diary; or Almanack for . . . 1772* (Boston: Kneeland & Adams).

35. Titan Leeds, *The American Almanack for . . . 1740-1746;* Nathaniel Ames, *The Almanacks of Nathaniel Ames, 1726-1775,* ed. by Samuel Briggs (Cleveland: Short & Forman, 1891), p. 49.

was also known as Chronos, Phoenon, and Falifer—and listed some twenty-four ways in which the zodiac signs could be organized. For example, the barren signs were Gemini, Leo, and Virgo; the fruitful signs were Cancer, Scorpio, and Pisces; and so forth.[36] A later Virginia almanac, which listed the astrologically proper days to pick herbs, also listed a host of ways in which the signs were grouped, including Northern Signs, Southern Signs, Fiery Signs, Earthly Signs, Airy Signs, Watry Signs, Masculine Diurnal Signs, Feminine Nocturnal Signs, Feral Signs, Mute Signs, etc.[37]

A 1743 almanac attempted to explain astrological prognostications in detail to its readers. What made this especially unusual was that the author first stated that he did not believe in astrology but had merely "scattered some Fragments of Astrology: the double Use whereof may be seen in two Lines of Pope's Essay on Criticism:"

> Such labour'd Nothings in so strange a Stile
> Amaze th' Unlearn'd, and made the Learned smile.

Taylor's almanac then presented and explained sample prognostications for several months. In January there would be a conjunction of Mars and Saturn, the *"Infortunes,* or malevolent Planets." Mercury was in the house of Saturn (Capricorn or Aquarius), which meant rumors and false reports. Fortunately, as the almanac pointed out, the conjunction of Mars and Saturn was in Virgo, which lessened its effect because Mars was mildest in Virgo. Thus there would be quarrels and thefts rather than great disasters. The almanac also explained to its readers such astrological facts as "a Trine is called an Aspect of perfect Love and Benevolence," and that it did not use "those call'd the new Aspects, or the Semisextile, &c. they being little regarded by the best Astrologers." [38]

In an almanac for 1739, Titan Leeds, who did believe in astrology, explained the significance of several of the planets in a series of verses.

---

36. John Warner, *Warner's Almanack . . . for . . . 1742* (Williamsburg: Wm. Pares). Almanacs usually do not list the date of publication but it can usually be assumed that they were printed the year prior to their year of use.

37. *The Virginia Almanack for . . . 1751* (Williamsburg: Hunter).

38. Jacob Taylor, *An Almanack . . . 1743* (Philadelphia: Isaiah Warner).

> *Mars* must not be forgot, not but I know
> The Hurly-Burlies he forments below,
> Parent of Broils, and Master of Disorders,
> Grand Disturber of States, Prompter of Murders:

He also discussed some of the effects of Venus:

> But when ill Dignifi'd oft surprize
> With raging Lusts and close Adu'teries

Mercury and the moon were not forgotten.

> Mercury is a Trimmer, turns his Coat
> And with the rising side still joins his Note;
> Supplies good Authors Fancies with rich Sense,
> And supplies Praters with Impertinence
> The Mobb are ruled by the *Moon,*
> Whose Humours suit her, and will change as soon.[39]

A few scholars of astrology may have even studied from formal texts on the subject such as the copy of "Parker's Tutor to Astrology" advertised in the *Pennsylvania Gazette.*

This book, which was actually George Parker's corrected edition of *Eland's Tutor to Astrology: or Astrology Made Easy,* was a primer for would-be astrologers. It opened with the most basic material—the definition and significance of the individual planets and signs of the zodiac. It soon grew more complex as it explained the significance of each planet in each of the twelve signs. The *"Moon in Aquarius* represents a Person of middle Stature, and a well shap'd corpulent Body, the Hair of a light Brown . . . a Lover of Curiosities and moderate Recreation, an Abhorrer of base and unhandsome Actions . . . ." There would be no mere "tall, dark, and handsome" answers from astrologers trained on *Eland.*

The textbook continued with detailed discussions of planetary aspects, essential and accidental dignities and debilities, the parts of the body

39. Titan Leeds, *The American Almanack for . . . 1739* (Philadelphia: Bradford).

governed by each planet in each of the twelve signs, and a glossary of technical terms. It then moved on to a discussion of the twelve houses, the erection of a figure, planetary hours, the answering of horatory questions, and the rectification of a nativity.

There can be little doubt that a student who mastered *Eland,* if supplied with the appropriate ephemeris (tables showing the positions of the planets at specific times), was well prepared to start on a career as a practicing astrologer.[40]

II

Natural astrology in colonial America dealt with medicine, farming, and weather-predicting. One popular source of astrological medical information was several old works of Nicholas Culpeper. His most popular works in the colonies included the *Pharmacopoeia Londinensis; or the London Dispensory,* first published in England in 1653, and the *English Physician Enlarged,* first published in 1653 (his *English Physician* was first published in 1652). Both were reprinted in Boston, the *Pharmacopoeia Londinensis* in 1720 and the *English Physician Enlarged* in 1708, but the colonies appear to have depended primarily upon imports from England for their supply. One scholar has noted that "the smallest collections of books in Tidewater Virginia early in the [eighteenth] century were likely to contain Nicholas Culpeper's *English Physician.*"[41] Another scholar reported, regretfully, that in late seventeenth- and early eighteenth-century New England "the commonest work on medicine was the ancient *Culpepper's London Dispensatory.*"[42] The popularity of these works is also indicated by the large number of advertisements for them and the numerous estate inventories which included them throughout eighteenth-century America. Other works by Culpeper found in the colonies

40. *Pennsylvania Gazette,* March 14, 1748/49. *Eland's Tutor to Astrology: or Astrology Made Easy,* ed. by George Parker (10th ed.; London: Printed for G. Conyers, 1704).

41. Whitfield J. Bell, Jr., "Medical Practice in Colonial America," *Bulletin of the History of Medicine,* XXXI (September-October 1957): p. 447.

42. Clifford K. Shipton, "Literary Leaven in Provincial New England," *The New England Quarterly,* IX (June 1936): 212.

included his *Legacy* and *Midwives*.[43] The latter, in the early eighteenth century, had been sufficiently fashionable in London to be found in "Leonora's library," in the *Spectator*.[44] These books were clearly in the astrological tradition. The *Pharmacopoeia Londinensis* explained that the procreative virtue was

> governed principally by the influence of *Venus.*
> It is augmented & increased by the strength of *Venus*, by her Herbs, Roots, Trees, Minerals, &c.
> It is deminished & purged by those of *Mars*, and quite extinguished by those of *Saturn.*
> Observe the Hour and Medicines of *Venus* to Fortifie: of *Mars* to Cleanse this Virtue: of *Saturn* to Extinguish it.[45]

The *Pharmacopoeia* discussed which medicines should be taken under what signs, and warned that "He and he only is a Physitian that knows which of the Qualities [heat, cold, dryness, and moisture] offends, by which of these Celestial Bodies it is caused, and how safely but speedily to remedy it: all the rest that practise Physic are but Montebanks." [46] This work, and others by Culpeper, included a signature by him as a "Student in Physick and Astrology."

The contents of the several editions of Culpeper's *English Physician Enlarged* vary, but the core of the book appears to be an herbal which often includes astrological details. Thus his description of "Adder's Tongue" states:

> It is an herb under the dominion of the Moon and Cancer, and therefore if the weakness of the retentive faculty is caused by an evil

43. *William and Mary Quarterly,* 1st Series, VIII (July 1899): 20, (October 1899): 78; *Virginia Gazette* (Purdie and Dixon) Nov. 29, 1770, Dec. 13, 1770; Francisco Guerra, *American Medical Bibliography, 1639-1783* (New York: Lathrop C. Harper, Inc., 1962), pp. 44, 74-75, 104-5, 170, 194, 204, 288, 290, 322, 331, 436-38, 440-41, 460-61, 540, 546, 604.

44. Joseph Addison and Richard Steele, *The Spectator,* No. 37.

45. Nicholas Culpeper, *Pharmacopoeia Londinensis; or the London Dispensatory* (Boston: Nicholas Boone, 1720), p. [iv].

46. *Ibid.,* pp. [ix-x, xviii].

influence of Saturn, in any part of the body governed by the Moon, or under the dominion of Cancer, this herb cures it by sympathy; and it cures the following diseases of the body under the influence of Saturn, by antipathy.[47]

Some editions of this book also included Culpeper's *Astrological Judgment of Diseases,* first published in 1665. Readers of those editions would learn how to calculate critical days and were told that on such days, "if the Moon be well aspected with good planets, it goes well with the sick; if, by ill planets, it goes ill." (Such readers also learned a number of reasons why these calculations were not always correct).[48] They would also learn the sympathies and antipathies of the planets, for example, that Jupiter and Mars were enemies, and how to cast horoscopes for diseases.[49] Those who had Culpeper's *A Directory for Midwives* could read the chapter on "The Formation of the Child in the Womb astrologically handled." [50]

Culpeper was not received without opposition. Cotton Mather may have been reacting to the Boston reprint of the *Pharmacopoeia Londinensis* when he warned against looking "up unto the *Stars,* with the foolish *Astrology* of the *Star-gazers,* who try to *read,* what the Great GOD that made them has not *written* there." [51] He left no doubts about whom he was attacking in his unpublished "Angel of Bethesda," written in the

47. Nicholas Culpeper, *Culpeper's English Family Physician or, Medical Herbal Enlarged* (London: W. Locke, 1792), I, 132 and Nicholas Culpepper [sic], *The English Physician Enlarged* (London: S. Ballard, 1765), p. 5. There is no adequate bibliographic study of the various editions of Culpeper which differ in title, contents, and even the spelling of the author's name.

48. Culpeper, *English Family Physician,* I: 53-64.

49. *Ibid.,* 63-94.

50. Nicholas Culpeper, *A Directory for Midwives* (London: C. Hitch, 1762), pp. 53-60. For further studies of Culpeper see F. N. L. Poynter, "Nicholas Culpeper and His Books," *Journal of the History of Medicine and Allied Sciences,* XVII (January 1962): 152-67, and David L. Cowen, "The Boston Editions of Nicholas Culpeper," *Journal of the History of Medicine and Allied Sciences,* XI (April 1956): 156-65.

51. Cotton Mather, *The Christian Philosopher: A Collection of the Best Discoveries in Nature with Religious Improvements* (London: Eman. Mathews, 1721), p. 24. This did not prevent Mather from believing in the "very wonderful" influences of the moon on medicine and agriculture. *Ibid.,* pp. 51-52.

1720s. Mather warned that "the assigning of particular Plants to particular Planets, or to say, as your Culpepper continually does, that such an
Herb is governed by Saturn, and such an one is under the Dominion of
Jupiter, and the Rest; it is a Folly akin to the Idolatry and Superstition of
the Roman-Catholicks, in looking to Saints, for their Influences on our
several Diseases." [52] This attitude was also reflected in a 1728 Harvard
master's thesis which answered in the negative the question, "Do medicinal herbs operate by planetary power?" [53]

Another set of seventeenth-century medical books still popular in the
colonies in the eighteenth century were three apocryphal works ascribed
to Aristotle: *Aristotle's Last Legacy*, *Aristotle's Master-Piece*, and *Aristotle's
Compleat & Experienced Midwife*. (Two similar books—*Aristotle's Physiognomy* and *Aristotle's Book of Problems*—were older and less medical in
content). These medical works, which seem to have served the colonies as
sex manuals, were apparently popularized by a number of men in the
seventeenth century, including Nicholas Culpeper.[54] They too contained
some astrology. One explained that children born in their eighth month
were more likely to die than those born in the seventh because the eighth
month was ruled by the moon, a cool planet.[55] However, another work
ascribed to Aristotle, which stated that the eighth month was ruled by
Saturn, refuted the astrological explanation.[56] *Aristotle's Master-Piece* included a detailed survey of astrological physiognomy. In this science each

52. Otho T. Beall, Jr. and Richard H. Shryock, *Cotton Mather: First Significant
Figure in American Medicine* (Baltimore: Johns Hopkins University Press, 1954),
p. 234.

53. Young, "Master's Degree in Harvard College," p. 133.

54. Otho T. Beall, Jr., *"Aristotle's Master Piece* in America: A Landmark in the
Folklore of Medicine," *William and Mary Quarterly*, 3rd Series, XX (April
1963): 208-12, and Vern L. Bullough, "An Early American Sex Manual, Or,
Aristotle Who?," *Early American Literature*, VII (Winter 1973): 236-46.

55. Aristotle [pseud.], *Aristotle's Problems* in *Works of Aristotle* (A New Edition;
Philadelphia: Printed for the Booksellers, 1798), p. 44.

56. Aristotle [pseud.], *Aristotle's Master-Piece Completed* (New York: Company
of Flying Stationers, 1798), p. 88.

A non-astrological explanation had also been offered by Culpeper, who explained that it was due to the "perfection of the Number [seven], which, if I were
writing Divinity, I could prove by Scripture to be the perfectest Number that is."
Culpeper, *A Dictionary for Midwives*, p. 60.

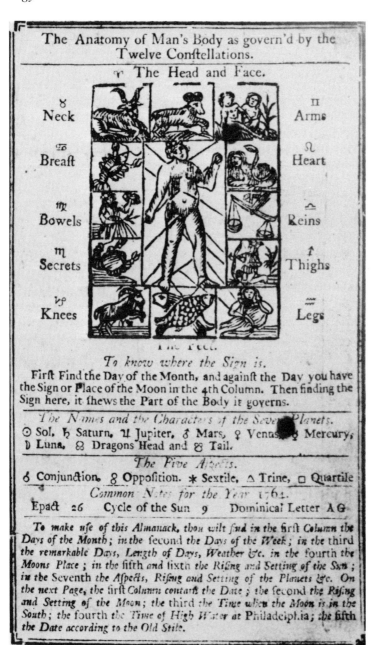

The Anatomy of Man's Body as govern'd by the Twelve Conftellations.

♈ The Head and Face.

♉ Neck

♊ Arms

♋ Breaft

♌ Heart

♍ Bowels

♎ Reins

♏ Secrets

♐ Thighs

♑ Knees

♒ Legs

The Feet.

*To know where the Sign is.*

Firft Find the Day of the Month, and againft the Day you have the Sign or Place of the Moon in the 4th Column. Then finding the Sign here, it fhews the Part of the Body it governs.

*The Names and the Characters of the Seven Planets.*
☉ Sol. ♄ Saturn, ♃ Jupiter, ♂ Mars, ♀ Venus, ☿ Mercury, ☽ Luna, ☊ Dragons Head and ☋ Tail.

*The Five Aspects.*
☌ Conjunction, ☍ Oppofition. ⚹ Sextile, △ Trine, ▫ Quartile

*Common Notes for the Year* 1764.

Epact 26  Cycle of the Sun 9  Dominical Letter A G

*To make ufe of this Almanack, thou wilt fnd in the firft Column the Days of the Month; in the fecond the Days of the Week; in the third the remarkable Days, Length of Days, Weather &c. in the fourth the Moons Place; in the fifth and fixth the Rifing and Setting of the Sun; in the Seventh the Afpects, Rifing and Setting of the Planets &c. On the next Page, the firft Column contains the Date; the fecond the Rifing and Setting of the Moon; the third the Time when the Moon is in the South; the fourth the Time of High Water at Philadelphia; the fifth the Date according to the Old Stile.*

*Fig. 1.* Zodiac man.

part of the face was governed by an astrological body—the forehead by Mars, the right eye by the sun, the right eyebrow by Leo, etc.[57]

The most popular source of astrological-medical information, however, was probably the almanac. Most almanacs displayed the "Anatomy," or zodiac man (Fig. 1). This consisted of a picture of a man's body together with the signs of the zodiac which ruled each part of the body. Thus the sign for Aries would be shown next to the head and face, while that for Pisces would be found next to the feet. The reader would be told to check the calendar portion of the almanac where, for each day, was listed the sign of the zodiac which the moon was "in." Then, by checking the anatomy, one could determine which part of the body the moon governed, or was "in," that day. There were some minor variations on this format. Some almanacs included a picture as well as the sign. Thus the symbol for Pisces would be accompanied by two fish.[58] Other almanacs gave the name of the sign,[59] some simplified matters by listing the part of the body instead of the sign in their calendar for each day,[60] while others omitted the sketch of the anatomy but listed all the necessary information in a chart instead.[61] The most common form, however, was the picture of the anatomy and the signs. (It can be more conveniently consulted in the Labaree edition of Franklin's *Papers*.[62] ) In one form or another it was a traditional and standard feature of colonial almanacs. First introduced into the colonies in 1678, one student of colonial medical literature states that it is found in over 90 percent of the colonial almanacs; [63] my own survey indicates that about 75 percent of the almanacs published in 1760 still carried it.

The function of the anatomy is clear from Renaissance medical theory.

57. Aristotle [pseud.], *Aristotle's Master-Piece* in *The Works of Aristotle*, p. 55.

58. John Tobler, *The Pennsylvania Town and Country Man's ALMANACK, for . . . 1761* (Germantown, [Pennsylvania]: Sower for Fussel, Marshall and Zone).

59. Roger More, *The American Country Almanack, for . . . 1761* (New York: James Parker, and Company)

60. Edmund Freebetter [Nathan Daboll], *The New-England Almanack; for . . . 1778* (New London, Conn.: T. Green).

61. *The Pennsylvania Pocket ALMANACK for . . . 1761* (Philadelphia: W. Bradford).

62. Franklin, *Papers*, I: 289.

63. Francisco Guerra, "Medical Almanacs of the American Colonial Period," *Journal of the History of Medicine and Allied Sciences*, XVI (July 1961): 237.

One of the most common treatments was phlebotomy and, depending upon the illness, different veins were to be opened. Before opening a vein, however, it was necessary first to check the position of the moon, for, as Titan Leeds explained, "It is not good Bleeding in the Member where the Sign is for that Day; for example, on the fourth of *January* the Moon is in *Aries*, then it is not good Bleeding in the Head, and so of the rest." [64] The sixteenth-century *Kalendar of Shepherds* presented a more detailed statement of the same theory: "A man ought not to make incision nor touch with iron the member governed by any Sign the day the Moon is in it for fear of so great effusion of blood that might happen, nor in likewise also when the Sun is in it, for the danger and peril that might ensue." [65]

Some almanacs gave additional information concerning astrological medicine. The Leeds almanacs told their readers to "bleed when the [moon] is in [Cancer, Aquarius, or Taurus]; but not when the [Moon] is in the Sign that rules the Member where the Vein is to be opened." [66] They also explained that purging was best done in March and April and when the moon was in a watery sign (Cancer, Scorpio, or Pisces); [67] that ointments and plasters should be applied when the moon was in the sign that governed the part of the body to which the plaster was to be applied; [68] and that bleeding should not be done when the sun was in the part of the body to be bleed.[69] One set of Leeds almanacs explained which signs were in themselves good, bad, or indifferent when bleeding in the parts of the body they did not rule or, as the *Kalendar of Shepherds* had earlier succinctly put it, "Aries is good for blood letting when the Moon is in it, save in the part that it domineth." [70]

64. Titan Leeds, *The American Almanack for . . . 1739.*

65. *The Kalendar & Compost of Shepherds,* pp. 100-1. Manuscript booklets containing similar information were carried about by medieval doctors. See C. H. Talbot, "A Mediaeval Physician's Vade Mecum," *Journal of the History of Medicine and Allied Sciences,* XVI (July 1961): 228-29.

66. Titan Leeds, *The American Almanack . . . 1722* (Philadelphia: Andrew Bradford).

67. *Ibid.* See also Daniel Leeds, *The American Almanack . . . for 1713.* (New York: Bradford).

68. Daniel Leeds, *ibid.*

69. *Ibid.*

70. Titan Leeds, *Almanack for 1739-41* and Phila. ed. *1742-46; Kalendar & Compost of Shepherds,* p. 101.

The anatomy, despite its human form, also appears to have been used for veterinary medicine. One almanac explained that "FOR *the better Success in letting Blood, taking Physick, Cutting of Cattle, Sheep and Hogs, its necessary to know where, or in what Part of the Body the Sign is.* " [71] Benjamin Franklin's *Poor Richard's Almanack* completed a verse mocking the anatomy with "To purge, to bleed, or *cut,* thy Cattle, or *thy self.*" [72] A few almanac essays on astrological veterinary medicine explained that the best time for gelding cattle was when the moon was in Aries, Sagittarius, or Capricorn. The best time for shearing sheep was when the moon was increasing in Taurus, Virgo, or Libra, and if the moon was in a favorable aspect with Venus it was even better. These were also good days to have a haircut. [73]

Such advice was not found only in almanacs. John Smith's *The Husbandman's Magazine,* published in 1718, recommended that horses be gelded in the spring or fall, but if that were impossible, it should be done "in the waine of the *Moon,* the Signs being either in *Virgo* or *Aries;* . . ." [74] Rams and pigs were also to be gelded in the waning moon. [75] If, however, one wished to increase one's livestock, "about Candlemass (observing it to be in the Increase of the Moon) is the best time to let your Sows be Covered; . . ." [76]

The 1712 *Husband-man's Guide* told its readers that in May one should "Geld Sheep and other Cattle the Moon being in *Aries, Sagierary* or *Capricorn.* Sheer Sheep the *Moon* increasing in *Taurus, Virgo* or *Libra,* and their fleeces will grow the thicker and faster, the like observed in cutt[in]g hair; and if the Moon be in a friendly aspect to Venus 'tis much the better." [77] The *Guide* also informed its readers that "It is good to bathe, the Moon being in *Taurus Virgo* and *Capricorn;* it is best bathing

71. Felix Leeds, *The American Almanack for . . . 1730* (New York: William Bradford).

72. Franklin, *Papers,* I: 351.

73. Daniel Leeds, *The American Almanack . . . for 1713;* Titan Leeds, *The American Almanack . . . 1722.*

74. J[ohn] S[mith], *The Husbandman's Magazine* (Boston: Allen for Boone, 1718), p. 45.

75. *Ibid.,* pp. 86, 98.

76. *Ibid.,* p. 98.

77. *The Husband-man's Guide . . . ,* (2nd ed. Enlarged; Boston: Elea Phillips, 1712), pp. 7-8.

two or three days after, or at the full of the Moon, . . ." [78] In 1764 an enterprising colonist created, from a pair of late sixteenth- and early seventeenth-century books by Gervase Markham, a work entitled *The Citizen and Countryman's Experienced FARRIER*. It included some advice on how

To get horse colts

TAKE your mare to the horse before the full of the moon, and when the sign is a female. To get mare colts, cover after the full, and in the male signs. N.B. There be twelve signs, six male, and six female.[79]

Most almanacs, however, limited themselves in the field of astrological medicine (despite the fact that they often dealt with other medical matters) simply to printing the anatomy and the sign the moon was in. There was often resistance even to printing that much. A 1726 almanac introduced its anatomy as "the anatomy of Mans Body, as *imagin'd* to be governed by the Twelve Constellations." [80] In 1761 an almanac explained good-humoredly that

Since there's twelve Signs, Mans' Body we divide,
Into twelve Parts, that so we may provide
Each Sign a proper Share, as you may know,
If you consult the Figure down below:
But had there been more Signs, we must have cut
The Pieces smaller, that they might hold out.[81]

78. *Ibid.,* p. 30-31.

79. J. [Gervase] Markham, G. Jefferies, and Discreet Indians, *The Citizen and Countryman's Experienced FARRIER* (Wilmington: John Adams, 1764), p. 290; in another edition (Baltimore: Somes, 1797), p. 251. For the sources of this book see F. N. L. Poynter, *A Bibliography of Gervase Markham, 1568?-1637,* Oxford Bibliographical Society Publications, N.S., XI (Oxford: The Oxford Bibliographical Society, 1962): 190-93.

80. Jacob Taylor, *A Compleat Ephemeris . . . for 1726* (Philadelphia: Keimer).

81. Theophilus Wreg, *The Virginia Almanack, for . . . 1761* (Williamsburg: Hunter).

Nathaniel Ames, the author of some of the best eighteenth-century almanacs and a strong advocate of astrology but an opponent of the anatomy, explained his reasons for printing it:

> The Blackmoor may as eas'ly change his Skin,
> As Men forsake the ways they'r brought up in;
> Therefore I've set the Old Anatomy,
> Hoping to please my Country men thereby,
> But where's the Man that's born & lives among,
> —— —— —— Can please a Fickle throng? [82]

Jacob Taylor, in the midst of a sharp attack upon all forms of astrology, bitterly explained why he printed the anatomy:

> The old Fable of the Sign in the Body of Man and Beast, has obliged me to make a short Dissertation on it, in my own Defense: The Omission of the Anatomy being tho[ugh]t an unpardonable Defect by some, who esteem the pretty picture the Beauty and Ornament of their annual Bargain. *Billy* and *Dicky, Peggy* and *Molly* must see the Man on the Moon; and when the little Child cries, the great one runs for the Almanack, to bless the House with Peace. [83]

A 1770 almanac stated the almanac maker's reason for including the anatomy quite clearly:

> Should I omit to place this Figure here,
> My Book would hardly sell another Year:
> *What* (quoth my Country Friend) *D'ye think I'll buy*
> *An* ALMANACK *without th'* ANATOMY?
> As for its USE, nor he, nor I can tell;
> However, since it pleases all so well,
> I've put it in, because my Book should sell. [84]

---

82. Ames, *The Almanacks of Nathaniel Ames,* p. 60.

83. Jacob Taylor, *An Almanack . . . 1743* (Philadelphia: Isaac Warner).

84. Thomas More, *Poor Tom Revived: Being More's Almanack, for . . . 1770* (Charles Town, South Carolina: Crouch).

Despite the demand for the anatomy, there are only a few documented examples of the actual application of some form of astrological medicine. A family Bible in Virginia had listed in it the days when it was safe to bleed: "April, to let blood in the left Arm on the 3rd, 12th, or 15th, but the head of bleeding on the 7th, 8th 10th, and 20th." [85] Were these notes jotted down perhaps in part from a borrowed almanac? In 1764 Dr. James Greenhill described his treatment of an epileptic slave. After experimenting with vomits, purges, and electric shock, he tried blisters and more internal medicine.

> This succeeded and the next Change of the Moon expecting the fit, as usual, he missed them. The Medicines has been continued and he has missed the fits this last full moon again. The Blister is almost dry but I intend if the fellow stays with me to draw a fresh one. It is something remarkable that the fits has Usually returned when the Moon was in the Sign Capricorn Even When it was a week before or after the full or change. [86]

A Captain Jenks noted that smallpox kept "breaking out every full & change of the moon. . . ." [87] A New Jersey medical student studying with Christopher Witt received a certificate stating that he had been trained in the "Arts & Mysteries of Chemistry, Physick, & the Astral Sciences, whereby to make a more perfect Discovery of the Hidden causes of more Occult & uncommon Diseases, not so easily to be discovered by the Vulgor Practice." [88] There can be little doubt that Witt and his students took the planets and signs into account in treating their patients. At least one New England minister, a Harvard graduate of the class of 1714, "dabbled" in astrological medicine. [89]

85. Wyndham B. Blanton, *Medicine in Virginia in the Eighteenth Century* (Richmond, Virginia: Garrett & Massie, Incorporated, 1931), p. 6.

86. *Ibid.*, pp. 6-7.

87. Samuel Jenks, "Journal of Captain Jenks," *Proceedings of the Massachusetts Historical Society*, Series 2, V (1889-90): 386.

88. Francis R. Packard, *History of Medicine in the United States* (New York: Paul B. Hoeber, Inc., 1931), I: 277. For more on Christopher Witt see chap. 3 below.

89. John Langdon Sibley and Clifford K. Shipton, *Sibley's Harvard Graduates* (Boston: Massachusetts Historical Society, 1873- ), V: 566.

As late as 1801, an outraged observer, perhaps himself a physician, noted:

> This calculation of nativities, and the delineation of their horo-
> scopes, have become unfashionable, and have been generally
> deemed foolish, since astronomy, from a collection of desultory
> facts, has been improved to a science. But a miserable relic of it still
> exists among us, and disgraces and disfigures some of our most
> popular pamphlets. We fear it will be hardly credited in Europe, and
> in the distant parts of America, that in the city of New-York, famous
> as it is for enterprise, genius, learning and talents, the almanacks
> teach the people who read them, that each constellation in the zodiac
> presides over a particular part of the animal body. . . . This miser-
> able doctrine, propagated in publications more generally spread
> among the people than perhaps any other kind of books, has such
> sway in many parts of the country, that a citizen will not castrate a
> lamb or a pig, nor suffer himself nor any of his family to be bled from
> the arm, without inspecting the almanack in the first place, to find
> what the philomath who compiled it has certified about the astral and
> lunar influence on the body for that day. . . . These, with trines, and
> quartiles, and sextiles, and similar astrolgical nonsense, are not only
> tolerated from year to year, but, from long habit, regularly expected
> as a most important part of these periodical productions.[90]

Despite this popularity, it is clear that the status of astrological medicine was not high. Its literature appears to have been largely limited to
almanacs and reprints of previous centuries' works. It is quite evident that
astrology played no role in the modern medicine of the eighteenth
century. Even the almanac essays on astrological medicine appear limited
to the first half of the eighteenth century despite the continued interest
almanacs took in medical affairs.[91] Many, probably most, almanac makers

90. "Observations on the Influence of the Moon on Climate and the Animal
Economy . . . ," *Medical Repository and Review of American Publications,* IV,
(1801): 286-87.

91. For medicine in almanacs see Guerra, *American Medical Bibliography,* pp.
275-417. None of the standard studies of eighteenth-century colonial medicine
discusses astrology.

of the eighteenth century clearly did not believe in any aspect of astrological medicine. The fact that, despite this disbelief, the majority of almanacs carried the anatomy is highly significant. It, together with the open complaints of some of these disbelieving almanac makers, clearly indicates that there was somewhere a strong popular desire for the anatomy. (This situation can be contrasted with twentieth-century astrology in which the anatomy is rare, although it was carried by a few almanacs including at least one published by a pharmaceutical house which had an astrology department.[92] It is thus clearly of limited popular interest. The popularity of personal predictions based on the signs which are found in booklets and so much of the popular press, however, indicates a strong popular interest in this form of astrology, although it may not necessarily indicate anything about the personal beliefs of the newspaper publishers.)

Some further, rather tenuous, judgments can be made about the people who used astrological medicine. The very limited use of this topic in new books, as opposed to reprints of "how to" books of the previous century, when contrasted with the popular demand for the anatomy, indicates that its users were not part of the book-buying public. Even the reprints of seventeenth-century books were utilitarian works which could, and no doubt were, used by many without any regard for their astrological content. The almost total absence of any mention of astrological medicine in private letters and diaries, despite the fact that they often dealt with diseases and their cures (with bleeding quite prominent), indicates that its practitioners were not prolific writers. Of course, what is here just drawn is a sketch of the "inarticulate." In this instance, however, we are fortunate in that even though we must work with material which was written for them rather than by them, it appears from the complaints of the almanac makers, that what they received was what they demanded rather than what others thought was good for them and wished them to believe

The planets and signs were used not only in medicine and animal husbandry but also in various phases of agriculture. *The Husband-man's Guide* recommended that trees be set and removed in winter, "especially

92. Ernest Wickersheimer, "Le Médecine Astrologique Dans Les Almanachs Populaires Du XXe Siècle," *Bulletin de la Société Francaise D'Histoire De La Médecine*, X (1911): 27-29.

at new Moon." [93] *The Husbandman's Magazine* stated that the planting and grafting of fruit trees should be done in the moon's increase. Transplanted trees, however, were to be set in the waning moon. This is a clear instance of the use of the phases of the moon as a form of sympathetic magic. The waning or declining moon helped a plant set its roots down in the earth just as the rising moon helped plants grow upward toward the sky. [94]

Jared Eliot, a leader in the rather weak colonial movement for scientific agriculture, stated that the best times for cutting bushes were "in the Months of *June, July,* and *August, in the old Moon that Day the Sign is in the Heart [Leo]*." This was clearly as astrological folk-belief which Eliot had learned from local farmers. He argued, however, that one could accept this statement without believing in occultism. The use of the sign merely indicated a time and the effectiveness was due to the moon's influence on fluids. [95] That is, Eliot tried to reinterpret this astrological belief in terms of Newtonian gravity. (At the times indicated, the sun and moon are, roughly, lined up with the earth).

This belief was refuted by a later agricultural writer, Samuel Deane, who did, however, attest to its widespread acceptance.

> It has often been asserted, that when the sign is in the heart, and the moon in her wane, in June, July, or August, if the bushes are cut they will certainly die. But, by a sufficient trail, I have found this to be a great mistake. In August, 1782, on the day recommended, I cut several acres of alder bushes. And on the following day, when the moon was in the next sign, I cut a large quantity more of the same kind, and in the same swamp. The former are sprung up very generally, and become tall now in the year 1789; and so are the latter. The cutting was as ineffectual on the one day as on the other. [96]

This was apparently quite scientific, even to the use of a control, but it

93. *The Husband-man's Guide*, p. 13. See also p. 3.

94. Smith, *The Husbandman's Magazine,* pp. 117, 119.

95. Jared Eliot, *Essays upon Field-Husbandry in New-England* (Boston: Edes and Gill, 1760 [1761?]), pp. 123-24. It was repeated in Nathan Daboll, *The New England Almanack . . . for . . . 1794* (New London: Green).

96. Samuel Deane, *The New England Farmer, or Georgic Dictionary* (2nd ed.; Worcester, Mass.: Isaiah Thomas, 1797), p. 38.

would not have necessarily refuted Eliot's reinterpretation, since he treated the sign as merely a time indicator rather than a source of some occult power, and thus a single day's difference might be too slight to have any measurable effect. But no doubt more significant in neutralizing such scientific refutations of old beliefs was the fact that it offered no usable alternative. The farmer still had no better way to attempt to destroy bushes than to follow his old traditions and beliefs and diligently consult his almanac for the day the sign was in the heart.

If Deane ignored the planets while weeding, he consulted the heavens when gathering apples. He picked them in late September or early October about noon, on a day which had a full moon.

> Some may think it whimsical to gather them on the day above mentioned. But, as we know both animals and vegetables are influenced by the moon in some cases, why may we not suppose a greater quantity of spirit is sent up into the fruit, when the attraction of the heavenly bodies is greatest? If so, I gather my apples at the time of their greatest perfection, when they have most in them that tends to their preservation.—I suspect that the day of the moon's conjunction with the sun may answer as well; but I have not had experience of it. The same caution, I doubt not, should be observed in gathering other fruits, and even apples for cyder: But I have not proved it by experiments.[97]

Here Deane attempted to reinterpret an astrological belief, the influence of the full moon, in terms of Newtonian physics.

Cotton Mather, without any effort at interpretation, noted that "the Influences of the *Moon* upon *Sublunary* Bodies are very wonderful" and described two apparently novel instances of it which were furnished him by the *"Georges* of my Neighbourhood." Chestnut wood had to be cut in the waning moon, for if it were cut in the waxing moon it would sparkle dangerously in the fire. All timber should be cut in the waning moon in August or February, for timber cut at this time would remain forever free of worms.[98]

97. *Ibid.*, p. 14.
98. Mather, *The Christian Philosopher,* pp. 51-52. See also George Lyman Kittredge, "Cotton Mather's Scientific Communications to the Royal Society," *Proceedings of the American Antiquarian Society,* N.S., XXVI (1916): 29-30.

Mather's pun upon Virgil's *Georgics* was not, as one might easily assume, merely an attempt to embellish a sentence with an irrelevant classical allusion. The eighteenth century not only highly regarded the *Georgics* as a poem but also considered it to be a didactic work upon scientific agriculture. This viewpoint, already common by the mid-seventeenth century, was reinforced in eighteenth-century England by Dryden's translation and the accompaning laudatory "An Essay on Virgil's Georgics" by Addison. He described it as falling into "that class of Poetry, which consists in giving plain and direct instructions to the reader. . . ." [99] In the colonies, in 1718, *The Husbandman's Magazine* was obviously modeled upon the *Georgics* and cited Virgil as an authority. [100] A paper upon scientific agriculture, read before the Philadelphia Society for Promoting Agriculture in 1786, noted that a few years ago it had been observd "that VIRGIL and COLUMELLA, old as they are, remained almost the only writers worth consulting on this subject." [101] As late as 1799, Benjamin Smith Barton, professor of botany at the University of Pennsylvania, was willing to call Virgil "at once a naturalist and a poet." [102] But no doubt by this time America was following the lead of England in deprecating the scientific value of the *Georgics*. In 1803 John Quincy Adams doubted that it had ever had any value for farmers, even in Virgil's own time, and certainly saw no such value for it for in contemporary America. [103]

The temporary scientific reputation of the *Georgics* could have only

99. For the *Georgics* in England see Stearns, *Science,* p. 90; L. P. Wilkinson, *The Georgics of Virgil* (Cambridge: University Press, 1969), pp. 299-309; John Chalker, *The English Georgic: A Study in the Development of a Form* (Baltimore: Johns Hopkins University Press, 1969), *passim,* and p. 17 for the role of Addison's essay. For the quotation from Addison see Joseph Addison, *The Miscellaneous Works of Joseph Addison,* ed. by A. C. Guthkelch (London: G. Bell and Sons Ltd., 1914), II: 4.

100. Smith, *The Husbandman's Magazine,* pp. 85-87; see also p. 138.

101. William Darlington, *Memorials of John Bartram and Humphry Marshall* (Philadelphia: Lindsay & Blakiston, 1849), p. 583.

102. Benjamin Smith Barton, *Fragments of the Natural History of Pennsylvania* (Philadelphia: Way & Groff, 1799), p. xi.

103. *Port Folio,* Feb. 26, 1803, p. 66. John Quincy Adams is identified as the author in Linda K. Kerber, *Federalism in Dissent: Imagery and Ideology in Jeffersonian America* (Ithaca, N.Y.: Cornell University Press, 1970), p. 119.

helped to reinforce a belief in astrological agriculture in colonial America. From its opening invocation to Maecenas, "What makes the crops joyous, beneath what star, Maecenas, is it well to turn the soil, and wed vines to elms, . . ." to its discussion of lunar lucky days, to its discussion of weather and other omens, it made use of astrology.[104]

Not all colonial agricultural astrology was classical or given a gloss of Newtonian science. A few almanacs listed the appropriate days to gather certain herbs according to the planets which ruled them. "Gather Chestnut, Scurvey-Grass, Balm, Cinquefoil, Sage, and all Herbs of *Jupiter,* May 6, June 16, 22, 29, July 8, 12, 17."[105] We have already seen how Culpeper prescribed the herbs of different planets for different illnesses.

*The Husband-man's Guide* merely recommended that herbs be picked on a full moon in June and July.[106] Undoubtedly most of the popular agricultural astrology was of this nature—emphasizing the phases of the moon and ignoring the other more elaborate elements of formal astrology. An intriguing question concerns the extent of lunar astrology, especially in planting crops. *The Husband-man's Guide* recommended that peas, beans, and parsnips be set when the moon is declining.[107] *The Husbandman's Magazine,* on the other hand, gave the more customary advice that "the best time to Sow . . . Seeds is in the Increase of the Moon. . . ."[108] Deane opposed this belief and again implied that he had known people to follow it. He warned that peas should be planted

104. Virgil, *Georgics* 1. 1-5, 276-86, 335-497. Dryden's translation omits "beneath what star," which some colonists presumably still read in the Latin text, but included the other astrological allusions. John Dryden, trans., *The Georgics of Virgil* (New York: Cheshire House, 1931), 1. 371-82, 459-693.

105. Felix Leeds, *The American Almanack . . . for 1730;* Titan Leeds, *The American Almanack for . . . 1730* (Philadelphia: Nearegress & Arnot); Titan Leeds, *The Genuine Leeds Almanack for . . . 1730* (Philadelphia: Harry). A similar chart appeared in *The Virginia Almanack for. . . 1751.*

106. *The Husband-man's Guide,* p. 9.

107. *Ibid.,* p. 3. Nourry interprets this as meaning the period just before the moon starts to increase, the so-called *lune paresseuse.* P. Saintyves [Emile Nourry], *L'Astrologie Populaire: Estudiée Spècialement dans les Doctrines et les Traditions Relatives à L 'Influence de la Lune* (Paris: Librairie Emile Nourry, 1937), p. 113.

108. Smith, *The Husbandman's Magazine,* p. 128. To sow hemp the same moon was required with the additional recommendation of a southwest wind. *Ibid.,* p. 136.

"without any silly regard to the time of the moon; by which I have known some miss the right time of sowing, and suffer much in their crop." [109]

It appears to be impossible to say how widespread this practice was. It was ignored by the almanacs and most of the other literature of the period. On the other hand, *The Husbandman's Magazine* and the *Guide* were meant as handbooks on agriculture, and Deane treated it as a living belief in the 1790s. Moreover, these and other similar beliefs continued to be very strong in rural America into the twentieth century, and it seems probable that they have held a firm position in the folk-beliefs concerning agricultural practices from the time of the migration from England into the twentieth century.[110]

Besides medical and agricultural astrology, one other form of natural astrology was practiced in the colonies: astrological weather-predicting.

109. Deane, *New England Farmer,* p. 252. In 1767 he was apparently testing this belief, for in his diary he carefully noted the state of the moon when he planted (George Lyman Kittredge, *The Old Farmer and His Almanack* [New York: Benjamin Bloom, 1967], p. 309).

110. See Dixon Ryan Fox, "The Old Farm," *New York History,* XIX (January 1938): 24-25, for the 1790s. For the late nineteenth and twentieth centuries see, "By the Signs," *Foxfire,* I (Fall 1967): 14-23, 56-61; Mandel Sherman and Thomas R. Henry, *Hollow Folk* (New York: Thomas Y. Crowell, [ca. 1933]), pp. 89-94; Vance Randolph, *Ozark Superstitions* (New York: Columbia University Press, 1947), pp. 34-52; W. J. Hoffman, "Folk-Lore of the Pennsylvania Germans," *Journal of American Folk-Lore,* I (July-Sept. 1888), 130-31; Gertrude Barnes, "Superstitions and Maxims from Dutchess County, New York," *The Journal of American Folk-Lore,* XXXVI (January-March, 1923): 17; Newman Ivey White, general ed., *The Frank C. Brown Collection of North Carolina Folklore,* ed. by Wayland D. Hand, Vol. VII, *Popular Beliefs and Superstitions from North Carolina* (Durham, N.C.: Duke University Press, 1964), VII: 501-6; N. C. Hoke, "Folk-Custom and Folk-Belief in North Carolina," *Journal of American Folk-Lore,* V (April-June 1892): 113; D. C. Brinton, "Reminiscences of Pennsylvania Folk-Lore," *Journal of American Folk-Lore,* V (July-September 1892): 178-79; Daniel Lindsey Thomas and Lucy Blayney Thomas, *Kentucky Superstitions* (Princeton, N.J.: Princeton University Press, 1920), pp. 172-82; Edwin Miller Fogel, *Beliefs and Superstitions of the Pennsylvania Germans* (Philadelphia: American German Press, 1915), pp. 194-202; Herbert Passim and John W. Bennett, "Changing Agricultural Magic in Southern Illinois," in Alan Dundes, ed., *The Study of Folklore* (Englewood Cliffs, N.J.: Prentice-Hall, Inc., 1965), pp. 314-28; *New York Times,* June 16, 1974, sec. 2, p. 42.

Both Morton's *Compendium* and Chambers's *Cyclopedia* devoted most of their discussion of natural astrology to the effects of the planets upon the weather. Colonial almanacs (as well as some modern ones) routinely included weather predictions in the calendar portion of the almanac. Some, perhaps most, colonial almanac makers used weather predictions merely as fillers to use for days which had no historical event or church holiday to commemorate.[111] Some, however, took their predictions more seriously. Nathaniel Ames twice attempted to explain and justify his weather predictions, first in 1727 and again, with less assurance of accuracy, in 1745.

As to what I have predicted of the Weather, it is from the Motions & Configurations of the heavenly Bodies, which belongs to Astrology: Long Experience testifies that the Sun, Moon and Stars have their Influence on our Atmosphere, for it hath been observed for Seventy Years past, That the Quartile & Opposition of Saturn & Jupiter produce Wet Seasons; and none will deny but that the Sun affordeth us his benign Rays & kind influence, and by his regular Motion causeth Spring, Summer, Autumn & Winter; and if the Moon can cause the daily Ebbing and Flowing of the Tide, and has the vast Ocean subject to her government, she can certainly change the Air which is Thin, and Tenuious.[112]

With Regard to my Judgment of the Weather, I have only this to say, namely, that I have endeavoured to observe what Aspects of the Planet affect the Country most, & have the Advantage of this same

---

For similar beliefs in other parts of the world, see James George Frazer, *The Golden Bough,* Part IV, *Adonis Attis Osiris* (3rd ed.; New York: Macmillan Co., 1935), VI: 131-50; Nourry, *L'Astrologie Populaire,* pp. 113-15; Joshua Trachtenberg, *Jewish Magic and Superstition: A Study in Folk Religion* (New York: Atheneum, 1974), p. 186.

For an interpretation of this belief as sympathetic magic see Frazer, *The Golden Bough,* VI: 132-50; Nourry, *L'Astrologie Populaire,* p. 113; Passim, "Changing Agricultural Magic in Southern Illinois," p. 318n.

111. Some New England almanacs, especially in the early eighteenth century, did not print church holidays.

112. Ames, *The Almanacks of Nathaniel Ames,* pp. 53-54.

20 Years Experience; but after all, the Weather is uncertain even to
a Proverb—*As Fickle as the Wind,* or *as uncertain as the Weather.*[113]

A similar explanation was made by Nathaniel Low in 1762: "With
Regard to what I have said of Weather, I have observed the best rules
that the most experienced Astrologers, both Ancient and Modern, dic-
tates on this Occasion:—But however the Weather is uncertain.—"[114]
*The American Almanac* in 1743 explained that the weather was predicted
by the positions and aspects of the planets but that these predictions could
not be perfect because "of the many contrary Causes happening at or
near the same time" and because it sometimes rained at one location and
was clear a few miles away.[115]

It is difficult to determine what "the best rules of the most experienced
Astrologers" were. The fullest listing of the factors to be taken into
consideration, however, was given us by Daniel Leeds. "Though our
Prognosticator judge of the Weather by considering the Sun's ingress's,
the Luminations, the Cosmical and Chronical Rising of the Sta[rs] &c the
mutual and Lunar Aspects, and several other things, yet they miss as
often as they hit the truth, as we very well know; . . ."[116]

Leeds followed this with a traditional excuse: "Therefore when you
think I miss the truth in judging the weather, pray show so much favour as
to let the Prognosticators general answer speak for me *viz: That it [is such]
Weather [so]me where, though not here,* and you will oblige me another
Year:"[117] This explanation was given a light-hearted nationalistic twist by
a 1764 almanac. "Whereas his Majesty's dominions have been considerably enlarged in these latitudes, it appeared reasonable not to overlook
this circumstance; accordingly it is expected, that if, at any time, or

113. *Ibid.,* p. 179.

114. Nathaniel Low, *An Astronomical Diary, or, an Almanack for . . . 1762*
(Boston: Kneeland).

115. John Jerman, *The American Almanack for . . . 1743* (Philadelphia:
Bradford).

116. Daniel Leeds, *An Almanack and Ephemerides for . . . 1693* ([Philadelphia:]
William Bradford). For a further study of almanac weather predictions see Silvio
A. Bedini, *The Life of Benjamin Banneker* (New York: Charles Scribner's Sons,
1972), pp. 221-29.

117. Daniel Leeds, *An Almanack and Ephemerides for . . . 1693.*

in any place, the weather and our predictions should not agree, it will be taken for granted that for that day we had calculated for some other place, . . ." [118]

But perhaps the viewpoint of many almanac makers who did not bother to comment on their weather predictions was expressed by Jacob Taylor, an inveterate opponent of astrology, in a verse reminiscent of Pope:

> The Weather here premis'd without pretence
> To Truth, Fore-knowledge, Art or common Sense
> Inserted only in a feigned Style.
> To please the Weak, and make the wiser smile.

He coupled this with a sharp attack upon all forms of astrology, calling it a "meer cheat, a Brat of *Babylon*, brought forth in *Chaldea*, a Place Famous for Idolatry." [119]

## III

Some judicial astrology was found in eighteenth-century America. Joseph Stafford's almanacs warned of direful events, but always with a saving phrase in case they did not materialize. Two eclipses in 1738 were to cause the destruction of sheep and cattle, political disorders, wars, etc. "These things will, or may, happen principally, in those Countrys or Regions that are subject to the Sign Eclipsed." [120] In 1740 he gave his readers a detailed analysis of a forthcoming eclipse.

> *Now as to the Effect of the Eclipse of the Moon on the second Day of January, 1740, it being celebrated in the third face of* [Cancer] *a Sign of a watry triplicity, and the* ☽ *in* ♂ *of* ♄ [moon in conjunction with Saturn] *who is the great Infortunate; this signifies the Death of the*

118. John Tobler, *The South-Carolina and Georgia Almanack, for . . . 1764* (Savannah: James Johnston).

119. Jacob Taylor, *An Almanack and Ephemeris . . . for the Year 1746* (Philadelphia: W. Bradford).

120. Joseph Stafford, *The Rhode-Island Almanack for . . . 1738* (Newport: Widow Franklin, 1738).

*common People by Wars and other Destructions, and also of Fish and
Fowls, and all Creatures that live in or near the Water: There may
happen a great Destruction among them in some part of the World,
which I do believe will come to pass, without it should please God to
withdraw his Hand.*[121]

Titan Leeds warned that a forthcoming eclipse of the sun would occur
in Pisces near the dragon's tail, and "therefore it will not produce any
good."[122] On the other hand, an earlier eclipse had occurred "so near the
*Dragon's Head,* it will not be of ill Consequence."[123] He reported that the
1742 conjunction of Saturn and Jupiter in the fiery sign Leo was to cause
trouble in religion, a safe prognosis to make in the midst of the Great
Awakening.[124] In 1744 Nathaniel Ames also explained that the religious
disputes of the period had been due to the conjunction in Leo, "a
Religious Sign."[125]

In 1730 Ames made a series of prognostications:

> Bright Scenes do change, three Posting Years shan't Cease
> Before stern Mars stares in the Face of Peace,
> Steel Glitt'ring Spears in the very Fields affright
> And Europe all seems fir'd with armour bright.
> Saturn & Jove contend and will not yield
> So dead & Wounded pave the Bloody Field.

Concerning the Eclipses this year, the Author would observe,
that according to Authors the Eclipse of the Moon (Jan. 22) which
happens in Leo the 2nd Sign of the Fiery Triplicity, threatens more
Grudgings, Repinings, discord and hatred, murmuring, complaints

121. Joseph Stafford, *An Almanack for . . . 1740* (Boston: T. Flees).

122. Titan Leeds, *The American Almanack for. . . 1737* (Philadelphia: Andrew Bradford).

123. Titan Leeds, *The American Almanack for. . . 1731* (Philadelphia and New York).

124. Titan Leeds, *The American Almanack for . . . 1742* (New York: Wm. Bradford).

125. Ames, *The Almanacks of Nathaniel Ames,* p. 176.

of the Common People, motions of Armies, Wars, burning of Houses, sharp Fevers, Pestilential Diseases, etc.

As as for the Eclipse of the Sun of the 3rd of *July*, *Mars* casts his Malign Rays to both the Luminaries, which portends much Mischief to those Places and Countries, that are subject to the Sign Eclipsed.

*Note*. In the last preceding Years, the Superior Planets have been within the benevolent Rays, but in the three succeeding Years they will be malevolently Affected and near the AEquinox, which perhaps may affect the bigger part of the Earth, with War and Tumults.[126]

The following year Ames continued in the same vein, but with the vagueness that opponents of astrology loved to mock.

I doubt not but the Oppositions of the Superiours *Saturn* and *Jupiter* will have their malign Effects, especially those which are celebrated in Cardinal and AEquinoctial Signs. I do not pretend to determine the Event of these things: yet doubtless he who lives a few years, and observes the Mutations, Alterations, and Vicissitudes of things, and Accidents of Mundane Affairs, may be able to judge from his own experience, whether these *Phaenomena* forbode Good or Ill.[127]

Of great interest to both Leeds and Ames was the 1762 conjunction of Jupiter and Saturn in Aries. The conjunction, similar to one which had made a great stir in England in the sixteenth century (although with somewhat less astrological import),[128] encouraged Leeds as early as 1738 to start making eschatological predictions: "and perhaps then will be the beginning of the pouring forth of the seven vials or last Plagues upon *Babylon* or *Tyrus* i.e. the Papacy, . . ."[129] Ames, despite some uncharac-

---

126. *Ibid.*, pp. 65, 68.

127. *Ibid.*, p. 75.

128. Margaret E. Aston, "The Fiery Trigon Conjunction: An Elizabethan Astrological Prediction," *Isis*, LXI (Summer 1970): 159-87. See also Giorgio De Santillana and Hertha von Dechend, *Hamlet's Mill: An Essay on Myth & the Frame of Time* (Boston: Gambit, 1969), pp. 399-401.

129. Titan Leeds, *The American Almanack for . . . 1738* (Philadelphia: Bradford).

teristic hedgings on the validity of his prognostications, also saw this conjunction as very important, although not quite so transcendentally important as Leeds had thought.

> Dire Wars and mutual Rage are surely come,
> E're any Comet blaz'd the threatned Doom!
> Kingdoms and States impatiently attend,
> The great Events now verging to an End;—
> When three Times more the Sun has chear'd the Spring,
> A new important AEra will begin:
> From which young Date and settled State of Things
> A Train of Strange Events and Wonder springs.[130]

In 1762 Ames asserted that his predictions had been vindicated by the death of George II, the accession to the throne of George III, and the victories of the French and Indian War.[131] In the same year, Nathaniel Low's first almanac devoted over a page to this conjunction and explained that "the Learned are of the Opinion that these Aspects may stir up great Politicians in contriving some new Ways and Methods of regulating the Affairs of Governments." (A most auspicious prognostication for the eves of the American and French revolutions.) He then threatened the world with a whole host of miscellaneous disasters including famine, drought, mortal disease, violent death by accident, war, deluge, inudations, earthquakes, and alterations of oceans and river channels.[132]

Some almanacs, perhaps following the tradition of English "mock almanacs," made fun of astrology. Much of this, as one might expect, is found in Benjamin Franklin's *Poor Richard's Almanack.* Many of Franklin's comments on astrology were merely short and not overly inspired "gags."

> When ♂ and ♀ in ☌ lie [When Mars and Venus in Conjunction lie]
> Then, Maids, whate'er is ask'd of you, deny.[133]

130. Ames, *The Almanacks of Nathaniel Ames,* pp. 289-90.
131. *Ibid.,* 323.
132. Low, *An Astrological Diary, or an Almanack for . . . 1762.*
133. Franklin, *Papers,* II: 7.

He did, however, perpetrate an elaborate astrological hoax upon Titan Leeds, an unfortunate rival Philadelphia almanac author. Franklin predicted the death of Leeds, proved his death, and then refuted Leeds' claim to still be alive. This hoax was clever and well carried out, but hardly original. It was obviously inspired, in both theme and detail, by a famous hoax of the English satirist Jonathan Swift. Swift, writing under the name Isaac Bickerstaff, had in just this way attacked the London astrologer and almanac author John Partridge.[134]

The first indications of the hoax appeared in late 1732 in an advertisement for Franklin's very first almanac. Among a long list of the contents of the new almanac was the "Prediction of the Death of his friend Mr. Titan Leeds." This teaser was followed in Franklin's *Poor Richard's Almanack for 1733,* which of course was written under the persona of Richard Saunders, by a claim that he, Saunders, had not written an almanac before, despite his great need for money, because he did not want to compete with his good friend Titan Leeds.

> But this Obstacle (I am far from speaking it with Pleasure) is soon to be removed, since inexorable death, who was never known to respect Merit, has already prepared the mortal Dart, the fatal Sister has already extended her destroying Shears, and that ingenious Man must soon be taken from us. He dies, by my Calculations made at his Request, on *Oct.* 17. 1733. 3 ho. 29m. P.M. at the very instant of the ♂ of ☉ and ☿ [conjunction of the sun and Mercury]: By his own Calculation he will survive till the 26th of the same Month.

Although Saunders declared that the only disagreement between the two learned astrologers was over nine days, Leeds strongly disagreed. In his 1734 almanac Titan Leeds replied to Saunders's prediction, denouncing it, denying that he had predicted he would survive until the 26th of October, and claiming that "I have lived to survive this conceited Scriblers Day and Minute whereon he has predicted my Death. . . ."

---

134. For Swift see Jonathan Swift, *Satires and Personal Writings of Jonathan Swift,* ed. by William Alfred Eddy (London: Oxford University Press, 1965), pp. 161-91, and Richmond P. Bond, "Isaac Bickerstaff, Esq.," in Carrol Camden, ed., *Restoration and Eighteenth-Century Literature: Essays in Honor of Alan Dugald McKillop* (Chicago: University of Chicago Press, 1963), pp. 103-24.

This, by creating a continuing controversy, merely played into Franklin's hands. In his 1734 almanac, Franklin had Saunders gravely argue that Leeds must indeed be dead. Admittedly, what the stars predict are sometimes set aside "by the immediate particular Disposition of Providence," but

> there is the strongest Probability that my dear Friend is *no more;* for there appears in his Name, as I am assured, an Almanack for the Year 1734, in which I am treated in a very gross and unhandsome Manner; in which I am called *a false Predicter, an Ignorant, a conceited Scribler, a Fool, and a Lyar.* Mr. Leeds was too well bred to use any Man so indecently and so scurrilously, and moreover his Esteem and Affection for me was extraordinary: So that it is to be feared that Pamphlet may be only a Contrivance of somebody or other, who hopes perhaps to sell two or three Year's Almanacks still, by the sole Force and Virtue of Mr. Leeds's Name; but certainly, to put Words into the Mouth of a Gentleman and a Man of Letters, against his Friend, which the meanest and most scandalous of the People might be asham'd to utter even in a drunken Quarrel, is an unpardonable Injury to his Memory, and an Imposition upon the Publick.

Having been proved both dead and a writer of indecent and scurrilous literature, Leeds seems to have realized that he was outmatched. In his next almanac he merely managed a weak retort to the effect that Saunders and his wife had undoubtedly made profit from their new almanac, but "if Falsehood and Inginuity be so rewarded, what may he expect if ever he be in a capacity to publish that that is either Just or according to Art?" Although there is humor in Leeds's references to Saunders's new secondhand coat and his wife's new pot, he seems ready to drop the entire sorry matter.

Franklin, however, was not. His 1735 almanac was advertised as containing "Proofs of Titan's death," and it did.

> But having receiv'd much Abuse from Titan Leeds deceas'd, (Titan Leeds when living would not have us'd me so!) I say, having receiv'd much Abuse from the Ghost of Titan Leeds, who pretends to be still living, and to write Almanacks in spight of me and my Predictions, I cannot help saying, that tho' I take it patiently, I take it very

unkindly. And whatever he may pretend, 'tis undoubtedly true that he is really defunct and dead. First because the Stars are seldom disappointed, never but in the Case of wise Men, *Sapiens dominabitur astris,* and they fore-show'd his Death at the Time I predicted it. [This was not only sound astrological doctrine, but it also managed to imply that Leeds was not a wise man.] Secondly, 'Twas requisite and necessary he should die punctually at that Time, for the Honour of Astrology, the Art professed both by him and his Father before him. Thirdly, 'Tis plain to every one that reads his two last Almanacks (for 1734 and 35) that they are not written with that *Life* his Performances use to be written with; the Wit is low and flat, the little Hints dull and spiritless, nothing smart in them but Hudibras's Verses against Astrology as the Heads of the Months in the last, which no Astrologer but a *dead one* would have inserted, and no Man *living* would or could write such Stuff as the rest. But lastly, I shall convince him from his own Words, that he is dead, *(ex ore suo condemnatus est)* for in his Preface to his Almanack for 1734, he says, "Saunders adds another GROSS FALSHOOD in his Almanack, viz. that by my own Calculations I shall *survive* until the 26th of the said Month October 1733, which is as *untrue* as the former." Now if it be, as Leeds says, *untrue* and a *gross Falshood* that he surviv'd till the 26th of October 1733, then it is certainly *true* that he died *before* that Time: And if he died before that Time, he is dead now, to all Intents and Purposes, any thing he may say to the contrary notwithstanding.

Battered by this indisputable logic, Leeds remained quiet, and the hoax lay dormant until rasied by Leeds's printers, William and Andrew Bradford. In Leeds's almanac for 1739 they reported Leeds's death and the fact that he had left them predictions for the next seven years, and referred to the earlier false prediction. This was too good an opening for Franklin to ignore, and in his almanac for 1740 he reported that Leeds had died as predicted and the almanacs under his name since then had been prepared by others. He proved his point with the best possible evidence, a letter of Titan Leeds's ghost. That spirit, having found Saunders asleep, "entred your left Nostril, ascended into your Brain, found out where the Ends of those Nerves were fastned that move your right Hand and Fingers, by the Help of which I am now writing unknown to you; but when you open your Eyes, you will see that the Hand written is mine, tho' wrote with yours." Besides reiterating that he had died when predicted and that he had left no predictions for the Bradfords to use, he issued several new prognostications, including a claim that "J. J——n, Philomat, shall be openly reconciled to the Church of Rome. . . ."

The Bradfords replied to Franklin in Leeds's almanac for 1740, written when everyone acknowledged that Leeds was dead, with another letter from Leeds's overworked ghost. He identified R. Saunders as B. Franklin, acknowledged entering Franklin's nostril but solemnly chided Franklin for changing the text of the letter, and gave the original text of his letter. In it, the ghost exposed Franklin's alleged habit of publishing his almanac after his rivals were in print in order to "pick a little out of one and a little out of another, and so you patch up your almanack."

Finding himself finally answered in kind, Franklin let the somewhat overworked feud disappear, except for a casual allusion in 1742. He had, however, a new dispute underway with John Jerman, the putative convert to Catholicism. In his almanac for 1741, printed by one Benjamin Franklin, Jerman denied the prediction and called Poor Richard one of "Baal's *false Prophets.*" This not very serious feud continued in 1742 when Saunders proved Jerman to be a crypto-Catholic from a poem which Jerman had printed in his 1741 almanac. In it Jerman had called November 1 All Hallows' Day: "Reader; does not this smell of Popery?" Also in the poem were the lines "When any Trouble did me befal / To my dear *Mary* then I would call." Obviously, said Saunders, a reference to the Virgin Mary. Although clever, this was perhaps not in the best of taste. The poem had been written by Jerman "when I was almost overcome with Grief and Distress" over the recent death of his wife. For whatever exact cause, in 1743 Jerman's printer was William Bradford, and Jerman firmly declined to continue playing the game. And with a final attack in 1744, Franklin too ended his interest in this particular set of hoaxes.[135]

135. Franklin, *Papers,* I: 280, 281, 288 (repeated on 311), 343, 347, 350-51, 382; II: 3-4, 245-47, 331-33, 393-94; Titan Leeds, *American Almanack for 1734, 1735, 1739, 1740;* John Jerman, *The American Almanack for . . . 1741, 1743.* See also John F. Ross, "The Character of Poor Richard: Its Source and Alteration," in Esmond Wright, ed., *Benjamin Franklin: A Profile* (New York: Hill and Wang, 1970), pp. 27-35.

Others also parodied astrology, even if none did it so elaborately. Nathaniel Ames effectively mingled his serious prognostications with the humor of mock almanacs, by making such comments as "the *Planet Saturn* informs me of Snow and Cold Weather in the Winter Season." [136]

> The Year to come shall wondrous Things behold.
> But what? to me the Stars have not fortold. [137]

A 1750 almanac made such mock predictions as "January:—I find by the stars that the greatest disease incident to this month is want of money, caused by the great consumption of Woods, Candles, and Canary, three valuable things in this cold Season. . . ." [138] A somewhat more successful attempt at crude humor was made by a Virginia almanac.

> Although we are not so curious in the study of judicial astrology as was the father of Firminus, who calculated the very horoscope of cats and dogs that were whelped in his house, yet this we can positively affirm that those who have no money shall be much more subject to want content, and other incommodities incident to an empty purse. Those millers shall be very honest who have no corn to grind, and women exceedingly quiet who are fast asleep.
>
> If you will believe our learned ass-trologers, it is better taking money this month [June] than physick, and more seasonable for lusty *Ralph* to entertain sweet-lipped Susan with a love sonnet under a green bower than to slide upon the ice. [139]

Even Titan Leeds, for a time badly shaken by Franklin's hoax, turned against some uses of astrology:

> Some calculate the hidden Fates
> Of Monkeys, Puppy-Dogs, and Cats;

136. Ames, *The Almanacks of Nathaniel Ames,* p. 174.
137. *Ibid.,* p. 195.
138. N. W. Lovely, "Notes on New England Almanacs," *New England Quarterly,* VIII (June 1935): 267.
139. T. T. Philomath, *The Virginia Almanack for . . . 1769* (Williamsburg: Purdie & Dixon).

Some Love, Trade, Law-suits, and the Pox;
Some running Nags, and fighting Cocks.
Some take a Measure of the Lives,
Of Fathers, Mothers, Husbands, Wifes.[140]

As this verse and the similar protest below by Ames indicate, some
people wanted more specific and personal prognostications than the
yearly almanac could offer them.

—— —— Nor think I can fortel
Those Secrets that the Stars do not reveal:
One asks how soon Panthea may be won,
And longs to feel the Marrage Fetters on:
Others convinc'd by melancholy Proof
Inquire when courteous Fates will strike 'em off.
Some by what Means they may redress the Wrong,
When Fathers the Possession kept too long:
And some would know the issue of their Cause
And whether Gold can sodder up its Flaws.[141]

One man who did indeed ask "how soon Panthea may be won" was
William Byrd of Virginia. In 1718, in London, he several times consulted
"a conjuror called Old Abram," probably an astrologer although possibly
only a "cunning man," who "gave me hope that my mistress would be
kind again." [142] (This did not prevent Byrd from writing a few years later
a satire called "The Female Creed," a tenet of which was, "I believe in
astrologers, coffee-casters, and Fortune-tellers of every denomi-
nation, . . ." [143] )

140. Titan Leeds, *The American Almanack for . . . 1735* (Philadelphia: Andrew
Bradford). It was copied, as Franklin indicated, from Samuel Butler's *Hudibras*,
pt. 2, canto III, ll. 933-38.
141. Ames, *The Almanacks of Nathaniel Ames*, p. 187.
142. William Byrd, *The London Diary (1717-1721) and Other Writings*, ed. by
Louis B. Wright and Marion Tinling (New York: Oxford University Press,
1958), pp. 78, 102. See also pp. 79, 115. For more on "cunning men," see chap.
3, below.
143. William Byrd, *Another Secret Diary of William Byrd of Westover for the
Years 1739-1741,* ed. by Maude H. Woodfin and decoded by Marion Tinling
(Richmond, Va.: The Dietz Press, Inc., 1942), p. 452.

Another Virginia diarist was Colonel Landon Carter, who made an obscure astrological comment in his diary: "Rode out this day. As dry everything as Usual, and nothing has grown this whole week. Its my 3d plannet that governs and I shall not this year amount to a Groat." [144] "My 3d plannet" may have been, counting inward from Saturn, Mars the infortunate planet, dry and barren.

In 1728 a Connecticut Presbyterian minister, Joseph Morgan, was accused by his congregation of "making two experiments in judicial astrology." In 1781 the deacon of a Marblehead, Massachusetts, church introduced a millennial pamphlet by explaining that he had first waited to hear "what the Wise Men and Astrologers opinion was of that remarkable Phenomenon or DARK DAY . . . and would let the world know that it was the forerunner of some extraordinary event or period."[145]

In the last third of the eighteenth-century, William Paterson, a future United States Senator and justice of the Supreme Court, while speaking of omens mentioned a comet and stated: "those who are skilled in matters of this nature, (one of whom without vanity I count myself), looked upon it as a token of some terrible disaster, . . . ." [146]

One of the most intriguing evidences of the practical use of judicial astrology comes from Rhode Island. Ezra Stiles noted in his *Diary*, after referring to the biblical prohibitions against witches, wizards, and necromancers as well as to Indian "Poways," that "Something of it subsists among Almanack Makers and Fortune Tellers, as Mr. Stafford of Tiverton lately dead who was wont to tell where lost things might be found and what day, hour and minute was fortunate for vessels to sail &c." [147]

144. Landon Carter, *The Diary of Colonel Landon Carter of Sabine Hall, 1752-1778*, ed. by Jack P. Greene (Charlottesville, Va.: University Press of Virginia, 1965), II: 730.

145. Whitfield J. Bell, Jr., "The Reverend Mr. Joseph Morgan, An American Correspondent of the Royal Society, 1732-1739," *Proceedings of the American Philosophical Society*, VC (1951): 255; Samuel Gatchel, *The Signs of the Times* (Danvers: 1781), p. 1.

146. John E. O'Connor, "William Paterson and the American Revolution, 1763-1787" (Unpublished Ph.D. dissertation, The City University of New York, 1974), p. 63; and a typescript of William Paterson, [On Doctors], n.d., Paterson Papers, Library of Congress, furnished by Dr. O'Connor.

147. Ezra Stiles, *The Literary Diary of Ezra Stiles*, ed. by Franklin Bowditch Dexter (New York: Charles Scribner's Sons, 1901), I: 385-86. (Hereinafter referred to as *Diary.*)

The most interesting part of this statement concerns vessel departures. At first thought it would seem highly unlikely that the vigorous Rhode Island shipping industry utilized astrology, but this is confirmed by two nineteenth-century historians. One local historian has told us, referring to the sailing of two Rhode Island privateers in 1745, that "According to the custom of the time their horroscope [sic] was cast, and the figure had disclosed that they should sail on Friday, the 24th of December, 1745." Unfortunately, a snowstorm was raging at that time and both vessels were lost.[148] Another Rhode Island historian has stated that when ships were ready to sail, "an astrologer or 'conjurer,' as they were frequently called, was sometimes employed 'to cast a figure,' to ascertain the proper moment for the vessel to depart." This historian stated he had seen hundreds of such horoscopes and reproduced one which had been cast in 1752.[149] Even Benjamin Franklin, in Philadelphia, included as one of the "1000 trifling Questions" asked of an astrologer: "*Will* my Ship return safe?"[150]

It would thus appear that many merchants may have routinely dealt with astrologers in the course of their business during the eighteenth century. Whether this practice extended beyond Rhode Island is a moot point. If common in other colonies it would be odd that all the evidence for it comes from Rhode Island. One is tempted somehow to try to connect the apparent prevalence of astrology in Rhode Island with its notorious toleration of all sects and believers. This may have simply made Rhode Island a colony in which astrologers could work more openly than in other places. Yet, were this true, one would have expected other colonists, never loath to point out the deviant behavior of Rhode Islanders, to have sharply attacked it.

The extent of this practice in colonial America is thus an unsettled

---

148. William P. Sheffield, *An Address delivered by William P. Sheffield Before the Rhode Island Historical Society in Providence, February 7, A.D., 1882* (Newport, R.I.: John P. Sanborn, 1883), p. 18. I was informed of this *Address* by a private communication from J. C. Furnas. See J.C. Furnas, *The Americans: A Social History of the United States, 1587-1914* (New York: G. P. Putnam's Sons, 1969), p. 319.

149. George C. Mason, "The African Slave Trade in Colonial Times," *The American Historical Record and Repertory of Notes and Queries*, I (July 1872): 319.

150. Franklin, *Papers*, II: 332.

question. We have, however, a guide as to how it was done in seven-teeth-century England in John Gadbury's *Nauticum Astrologicum: or, the Astrological Seaman; . . .* It explained that a ship's true nativity, necessary for the casting of the ship's horoscope, was the moment it was first launched into the water; it gave examples of electionary figures cast to determine the propitious moment for the ship to sail; and it gave examples of horary figures cast to determine if a ship was safe, should it be sold, should it be insured, and would the voyage be prosperous.[151]

The overall significance of judicial astrology in this period is limited. Serious prognostications, when contrasted with the extensive use of the anatomy, occurred in only a few almanacs. In 1762 only two almanacs discussed the conjunction of Jupiter and Saturn in Aries, a major astro-logical event. In 1778 the almanacs dutifully reported an almost complete eclipse of the sun, but none of them took advantage of this golden opportunity to make an appropriate prognostication of the outcome of the American Revolution. However, someone, probably a Massachusetts Loyalist in exile in London about 1786, amused himself by casting predated horoscopes of John Hancock and Joseph Warren, which showed that both men, in the 1760s, fell under the malignant influence of Saturn.[152] With the probably exception of an uncertain amount of ship-ping, judicial astrology did not appear to influence any major decisions, although it should be pointed out that what evidence we have indicates that its use may have been among a broader spectrum of society than the more important, but possibly class linked, use of natural astrology in blood-letting and agriculture.

## IV

Although there was little theoretical literature on astrology in eigh-teenth-century America, there is enough to give us some idea of what the

151. John Gadbury, *Nauticum Astrologicum: or, the Astrological Seaman; . . .* (London: George Sawbridge, 1710). See also E. G. R. Taylor, "Sir William Monson Consults the Stars," *Mariner's Mirror,* XIX (January 1933): 22-26.

152. Francis J. Hurtubis, Jr., "First Inauguration of John Hancock," *The Bostonian Society Publications,* 2nd series, I (1926): plate opposite p. 57, and John W. Farwell, "A Horoscope of Joseph Warren," *Transactions of the Colonial Society of Massachusetts,* XX (1917-19): 18-20.

astrologers believed. Two basic theories were in circulation in this period. The first "explained" the influences of the heavenly bodies as the result of occult forces and the intimate relationship between man and the entire universe. This Renaissance theory of astrology is found, not surprisingly, in the previously discussed works of Nicholas Culpeper. The *Pharmacopoeia Londinensis* explained that

> . . . if you do but consider the Universe as one united Body, and Man an Epitome of this Body; it will seem strange to none but Mad-men and Fools, that the Stars should have an influence upon the Body of Man, considering he being an Epitome of the Creation; must needs have a Celestial World within himself. . . .[153]

Ames approvingly quoted a poem which had originally been written for Henry Coley, a late seventeenth-century astrologer who was the adopted son and professional heir of William Lilly.[154]

> When the Divine Idaea's first unfurl'd
> Themselves to raise this glorious Frame the World,
> Almighty Wisdom by a Mistique Tye,
> Spread through the whole a secret Sympathy;
> Impregnating Superiors to dispense,
> On lower Bodies daily influence;
> Which Train, if Causes that in order fall
> The Wiser Nature, others Fortune call:
> And whilst Man did in Innocence remain;
> He knew ('tis like) each Link of that great chain;
> But when Sin Blurr'd his Soul, that Light was Damp't
> Affected Knowledge made him Ignorant;
> Heaven's Language then no longer he could spell,
> But rudely guess at what he could not tell:

(The rest of the poem dealt with man's attempt to relearn astrology.)[155]

---

153. Culpeper, *Pharmacopoeia Londinensis*, p. [xv].

154. *Dictionary of National Biography*, "Henry Coley," and Ames, *The Almanacks of Nathaniel Ames*, p. 70.

155. Ames, *The Almanacks of Nathaniel Ames*, pp. 68-69.

A second explanation, however, was more popular than that of occult forces and a "Mistique Tye." An attempt was made to fit astrology into the rational scientific world of the late seventeenth and the eighteenth centuries. Thus Morton's *Compendium* explained that all planets, "by motion and inward fermentations," produced and sent forth particles which affected the earth. Moreover, the effect of these particles was altered by the relationships between the planets, by their aspects. The particles of the moon are cool and moist and, as the sun stimulates their production, during a full moon these particles are more plentiful, and thus cool and moist weather usually accompanies a full moon. But when the sun and moon are in conjunction, the sun draws these particles to itself and away from the earth, and drier weather results. Similar explanations could presumably be given, although Morton does not actually do so, for the other planets and their assorted aspects. Through their fermented particles the planets could affect the air and then, indirectly, man's body and even his mind. However, Morton denounced judicial astrology and denied that the position of the planets at one's birth was important, for the air was not so changed in an hour or two "as that Honour or hanging depends thereon," which might indeed be the case in a horoscope.[156]

Chambers's *Cyclopedia* cited Robert Boyle, the seventeenth-century chemist, in support of natural astrology. The "effluvia" and light of the planets, which were distinct for each planet, determined the rarefication and condensation of the air on earth. This in turn controlled not only the weather but also generation and corruption on earth. As with Morton, the angles and relationships of the planets helped to determine their influence on earth.[157] (This explanation was considered scientific enough in the eighteenth century to be included in Diderot's *Encyclopédie*.[158]) It should be noted, also, that while the Chambers article "Astrology" appeared to be favorable to natural astrology it, to enable its readers to judge astrology's "foundation and merits," gave cross reference to the articles "Air," "Atmosphere," and "Weather." While there is no mention of astrology in the last two articles, the one on air, although not mentioning astrology per se, does state that one of the two constituents of air is "The

---

156. Morton, *Compendium Physicae*, pp. 27-30. This was omitted from the 1720s versions.

157. Chambers, *Cyclopedia* (7th ed.), "Astrology."

158. Diderot and D'Alembert, *Encyclopédie, ou Dictionnaire Raisonné Des Sciences, des Arts et des Métiers*, "Astrologie."

matter of light, or fire, which is continually flowing into it from the heavenly bodies." [159] Thus this cross reference is in accord with Boyle's justification of astrology, as both accept the importance of planetary light on the air.

Nathaniel Ames, when not quoting old authorities, attempted scientific explanations for astrology. "No doubt but their Radiations act upon us according to the strictest Laws of Nature though we are ignorant thereof." He considered planetary "effluvia" as a possible, though not necessarily certain, means by which the planetary influences were transmitted. (No doubt it was easier and more respectable to admit to influences carried by unknown, though natural, forces after the example of Newtonian gravity.) Although Ames couples this explanation with a denial of being "a Superstitious Bigot to Judicial Astrology," this did not prevent him, in the same almanac, from predicting much pilfering and stealing because Mercury was the Lord of the Ascendant during a solar eclipse.[160]

He also made an effort to adapt medical astrology to current medical theories. Whereas the use of astrology in bleeding had been based upon the doctrine of the four humors, Ames explained that "the caelestial Powers that can and do agitate and move the whole Ocean, have also the Force and Ability to change and alter the Fluids and Solids of the humane Body." He thus explained astrological medicine in terms of the popular eighteenth-century theories of Hermann Boerhaave, which saw disease as stemming from the contractions and relaxations of the fluids and solids of the body.[161]

In a long and interesting poem, Ames also incorporated astrology into the new astronomy, which assumed all stars to have planets and all planets, the others of this solar system included, to have life.

> Their noblest Uses by themselves enjoy'd,
> For more remote are mutually employ'd
> To serve each other. Daily they dispense
> On us, and we on them kind Influence:

159. Chambers, *Cyclopedia* (7th ed.), "Air."
160. Ames, *Almanacks of Nathaniel Ames*, pp. 120-22.
161. *Ibid.*, p. 347.

Their Trines, their Squares, the great Creator drew,
To intimate what he intends to do.[162]

None of the colonial astrologers attempted to explain judicial astrology. The closest perhaps was Nathaniel Ames, who after all did make judicial prognostications in his almanac, when he wrote that "that which can alter and change the Fluids and Solids of the Body, must also greatly affect and influence the Mind; and that which can and does affect the Mind, has a great Share and Influence in the Actions of Men." [163] This is rather far along the road to judicial astrology, but it is, after all, little more than what Morton had previously said, although in a different "scientific" idiom. Even Culpeper had strongly opposed judicial astrology, pointing out "that every inferior World is governed by its superiors, and receives influences from it." This cosmic hierarchy extended from God to the intellectual world, to the celestial world, to the elementary world and bodies. Thus the stars, as part of the celestial world, were superior to bodies and could influence them. The human mind, however, was an epitome of the intellectual world, and thus superior to the stars and uninfluenced by them.[164]

Even those who practiced judicial astrology did not claim absolute knowledge, although there is no way of knowing what claims a practicing fortune teller such as "Mr. Stafford of Tiverton" made to his clients. Titan Leeds, after discussing the influence of Mars, sternly warned:

Forgive not what thou dost, provok'd by Wine,
'Tis not the Liquor's fault, to drink was thine.[165]

Ames denied the possibility of being certain even of astrological weather predictions and explained that "The Book of Fate is hid from all created Beings." [166] A 1746 article in *The American Magazine* argued that not only lunacy but inconstancy were caused by the moon.

162. *Ibid.*, pp. 156-57. For the new cosmology, see chap. 6, below.
163. *Ibid.*, p. 347.
164. Culpeper, *Pharmacopoeia Londinensis*, p. [xvi].
165. Leeds, *The American Almanack for . . . 1739*.
166. Ames, *The Almanacks of Nathaniel Ames*, p. 334.

But when I say this, I would not be mistaken, as if I thought it an
incurable Distemper; for if we strive against it, we may overcome it:
Right Reason and good Resolution being capable of curing it, and
reducing us to a more steady and uniform Method in our
Proceedings.[167]

Benjamin Franklin ironically but accurately mirrored this viewpoint
when he explained that Titan Leeds was undoubtedly dead "because the
Stars are seldom disappointed, never but in the Case of wise Men, . . . and
they fore-show'd his Death at the Time I predicted it." [168]


V


   Astrology in eighteenth-century America was clearly a subject in a
state of decline. It did not have the prestige or importance it had had in
Renaissance Europe. Its primary vehicle was the lowly almanac, the
literature of the semiliterate. No learned tracts were written about it in
the colonies and those which mentioned it in passing are found only early
in the century. But, if astrology no longer had a dominant role in the
eighteenth century, it had survived. Medical astrology, at least in governing phlebotomies, was still used by many, even if it was no longer a
part of contemporary medical theory. Almanac prognostications may not
have influenced many persons, but some individuals in all classes consulted astrologers.
   The decline of astrology was not accompanied by any great disputes or
polemics. Although casual attacks were occasionally made on astrology,
only one man, and he a reformed astrologer with the proverbial zeal of an
apostate, devoted much effort to doing so.[169] Perhaps the best symbol of
astrology's decline in the colonies is Samuel Johnson who, after 1716,
never again mentioned astrology either in revisions of his encyclopedia or
in the rest of his long career. The colonial decline of astrology is similar to
the pattern found by one scholar in Europe; it is not disproved (the efforts

   167. "Reflections on Inconstancy," *The American Magazine and Historical
Chronicle*, III (1746): 121.
   168. Franklin, *Papers*, II: 3.
   169. Jacob Taylor, *Almanacks for 1740, 1741, 1743, 1745*.

of Boyle, Morton, and Ames show that it could be made to agree with eighteenth-century science), but is simply displaced from the center of attention by new ideas.[170] This process was already underway in New England, at least, by the start of the eighteenth century.[171]

In astrology, as in other sciences both old and new, the colonies were clearly dependent upon and imitative of Europe. The use and the form of the almanac, the astrological terminology and beliefs, and the continued use of Culpeper all display a colonial dependency upon an earlier English tradition. Such items as Swift's satire, the constant availability of British reprints of Culpeper, the use by Chambers's *Cyclopedia* of Boyle's defense of astrology, and the many English astrological almanacs [172] all point to colonial astrology as being not a provincial relic of an outdated idea but an integral part of a continued British interest in astrology.

170. Mark Graubard, "Some Contemporary Observations on Ancient Superstitions," *Journal of American Folklore*, LIX (January-March 1945): 125.

171. See Michael G. Hall, "Renaissance Science in Puritan New England," in Archibald R. Lewis, ed. *Aspects of the Renaissance: A Symposium* (Austin, Tex.: University of Texas Press, 1967), p. 135.

172. See, for example, William Andrews, *Remarkable News from the Stars: Or, an Ephemeris for . . . 1738* (London: A. Wilde); Henry Coley, *Merlinus Angelicus Junior: Or the Starry Messenger, for . . . 1738* (London: J. Read); Francis Moore, *Vox Stellarum: Or, a Loyal Almanack for . . . 1738* (London: Samuel Idle).

# 3

## Witchcraft

*The giving up of witchcraft is, in effect, giving up the Bible. . . .*
—John Wesley, *Journal,* 1768

## I

Although the scholarly study of witchcraft is clearly undergoing a renaissance,[1] the nineteenth-century complaint of Samuel G. Drake about the study of colonial American witchcraft still has considerable validity: "So much Prominence has been given to what is called the *Salem Witchcraft,* that what had occurred in the Country before and since 1692 is, and has been, overlooked or almost entirely lost sight of." [2] Thus, such recent prominent works on colonial witchcraft as John Demos's "Underlying Themes in the Witchcraft of Seventeenth-Century New England," [3]

1. H. C. Erik Midelfort, "Recent Witch Hunting Research, or Where Do We Go from Here?" *Papers of the Bibliographical Society of America,* LXII (3rd Quarter, 1968): 373-420; Lawrence Stone, "The Disenchantment of the World," *New York Review of Books,* Dec. 2, 1971, pp. 17-25; W. R. Jones, "Abracadabra—Sorcery and Witchcraft in European Witchcraft," *History Teacher,* V (November 1971): 26-36.

2. Samuel G. Drake, *Annals of Witchcraft in New England and Elsewhere in the United States* (New York: Benjamin Bloom, 1967), p. viii.

3. John Demos, "Underlying Themes in the Witchcraft of Seventeenth-Century New England," *The American Historical Review,* LXXV (June 1970): 1311-326.

66

Chadwick Hansen's controversial *Witchcraft at Salem,*[4] and Boyer and Nissenbaum's *Salem Possessed*[5] continue the traditional emphasis upon the events at Salem. Other episodes of seventeenth-century witchcraft, however, have also received some scholarly attention. Several studies have adequately discussed seventeenth-century witchcraft in specific colonies,[6] and recently there has appeared a sophisticated study of colonial witchcraft before Salem.[7]

For the eighteenth century, however, Drake's complaint is still valid. With one exception, there exists no study which even attempts to discuss the period adequately.[8] There are several probable causes for this, including what appears to be an implicit assumption that the aftermath of Salem and the coming of the Enlightenment struck a fatal blow to the belief in witchcraft. Perhaps it is even more important to note the change which occurs in the nature of the available evidence when one reaches the eighteenth century. The seventeenth century provided historians with a type of evidence that they could use with confidence, namely, court records. These are contemporary with the event, have a definite date, and are presumably accurate as to what was said and done in court, although historians view the objective reality of such testimony and confessions with almost complete disbelief. Moreover, for "social-science"-oriented historians, such records contain data which can be used to analyze the social relationships involved in the witchcraft disputes, and thus the

4. Chadwick Hansen, *Witchcraft at Salem* (New York: George Braziller, 1969).

5. Paul Boyer and Stephen Nissenbaum, *Salem Possessed: The Social Origins of Witchcraft* (Cambridge: Harvard University Press, 1974).

6. Francis Neal Parke, *Witchcraft in Maryland* (n.p.: n.p., 1937); Richard Beale Davis, "The Devil in Virginia in the Seventeenth Century," *Virginia Magazine of History and Biography,* LXV (April 1957): 131-49; John M. Taylor, *The Witchcraft Delusion in Colonial Connecticut, 1647-1697* (New York: The Grafton Press, 1908). See also Drake, *Annals of Witchcraft.*

7. Frederick C. Drake, "Witchcraft in the American Colonies, 1647-62," *American Quarterly,* XX (Winter 1968): 694-725.

8. Richard M. Dorson, *Jonathan Draws the Long Bow* (Cambridge: Harvard University Press, 1946), chap. ii. This work, by a prominent folklorist, makes extensive use of New England town histories, and I have used it extensively as a guide to such works.

societal causes and functions of witchcraft.[9] In the later nineteenth and the twentieth centuries a new form of evidence appeared as folklorists began collecting such beliefs and stories in the field.[10]

As we have neither of these sources in a satisfactory form for the eighteenth century, it will be well worth our while to examine two well-documented witchcraft cases near the turn of the century: the Salem witch-hunt in the 1690s and the Grace Sherwood affair in Virginia in 1705-6. The witch-hunt in Salem, Massachusetts (actually not the town of Salem but, rather, the outlying parish of Salem Village, which in 1757 finally became the independent town of Danvers), originated in the household of the Reverent Samuel Parris, minister of the Salem Village church. Samuel Parris's daughter Betty and his niece Abigail Williams, aged nine and eleven respectively, spent much of the time with Parris's West Indian slave Tituba, who taught them minor spells and fortune-telling techniques. They were soon joined by a group of friends in this forbidden lore, mostly unmarried girls between the ages of twelve and twenty.

These activities came to the notice of the community at large, not

9. Thus a major reason for MacFarlane's concentrating upon Essex County, England, was that "it possessed very good series of all the important court records," while Thomas's study of English witchcraft continued only through the seventeenth century because "the sources also dictate a halt at the end of the seventeenth century, since the records of both lay and church courts cease around that time to be so informative on the matters with which I am concerned." Alan D. J. MacFarlane, *Witchcraft in Tudor and Stuart England* (New York: Harper & Row, 1970), p. 7; Keith Thomas, *Religion and the Decline of Magic* (New York: Charles Scribner's Sons, 1971), p. ix.

10. For a few random examples see Thomas, *Kentucky Superstitions*, pp. 277-83; Wheaton P. Webb, "Witches in Cooper Country," *New York Folklore Quarterly*, I (February 1945): 5-20; W. J. Hoffman, "Folk-Lore of the Pennsylvania Germans," *Journal of American Folk-Lore*, II (January-March 1889): 32-33; Emelyn Elizabeth Gardner, *Folklore from the Schoharie Hills, New York* (Ann Arbor: University of Michigan Press, 1937), pp. 44-84; Newman Ivey White, general ed., *The Frank C. Brown Collection of North Carolina Folklore*, vol. I, *Games and Rhymes, Beliefs and Customs, . . . Tales and Legends*, ed. by Paul G. Brewster (Durham, N.C.: Duke University Press, 1952): 643-68; vol. VII, *Popular Beliefs and Superstitions from North Carolina*, ed. by Wayland D. Hand (Durham, N.C.: Duke University Press, 1964): 99-181.

through discovery of the girls' "little sorceries," which probably would have merely earned them a lecture and a beating that would have ended the entire affair, but rather, through the strange actions of the children. First Betty, the youngest and perhaps the most guilt-ridden over their illicit activities, then Abigail, then the other girls not of the Parris household all started acting most oddly. They went into apparent trances, made strange barking sounds, ran around on all fours, went into convulsions, screaming and writhing, screamed at the sound of prayers, and interrupted services. The local doctor was consulted and gave his diagnosis: "The evil hand is on them."

The problem having been diagnosed as witchcraft, it was now a spiritual rather than a medical problem. A half-dozen ministers from nearby communities came, observed with horror, and prayed, but to no avail. Some of the girls sat dully through it, but others, especially Abigail, shrieked and disrupted the service.

The next step was obvious. Medicine and prayer having proved useless, the law must be invoked to identify the witches and deal with them. Constant questioning of the afflicted girls as to who was tormenting and bewitching them finally brought answers. First named was Tituba, and then the names of Sarah Good and Sarah Osburne followed. All three were natural scapegoats. Tituba, who was first named by a hysterical Betty and then confirmed by the other girls, was an Indian slave from the West Indies, an outsider, who had in fact been teaching the girls magic. Sarah Good fitted the popular image of a witch, an old hag, to perfection. She looked old and weatherbeaten; she was shrewish, idle, and slovenly; she had the dangerous habit of muttering under her breath, which could easily, and perhaps rightly, be construed as cursing; and as a penniless beggar she was a nuisance to the community. Sarah Osburne was neither as much of an outsider as Tituba nor as obvious a stereotype as Sarah Good, but she too was a subject of hostile village gossip. She had married an indentured servant who had been living with her on her farm, and she had frequently missed church services.

With the witches identified—and at this point it was thought that these three were all that were involved—the next step was a series of hearings and trials to decide their fate. At this step in the proceedings, what had been a relatively routine episode of witchcraft exploded into a witch-hunt. From these three witches the affair spread until probably about one hundred were imprisoned upon suspicion or conviction of witchcraft.

People of both sexes, various social stations, and all ages were accused. The youngest imprisoned witch was the four- or five-year-old daughter of Sarah Good. Described as "hale and well looking" when jailed, she, unlike her mother, survived; but eighteen years later her father stated: "She hath ever since been very chargeable, having little or no reason to govern herself."

Just why a witch-hunt happened in this place at this time has been the subject of much discussion. It has been attributed to the unsettled conditions of Massachusetts at this time, due to the lose of the charter and uncertainty over the aftermath of the overthrow of the Dominion of New England; it has been attributed to generational conflicts between girls and older women in New England towns; and it has been attributed to the unusually sharp and bitter factionalism within Salem Village. But equally important in explaining the wild spread of the witch-hunt were the procedures and methods used in the formal hearings and trials of the alleged witches.

One of the most controversial aspects of those proceedings was the use of spectral evidence: that is, claims by the afflicted girls that they had been assaulted by the image or specter of an individual, although that specter was invisible to all but the witches and afflicted girls, was accepted as eyewitness evidence against the accused witch. This virtually eliminated any possible defense, for the physical body of the witch could be miles away from where the actual witchcraft was said to occur. In the case of the Reverend George Burroughs, who had the great misfortune of having previously served as a minister in Salem Village, his spectral image was seen assaulting the girls in Salem while he himself was ministering in Wells, Maine.

In court itself, the afflicted girls were a constant reminder and proof of the guilt of the accused. When suspected witches were on the stand the girls would be publicly bewitched by them. They would suffer fits, be choked, be pinched, and claim that it was done by the witch on the stand. When Martha Corey bit her lip, the girls claimed that she had bitten them, and rushed to show the magistrate their blood. When Rebecca Nurse made any movement in court, the girls claimed they were forced to follow it. When the girls had fits, they were brought to the accused witch who was forced to touch them, and if they recovered, as they always did, this proved that the accused had in fact been the one who had bewitched them in the first place. All but one of those who thus faced the girls in court failed the various tests and were proved witches. (Actually the jury also found Rebecca Nurse innocent, but the girls immediately had fits, and the chief justice then told the jury to reconsider. They did, found her guilty, and Rebecca Nurse was later hanged for witchcraft.)

Nearby Andover made the mistake of calling in two of the afflicted girls to identify the supposed handful of witches troubling Andover. The girls acted as they had in court, falling into fits and then touching various individuals. If they recovered from the fit, the individual they had touched was identified as a witch. Unfortunately, virtually everyone they touched was identified as a witch, and before the proceedings were ended, warrants had been issued for the arrest of forty people as witches.

The children were not the only evidence of course. The witches were tested for witches' marks, and neighbors told of suspicious illnesses, injuries to cattle, etc. More important than this, however, in spreading the witch-hunt was another form of proof extensively used, the confession of accused witches. The first to follow this path was Tituba. She, reportedly after being well beaten by her master, the Reverend Samuel Parris, not only confessed to witchcraft but also stated she had seen nine names in the Devil's Book. This book played a major role at Salem. The afflicted girls frequently had to resist being forced or talked into signing it. Sometimes it was offered by a black man (the devil), other times it was offered by one of the witches. Its purpose was explained in a sermon at Salem by Deodat Lawson, a former minister at Salem Village and an interested spectator at the trials: "So far as we can look into those hellish mysteries, and guess at the administration of that kingdom of darkness, we may learn that witches make witches by persuading one the other to subscribe to a book. . . ." But the shock over Tituba's testimony was not about the existence of the Devil's Book but the fact that there were nine names in it. Only three witches had been identified at that time; therefore six more witches remained unknown and at large. Pressure was again brought to bear on the girls to name more witches. They did, and the witch-hunt spread. So too the mythology of Salem witchcraft grew. The testimony of the afflicted girls and the confessions of the accused witches painted a picture not only of witches attacking people and livestock but also of formal contracts with the devil and witches' Sabbaths.

Why did witches confess? For one thing, it was the only path to safety. Persons accused of witchcraft who confessed fully, including the naming of their fellow witches, were left unharmed; those who claimed to be

innocent were jailed and faced trial with an apparently inevitable conviction and execution to follow. Several confessed witches recanted and then
attempted to explain why they had confessed in the first place. Margaret
Jacobs, who in confessing had implicated the Reverend George Burroughs and her own grandfather, recanted, and said, "They told me, if I
would not confess, I should be put down into the dungeon, and would be
hanged, but, if I would confess, I should have my life: the which did so
affright me, with my own vile, wicked heart, to save my life, made me
make the like confession I did, which confession, may it please the
honored Court, is altogether false and untrue." Happily, Margaret Jacobs
was then forgiven by Burroughs and apparently reconciled with her
grandfather, who inserted a gift to her in his will after learning of her
recantation. Less happily, it did not "please the honored Court," and she
was jailed. Burroughs and her grandfather were executed.

A recantation by six Andover women illustrates not only the desire for
self-preservation but also the total confusion that led to confessions.

> Whereupon we were all seized as prisoners, by a warrant from the
> justice of the peace, and forthwith carried to Salem; and by reason of
> that sudden surprisal, we knowing ourselves altogether innocent of
> that crime, we were all exceedingly astonished and amazed, and
> consternated and affrighted, even out of our reason; and our nearest
> and dearest relations, seeing us in that dreadful condition, and
> knowing our great danger, apprehended there was no other way to
> save our lives, as the case was then circumstanced, but by our
> confessing ourselves to be such and such persons as the afflicted
> represented us to be, they, out of tenderness and pity, persuaded us
> to confess what we did confess. And, indeed, that confession that it is
> said we made was no other than what was suggested to us by some
> gentlemen, they telling us that we were witches, and they knew it,
> and we knew it, which made us think it was so; and, our under-
> standings, our reason, our faculties almost gone, we were not capa-
> ble of judging of our condition; as also the hard measures they used
> with us rendered us incapable of making our defence, but said any
> thing, and every thing which they desired, and most of what we said
> was but in effect a consenting to what they said.

Exactly what "hard measures" refers to is unclear. Perhaps it refers to
extended cross examination and being bound with manacles and chains

even while in jail. But for at least some of the men a more straightforward form of torture was used. They were tied neck to their feet until they confessed or until blood ran from their nostrils.

Even some of the afflicted girls tried to recant, but with no success. Mary Warren attempted to do so when John Procter, her master, was accused of witchcraft. She said that the girls "did but dissemble." That earned her accusations from the other girls that now she was a witch. She was summoned before a magistrate, and when she attempted to recant she was called a witch and all the other girls went into their customary fits. She tried several times to tell the truth, but was always so shaken by the sharp attack of the examining magistrates that she eventually gave up and was restored to the ranks of the afflicted girls.

Another of the afflicted girls who attempted to recant was Sarah Churchill. She had previously stated that she had signed the Devil's Book, but told Sarah Ingersoll that that was false. The latter in turn gave a deposition to the court about what Sarah Churchill had told her. Sarah Churchill had said that she signed the Devil's Book "because they threatened her, and told her they would put her into the dungeon, and put her along with Mr. Burroughs." She had also explained the uselessness of recanting. "If she told Mr. Noyes [a minister from Salem who was active in the prosecution of the witches] but once she had set her hand to the book, he would believe her; but, if she told the truth, and said she had not set her hand to the book a hundred times, he would not believe her." Her forbodeings were correct, and this deposition seems to have been ignored.

After trial and conviction came execution. Nineteen witches were hanged at Salem. (Burning in colonial America seems to have been reserved for the one offense considered even more heinous than witch-craft—slave revolts.) One old man, Giles Corey, was pressed to death. This was an English legal procedure designed to force a defendant to plead either guilty or not guilty at the start of a trial, for without a plea the trial could not proceed. Giles Corey refused to plead. Perhaps by thus preventing himself from being convicted of witchcraft he hoped to prevent his property from being sequestered, or perhaps he simply did it out of contempt for the court. He was then pressed. Stones were put on his chest to force him to plead. Tradition has it that he was silent except for a muttered "more weight"; he remained mute until crushed to death.

Finally the witch-hunt came to an end. First spectral evidence was no longer accepted, which resulted in a sudden rash of not guilty verdicts. Then the trials were stopped, the jails emptied, and eventually even pardons and compensation were given to the convicted witches and their families. Why did it end? Some think that it was due to the oppostion of the clergy to spectral evidence, but this opposition had existed earlier. Probably the best explanation is one that has recently been offered to explain the ending of similar witch-hunts in Germany.

> Large panic trials were basically different from the smaller trials in that they depended on masses of denunciations whose truth was hardly doubted. As a series of witch trials progressed, the typical stereotype of the old woman, living a solitary and eccentric exis-tence, usually began to break down. As witches were tortured into denouncing others whom they had seen at the sabbath, age and sex barriers crumbled until anyone, even the magistrates, could be accused of witchcraft. This progress towards anarchy corrected itself by controls within society in every large hunt known in the German Southwest. Not the Swedes, but a crisis of confidence in the judicial procedures, brought panic to a halt. We found signs of this crisis in the statements of magistrates as well as from members of the popu-lace who came to realize that if the law were given free rein, no one would be safe from its relentless grasp. We suggested that this crisis was especially evident where stereotypes broke down most completely. . . .
>
> . . . The crisis of confidence in judicial procedures may have forced men to search their traditions for a new understanding of the interrelations of God, the devil, and the world. Only rarely did such reevaluation produce a genuine disbelief in the devil or a denial of witchcraft. We know of no such denials in the German Southwest. Men had lost instead the ability accurately to detect witches. From their own experiences men had learned that the attempt to purge the body politic was not worth the agony that resulted.

This interpretation appears to reflect accurately what happened at Salem. The stereotype was broken by the accusation and conviction of large numbers of men and women of all ages including respectable church members, a minister, and people of even higher station. Many such accusations may have been officially ignored by the magistrates who knew the accused personally, but nevertheless the charges against respectable people were bruited about and so had their impact against the stereotype.

This effect of breaking the stereotype was recognized by Parris even as he argued against it in a sermon.

> It may serve to reprove such as seem to be so amazed at the war the Devil has raised amongst us by wizards and witches, against the Lamb and his followers, that they altogether deny it. If ever there were witches, men and women in covenant with the Devil, here are multitudes in New England. Nor is it so strange a thing that there should be such; no, nor that some church-members should be such. Pious Bishop Hall saith, "The Devil's prevalency in this age is most clear in the marvelous number of witches abounding in all places. Now hundreds (says he) are discovered in one shire; and, if fame deceive us not, in a village of fourteen houses in the north are found so many of this damned brood. Heretofore, only barbarous deserts had them; but now the civilized and religious parts are frequently pestered with them. Heretofore, some silly, ignorant old woman, &c.; but now we have known those of both sexes who professed much knowledge, holiness, and devotion, drawn into this damnable practice.

But despite all that Parris could say, and all the citations from the "Pious Bishop Hall" he could muster, the stereotype was too shattered and the danger of continuing trials too clear, for the witch-hunt to go on. And, curiously enough, the ending of the witch-hunt and the sharp doubts about the validity of the procedures used at Salem were about the only results. Many colonists, as we shall see, continued to believe in the reality of witchcraft and even in the reality of the witches at Salem. Many would have agreed with the statement made by Dr. Isaac Watts, the famous English author of hymns and other religious and educational works, in a 1720 letter to Cotton Mather: "I am much persuaded that there was much immediate agency of the Devil in these affairs [the Salem witch-hunt], and perhaps there were some real witches too." [11]

11. The best narrative treatments of Salem are the nineteenth-century study by Charles W. Upham, *Salem Witchcraft* (New York: Frederick Ungar Publishing Co., 1966), and the more modern study by Marion L. Starkey, *The Devil in Massachusetts* (Garden City, N.Y.: Doubleday & Company, Inc., 1969). With one exception, all of my quotations from Salem come from these works. The excep-

With the Grace Sherwood affair in Virginia in 1705-6 we reach the last well-documented witchcraft trial in America (although there are later cases involving slander suits brought by accused witches against their accusers). In February 1697/98 Grace Sherwood and her husband sued Richard Capp for defamation in a case which was eventually settled out of court by a private agreement. The exact nature of the defamation was not stated, but her next set of suits make her reputation quite clear. In September 1698 the Sherwoods sued John and Jane Gisburne for saying that Grace "is a Witch and bewitched their piggs to Death and bewitched their Cotton. . . ." In the same month the Sherwoods also sued Anthony and Elizabeth Barnes for saying that "Grace came to her [Elizabeth Barnes] one night and rid her and went out the key hole or crack of the door like a black Catt. . . ." The Sherwoods lost both suits and were required to pay court costs. It is of course possible that they were merely unable to prove their case, but in view of what happened soon after, it is far more likely that the juries were in fact influenced by the possibility that the statements had been true.

Having failed to vindicate herself by slander suits, Grace Sherwood was soon forced onto the defensive. In 1705-6, Luke and Elizabeth Hill, who had just been involved in a civil action for assault and battery against Grace Sherwood, accused her of witchcraft. A jury of women were summoned to examine her for witch's marks and found "Two things like titts with Severall other Spotts. . . ." The Virginia attorney general found the case against her defective because it failed to specify any specific act of witchcraft by her, but as there was so much suspicion against her she was reexamined.

---

tion is the description of Sarah Good's daughter after being imprisoned, which came from Boyer, *Salem Possessed,* p. 5. This work, together with Demos, "Underlying Themes," and Hansen, *Witchcraft at Salem,* are the major interpretive studies. The quotations about the breaking of the stereotype come from H. C. Erik Midelfort, *Witch Hunting in Southwestern Germany, 1562-1684: The Social and Intellectual Foundations* (Stanford, Calif.: Stanford University Press, 1972), pp. 194, 196. For the argument that Tituba was wholly of West Indian origin rather than being part-Indian and part-black, as has been traditionally believed, see Chadwick Hansen, "The Metamorphosis of Tituba, or Why American Intellectuals can't Tell an Indian Witch from a Negro," *The New England Quarterly,* XLVII (March 1974); 3-12.

This time she was accused in sworn testimony of "Many Cercumstances in which She could not make any excuse or Little or nothing to say in her own Behalf...." Apparently in desperation, Grace Sherwood agreed to the popular but extralegal test of swimming. In this procedure the suspect was bound and cast into the water. If she sank she was innocent (and she would, hopefully, be fished out of the water before drowning), but if she stayed afloat it was taken as evidence of guilt. The first effort to apply the water test was called off because the weather was so bad that "it might endanger her health." But the second attempt was completed, and she remained afloat. She was also reexamined by "ffive antient weoman who have all Declared on Oath that She is not like them nor noe Other woman that they know of having two things like titts on her private parts of a Black Coller being Blacker than the Rest of her Body...." Under these extremely suspicious circumstances, she was ordered held for trial, but the court records for the following year are unfortunately lost. Somehow, however, she either managed to be found not guilty or else escaped with a relatively mild punishment, for we know that she was alive in 1733 and her will was not probated until 1740.[12]

Unfortunately, for the eighteenth century we rarely have such extensive documentation. Instead we have some laws and lawbooks, a few scattered literary and personal accounts, and legends. The latter is a rich source, especially for New England where it was mined early by John Greenleaf Whittier,[13] and where many town and local histories written in

12. The documents concerning Grace Sherwood are printed in the *William and Mary Quarterly*, 1st Series, III: 96-101, 190-92, 242-45; IV: 18-22. Some of them can also be found in George Lincoln Burr, ed., *Narratives of the Witchcraft Cases, 1648-1706* (New York: Barnes & Noble, Inc., 1968), pp. 438-42. See also Davis, "The Devil in Virginia," pp. 146-47.

Abbreviations using thorns and superscripts, such as "y$^e$" for "that," have been expanded.

For swimming witches see George Lyman Kittredge, *Witchcraft in Old and New England* (New York: Russell & Russell, 1956), pp. 232-38, and Christina Hole, *Witchcraft in England* (London: Collier-Macmillan, Ltd., 1966), pp. 86-89.

13. [John Greenleaf Whittier], *The Supernaturalism of New England* (London: Wiley and Putnam, 1847); *idem, Legends of New England (1831): A Facsimile Reproduction*, introduction by John B. Pickard (Gainesville, Florida: Scholars Facsimiles Reprints, 1965); *idem, Moll Pitcher. A Poem* (Boston: Carter and Hendee, 1832).

the nineteenth and twentieth centuries devote a few pages to local legends of the supernatural. But this lore lacks much in the way of details and specificity. Often it lacks dates, and is vague and unverifiable. One such story, before being used by George Lyman Kittredge, was first printed in a local newspaper, after being related by the grandson of a shipmate of the victim.[14] Legends transmitted orally in this manner obviously cannot be used in the same way as can orthodox historical sources. Many details must have been lost, added, or distorted in the transmittal. Thus, for example, the type of sociological analysis done by Demos, Macfarlane, and Boyer and Nissenbaum on the relationship of the accused and the accuser (inverted in such historical analysis from the relationship of the witch and the victim) cannot be performed with such data. Nor is there enough precision in the dating of these legends to permit the creation of a chronological analysis of instances of witchcraft, such as has been done recently for part of the seventeenth century.[15] The survival of legends appears to have been too haphazard to permit even an analysis of the spatial distribution of eighteenth-century witchcraft. Yet the legends cannot be ignored. That would result in a much more serious distortion of reality than would result from an uncritical acceptance of them. These legends, if corroborated by other data, help illustrate the general character of eighteenth-century witchcraft. Moreover, although no meaningful count can be made of them, yet their prevalence at least indicates that the examples of witchcraft found in more reliable sources are not isolated archaisms, but rather, are the tip of the iceberg extending above the waterline of literacy.

## II

The legal history of colonial witchcraft in the eighteenth century can be traced back to seventeenth-century England where there had been passed in 1604 the most famous of all English witchcraft statutes, 1 James I, ch. 12. It provided the death penalty for all those who "practise, or exercise any invocation, or conjuration of any evil and wicked spirit, or shall consult, covenante with, entertaine, employe, feede, or rewarde any evil and wicked spirit, to, or for any intent or purpose, . . ." or who dug

14. Kittredge, *Witchcraft in Old and New England,* pp. 219, 528.
15. Frederick C. Drake, "Witchcraft in the American Colonies, 1647-62."

up a corpse to use in magical rites, or who used any form of magic whatsoever "whereby any person shall be killed, destroyed, wasted, consumed, pined or lamed in his or her bodie, or any part thereof. . . ." For using magic to find treasure or lost or stolen property, to provoke unlawful love, to harm cattle or other property, or unsuccessfully to attempt to harm an individual, the penalty was a year's imprisonment, with the prisoner to be displayed once in each quarter at the pillory. For the second offense the penalty was death. In 1736 Great Britain replaced this statute with 9 George II, ch. 5, which merely provided for a year's imprisonment for those who "pretend to exercise or use any kind of witchcraft, sorcery, inchantment . . . ." It was a law directed against those who fraudulently claimed to be a witch. Witchcraft itself was no longer a criminal offense.[16]

During the late seventeenth and early eighteenth centuries, the Jacobean statute on witchcraft was adopted by a number of colonies. The first to do so was Massachusetts, which in late 1692, when the Salem witchcraft craze was drawing to a close, replaced its previous legislation on the subject with a statute that, although not specifically citing it, was a close copy of the Jacobean statute. It added a distinctive New England note, however, by requiring that those exposed at the pillory each quarter should publicly confess their offense and wear a placard upon which their offense was to be "written in capital letters and placed upon . . . [their] breast."[17] This law, however, was disallowed by England in 1695. This disallowance, one should hasten to add, was not caused by any doubts about the propriety or legitimacy of witchcraft acts in general; rather, it was due to a somewhat technical conflict between the Massachusetts act and the relevant English act, 1 James I, ch. 12. The Massachusetts act, unlike the Jacobean one, did not protect the rights of widows and heirs of

16. Both statutes are printed in full in Thomas Cooper, ed., *The Statutes at Large of South Carolina* (Columbia, S.C.: A. S. Johnson, 1836-39), II: 508-10. For a discussion of earlier English witchcraft legislation, see MacFarlane, *Witchcraft in Tudor and Stuart England,* pp. 14-20, and Kittredge, *Witchcraft in Old and New England,* pp. 281-84.

17. For the text of the statute see *The Charters and General Laws of the Colony and Province of Massachusetts Bay* (Boston: T. B. Wait and Co., 1814), pp. 735-36. See also Sanford J. Fox, *Science and Justice: The Massachusetts Witchcraft Trials* (Baltimore: Johns Hopkins University Press, 1968), p. 41.

convicted witches to their dower and inheritance from the witches' estates. It is also worth noting that although Massachusetts repassed with perfecting amendments a number of other statutes which had been disallowed at the same time for similar technical reasons, it choose, in the aftermath of Salem, not to bother reenacting the witchcraft act.[18]

In 1712 South Carolina had passed an omnibus act which cited and put into effect in that province numerous English statutes, including the Jacobean witchcraft act. It was apparently never formally repealed or replaced during the colonial period, although it was omitted from a 1761 legal handbook and listed as obsolete in a 1790 compilation of the laws of the state.[19] In Pennsylvania a 1718 omnibus act adopted the witchcraft law, and in 1719 the commissions for at least some Pennsylvania justices of the peace authorized them to inquire about "witchcrafts, enchantments, sorceries, and magick arts." [20] In 1754 a committee to inspect the laws recommended that as the law had been repealed in England and "seems unnecessary here," it be replaced by 9 George II, ch. 5.[21] Apparently, however, nothing was done at this time, for a late eighteenth-century compilation of Pennsylvania statutes noted that this law had remained in force until 1794.[22]

Delaware, following the precedent of her larger sister colony, had

18. *Copy of the Orders for Repealing of Several Acts* (Boston: Printed by Order of the Honorable the Lieutenant Governor and Council; by Bartholomew Green, and John Allen, 1697); *Acts of the Privy Council of England. Colonial Series* (Hereford: Printed for His Majesty's Stationery Office by the Hereford Times Co., Ltd., 1910), II: 842; A. G. Dorland, *The Royal Disallowance in Massachusetts* (Bulletin of the Departments of History and Political and Economic Science in Queens University, Kingston, Ontario, Canada, No. 22, January 1917), p. 14.

19. *The Public Laws of the State of South Carolina* (Philadelphia: Aitken and Son, 1790), p. 73; Cooper, *The Statutes at Large of South Carolina,* II: 508-10, argued that the repeal of the Jacobean act extended only to England and Scotland and did not affect its validity elsewhere. William Simpson, *The Practical Justice of the Peace . . . of His Majesty's Province of South-Carolina* (Charleston: Robert Wells, 1761).

20. *Laws of the Commonwealth of Pennsylvania* (Philadelphia: Hall and Sellers, 1797), I: 137; Lawrence Lewis, Jr., "The Courts of Pennsylvania in the Seventeenth Century," *Pennsylvania Magazine of History and Biography,* V (1881): 171.

21. *Pennsylvania Archives,* 8th Series, V, 3648.

22. *Laws of the Commonwealth of Pennsylvania,* I: 137n.

enacted the Jacobean statute in a 1719 omnibus act.[23] It was quicker to change, however, and repealed the law in 1779, replacing it with an act which punished fraudulent claims to magical powers. The act provided for payment of double damages to defrauded victims, and carefully provided that those who failed to pay would be sold for up to seven years of servitude.[24] The last colony to pass an act punishing witchcraft was Rhode Island, which in 1730 passed an omnibus act which stated "That Witchcraft is, and shall be Felony; and whosoever shall be lawfully convicted thereof, shall suffer the Pains of Death," thus maintaining the harshness, simplicity, and lack of detail typical of seventeenth-century New England witchcraft legislation.[25]

Nor did failure to enact a specific legislation concerning witchcraft necessarily leave a colony without legal recourse. Colonies that customarily used English common law, or that used English statutes when their own laws were silent, were well protected.[26] It may be significant that only in colonies which lacked specific witchcraft legislation did some legal handbooks follow the precedent of Michael Dalton's *The Country Justice* by noting that under the common law all witches were to be burnt.[27]

More frequently used, perhaps, than the statutes themselves were legal

23. *Laws of the State of Delaware* (Newcastle: Samuel and John Adams, 1797), I: 68.

24. *Ibid.,* II: 669.

25. *The Charter . . . of Rhode-Island. Acts and Laws . . . of Rhode-Island* (New Port: James Franklin, 1730), p. 170. According to Drake this law was enacted in 1728. See Samuel G. Drake, *Annals of Witchcraft,* p. 217.

26. Paul Samuel Reinsch, "English Common Law in the Early American Colonies," *Bulletin of the University of Wisconsin,* vol. II, no. 31, pp. 34, 43, 49-50, 54; Herbert Alan Johnson, "The Advent of Common Law in Colonial New York," George Athan Billias, ed., *Law and Authority in Colonial America* (Barre, Mass.: Barre Publishers, 1965), p. 86; Joseph H. Smith, "The Foundations of Law in Maryland: 1634-1715," Billias, ed., *Law and Authority in Colonial America,* pp. 97-100; Julius Goebel, Jr., *Law Enforcement in Colonial New York* (New York: The Commonwealth Fund, 1944), pp. xvii-xviii.

27. Michael Dalton, *The Country Justice* (In the Savoy: E. & R. Nutt, and R. Gosling, 1727), p. 513; George Webb, *The Office and Authority of a Justice of the Peace* (Williamsburg, William Parks, 1736), p. 361; James Davis, *The Office and Authority of a Justice of Peace* (Newbern, N.C.: James Davis, 1774), p. 374. Davis probably copied Webb. See *infra,* p. 84.

handbooks written to aid the often untrained justices of the peace. Among the most popular of these in the seventeenth and early eighteenth centuries (Maryland ordered it for the use of her county courts) was Dalton's *The Country Justice*.[28] This English work, first published in 1618 and reprinted over twenty times before the end of the eighteenth century, included both a summary of the Jacobean witchcraft statute and detailed instructions on how to identify a witch. Witches could be identified by their possession of a familiar spirit with which they conversed. Familiar spirits could appear in a multitude of forms: "in the Shape of a Man, Woman, Boy, Dog, Cat, Foal, Hare, Rat, Toad, &c." These familiars were fed from "witches teats" (any unnatural growth on the witch's body) and often left marks similar to flea bites. "And these the Devil's Marks be insensible, and being pricked will not bleed, and be often in their secretest Parts, and therefore require diligent and careful Search." While these were the most common conclusive proofs of witchcraft, there were others, such as the ownership of clay or wax images which could be used to bewitch victims.

Other facts, although not conclusive in themselves, could at least indicate that a person was a witch. These included cursing; a too diligent inquiry after sick people and going to visit them "especially being forbidden the House"; spectral images or the testimony of a victim; common repute, especially if the accused was a friend or relative of known witches; the testimony of other witches; and the bleeding of a corpse when touched by the suspect.

Michael Dalton, in *The Country Justice,* had also attempted to define the various terms used to denote different types of illicit magicians. Witches were those who made voluntary agreements with the devil and were inspired by sheer malice and the desire to harm others and gain revenge. Conjurers also made pacts with the devil but they fondly believed that they could compel and control the devil and were motivated by curiosity and

28. Parke, *Witchcraft in Maryland,* pp. 16-21; Tom Peete Cross, "Witchcraft in North Carolina," *Studies in Philology,* XVI (July 1919): 221-22; Shipton, "Literary Leaven in Provincial New England," p. 213; *William and Mary Quarterly,* 1st Series, VIII (July 1899): 20, and (October 1899): 78, Walter B. Edgar, "Some Popular Books in Colonial South Carolina," *The South Carolina Historical Magazine,* LXXII (July 1971): 176; George K. Smart, "Private Libraries in Colonial Virginia," *American Literature,* X (1938-39): 49, 51.

the desire to know secrets and work miracles. Soothsayers, wizards, enchanters, charmers, and sorcerers had no direct personal dealings with the devil, but they performed their feats "(seemingly at the least) by certain superstitious and ceremonial Forms of Words (called Charms) by them pronounced; or by Medicines, Herbs, or other Things applied, above the Course of Nature, and by the Devil's Help, and [implicit] Covenants made with him." [29]

A later edition of Dalton's *The Country Justice,* noting that 9 George II, ch. 5, had ended prosecutions for witchcraft, omitted "the Account and Description of Witches and Witchcraft, inserted in the former Editions of this Work." It did, however, summarize the new law against the "pretenders to Witchcraft and Fortune-tellers, &c. . . ." [30]

Some legal handbooks printed in the colonies also dealt with witchcraft, although with less detail than Dalton. The first was the anonymous *Conductor Generalis,* printed in Philadelphia in 1722 and reprinted in 1749, which included a condensed version of 1 James I, ch. 12.[31] By 1736 some doubt (if not confusion) became evident in a Virginia handbook written by George Webb, *The Office and Authority of a Justice of the Peace.* It stated that witchcraft "has been a subject of Controversy among learned Men; and latter Ages have produced very few Instances of Conviction of Witchcraft: But nevertheless, 'tis a Capital Offense, and, by the Common Law, such Offenders were to be burnt." This uncertainty over the reality of witchcraft was compounded by confusion over the proper attitude to take when confronted with an alleged incident of witchcraft. It warned that no action should be taken "without strong and apparent Cause, proved by sufficient Witnesses upon Oath . . . ," yet it contradicted itself in the very next paragraph where, citing Dalton, it pointed out quite logically that "plain and direct Evidence is not to be expected in these Works of Darkness, where no Witnesses are admitted, and therefore we can have only, either the Confession of the Offender, or pregnant and convincing Circumstances, whereupon to found an Indictment, or Conviction." [32]

29. Dalton, *The Country Justice* (1727), pp. 513-16.
30. Michael Dalton, *The Country Justice* (London: H. Lintot, 1742), p. 360.
31. *Conductor Generalis* (Philadelphia: Andrew Bradford, 1722), pp. 51-52; *Conductor Generalis* (2nd ed.; Philadelphia: Franklin & Hall, 1749), p. 53.
32. Webb, *The Office and Authority,* pp. 361-62.

After 1736, with the enactment in England of 9 George II, ch. 5, the discussion of witchcraft in the colonial legal handbooks naturally changed. Only the previously mentioned uncorrected 1749 edition of the *Conductor Generalis* continued to cite the now obsolete Jacobean statute as binding. In 1764 a New Jersey justice of the peace wrote another legal handbook entitled *Conductor Generalis*, which cited the new Georgian law.[33] A more complex and confused treatment of witchcraft is found in a 1774 North Carolina legal handbook authored by James Davis, *The Office and Authority of a Justice of Peace.* It repeated what Webb, in the Virginia work of the same title, had previously said about witchcraft; and it, too, summarized the old Jacobean law. However, it then noted the law's replacement by the new Georgian statute, but further confused matters by again following Webb in noting that witchcraft was still an offense at common law, punishable by burning.[34] This work might well have left its users confused as to the current status of witchcraft as a criminal offense. It is clear, however, that this confusion was not due to a desire by Davis to claim that witchcraft was still a criminal offense punishable by death. Rather, it was the result of a too slavish copying of Webb's work, which was now totally obsolete on the subject. Most post-1736 legal handbooks, however, simply ignored the topic of witchcarft entirely.[35] It is clear that this elimination of witchcraft from many colonial legal handbooks was the result not of a reaction against Salem or a growing rationalism and skepticism in the colonies (although the latter was clearly evident in Webb's work), but was simply a matter of conforming to the change in English statutory law.

## III

A few cases involving witchcraft did reach the courts even after the Grace Sherwood affair. In 1707, Francis Le Jau, a Huguenot turned

33. James Parker, *Conductor Generalis* (Woodbridge, N.J.: Parker for Hall, 1764), p. 467.

34. Davis, *The Office and Authority,* p. 374.

35. Richard Starke, *The Office and Authority of a Justice of Peace* (Williamsburg: Alexander Purdie and John Dixon, 1774); [Richard] Burn, *An Abridgment of Burn's Justice of the Peace and Parish Officers,* abridged by J.Greenleaf (Boston: Joseph Greenleaf, 1773), "Preface"; [Jacob, Giles], *Every Man His Own Lawyer* (7th ed.; New York: Hugh Gaine, 1768).

Society for the Propagation of the Gospel missionary in South Carolina, indignantly reported Carolina's laxness in prosecuting witches: "A notorious Malefactor evidently guilty of Witchcraft, & who has kill'd several Persons by the Devils was lately return'd Ignoramus by the Grand Jury; this makes me stand amazed that the Spirit of the Devil shou'd be so much respected, as to make men call open Witchcraft Immagination and no more." But this laxness, if it existed, could hardly be justly charged against the chief justice of South Carolina, Nicholas Trott, who warned a jury that although he did not want them "to be over credulous" about witchcraft, "yet that there are such creatures as witches I make no doubt: neither do I think they can be denied without denying the truth of the Holy Scriptures, or most grossly perverting them." [36]

In 1718 a man took the unusual step of accusing his mother of witchcraft before the church in Milton, Massachusetts. It backfired, and the accuser was instead declared guilty of violating the fifth, sixth, and ninth commandments.[37] In 1712 the Maryland Provincial Court indicted "Virtue Violl of Talbott County Spinster" for witchcraft. She was accused of causing Ellinore More to become speechless and her tongue to be "lame." Despite this grievous offense, she was acquitted.[38] Even as late as the 1740s, a correspondent of William Johnson of New York reported that "a Cart Loade of Old Dutch People" were seized by a constable on charges of witchcraft.[39]

---

36. Francis Le Jau, *The Carolina Chronicle of Dr. Francis Le Jau, 1706-1717,* ed. by Frank J. Klingberg (Berkeley and Los Angeles: University of California Press, 1956), pp. 25, 30; Edward McCrady, *The History of South Carolina Under the Proprietary Government, 1670-1719* (New York: The Macmillan Company, 1897), p. 450.

37. Emil Oberholzer, Jr., *Delinquent Saints* (New York: Columbia University Press, 1956), p. 75.

38. Parke, *Witchcraft in Maryland,* pp. 37-39.

39. Johnson, *The Papers of Sir William Johnson,* I: 44-45. There also exists a reported case of the judicial execution of a slave witch, by burning, in Virginia-governed Illinois, in the last quarter of the eighteenth century. John Reynolds, *The Pioneer History of Illinois* (2nd ed.: Chicago: Fergus Printing Company, 1887), p. 175; John Ashton, *The Devil in Britain and America* (n.p.: Ward and Downey, 1896), pp. 311-13. It has, however, been proved that the sentence was for poisoning, and the penalty was commuted to hanging. Clarence Walworth Alvord, ed., *Collections of the Illinois State Historical Library,* vol. II, *Virginia Series,*

In some instances, the alleged witch went to court herself. In 1724 Sarah Spencer was accused by the Ackleys of being a witch and of "riding and pinching." She replied by suing them for £500, and received £5 which on appeal was reduced to a token shilling. The Ackleys also received a formal acknowledgment from the court that they were not insane.[40]

A similar incident occurred in Maine in the 1720s in which John Spinney was first convicted, and then had the conviction reversed, on a charge that he "did Scandalize & abuse the sd Sarah Keen in Saying She was a witch & Said he could prove it. . . ." Both Spinney's accusation and the resulting libel suit were apparently part of an old local feud, but Sarah Keene seems to have already had a reputation as a witch. Much of the evidence at Spinney's trial was, in effect, an attempt to prove that Keene was indeed a witch. She had been seen in strange company, apparently riding with fairy folk; she was reputed to "ride" people; she had had an extra nipple on her breast; and strange sucking sounds had been heard at her house. Nor had she been loath to use her reputation for her own purposes. One witness told of an incident in which Sarah Keene

> having a Bridle in her hand Said She Could not find her mare and She Would Ride the Said Jno: Speney Down to Collonel Pepperells. The said Williams [the witness] further Saith that her Dafter Easter Came Took the Bridle from her mother Saying She would make the head of the Bridle Shorter and fit it for Said Spineyes head, and ride him her Selfe.

It may be, as the historian who has studied this case has argued, that the reversal of Spinney's conviction for slander was due to some doubt about what he actually had said and to the court's realization that this was merely an incident in an old quarrel. But it would be wrong simply to asume that the court could not find that Spinney had ample grounds for his accusation, and the reversal must have confirmed the belief of those who had testified against Sarah Keene that she was, in fact, a witch.[41]

---

vol. I, *Cohokia Records, 1778-1790* (Springfield, Ill.: Trustees of the Illinois State Historical Library, 1907), pp. 12-21.

40. Taylor, *The Witchcraft Delusion in Colonial Connecticut*, p. 155.

41. Neal W. Allen, "A Maine Witch," *Old-Time New England,* LXI (Winter 1971): 75-81.

In some instances, reputed witches may have gone to court not for damages, not in an aggressive counterattack against their enemies, but as a desperate attempt to clear their name. This is illustrated by the following pathetic letter, written somewhere in eighteenth-century America.

Pleas your Worships gentlemen Pray doo have some charety for me A Poor Distrest man that is become now old and Scars able too muntain my family at the best and Now Sum People has Raised a Reporte that My Wife is a Witch by Which I and my famely must Sartenly Suffer if She Cant be Clerd of the things and a Stop Poot to the Report for People not have no Delings with me on the account Pray Gentel men I Beeg the favor of you that one or more of you wood trie her for She is Desiros that She may be tried by all Maner of ways that Ever a Woman was tried so that she can git Clear of the Report.

from Your Poor and Humble Sarvent
Jearns Moor.[42]

One of the fullest descriptions of a witchcraft incident in eighteenth-century America comes not from court records but from an unprinted manuscript by the Reverent Ebenezer Turell of Medford, Massachusetts.[43] One of his parishioners, a woman identified only as "E—h," had been the central figure in a witchcraft scare at Littleton, Massachusetts, in the 1720s.[44] Overcome by conscience (on the eve of admittance

42. Whittier, *The Supernaturalism of New England*, pp. 50-51n, has it written presumably in New England, in the late eighteenth century. Amelia Mott Gummere, *Witchcraft and Quakerism* (Philadelphia: The Biddle Press, 1908), p. 56, has it written in Burlington, N.J., sometime before 1730.

43. E.T. [Ebenezer Turell], "Detection of Witchcraft," *Massachusetts Historical Society Collection*, Series 2, X (1823): 6-22. Turell wrote this account as something he owed "to his own generation, and to posterity" (p. 7), but never published it. The comment in Samuel Sewall's *Diary*, which its editors took to relate to a printed edition of this work, related instead to *Early Piety Exemplified in Elizabeth Butcher of Boston. . . .* Samuel Sewall, *Diary*, *Massachusetts Historical Society Collection*, 5th Series, VII: 226.

44. The various individuals involved are identified in Herbert Joseph Harwood, "Littleton," in D. Hamilton Hurd, compiler, *History of Middlesex County, Massachusetts* (Philadelphia: J. W. Lewis & Co., 1890), II: 866-67.

to full church membership she had heard a sermon on the sin of lying), E—h told and confessed what had truly happened. When about eleven years old, she and her two younger sisters had acted as if possessed. Strange noises and events had occurred about their house. E—h had torn her clothing and bit and spat at her attendants. She had been found in the pond crying that she would drown, and in a tree, afraid of falling, and claiming she had flown there. "She did frequently complain of wounds and pinches and prickings, which she said she received by invisible hands and the usual marks of such things were seen upon her."

E—h had accused a certain woman, D—y, of causing her afflictions and claimed to have often seen her even when she was invisible to anyone else. Once E—h claimed a bird was in the room with her, and her mother struck at the space where she said the bird was. The girl claimed the bird had been struck on the head, and D—y was found to be injured upon one side of her face. Another time the girl claimed she saw D—y approaching, and her mother again struck at the indicated position. This time, according to E—h, the blow had struck the spectral image in the bowels. D—y, then pregnant, became ill, took to bed, and soon died. E—h, and her two sisters who had become afflicted a few months after her, then fully recovered. However, while E—h and one of her sisters recovered as soon as they heard of D—y's death, a day or two after it occurred, the youngest sister, only about five years old, continued to be "afflicted" for several months before recovering.

At this point in his narrative, Turell posed a problem for his readers. He asked them to "judge whether this be witchcraft or not . . . ?" Turell soon answered this question himself. It had all been a fake, done by the girl for "pride" and the desire to attract attention.

There are a number of interesting aspects to Turell's account. One is the similarity of the girls' actions to those which had earlier occurred at Salem. The children's actions and afflictions, their age and sex, and the spectral evidence, are all very similar to the events at Salem. This poses a problem for us, for Turell argues, using E—h's own confession, that it was all a fake, and strongly hints that Salem was no better. Modern historians, however, continue to accept the "afflictions" of the victims at Salem as subjectively true, although admittedly the result of clinical hysteria rather than witchcraft. This discrepancy may simply be the result of viewing similar events from within different psychological frameworks. Modern historians, following modern psychology, can comfortably use the concept of the subconscious, uncontrolled and unrecognized by the conscious mind. Turell (and even E—h when reflecting upon her own actions) lacked this concept, and thus had to assume voluntary lying and faked afflictions.[45] It is quite possible, however, that the events of Littleton, unlike those at Salem, were not the result of true hysteria but, rather, were consciously faked and derived from the general culturally accepted behavior for witchcraft victims. Supporting this possibility is the fact that one of the most common and indicative symptoms of hysteria, a choking sensation, the "mother" of seventeenth-century accounts,[46] is absent from Turell's description of the children's actions.

The isolated actions of three young girls, although probably illustrating a generally accepted pattern of bewitchment, would of itself be of limited historical significance. More significant is the reaction of the community to their claims, and on this point, too, Turell gives us valuable information. (However, remember, as Turell did, that his information came from the eight-year-old memories of a girl who was only eleven when the events occurred.) Some in the community thought the children sick, or insane, or feebleminded, or simply bad, but the majority "said they were under an evil hand, or possessed by Satan." Many, especially those who lived at some distance from the town (who perhaps did not know that D—y was a pious woman) "plumply pronounced it witchcraft as much as that which was formerly acted at Salem. . . ."

Thus, if this last passage is at all accurate, Salem was still for many a paradigm rather than a disparagement of witchcraft. Indeed, Thomas Hutchinson, who regarded Salem as "a scene of fraud and imposture," reported in 1767 that

> The opinion which prevailed in New-England, for many years after this tragedy, that there was something praeternatural in it, and that it was not all the effect of fraud and imposture, proceeded from the reluctance in human nature to reject errors once imbibed. As the principal actors went off the stage, this opinion has gradually lessened, and perhaps it is owing to a respect to the memory of their

45. Eighteenth-century faculty psychology understood the importance of the passions and the irrational, but these were not the same as the subconscious.

46. Hansen, *Witchcraft at Salem,* pp. 1-3, 15-16.

immediate ancestors, that many do not yet seem to be fully convinced.[47]

One who was not convinced was Jonathan Sayward, one of Governor Hutchinson's strongest political supporters in the years before the Revolution and a man who had held several judicial and legislative posts in colonial Massachusetts. John Adams reported in 1774 that Sayward had said that

> there was but one point in which he differed, in Opinion from the late Governor Hutchinson and that was with Regard to the Reality of Witchcraft, and the Existence of Witches. The Governor he said would not allow there was any such Thing. He had so great a Regard for him, and his opinion that he was willing to *give up* almost every Thing, rather than differ with him, but in this he could not see with him.

John Adams was not impressed by this display of intellectual independence on the part of a political enemy and commented, "Such is the Cant of this artfull, selfish, hypocritical Man." [48]

Yet this is not to say that Salem had had no cautionary effect even at this time. Many who believed the girls at Littleton to have been possessed by devils "were not so uncharitable as to judge or condemn Mrs. D—y as afflicting them, or to censure her as in covenant with the devil, (having sufficient reason to believe the accused are not always the guilty persons); yet they scrupled not to say, some evil spirit afflicted them in her shape." Others, it is true, did believe D—y to be a witch, at least until her pious death and the continued afflictions of the children after she had died had dissuaded many of them. Nevertheless, it appears evident that Salem was the "sufficient reason to believe the accused are not always the guilty persons." If it had not discredited the concept of witchcraft, it had at least damaged the credibility of spectral evidence.

---

47. Thomas Hutchinson, *The History of the Colony and Province of Massachusetts-Bay* (New York: Kraus Reprint Co., 1970), II: 47.

48. *The Adams Papers*, L. H. Butterfield, ed.-in-chief: Series II, *Adams Family Correspondence*, L. H. Butterfield, *et al.*, ed. (Cambridge: Harvard University Press, 1963), I: 121.

Indicative of the popular acceptance of witchcraft is the difficulty Turell himself has in attempting to deny it. He had made his position quite clear: this episode was a fraud. Moreover, he had implied that Salem may have been a fraud also. Salem "it may be, arose from as small a beginning, though attended and followed with more fatal effects." Despite all this, he does not, cannot, deny the reality of witchcraft:

> Although I am as far as any one from holding or maintaining the doctrine of the Sadducee; and firmly believe the existence of spirits, and invisible world, and particularly the agency of Satan, and his instruments, in afflicting and tormenting the children of men, (when permitted by God;) yet I fear the world has been wretchedly imposed upon by relations of such matters. . . . Where one relation is exactly according to the truth, there are two, at least, that are wholly the fruit of wild imagination, or intolerably mixt with deceit and falsehood.

Such a statement differs in emphasis (which is of importance itself) but not in basic belief from Cotton Mather's warning, "Though it be Folly to impute every dubious Accident, or unwonted Effect of Providence, to Witchcraft; yet there are some things which cannot be excepted against, but must be ascribed hither." [49]

Yet this tension between disbelief in specific instances of witchcraft and belief in the theoretical existence of witchcraft led some in the eighteenth century to what can best be called "skeptical belief." In 1697 James Johnston, who had been educated in civil law in Holland and who had served for a time as secretary for Scotland, stated:

> So as to witches that there may be such I have noe doubt, nor never had, it is a matter of fact that I was never judge of. But the parliaments of France and other judicatories who are perswaded of the being of witches never try them nou because of the experience they have had that its impossible to distinguish possession from nature in disorder, and they chuse rather to let the guilty escape than

49. Cotton Mather, *Memorable Providences,* in Burr, ed., *Narratives of the Witchcraft Cases,* p. 95.

to punish the innocent. If indeed there be malifics, they punish those malifics according to the laws and nature of them, without respect to the principalls whence they proceed . . . ."[50]

Others attempted to reconcile this conflict by accepting the reality of witchcraft in the past but denying that it occurred in the modern world. Daniel Defoe argued that "the Devil's possessing power is much lessened of late, and that he either is limited, and his fetter shortened more than it has been, or that he does not find the old way . . . so fit for his purpose as he did formerly. . . ."[51] Samuel Johnson, the English lexicographer, stated in reply to the argument that the repeal of the witchcraft act put an end to witchcraft:

> No, sir; witchcraft had ceased; and therefore an act of parliament was passed to prevent persecution for what was not witchcraft. Why it ceased, we cannot tell, as we cannot tell the reason of many other things.[52]

Yet the best-known statement of this problem, one that was undoubtedly read in the colonies, highlighted rather than attempted to explain away the inherent conflict in this position. *The Spectator* gave the classic formulation of this problem for the eighteenth century.

> When I hear the Relations that are made from all Parts of the World, not only from *Norway* and *Lapland,* from the *East* and *West Indies,* but from every particular Nation in *Europe,* I cannot forbear thinking that there is such an Intercourse and Commerce with Evil Spirits, as that which we express by the Name of Witchcraft. But when I consider that the ignorant and credulous Parts of the World

50. Historical Manuscripts Commission, *Fourteenth Report, Appendix III,* p. 132.

51. Daniel Defoe, *The Political History of the Devil,* quoted in Rodney M. Baine, *Daniel Defoe and the Supernatural* (Athens, Ga.: University of Georgia Press, 1968), pp. 66-67.

52. James Boswell, *The Journal of a Tour to the Hebrides,* in vol. V. of *Boswell's Life of Johnson Together with Boswell's Journal of a Tour of the Hebrides and Johnson's Diary of a Journal into North Wales,* ed. by George Birkbeck Hill and revised by L. F. Powell (Oxford: Clarendon Press, 1964), p. 46.

abound most in these Relations, and that the Persons among us who are supposed to engage in such an Infernal Commerce are People of a weak Understanding and crazed Imagination, and at the same time reflect upon the many Impostures and Delusions of this Nature that have been detected in all Ages, I endeavour to suspend my Belief till I hear more certain Accounts than any which have yet come to my Knowledge. In short, when I consider the Question, Whether there are such Persons in the World as those we call Witches? my Mind is divided between the two opposite Opinions, or rather (to speak my Thoughts freely) I believe in general that there is and has been such a thing as Witch-craft; but at the same time can give no Credit to any Particular Instance of it.[53]

This elaborate quibble was reaffirmed toward the end of the colonial period by another oft-read English author, the famous legal authority, William Blackstone. After admitting that "one knows not well what account to give" of witchcraft, he approvingly cited and quoted from the above statement by Addision.[54] Yet this statement is logically untenable. If one believes witchcraft to be theoretically possible (an important point in itself), then one may meet a situation which appears to be a concrete illustration of just such a theoretical possibility. Thus, the Anglo-Irish philosopher George Berkeley in 1711 stated, "I do not believe one in a thousand of these stories to be true, so neither on the other hand do I see sufficient grounds to conclude peremptorily against plain matter of fact well attested." When he said this, he was approving the decision of a court which had convicted eight women on charges of witchcraft.[55]

Clearly, many in the eighteenth century who would have preferred to disbelieve in witchcraft were forced, or rather forced themselves, to take an equivocal position, for reasons best expressed late in the century by Blackstone: "to deny the possibility, nay, actual existence, of witchcraft, and sorcery, is at once flatly to contradict the revealed word of God, in

53. *The Spectator,* no. 117.

54. William Blackstone, *Commentaries on the Laws of England* (Philadelphia: Robert Bell, 1771-72), IV: 60.

55. George Berkeley, *The Works of George Berkeley, Bishop of Cloyne,* ed. by A. A. Luce and T. E. Jessop (New York: Thomas Nelson and Sons Ltd., 1955), VIII: 46-47; IX: 15.

various passages both of the old and new testament [sic]: and the thing itself is a truth to which every nation in the world hath in it's turn borne testimony. . . ." [56] The two great sources of knowledge for the eighteenth century, revelation and reason based on experience, both argued for the reality of witchcraft. Thus Daniel N. Brinsmade, while a student at Yale in 1771, after hearing a classroom disputation which made just these points, decided that "from these arguments I think it is evident that there are witches." [57]

Turell had had to face another problem in discussing this case of alleged witchcraft. His essentially rationalistic viewpoint, his literal acceptance of E—h's confession, forced him to attempt to explain away the facts, even though some of the "facts" were unexplainable. True, many of them could be easily disposed of as the deliberate fakings of the children. What, however, was to be done with the injuries and death of D—y which had followed attacks on her spectral image? Turell attempted to answer this by claiming coincidences. When she had suffered an injury to her face it was the result of an ague and the overly harsh medicine used to treat it. When she had "something break within her," followed by her death, it was due to an accidental injury incurred by riding while pregnant. In both cases the child had previously lied to her mother about seeing a spectral image; but, unfortunately, this failed to explain away the coincidence, the fact that the child had seen the spectral image struck, or rather had lied about it, just before D—y was injured. Turell simply had to accept this as a coincidence and, as a result, his explanation was so strained as almost to make the occult explanation appear almost reasonable. Indeed, the unsatisfactory nature of this part of the tale may have been part of the reason why Turell himself never had it published. [58]

56. Blackstone, *Commentaries*, IV: 60. A possible source of this argument was the decision of Sir Matthew Hale in 1664 in the Bury St. Edmunds case. See Kittredge, *Witchcraft in Old and New England,* p. 332.

57. Daniel N. Brinsmade, "Book of Disputes," Question 1, MS, Yale University Manuscripts and Archives Division. The impossibility of refuting witchcraft by an appeal to the "Facts" is noted by E. William Monter, who also cites W. E. H. Lecky on the same point. E. William Monter, "Inflation and Witchcraft: The Case of Jean Bodin," *Action and Conviction in Early Modern Europe,* ed. by Theodore K. Rabb and Jerrold E. Seigel (Princeton: Princeton University Press, 1969), p. 380.

58. See Kittredge, *Witchcraft in Old and New England,* pp. 338-57, for an analysis of seventeenth- and eighteenth-century antiwitchcraft literature. He

Other more convincing explanations are in fact possible. The practice of striking out at the spectral image was after all quite common. John Hale may have devoted a rather lengthy passage to attacking the belief that striking the spectral image would wound the witch, but nevertheless it long continued as a popular method of countermagic.[59] Thus it is quite probable that the child's mother had often struck at the spectral image, especially as we are told that E—h was accustomed to "often cry out to her mother—There she is! there she is! there's Mrs. D—y." If this was the case, the coincidences may well have been the result of a selective memory. When a blow had no effect it was soon forgotten; after all, not every blow was effective, but if it were followed by any harm to the suspected witch (and perhaps the time of the blow and the injury could, if necessary, be appropriately rearranged in the memory), then cause and effect were promptly recognized.

In any case, Turell's account illustrates the continued belief of many people in a style of witchcraft identical to that of Salem, a full generation after Salem. It also illustrates the theoretical difficulties experienced by many in the eighteenth century who desired to disprove or explain away witchcraft.

A number of other accounts of witchcraft were published in the colonies which further illustrated similar points, although, as we will see, the incidents were often of doubtful reality. One of these accounts, published as a broadside ballad in 1776, described an incident which had allegedly occurred three years earlier in England. Its five-stanza description of an afflicted girl followed the classical Salem syndrome.

---

points out the weaknesses and logical contradictions involved in affirming, as all who were orthodox Christians must, the reality of Satan and evil spirits while denying the reality of their best-known and most spectacular manifestation—witchcraft. Only a radical revision of biblical exegesis, which would explain away the occurrence of witchcraft in the Scriptures, would permit one to deny absolutely the reality of witchcraft. Balthasar Bekker's attempt to do so, in the 1690s, met with a storm of reproach.

59. John Hale, *A Modest Enquiry into the Nature of Witchcraft* (Boston: Kneeland and Adams, 1771), pp. 55-59. Other examples of a witch being harmed when her spectral image was struck can be found in Dorson, *Jonathan Draws the Long Bow*, p. 40; Hole, *Witchcraft in England*, pp. 71-73; Kittredge, *Witchcraft in Old and New England*, pp. 174-79.

O then, alas! this pretty child so dear,
Was seiz'd with frantic fits we hear;
Which did her parents doubtless grieve,
While nothing could her pain relieve.
        Some neighbors they are apt to say,
This child's bewitch'd both night and day;
Sometimes she'll jump and climb the chair,
And there she'll be, tho' no one's near.
        Sometimes she'll jump and dance the room about;
And like one craz'd she'll make a fearful rout;
Sometimes she'll jump and climb the chair,
And there she'll be, tho' no one's near.
        Sometimes she sees black cats and crows that fly,
And other fearful sights just by;
Sometimes she's bit & scratch'd by hands unknown,
Which makes this child to sigh and groan.
        But alas! alas! to tell you all,
That doth unto this child befall,
Would take more lines than two or three,
Therefore I pray you to quit me.[60]

As with the case previously related by Turell, some thought the child ill, but others blamed witchcraft. The pattern of accusations followed a familiar path. Some "say it is some neighbour near" while others were sure it was "some near relation."[61] The conclusion was something less than a successful climax but it was pious, edifying, and undoubtedly good advice. All were urged to "forbear to tell the name,/And you'll be clear from any blame," and "not think to ease the smart,/By conjure or by foolish art." Instead, all were urged to pray to God for relief and to

60. *A New and True Relation, of a Little Girl in the County of Hartford, at Salmon-Brook in Simsbury who Acted in a Strange Manner, Supposed to be Bewitch'd, on March 1763* (Boston: n.p., 1766).

61. The accusation of neighbors of witchcraft was common. See MacFarlane, *Witchcraft in Tudor and Stuart England,* pp. 168-77; Demos, "Underlying Themes," p. 1318. It was unusual, however, for a relative to be accused, at least by the victim, possibly because witchcraft was believed to be hereditary. MacFarlane, *Witchcraft in Tudor and Stuart England,* pp. 170, 212-13.

"preserve our British land,/From witchcraft, witches and their band."

The witchcraft of Sarah Green was discussed in a 1762 pamphlet, *A Most Unaccountable Relation,* which was allegedly another account of English witchcraft. The substance of her witchcraft appears to have been of the traditional kind. People she quarreled with "commonly receiv'd Damage, either by Hurt to their Cattle or other Things," but the pamphlet also contained other less common themes which may have reflected literary or Continental influences. Sarah was said to have made a pact with the devil for fourteen years of wealth and pleasure on Earth, but after the specified period passed, even though she confessed her sins, the devil came upon her in the form of a bear and killed her! [62]

Another dubious tale of witchcraft, this one consisting entirely of traditional English motifs, was the account in the 1730 *Pennsylvania Gazette,* Franklin's paper, of witch-testing at Mount Holly, New Jersey. Some three hundred people were said to have gathered to see the testing of two "witches" accused of "making their Neighbours Sheep dance in an uncommon Manner, and with causing Hogs to speak, and sing Psalms, &c. to the great Terror and Amazement of the King's good and peaceable Subjects in this Province. . . ." The accused were weighed against a great Bible but all outweighed it. Together with their accusers, a woman and a man, they then were bound and cast into the water. The result was unexpected. Not only the accused witches but also one of their accusers, the woman, were rejected by the water and floated. Only the male accuser, a thin man, sank. The spectators, however, despite this unexpected denouement, neither rejected the test, nor considered the accused vindicated, nor even wondered about exactly who was the witch. Instead, the spectators decided "that the Womens Shifts, and the Garters with which they were bound help'd support them; it is said they are to be tried

62. *A Most Unaccountable Relation of one Miss Sarah Green* (1762). The authenticity of this account is dubious. It was attested by four men, two of whom were baronets. However, neither of these gentlemen, Sir John Aldridge, Bart. and Sir George Scroope, Bart., appear in either John Burke, *A Genealogical and Heraldic History of the Extinct and Dormant Baronetcies of England* (London: Scott, Webster, and Geary, 1838) or G.[eorge] E.[dward] C.[okayne], *Complete Baronetage* (Exeter: William Pollard & Co., 1900-6).

Very possibly this tale, which has no indication as to its publisher, was simply written to be an interesting tale which would sell well.

again the next warm Weather, naked." This account is a cleverly written spoof of popular beliefs about witchcraft, and was almost certainly written by Benjamin Franklin. There is no independent verification of this story, and it appears probable that it was not a satirical account of a real incident but, rather, an early Franklin bagatelle.[63]

Other probably more reliable tales of witchcraft were recorded in eighteenth-century newspapers. They sometimes carried accounts of witchcraft in England.[64] Other tales of witchcraft in England, and a spirited defense of the reality of witchcraft, could be read in the published *Journals* of John Wesley, the founder of Methodism.[65] In 1787 a number of American newspapers carried disapproving reports of the mobbing and death of a woman in Philadelphia who was believed to be a witch.[66] In 1802 a Boston magazine reprinted a report from New York about a Poughkeepsie man who had been prosecuted for slashing an "old lady upwards of 80 years of age" across the forehead three times. He had done this in the belief that he would thus "screen himself from her sorceries." He was convicted, but after coming to an "accommodation" with the victim's family, he was fined only one dollar and court costs.[67]

63. It is reprinted in *Archives of the State of New Jersey*, Series 1, XI: 220-23 and Franklin, *Papers*, I: 182-83. Both discuss the possibility that Franklin wrote the essay, although Labaree is rather noncommittal on that point. It is a beautifully written satire which can be appreciated only if read in full, and it is hard to believe that the *Gazette* had two such masters of the genre. See also the discussion of this hoax in Gummere, *Witchcraft and Quakerism*, pp. 54-55. For weighing witches against a Bible see Hole, *Witchcraft in England*, p. 86.

64. Judith Ward-Steinman Karst, "Newspaper Medicine: A Cultural Study of the Colonial South, 1730-1770" (unpublished Ph.D. dissertation, Tulane University, 1971), pp. 62-63.

65. John Wesley, *The Journal of the Rev. John Wesley*, ed. by Nehemiah Curnock (London: Charles H. Kelly, 1909-16), III: 250-51; V: 265-66, 374-75; VI: 109.

66. *Independent Journal or, the Central Advertiser* (N.Y.C.), July 18, 1787; *Massachusetts Centinel*, Aug. 1, 1787, cited in Burr, *Narratives of the Witchcraft Cases*, p. 88; *Columbian Magazine*, I (1786-87), cited in Brooke Hindle, *The Pursuit of Science in Revolutionary America, 1735-1789* (Chapel Hill: University of North Carolina Press, 1956), p. 253.

67. *Boston Weekly Magazine*, I (Dec. 18, 1802): 31. For English and seventeenth-century instances of drawing blood from a witch in order to break her

Although published accounts are of interest and value, many accounts of eighteenth-century witchcraft, such as Turell's, remained in manuscript throughout the century. Thomas Clap, the future president of Yale, was involved in one such incident, which has survived only as a passing comment in a letter written by Ebenezer Wheelock. "It is common talk at Windham that old Goody Fullsom . . . is a W—ch & indeed there are many Stories which Mr. Clap has told me of her that Look very Dark." Wheelock retold one such story. Goody Fulsome had been tormenting an old sick woman, and one day "an ill looken Dog" entered the old woman's room but was driven out by a blow from a broom. "At the very instant" Goody Fulsome suffered a pain in her shoulder and the next day it was learned that her shoulder was badly broken. One of the fascinating aspects of this letter is its tone—witchcraft was treated merely as a shocking item of local gossip, perhaps on a par with a not totally unexpected case of bastardy, not as anything truly extraordinary.[68]

In 1789 the New England Baptist leader Isaac Backus came across what had for a time been thought to be a case of witchcraft. It was a false alarm, however, for it was merely the ghost of a murdered woman summoning a witness to Nova Scotia for the trial of her murderer.[69] In 1776 William Duke, a Methodist minister, noted that the devil had nearly convinced the people of Penn's Neck, New Jersey, that one of their number was a witch.[70] In 1760 the Goshen Monthly Meeting of Penn-

---

spell, see Kittredge, *Witchcraft in Old and New England,* pp. 47, 169, 236, 290; Hansen, *Witchcraft at Salem,* p. 66; William Renwick Riddle, "A Curious 'Witchcraft' Case," *American Institute of Criminal Law and Criminology Journal,* XIX (August 1928): 233-35; Thomas, *Religion and the Decline of Magic,* pp. 531, 544.

68. Louis Leonard Tucker, *Puritan Protagonist: President Thomas Clap of Yale College* (Chapel Hill: University of North Carolina Press, 1962), pp. 42-43; letter from Eleazar Wheelock to Stephen Williams, August 18, 1737, MS, Dartmouth College Archives.

69. William G. McLoughlin, *Isaac Backus and the American Pietistic Tradition* (Boston: Little, Brown and Company, 1967), pp. 190-91. For a similar tale earlier in the eighteenth century, see Dorson, *Jonathan Draws the Long Bow,* p. 61.

70. Joseph Towne Wheeler, "Reading Interests of the Professional Classes in Colonial Maryland, 1700-1776: The Clergy," *Maryland Historical Magazine,* XXXVI (June 1941): 197.

sylvania disowned a member for having been one of a mob which had forced "a poor woman from her habitation (under a pretence of her bewitching a certain child), whereby she has suffered damage." [71] In 1746 the church in Salem Village, which had good cause to fear dabbling in magic and fortune-telling, took note of a report that several persons in the parish had "resorted to a woman of a very ill reputation, pretending to the art of divination and fortune-telling, &c.," and instructed the pastor to testify publicly "their disapprobation and abhorrence of this infamous and ungodly practice of consulting witches or fortune-tellers, or any that are reputed such; exhorting all under their watch, who may have been guilty of it, to an hearty repentance and returning to God, earnestly seeking forgiveness in the blood of Christ, and warning all against the like practice for the time to come." [72]

A rare example of white magic is found in a letter from the Virginian William Byrd to an English merchant, Mr. Hanbury. In this gossipy letter Byrd remarked: "I am glad to hear your ship the Williamsburg got home well, and that Crane agreed with a witch at Hampton for a fair wind all the way over." [73] Although from the tone of Byrd's remarks this was not the standard procedure, it was apparently not all that unusual either, and as Hampton was a fairly busy port,[74] it may well be that the Hampton witch (or witches) had a fairly steady business. Whether other ports provided this service can only be a matter for speculation. Not all "witch winds" were favorable, however, and a witch could send a wind to thwart a ship as easily as to aid it.[75]

A number of supernatural events around the time of the American Revolution were recounted by a New Yorker, William Hooker Smith. After expressing his belief in witchcraft and that "witcis and wizards are

71. J. Smith Furthey and Gilbert Cope, *History of Chester County, Pennsylvania* (Philadelphia: Louis H. Everts, 1881), p. 413.

72. Upham, *Salem Witchcraft*, II: 513.

73. William Byrd, "Letters of William Byrd, 2nd, of Westover, Va.," *Virginia Magazine of History and Biography*, IX (January 1902): 231.

74. Francis Carroll Huntley, "The Seaborne Trade of Virginia in Mid-Eighteenth Century: Port Hampton," *Virginia Magazine of History and Biography*, LIX (July 1951): 297-308.

75. Sibley, *Harvard Lines*, VI: 217-18, and Kittredge, *Witchcraft in Old and New England*, chap. viii.

always Poor distressd cretures thare master is Not able to do them any good they can onlay do Sum little Nasty durty Tricks," Hooker told of "a gang of witches" around Sing Sing, "who ware installed into that business by one martha chub, a noted hag." He also told of some men who found a nut tree being shaken by what appeared to be the image of a woman, but when the men investigated all they found was a blue hog, which left no tracks behind it. Another time, at Jacobs Plain, Smith himself was attacked by a cat that was actually a transformed witch. In still a third incident, this occurring in White Plains, a womam who had a "nervous fever" was attacked by the images of two women of another family (the images of course being invisible to everyone else), who pulled her arms and threatened to put red hot irons in her mouth. Eventually she died.[76]

Much eighteenth-century witchcraft did not leave even such fragmentary documentation as these but survived, if they survived at all, merely as local legends. Although these legends present quaint and picturesque details of bygone days, they are important for far more than that. They illustrate the widespread extent of witchcraft beliefs and provide valuable information as to the types of damage witches were believed to do and the folk countermeasures that were taken against them.

One such tale of witchcraft originated in Gloucester, Massachusetts, in 1745, where a company of forty-five Gloucester men were leaving for the siege of Louisburg. As if the dangers of war were not enough, several of the men annoyed Peg Wesson, the local witch. At Louisburg, the men saw a crow circling above them. Believing that it was probably Peg Wesson transformed, and thus impervious to common weapons, a silver button was loaded into a gun and fired at the bird. The bird was wounded, and, at the same time back in Gloucester, Peg Wesson fell and broke her leg. When her leg was treated, a silver button was found in it.[77]

A similar tale comes from Barnstable, Massachusetts, where some

76. William Hooker Smith, "Remarkable Acurances," MSS, N.Y., Westchester Co., Witchcraft, Manuscripts and Archives Division, New York Public Library, Astor, Lenox and Tilden Foundations.

77. James R. Pringle, *History of the Town and City of Gloucester, Cape Ann, Massachusetts* (Gloucester, Mass.: Published by the author, 1892), pp. 61-62, and Samuel Adams Drake, *A Book of New England Legends and Folk Lore* (Boston: Roberts Brothers, 1888), p. 260.

whalers saw a black cat swimming toward their vessel. They too shot a silver button at the cat and killed it, and at the same time a local woman reputed to be a witch also died.[78]

About 1789 a Grand Banks fishing schooner also had some trouble with witchcraft. One of its crew was found insensible in his berth. After hours he recovered, and explained that a witch had transformed him into a horse and had ridden him about Sable Island. His arms where black and blue where the witch had kicked him after he had attempted to bite her. He was not certain as to why he was bewitched, but he had once taken some doughnuts from an empty house, and while the witch had ridden him she had "twittered him of stealing the doughnuts." He continued to be harassed. When he tried to pump water from the cask it came up salt, although the next man to try would get fresh water. When he tried to stir dough, the bowl of his spoon would fall off. He became so annoyed that his health started to fail. Finally the captain of the vessel loaded a gun with his silver sleeve button and gave it to the bewitched man. One day he fired it in his cabin. The crew found him again insensible, and they also found a drop of warm blood. Presumably, although the account does not specifically say, he had shot the witch, because he was never troubled again.[79]

At Windham, New Hampshire, a somewhat similar tale is told of "Old Rif," said to have been the last slave in the state. Sometime around the start of the nineteenth century, he, his master, and a third man went hunting. They became lost, although they knew the terrain well, and found a rabbit which stood up on its hind legs and stared at them and could not be frightened away. Realizing it was probably a witch, "Old Rif" shot it with a silver sleeve button. The rabbit was killed and the path immediately became familiar to the three bemused men.[80]

In the 1750s Woodbury, Connecticut, had its own local witch, Moll Cramer. Her husband, a blacksmith, was careful to be good to her because if she became angry with him and came around while he was shoeing a horse, the shoe would invariably fall off. Finally, however, Moll's repu-

78. Donald G. Trayser, *Barnstable: Three Centuries of a Cap Cod Town* (Hyannis, Mass.: F. B. & F. P. Goss, 1939), p. 325.

79. The grandson of the captain of the schooner recounted this tale, which his father had told him, in a letter to the *Boston Herald,* Feb. 6, 1919, p. 10.

80. Leonard A. Morrison, *The History of Windham in New Hampshire* (Boston: Cupples, Upham & Co., 1883), p. 242.

tation became so bad that her husband drove her away, and she and her son lived in a cabin of boards and poles. She survived by begging; no neighbor would dare turn her away. If she asked for pork and it were denied her, a blight would settle upon the swine and they would never fatten. When she entered a house, the thread of the spinning wheel would break or some other domestic misfortune would occur. Some girls once picked grapes from near her cabin. They fled when she came, but the grapes were unfit to eat. Once Moll entered a house where cream was being churned into butter, and for the next two days the butter did not come. Finally, a heated horseshoe was put into the butter to burn the witch out, and the butter soon came.[81]

Salem, New Hampshire, had a similar witch in the person of Old Granny Ober. She was accustomed to asking Mrs. Wheeler for milk, but one day she was refused because there was none to spare. Old Granny Ober, angered, retorted, "You'll be sorry." The next day the cow was found lying on its back and two days later it was down again. Suspecting witchcraft, Mrs. Wheeler cut off the cow's tail and ears and threw them into the fire. About that time Granny Ober had an accident in which she badly scratched herself, burnt her ears off, and died in a fire.[82]

In Union, Maine, in 1813 Herny Esensa traded his horse to Samuel Daggett. Esensa's wife, unhappy about the trade, was overheard to say that the horse had "always been a plague and would never do the Daggetts any good." The horse, indeed, always came untied in the barn no matter how carefully it was tied up. This obvious case of witchcraft was solved by cutting off the horses ears and putting a red hot shovel to them. (Some, however, thought it was solved when the point of an awl broke off in the rope; for it was known that this too defeats witchcraft.) [83]

81. William Cothren, *History of Ancient Woodbury, Connecticut* (Waterbury, Conn.: Bronson Brothers, 1854), I: 159-61. For other examples of "burning the witch out of the cream," see Kittredge, *Witchcraft in Old and New England*, p. 167, and Dorson, *Jonathan Draws the Long Bow*, p. 35.

82. Edgar Gilbert, *History of Salem, N.H.* (Concord, N.H.: Rumford Printing Company, 1907), pp. 348-49.

83. John Langdon Sibley, *A History of the Town of Union, in the County of Lincoln, Maine* (Boston: Benjamin B. Mussey and Co., 1851), pp. 228-29. For another example of the use of an awl against witchcraft, see William Little, *The History of Warren* (Manchester, N.H.: William E. Moore, 1870), p. 434.

Fire in fact was frequently used as a cure for witchcraft. At Warren, New Hampshire, it was used in a dispute between Stillman Barker, whose wife was suspected of witchcraft, and Joseph Merrill. Merrill, who was superintendent of the turnpike, had an argument with Barker over a ditch which Barker had altered, and which now flooded the road. A few days later Merrill found one of his calves lying on the ground, trembling. Certain it was bewitched, he cut off its ear and threw it into the fire. The calf recovered, and the witch became ill.[84]

Another Merrill from Warren was involved in a witchcraft dispute that arose out of the quarrels of the American Revolution. The affair was somewhat unusual in that it concerned a male witch, or wizard, Simeon Smith. Smith was believed to have performed a variety of routine witcheries. He had bridled and saddled neighbors and ridden them around the countryside. He had stopped butter from coming. He had tormented cats. He had bewitched children. But with all that, he was a Patriot during the Revolution and had served his town as constable and tax collector. Stevens Merrill had been a moderate Tory, and he had especially objected to paying taxes for the war. This led to a lasting enmity between the two families, and when Merrill's deaf son Caleb starting acting strangely, it led to charges of witchcraft. Caleb ran up the sides of houses and spent hours writhing in agony. Using signs and pointing, he claimed that Simeon Smith caused his distress. Stevens Merrill, obviously not about to cut off his son's ear for a countercharm, bottled his son's urine and placed it under the hearth of his fireplace. Simeon Smith, the suspected witch, promptly suffered a very bad nosebleed. When it ended the urine was checked, and it was found that the cork had come out of the bottle allowing the urine to escape. Caleb's agonies returned and the entire procedure was repeated. The third time, however, something new was added. The cork of the bottle was stopped by a short sword. The next day Caleb indicated that he knew that Simeon Smith was dead. He was; and when the bottle was checked, it was found that the sword had penetrated the cork and reached the urine. Caleb was untroubled thereafter. Smith was buried under an apple tree which had formerly been frequently robbed by boys. They no longer came, but the apples turned bitter.[85]

84. Little, *The History of Warren,* pp. 433-34.

85. *Ibid.,* pp. 436-39, and Dorson, *Jonathan Draws the Long Bow,* pp. 44-45. For this procedure in England see Kittredge, *Witchcraft in Old and New England,* p. 102; Thomas, *Religion and the Decline of Magic,* pp. 543-44.

Warren, for some unknown reason, seems to have suffered a plague of witches. One witch, angered at the sale of some walnuts by Nat Turner, kept him up all night by mysteriously rattling walnuts. Another witch punished a man who had jilted her sister by invisibly rocking in a rocking chair whenever he went courting his new girlfriend. Despite this unique chaperone, the couple were eventually married. Mrs. Sarah Weeks of Warren was another witch whom it was unwise to refuse. When she was refused a ride, she warned the man who had refused her that he would not get home that night. Sure enough, the horse acted up and would not go on, and the man did not get home that night. When Mrs. Weeks's husband was refused some rum, she and her sister witches kept the stingy family up all night by making horrible noises on their roof and barn. When she was refused some flax by Nathaniel Clough, she merely laid her head on the table, and Clough's colt, usually a well-behaved beast, killed two lambs. The son of another Warren witch, when asked why he believed his mother to be a witch, replied quite simply, "Good Lord, if you had seen her coming over the ridgepole of the house in the air as many times as I have, in the shape of a hog, you would believe she was a witch." [86]

In eighteenth-century Pennsylvania, near West Chester, an old woman named Molly Otley was suspected of having bewitched the demented daughter of Joshua Ashbridge. A whole series of tests were held to see if she was indeed a witch. While she was being brought in for examination, silver bullets were fired at an image of her on a board, and the man bringing her in was ordered to observe her carefully to see if it had any effect on her. On arriving at their destination, she found the house prepared with two charms believed to block the passage of a witch—a horseshoe over the door and salt on the threshold. When she stopped to clean her shoes, the cry arose, "She's a witch, and can't pass over the salt until she performs some conjuration." They next weighed her against a Bible, but she outweighed it. A jury of women examined her to see if her body bore any indications of the silver bullets fired at her image, and presumably also checked her for witch's marks and teats, but found nothing. They considered swimming her, but were talked out of it. Finally, to break her spell over the girl, the girl was given a knife to cut Molly and draw her blood. Understandably, this upset Molly Otley and she called out, "Joshua, I will not let thy crazy child cut me; take it and cut

86. Little, *The History of Warren,* pp. 432-39.

me thyself." Instead of cutting her, the child scratched her face until it bleed. Finally, Molly prayed for the child, and the crowd, having used virtually every folk test and countermeasure possible, was satisfied and let her go.[87]

Various other colonial witchcraft tales also include such by now familiar themes as harming livestock, saddling and riding victims, and disrupting mechanical tasks. Still other colonial tales are not about malevolent witches but, rather, about "witches" who were seeresses and fortune-tellers.[88]

A number of themes and characteristics common to the eighteenth century can be found in these accounts and legends. The elaborations of Salem—witches' Sabbaths, the black man, signed agreements with the devil—do not reappear in the eighteenth century. The writhing and hysterics of demonic possession do occur, but they do not appear to be as prevalent or as dominant as they were at Salem. Far more common were minor harassments, misadventures concerning livestock, and the disruption of routine tasks such as churning butter. Spectral images and witches transformed into animals also remain fairly common.

These accounts provide us with some background on the accused witches. Several accused witches appear to have been old women who made a nuisance of themselves by their begging and general poverty. This, as we have seen, was also the description of Sarah Good, one of the first to be accused of witchcraft at Salem; and a recent sociological study has found it characteristic of sixteenth- and seventeenth-century English witchcraft.[89] In other instances we can see in the background of witchcraft accusations old feuds between the individuals or families concerned.[90]

87. Furthey, *History of Chester County,* pp. 413-14. For the use of horseshoes, see *William and Mary Quarterly,* 1st Series, XVII: 247-48, and Thomas, *Religion and the Decline of Magic,* p. 543. For the use of salt, see Cross, "Witchcraft in North Carolina," pp. 286-87; for weighing against a Bible see Hole, *Witchcraft in England,* p. 86.

88. Carolyn S. Langdon, "The Case of Lydia Gilbert (Witchcraft in Connecticut)," *The New-England Galaxy,* V (Winter 1964): 21; Edward C. Moody, *Handbook History of the Town of York* (Augusta, Maine: Kennebec Journal Company, 1914), pp. 183-84; Tayler, *The Witchcraft Delusion,* p. 156; Dorson, *Jonathan Draws the Long Bow,* p. 37; and Samuel Adams Drake, *A Book of New England Legend,* pp. 137-48.

89. See Macfarlane, *Witchcraft in Tudor and Stuart England,* pp. 147-99.

90. For such an analysis of Salem, see Boyer, *Salem Possessed.*

Even more interesting are the variety of protective countermeasures available to witchcraft victims. They could shoot the transformed witch with a silver bullet, hit and wound the spectral image of the witch, burn the witch out of the churn, burn a part of the bewitched animal, or break the spell by drawing blood from the witch.[91] Nor were they limited only to occult countermeasures even after witchcraft trials went out of fashion. Mob action and social pressure may have still been quite effective. Goody Fulsome, after all, eventually left town. In one unique case, the daughter of a male witch was simply able to persuade her father to cease his sorcery.[92] Some cures were very simple. In 1725 the New Hampshire minister Timothy Walker told a parish troubled by witchcraft that it would end if they simply stopped talking about it![93]

## IV

Most colonial witches and sorcerers were simple and unlearned, though no doubt in some instances malevolent, individuals. Although we know how countermagic was performed, indeed the tales describing it no doubt served a didactic purpose, yet there is a complete lack of detail as to how witches were believed to work their magic. It seems probable that at the most they muttered a charm or a curse, perhaps over an item belonging to or representing their victim. Most often they apparently worked their evil simply by the virtue of their sheer "maleficium," which Kittredge held to be the essence of witchcraft.[94] Except for the spectral images and familiars, there are no specific techniques associated with colonial witchcraft. Its magic was of a primitive and undefined nature.

There was, however, one group of colonial magic-workers who were very different, who clearly represented a more elaborate and learned form of occultism. These were the magicians, or magi, of the Pennsylvania German community, and their English followers. Probably the best known of these magi was Christopher Witt. Atypical in that he was an Englishman, he joined the German mystical and magic-working sect

91. For general discussions of defensive measures against witches, see Macfarlane, *Witchcraft in Tudor and Stuart England*, pp. 107-9; Hansen, *Witchcraft at Salem*, pp. 77-82; and Thomas, *Religion and the Decline of Magic*, pp. 543-45.

92. Moody, *Handbook History of the Town of York*, pp. 183-84.

93. Sibley, *Harvard Lives*, VII: 605-6.

94. Kittredge, *Witchcraft in Old and New England*, pp. 4-5.

headed by Magister Johannes Kelpius and continued to live in German-town even after the sect was dissolved.[95] The learned and scholarly nature of Witt's magic is indicated by a 1743 letter from John Bartram to Peter Collinson describing Bartram's visit to a mutual botanizing friend, Christopher Witt: "We went into his study, which was furnished with books containing different kinds of learning; as Philosophy, Natural Magic, Divinity, nay, even Mystical Divinity; all of which were the subject of our discourse within doors, . . ." Bartram was not at all convinced by Witt but remained polite due to his esteem for him.[96] Unfortunately, Witt's four or five volumes of "Rosecution philosophy," which might have furnished us with fascinating details about colonial Pennsylvania mysticism and magic, are apparently lost.[97]

Witt was not the sole surviving magus of the eighteenth century. His friend Christopher Lehman, though not a professional magician or astrologer, cast the nativities of all his children.[98] Witt's disciple, Mr. Fraily (commonly called "Old Shrunk"), apparently had a successful career curing bewitchments, finding lost, stolen, or hidden treasure, and in general acting as the "cunning man" for parts of Pennsylvania and New Jersey. He was connected with the use of protective magic circles, and probably engaged in ceremonial magic.[99] Another student of Witt's, Anthony Larry, also acted as a "cunning man" engaged in curing bewitched cattle, locating wells and running water, and finding lost treasure.[100] We have already seen that a New Jersey medical student studying with Witt was taught "the Astral Sciences, whereby to make a more perfect Discovery of the Hidden causes of more Occult and uncommon Diseases. . . ." [101]

95. Julius Friedrich Sachse, *The German Pietists of Provincial Pennsylvania, 1694-1708* (Philadelphia: privately printed, 1895), p. 403.

96. *Ibid.,* p. 407.

97. Letter from J. Watson to Darlington, May 8, 1848, MS, in the American Philosophical Society microfilm of Selections from the Darlington Papers filmed by the NYHS, film no. 627.

98. John F. Watson, *Annals of Philadelphia and Pennsylvania* (privately printed, 1850), I: 267.

99. *Ibid.*: I, 267-68; II: 32. For "cunning men," see *infra* pp. 120-21.

100. William J. Buck, *Local Sketches and Legends Pertaining to Bucks and Montgomery Counties, Pennsylvania* (privately printed, 1887), pp. 56-57.

101. Packard, *History of Medicine,* I: 277.

Other German magi included George Dresher, who cured victims of witchcraft with the aid of "a huge black letter MS volume, bound with heavy brass clasps . . . ," [102] and Paul Heym, a frontier magician who used his powers to battle the Indians. He, too, used a magic circle for protection and owned a magic book, *The Sixth and Seventh Books of Moses*.[103] Even in northwest New Jersey the descendant of a German immigrant cured people with the aid of a magic wand.[104]

These Pennsylvania German practices seem to have quickly spread to the neighboring Quaker communities.[105] As early as 1695-96 the Concord Monthly Meeting had to warn two young men who were involved in astrology, geomancy, chiromancy, and necromancy. They soon recanted all of these practices except astrology. Finally, one of the two, Robert Roman, was disowned after a committee of Friends who had spoken with him reported that he reserved the right to practice astrology "to Doe some great good by it from which beliefs of some great good may be Done by it wee could not remove him." This dispute resulted in a lengthy testimony directed primarily against astrology, but which also attacked "*Rabdomancy*, or consulting, with a *staff*, and such like things, . . ." A grand jury joined the attack by presenting "Robert Roman of Chichester for practicing Geomancy according to hidden, and divining by a stick." He was fined £5 and released upon his promise to "never practice the

102. William J. Buck, "Local Superstitions," *Collections of the Historical Society of Pennsylvania*, I (1853): 379.

103. D. C. Henning, *Tales of the Blue Mountains* (Pottsville, Pa.: Daily Republican Book Rooms, 1911), pp. 146-50.

A number of nineteenth-century German *Das Sechste und Siebente Buch Mosis*, some printed in Philadelphia, are in the Beinecke Library, Yale University. A brief description of an 1880 translation is found in J. Frank Dobie, *Coronado's Child: Tales of Lost Mines and Buried Treasure of the Southwest* (Dallas, Tex.: The Southwest Press, 1930), p. 338.

There may be some connection with the cabalistic belief that two extra books of the Pentateuch are hidden in this aeon. See Gershom G. Scholem, *On the Kabbalah and Its Symbolism*, trans. by Ralph Manheim (New York: Schocken Books, 1969), p. 81.

104. John Barber, *Historical Collections of the State of New Jersey* (Newark, N.J.: Benjamin Olds, [1852]), pp. 466-67.

105. See the discussion of their relationship in Gummere, *Witchcraft and Quakerism*, pp. 50-53.

arts." In addition, the grand jury presented and ordered brought to the next court (for burning?) "Hidons Temple of Wisdom which teaches Geomancy, and Scots discovery of Witchcraft,[106] and Cornelias Agrippas teach Necromancy." [107]

In 1723 the Philadelphia Yearly Meeting found it desirable to issue a warning against the use of magic for the discovery of lost treasure:

> such people as, by color of any art or skill whatever, do or shall pretend knowledge to discover things hiddenly transacted, or tell where things lost or stolen may be found: or if any under our profession, do or pretend to any such Art or Skill, we do hereby, in just abhorence of such doings, direct that the offender be speedily dealt with and brought under censure.

It was found necessary to repeat this warning in 1802. In addition, a copy of the 1723 warning was also found in the Quaker records of Dartmouth, Massachusetts, although it is not known if this reflected events at Dartmouth or merely the interest of the secretary.[108]

Many of these magical practices, including magic circles, books of magic, and magical treasure hunting, were satirized in a 1767 Philadelphia play, *The Disappointment: or, the Force of Credulity.* The probable author of this work, Thomas Forrest, was himself notorious for pretending to be a conjurer. Once "he made his Dutch girl give up some stolen money, by touching her with cow itch, and after laying down on his couch and groaning, &c., till she began to itch and scratch, he seemed to be enraged, and said, now I am putting fire into your flesh, and if you do not immediately tell how and when you took my money, I'll burn you up by conjuration, and make your ghost be pained and tell it out before your face." She confessed. Another time he was involved in a practical joke

106. The rather surprising condemnation of Reginald Scot's famous attack on witchcraft, the 1584 *Discoverie of Witchcraft*, undoubtedly referred to the 1665 edition which had added nine chapters that "appear to be, and are, practical directions for magic and necromancy." Kittredge, *Witchcraft in Old and New England*, pp. 342-43.

107. Gummere, *Witchcraft and Quakerism*, pp. 42-48; Furthey, *History of Chester County*, p. 413.

108. Gummere, *Witchcraft and Quakerism*, p. 48.

involving magic and treasure hunting, which was the basis of *The Disappointment.* In fact, it is said that the people involved were active later in preventing *The Disappointment* from actually being presented on the Philadelphia stage.[109]

The plot of the plot of the play was simple. Several men played a practical joke upon four "dupes" by leading them on a wild goose chase for the buried treasure of Blackbeard the pirate. One of the practical jokers, Rattletrap by name, pretended to be a conjurer. He prepared for his role by reading the canto of Hudibras and Sydrophel, to obtain some hard words "which added to his knowledge in the mathematicks, will sufficiently qualify him for a modern conjurer. . . ."[110] His accouterments included a "brass bound magical book," a "magnet nocturnal," a forestaff, and a hazel rod staff.[111] The magic book, most likely *The Sixth and Seventh Books of Moses,* was a standard feature of Pennsylvania German magic. Even when the mistress of one of the dupes had to pretend to be a conjurer (to explain away her boyfriend hiding under the bed), she did so by claiming that a German almanac was a book of magic originally owned by her uncle from Germantown, "a High-German doctor; who cou'd tell fortunes, detect lost maidenheads,[112] lay spirits, raise the devil, find stolen goods, and discover hidden treasure; and his whole art is contain'd in this little book."[113] Such a book of magic was characteristic of only the relatively learned and sophisticated occult tradition of the Germans. Simple witches in the rest of the colonies were never thought to have owned such a learned book. Even at Salem, the Devil's Book was used for recording pacts between Satan and his followers: it was not a "gramarye" of magic spells.

The climax of the play is a parody of magical treasure hunting. Rat-

---

109. Andrew Barton [Thomas Forrest(?)], *The Disappointment: or, the Force of Credulity. A New American Comic-Opera of Two Acts* (New York [Philadelphia]: [Goddard], 1767), p. iv; Watson, *Annals of Philadelphia,* I: 268-70.

The play is also of interest for its use of dialect and national characteristics for the four "dupes"—two Germans, a Scotsman, and an Englishman.

110. Forrest, *The Disappointment,* p. 11. For Sydrophel and Hudibras see Butler, *Hudibras,* pt. 2, canto III.

111. Forrest, *The Disappointment,* p. 11-12.

112. This difficult task is also found in Butler, *Hudibras,* pt. 2, canto III, l. 285.

113. Forrest, *The Disappointment,* p. 36.

tletrap, undoubtedly in full regalia, located the fake treasure with his divining rod.

> It draws excessive strong this way. I feel myself interrupted by invisibles—I can scarcely keep the rod in my hands—there—now I have it—it draws this way. . . . I know the rod to be good: I've try'd it's virtue—'T was cut on All-Hallow's Eve, at twelve o'clock at night, with my back to the Moon: and the Mercury injected while the sap was running.

After the treasure was located, Rattletrap drew a magic circle with his wand, and guarded it with twelve astrological lamins. He chanted a mixture of pseudo-astrological comments and Latin "incantations" to drive off the "invisibles," demons simulated by fireballs, who terrified the dupes as they dug for their, alas false, treasure.[114]

One of the most intriguing features of this magical treasure hunt was the use of the divining rod. This use, frequently known as dowsing or water witching, has an interesting history. It is a means of hunting for an object, usually one hidden in the ground. One takes the divining rod, usually a forked branch or twig although other shapes and substances have been used, over the terrain where the hidden object is believed to be. The rod is held with one fork in either hand and the third branch pointing straight up into the air. It thus looks like an inverted Y. When the rod passes over the hidden substance, it twists down and thus indicates where one should dig.

Such a magical rod seems to have been known in Germany by at least the eleventh century, and certainly by the sixteenth century it was used by German miners to locate mineral deposits. It soon spread to the rest of Europe where it diversified into a number of specialties including the one most common today, dowsing for water. By the midtwentieth century there were some twenty-five thousand dowsers in America, hunting mostly for water but also for oil and uranium. A new use for the dowsing rod was developed during the war in Vietnam, where marine engineers started using metal divining rods to detect enemy mines, tunnels, and booby traps. There exists, however, some uncertainty as to exactly when dowsing reached America. The standard monograph on the subject,

114. *Ibid.*, pp. 40-45.

although arguing that it reached this country in the seventeenth century, found no actual evidence for the period before the Revolution.[115]

We have already seen one such piece of evidence in *The Disappointment,* and there exists additional evidence which not only confirms the use of the divining rod in colonial America but also proves that Forrest's portrayal of the occult ceremonies accompanying its use was correct. Earlier in colonial Philadelphia, in 1729, corroboration can be found in "The Busy-Body," No. 8. This essay, written partly by a still young Benjamin Franklin and partly by Joseph Breintnall, and noticeably heavy-handed when compared to *The Disappointment,* discloses the same procedures later parodied by *The Disappointment.* Breintnall, writing as Titan Pleiades, described himself as a student of astrology who had read Scot, Albertus Magnus, and Cornelius Agrippa over three hundred times, but lamented

> that there are large Sums of Money hidden under Ground in divers Places about this Town, and in many Parts of the Country; But alas, Sir, Notwithstanding I have used all the Means laid down in the *immortal Authors* before-mentioned, and when they fail'd, the in-genious Mr. P-d-l with his *Mercurial Wand* and *Magnet,* I have still fail'd in my Purpose.

Franklin, explaining that the craze for treasure hunting was based on the belief that pirates had hidden their treasures along the banks of the Schuylkill River, described the procedure of the treasure hunters:

> They wander thro' the Woods and Bushes by Day, to discover the Marks and Signs; at Midnight they repair to the hopeful Spot with Spades and Pickaxes; full of Expectation they labour violently, trembling at the same Time in every Joint, thro' Fear of certain malicious Demons who are said to haunt and guard such Places. At

115. Evon Z. Vogt and Ray Hyman, *Water Witching, U.S.A.* (Chicago: University of Chicago Press, 1959), pp. 3, 12-35, figs. 2-14, 20-21. For a magical rod in medieval Germany, see Jacob Grimm, *Teutonic Mythology* (New York: Dover Publications, Inc., 1966), III: 974-77; IV: 1598. For recent discussions of dowsing and its use in Vietnam see *New York Times,* Oct. 13, 1967, p. 17, and Oct. 24, 1965, sec. II, p. 39.

length a mighty hole is dug, and perhaps several Carloads of Earth thrown out, but alas, no Cag or Iron Pot is found! no Seaman's Chest cram'd with Spanish Pistoles, or weighty Pieces of Eight! Then they conclude, that thro' some Mistake in the Procedure, some rash Word spoken, or some Rule of Art neglected, the Guardian Spirit had Power to sink it deeper into the Earth and convey it out of their Reach.[116]

Nor is evidence for the divining rod limited to German-influenced Pennsylvania. It had, after all, spread throughout Europe, and thus was also available to the colonists from English sources. Reginald Scot, cited by both the Pennsylvania grand jury and Franklin's "Busy-Body" essay, was quite possibly one such source for many colonial efforts at dowsing.

> THERE must be made upon a hazell wand three crosses, and certeine words both blasphemous and impious must be said over it, and hereunto must be added certeine characters, & barbarous names. And whilest the treasure is a digging, there must be read the psalms, *De Profundis, Missa, Misereatur nostri, Requiem, Pater noster, Ave Maria, Et ne nos inducas in tentationem, sed libera nos à malo, Amen. A porta inferi credo videre bona &c. Expectate Dominum, Requiem aeternam.* And then a certeine praier. And if the time of digging be neglected, the divell will carie all the treasure awai.[117]

In New England we find Peter Oliver, a future chief justice of Massachusetts, writing to Jared Eliot, the famous colonial expert on scientific agriculture, about an experiment in *"praeternatural Philosophy."* Two or three people in Middleborough, Massachusetts, practiced "what is called the *Virgula Divinatoria,* long since exploded." Using a twig shaped like an inverted Y with some "prepared matter" in it, they claimed to be able to find copper, silver, and gold objects and mines. Oliver at first did not believe in it, but he tried it, and found that it even "exceeded what I had heard." By using it one could "locate a single Dollar under ground, at 60

---

116. Franklin, *Papers,* I: 134-39.

117. Reginald Scot, *The Discoverie of Witchcraft,* introduced by Hugh Ross Williamson (Carbondale, Illinois: Southern Illinois University Press, 1964), p. 163.

or 70 feet Distance; & to a Quantity of Silver at a Miles Distance. . . ."
He carefully explained how it worked:

The Person holds the Twig by its two Branches in both Hands &
grasps them close with the upper Part erect. If any Metal or Mine is
nigh, its Fibres, tho' never so fast held in the hand will twist, till it
points to the Object; & if the Metal or Mine is under, will twist to a
perpendicular Situation.

He concluded his discussion of this topic by hazarding a guess that "it will
occasion as much Speculation as Electricity, & I believe will tend to
Publick Benefit." [118]
Although this account lacked any overt supernatural or occult accom-
paniments, they were found in most colonial accounts. More typical was
Silas Hamilton, a prominent inhabitant of Whitingham, Vermont. In the
1780s he recorded in his notebook both the suspected location of lost
treasure, often located in a dream, and "A method to Tak up hid
Treasure."

Tak Nine Steel Rods about ten or twelve Inches in Length Sharp or
Piked to Perce in to the Erth, and let them be Besmeared with fresh
blood from a hen mixed with hogdung. Then mak two Surkels
Round the hid Treasure one of Sd Surkles a Little Larger in
surcumference than the hid Treasure lays in the Erth the other
Surkel Sum Larger still, and as the hid treasure is wont to move to
North or South, East or west Place your Rods as is Discribed on the
other sid of this leaf.

[The diagram "on the other sid of this leaf" showed the rods placed
between the two circles with their heads alternately on the inner and
outer circle, totally surrounding the treasure.] [119]

At the turn of the century a traveler in New England reported the

118. Peter Oliver to Jared Eliot, March 1756, Beinecke Library, Yale
University.
119. Clark Jillson, *Green Leaves from Whitingham, Vermont* (Worcester,
Mass.: privately printed, 1894), pp. 114-19.

existence of extensive treasure hunting. Used in these hunts was a "mineral rod," a witch-hazel divining rod, which "must be cut in a certain quarter of the moon, and must be held by a person of an approved horoscope."[120]

Many similar features are found in a nineteenth-century tale about a certain "Commodore," a New Englander of Welsh origin, who used the divining rod in the first half of the nineteenth century. He had hunted pirate treasure in Maine with a divining rod, but his procedures grew even more elaborate when he moved west and started hunting lost Spanish mines. He obtained a special divining rod made of horn and bone and filled with various materials including quicksilver. The Commodore also learned to use a special ceremony for protection against the evil spirits which guarded the mines. He drew a large circle about the mine, so large that the dirt from the diggings would not overlap it, placed nine new nails in it, and walked about the circle sunwise, all the while reciting the verse from the Apocrypha where the angel Raphael exorcises a devil. Perhaps significantly, he had obtained these ceremonies from an old Hessian soldier.[121]

The widespread acceptance of these beliefs by many in the eighteenth century is evidenced by the career of Rainsford Rogers of Connecticut. He apparently played the role of a real Rattletrap, but for money rather than fun. He seems to have had little difficulty in finding "marks." He worked in Morristown, New Jersey; Adams County, Pennsylvania; Exeter, New Hampshire; and various locations in the south. In 1788-89 in Morristown, Rainsford started his career of fraud by claiming that the hobgoblins and spirits which guarded a buried treasure demanded money before they would permit the treasure to be uncovered. Rainsford kept his dupes busy with elaborate ceremonies, which often took place in magic circles for protection against the spirits, and managed to collect about five hundred pounds before being detected. In the late 1790s he came to Exeter, New Hampshire, with much the same modus operandi.

---

120. Edward Augustus Kendall, *Travels Through the Northern Parts of the United States in the Years 1807-1808* (New York: I. Riley, 1809), III: 84-104.

121. "The History of the Divining Rod; with the Adventures of an Old Rodsman," *The United States Magazine and Democratic Review*, XXVI (March 1850): 218-25. The verse from the Apocrypha was probably Tobit 3:16-17; 6:7-9; 6:17; or 8:2-4.

This time, however, he claimed that several hundred dollars was needed to purchase a special divining rod required to locate the treasure. He took the money, supposedly went off to Philadelphia to purchase the rod, which perhaps indicates a continuing association between Philadelphia and the divining rod, and was never seen again by the good people of Exeter.[122]

All these tales obviously share a number of common features. With only one exception they all relate to hunting buried treasure or its near equivalent, a lost mine, rather than minerals or water. The treasure hunt indeed became a common theme in early American tales and its motifs frequently included a treasure guarded by ghosts or other spirits, an expert with a divining rod, and readings from the Bible, the hymn book, or *The Sixth and Seventh Books of Moses.*[123] Perhaps the rarity of what is today the most frequent use of the divining rod in America, the search for water, was simply due to the fact that the relatively well-watered east coast had no great use for water dowsing, and thus other varieties predominated.

A second major feature of these tales is their association of dowsing with a host of other occult and supernatural phenomena. By combining the various accounts, a common pattern of American treasure-hunting magic can be discovered. The treasure is located by a divining rod, which sometimes contained mercury or was prepared at an especially propitious time; one or more protective circles, a common feature of European ceremonial magic, are drawn; magical charms, or religious verses used as charms, are recited to overcome the guardian spirits; and nails or metal rods are sometimes used to pin down the treasure because, as Franklin, Silas Hamilton, and a satirical midnineteenth-century account warned, the treasure was wont to move about and attempt to escape.[124]

122. Charles H. Bell, *History of the Town of Exeter, New Hampshire* (Exeter, N.H.: 1888), pp. 412-13, and [Rogers Ransford], "The Morris-Town Ghost Deliniated," in *A Collection of Essays on a Variety of Subjects in Prose and Verse* (Newark, N.J.: John Woods, 1797).

123. Gerald T. Hurley, "Buried Treasure Tales in America," *Western Folklore,* X (July 1951): 197-216. Pages 205-15 contain summaries and sources for 102 buried-treasure stories, a number of which can be conveniently consulted in Dorson, *Jonathan Draws the Long Bow,* pp. 173-87.

124. Caleb Butler, *History of the Town of Groton* (Boston: Press of T. R. Marvin, 1848), p. 256n.

It has been argued that the modern tenuous connection between dowsing and magic, which is found only in the common American term for dowsing—"water witching"—developed only after 1775.[125] It is clear, however, that this is incorrect, and that dowsing in fact entered America as part of a complex of magical beliefs which it only later shed.

It is also certain this belief was found throughout the colonies. The combination of German influence and the belief in pirate treasure along the Schuylkill combined to make Philadelphia a center of this belief; it is the only place from which we have detailed descriptions of dowsing for treasure during the colonial period. Similar beliefs, however, are found in the other colonies by at least the late eighteenth century, and it is perhaps more likely that they represented independent introductions from England rather than diffusion from Pennsylvania, although there is some evidence that the Pennsylvania German tradition continued to have special influence or prestige. The extent to which dowsing was believed in is uncertain, but probably represented a significant minority. The satires of Franklin and Forrest obviously had a reality upon which they were based. Some of the other stories, especially those recorded only in nineteenth-century secondary sources, may well have been influenced by the generally accepted theme for magical treasure hunting, but the existence of this theme itself indicates a general knowledge of dowsing, and enough evidence remains to leave no doubt that dowsing for treasure, including appropriate protective measures against hostile spirits, was a not unusual occurrence in eighteenth-century America.

## V

Excluding stage magicians,[126] one can distinguish four varieties of magic workers in colonial America. The Pennsylvania magus was a belated survival of scholarly Renaissance magic in Enlightenment

125. Edward Katz and Peter Paulson, "A Brief History of the Divining Rod in the United States," *Journal of the American Society for Psychical Research,* XLII (October 1948): 120.

126. See advertisements for "Sleight of Hand Artist" in Rita Susswein Gottesman, *The Arts and Crafts in New York 1726-1776,* Collections of the New-York Historical Society for the Year 1936, LXIX (New York: New-York Historical Society, 1938), pp. 312-14.

America. It was the type of magic which would have appeared most familiar to such seventeenth-century dealers in magic as John Dee, the Elizabethan court astrologer and magus. Unconnected with the devil or evil, at least as far as its adepts and users were concerned, it was apparently a combination of ceremonial white magic and natural magic. The latter, the use of occult powers inherent in natural objects, was not unknown elsewhere in the colonies. Sir Walter Raleigh's popular *History of the World* contained a spirited vindication of natural magic.[127] An eighteenth-century Long Islander had filled his commonplace book with its marvels,[128] and Edward Taylor penned a similar list in a 1703 Meditation.

> The Clock at Strasburgh, Dresdens Table-Sight
>     Regiamonts Fly of Steel about that flew.
> Turrian's Wooden Sparrows in a flight
>     And th' Artificial man Aquinas slew.[129]

That such natural magic had points of contact with eighteenth-century science, as well as basic disagreements with it, was symbolized by Bartram's visit to Witt, and Witt's relationship with the rest of the Anglo-American scientific community.

Nevertheless, this form of magic appears to have been largely limited to the Pennsylvania Germans and those they directly influenced. Although some of the achievements of natural magic may have been known throughout the colonies, there is no sign of any great interest in it. Ceremonial magic, except for that connected with treasure hunting, appears also to have been limited to the Pennsylvania Germans. It is not that this magic was necessarily distinctively German, although some elements of it such as perhaps *The Sixth and Seventh Books of Moses* were, but rather, it is that except for some German sects it does not appear to

127. Raleigh, *Works*, II, bk. I, chap. xi.

128. Nathanial Dominy, Commonplace Books (1729-80), MS, Long Island Collection, Queens Borough Public Library, pp. 113-18.

129. Edward Taylor, "Preparatory Meditations," 2nd Series, no. 56, in *The Poems of Edward Taylor*, ed. by Donald E. Stanford (New Haven: Yale University Press, 1968), 31-34. Unless otherwise noted, all future citation of Taylor will be to this edition.

have been significantly transmitted from the Old World to the New. Indeed, even among the Germans, after the collapse of Kelpius's mystical sect, the magi appear to have declined into little more than superior versions of the traditional "cunning folk."

Such cunning folk, the "white witches" of the traditional English peasant culture, are even more difficult to study than the evil witches. As few had any desire to accuse or prosecute them, they left little trace in court records, and, as their good deeds lacked the notorious interest of evil, they were perhaps less likely to remain alive in local legend.

We do know of a few cunning folk, most of them, perhaps by coincidence, connected with the sea. Moll Pitcher, a white witch and seeress, often told the fortune of ships going to sea.[130] As we have already seen, Mr. Stafford of Tiverton, "who was want to tell where lost things might be found," also cast horoscopes to determine the propitious moment for ships to sail.[131] All that is known of the Hampton witch was that upon occasion she sold favorable winds to sailors.[132] Apparently unconnected with the sea was seventy-year-old Granny Morgan, who accustomed herself on occasion "to a hocus pocus, & making Cakes of flour and her own Urine and sticking them full of pins and divining by them." Even she was located in Newport, Rhode Island, a busy seaport.[133]

Perhaps professional cunning men or white witches did concentrate on seamen; certainly if the resort to the use of magic is the result of an inability to control events rationally by natural means, then colonial sailors had the greatest need for it; but the evidence is too fragmentary to be certain.[134] Perhaps too, the cunning folk simply concentrated upon the wealthier centers of colonial life, all of which were seaports. Local New England legends indicate the ability of the inland farmers to counter evil witches without having to resort to the specialized help of cunning folk. Apparently rural colonists had to serve as their own magicians, as well as their own doctors and craftsmen. On the other hand, a purely urban concentration of cunning folk would have been contrary to English practice, and colonial cunning folk were a continuation of an old English

130. Samuel Adams Drake, *A Book of New England Legends*, pp. 137-48.
131. Stiles, *Diary*, I: 386.
132. Byrd, "Letters," p. 231.
133. Stiles, *Diary*, I: 386.
134. Thomas, *Religion and the Decline of Magic*, pp. 648-54.

tradition.[135] The witches or fortune-tellers that Salem Village was warned against in 1746 appear to have been this type of rural cunning folk.

John Hale's *A Modest Inquiry's* discussion of cunning folk, slim as it is, is the only extended discussion in eighteenth-century America. He describes them as people who have "such an ambition to excel in physic, and curing variety of wounds and diseases, that they will rather go to the devil, than fail of their desired skill and honour thereby." He had heard "many credible histories . . . of this kind . . . ," but unfortunately decided not "to enlarge in these things which have been so carefully handled by *Perkins*, and others." [136] One can assume with some confidence that the records grossly understate the number of cunning folk in the colonies; beyond that, little can be said with certainty about them.

The third, and quantitatively most important, variety of magic worker in colonial America was the traditional evil witch of folk belief, who dries up cows, prevents the milk from being churned into butter, and causes disruptions, illnesses, and death. Belief in these witches was not limited to the uneducated. We have seen several ministers accept the idea of witchcraft, and Samuel Locke, president of Harvard (1770-73), listed among his references on the subject of apparitions, Glanvill's *Saducismus Triumphatus* and Baxter's *World of the Spirits*.[137] There were, however, some direct attacks on the belief in witchcraft. Franklin and Forrest satirized the belief in witchcraft and magic, as we have already seen, and Josiah Cotton attacked it as a deception of the priests,[138] while Thomas Hutchinson called Salem "a scene of fraud and imposture." [139]

Probably even more important than overt attacks was the withdrawal of many of the upper class from active participation in witchcraft beliefs.

135. See MacFarlane, *Witchcraft in Tudor and Stuart England,* pp. 120-21.

136. Hale, *A Modest Inquiry,* pp. 130-31.

137. Samuel Locke, Notebook (1775-90), MS, Harvard University Archives, no. 25.

138. *Boston Evening Post,* Jan. 7, 1753. A rough draft of this essay, dated 1733, is found in Josiah Cotton, "Account of the Cotton Family," MS, Harvard University Library.

139. Hutchinson, *The History of . . . Massachusetts-Bay,* II: 47. Benjamin Wadsworth noted this opinion is his Commonplace Book, "An Abridgement of What I Extracted While an Undergraduate at Harvard College, 1767-69," MS, Harvard University Archives, p. 127.

The most obvious symptom of this was the decline in trials for witchcraft, which was manifest well before the repeal of the Jacobean witchcraft statute. This withdrawal of the upper classes was also indicated by the absence, after Salem, of any serious literature which attempted to defend the concept of witchcraft. They perhaps did not actively disbelieve in witchcraft, but they did not actively believe either. Thus a belief which in the seventeenth century had been common to all elements of society, was in the eighteenth century starting to become a belief that tended to separate the better educated from the less educated and less "enlightened" Americans.

Even in the seventeenth century, however, there had been a difference between the "folk" and the "scholarly" conceptions of witchcraft. The type of witchcraft beliefs seen at Salem and later at Littleton was in fact a fourth type of witchcraft, with features distinguishing it from the common folk-witch. Considerable modern scholarly emphasis had been placed upon proving that Salem was not a unique colonial aberration, but rather, was within the mainstream of the English witchcraft tradition and, except for its scope, had ample colonial precedents. All this is true, yet it is not the whole truth. Salem contained elements which never had a firm basis in English traditions and which failed to take root in the colonies.

At Salem, witchcraft had been linked with overt Satanism. Witches signed pacts with the devil, and potential witches were pursued by witches and the devil, who sought to gain their signatures on the fatal contract. This element was generally rare in the English folk tradition. "With the general run of English witches, who belonged to the illiterate class, the agreement with Satan was implicit only, or at the most oral . . . ," although on occasion a document was signed.[140] Thus too, in the colonies a formal contract between the devil and a witch rarely appeared except at Salem. Not that the Old Deluder never made a deal in the colonies but, when he did, he usually purchased souls with a promise of wealth rather than a promise of great magical powers.[141] The motif of a pact with the devil in order to obtain magical powers was undoubtedly known in the

140. Kittredge, *Witchcraft in Old and New England,* pp. 242-43.
141. Dorson, *Jonathan Draws the Long Bow,* pp. 47-58. However, see Samuel G. Drake, *Annals of Witchcraft,* pp. 62-63, 170.

colonies, through scholarly channels and from the popular legend of Faust,[142] but it was not usually associated with the local village witch.

Another exotic element at Salem had been the witches' Sabbaths. This doctrine had been a late introduction in England, and had never taken strong root either there or in the colonies, although a witches' coven was reportedly formed in Groton as late as 1797.[143] Also relatively new was the specific affliction caused by the Salem witchcraft, namely, possession by devils. Although simple possession by the devil had prominent biblical precedent, it had not been a major element in European witchcraft until some time about the beginning of the seventeenth century.[144] It too became largely quiescent in the colonies after Salem. While the traditional elements of English witchcraft, including the much maligned spectral evidence, continued as active beliefs and reappeared in numerous incidents of witchcraft throughout the eighteenth century, the scholarly imports of European concepts fell by the wayside, perhaps not actively disbelieved in by the people but without enough vitality to enter into the formation of new tales of witchcraft.

It was undoubtedly true that the Salem witch-hunt was the result of numerous factors: political uncertainty, personal and social tensions, and the traditional English and colonial belief in witchcraft. But one should not ignore the role of the imported Continental beliefs, which, if they never took root in the colonies, were nevertheless fully acceptable to the general population.[145] A witch who was in direct contact with her master,

142. Henry A. Pochman, *German Culture in America: Philosophical and Literary Influences, 1600-1900* (Madison: University of Wisconsin Press, 1957), p. 30. Doctor Faustus and Friar (Roger) Bacon were feature characters in a 1746 "magic Lantern" show in New York. Gottesman, *The Arts and Crafts in New York*, pp. 375-76.

143. Kittredge, *Witchcraft in Old and New England*, chap. xvi; Butler, *History of Groton*, p. 257n.

144. E. William Monter, "Witchcraft in Geneva, 1537-1662," *The Journal of Modern History*, XLIII (June 1971): 197-98. "The seventeenth century was the age of the *démoniaque*," p. 198.

145. Kittredge, *Witchcraft in Old and New England*, constantly pointed out the distinction between native English and imported Continental beliefs concerning witchcraft. For the argument that England did not have great witch-hunts similar

the devil, and working in league with her fellow witches, was a much different, a much more dangerous and terrifying, figure than a lone witch venting her malice on her own behalf. It was the difference between an isolated criminal, or even a crime wave, and a hellish anarchical conspiracy to overthrow the church, the state, and all human society. Consider, too, the difference it would have made at Salem had the children been diagnosed as suffering simply from demonic possession rather than from demonic possession induced by witchcraft.[146]

The eighteenth century, which generally lacks both the influence of scholarly beliefs about witchcraft and official action against witches, displays most clearly the structure of native folk beliefs concerning witchcraft. The isolated witch of folk belief was a threat to those she afflicted, but not an uncontrollable one. There were specific and effective cures for witchcraft, and the witch was singularly vulnerable to a magical counterattack. Any object she bewitched, be it man, beast, or butter churn, was a potential conduit for a magical counterattack against her. And the effectiveness of the counterattack was believed in as completely and with as much intensity as was the power of the witch herself.[147]

Moreover, if, as has been argued, the psychological basis of witchcraft was the projection of repressed hostility onto the witch by the accuser, and the direct manifestation of this hostility by verbal attacks upon the witch,[148] then folk countermagic permitted the expression of this hostility as well as, if not better than, a legal prosecution. One could still project the repressed hostility upon the witch, and attack her verbally by voicing

---

to those in the rest of Europe because it lacked the "superstructure" of belief connecting witches to Satan, see Norman Cohn, "The Myth of Satan and Human Servants," in Mary Douglas, ed., *Witchcraft Confessions & Accusations* (London: Tavistock Publications, Ltd., 1970), p. 12.

146. For example, see the case described in Increase Mather's *Remarkable Providences,* quoted in Burr, *Narratives of the Witchcraft Cases,* pp. 22-23.

147. A recent study of European witchcraft has argued that this dichotomy between popular and learned conceptions of witchcraft was true of medieval European witchcraft in general. See Norman Cohn, *Europe's Inner Demons: An Enquiry Inspired by the Great Witch-Hunt* (New York: Basic Books, Inc., 1975), pp. 205, 251-53, *passim.*

148. Demos, "Underlying Themes," p. 1322.

accusations of witchcraft to friends and neighbors, even if the latter could no longer be done formally in a courtroom. In addition, the most common modes of countermagic permitted one to attack the witch symbolically. She could be burned by burning something she had bewitched; struck by striking her spectral image; even physically attacked as one attempted to draw her blood. Such a magical duel would have been psychically as satisfying and effective as a trial, and no doubt safer to all concerned.

# 4

## Alchemy

*Doctor AEneas Munson shewed me another piece of Mercury which he had, fixt indeed, but not malleable. He told me that Capt. Phipps last year was shown the Experiment at Savanna by a Doctor Prentice thus—Phipps melted Lead, & when so far cold as to begin to grow hard, but while yet hot, he Phipps poured upon the congealing Lead, Mercury, which thus became fixt by the fumes of Lead. The Doctor then told him to melt the fixt substance, & gave him a small portion of grey Powder abot a pinch of Snuff, which Phipps took & cast on the Metal or Mercury in Fusion, & it coold & fixt. The Doctor told him, it would break in hammering, unless &c, & gave Phipps some corrosive sublimate. He melted it again, cast on the sublimate, & it then became malleable. Another Man told Doctor Munson, he himself had by Doctor Prentices Direction treated four Ounces of Mercury in the same manner, & made it also pfect Silver with the Loss of a few Grains only. This Doctor Prentice was son of a Doctor Prentice of Roxbury near Boston, was in New Haven at sesson of Assembly Oct. 1791, aet.30, had been cropt, & had been in Symsbury Mines or Newgate. Doctor Munson did not see him but his son did. Doctor Prentice associated with Major Prentice of this City, but no Relation; but the Major says he is a shrewd Fellow. He had made the Tour of Europe: and pretty freely & openly makes Projection, & says he cares Nothing for Money.*
—Ezra Stiles, *Literary Diary*[1]

Alchemy entered the eighteenth century with full academic approval. Morton's *Compendium* displayed both a knowledge of alchemical ter-

---

1. Abbreviations using superscripts, such as w$^c$ for "which" and Roxb$^y$ for "Roxbury," have been expanded.

minology and a cautious acceptance of their claims. Morton explained the alchemist's doctrine that the "soul" of every metal is gold, and therefore gold can be extracted from any metal.

> The Artiface of Gold by Alchymy came from the last consideration, [for] hence they took a Great Confidence of a transmutation of all mettals into Gold, by curing the Leprosities of them (as they Speak). This opperation is cal'd the finding of the Phylosophers stone; and tis affirm'd, that Some have done it, such are cal'd the Adepti; Sons of Art, Sons of Hermes, etc: Of this Number are Eminent Raimundus Lulius, who in the Dayes of our Henry 7th made (tis said) that Excellent Gold of which Rose-nobles ar[e] coyned. Yea Some say that afterwards he Communicated the [noble] art to the Senate of Venice, and that they Exersise the Art (at this day) in their St. Marks Tower from whence come forth Continually unaccountable Quantityes of Gold, besides Lullius ware famous Paracelsus, Vanhelmont, and others of whom we shall not farther Insist.[2]

It should be noted that this explanation of alchemy does not involve any transmutation of the original four elements—fire, air, water, and earth. That was the basis of an entirely different theory. Morton, in fact, had earlier explicity denied the possibility of transmuting those basic elements, and have called such theories "Goats wool." [3] Nor should it be assumed that belief in alchemy ended at Harvard when the *Compendium* was discarded. As late as 1771 a Harvard master's thesis affirmatively answered the question, "Can real gold be made by the art of chemistry?" [4]

At Yale, Samuel Johnson's early encyclopedias for once fail us. He made no mention of alchemy. He did, however, state the alchemical theory of the origin of minerals. They were composed of the principles of sulphur and mercury, with sulphur predominant in rocks and mercury in metals, while minerals were "of a middle nature as salt, etc." [5] From this one can learn little about Johnson's beliefs concerning the possible transmutation of metals, except for the fact that he was not very inter-

2. Morton, *Compendium Physicae*, pp. 120-21.
3. *Ibid.*, p. 41.
4. Young, "Subjects for Master's Degree in Harvard College," p. 131.
5. Johnson, *Works*, II: 147.

ested in it. Fortunately, however, we have a better source of information for the status of alchemy at early eighteenth-century Yale. A 1718 thesis upheld the proposition that metals could be transmuted.[6]

Some, of course, may have used alchemical terminology without necessarily being a practicing alchemist or even believing in alchemy. Benjamin Franklin mentioned the philosopher's stone while explaining Poor Richard's method of obtaining gold:

> Get what you can, and what you get hold;
> 'Tis the Stone that will turn all your Lead into Gold.[7]

Much less crassly he once wrote, "Content is the Philosopher's Stone, that turns all it touches into Gold." [8]

Several of Edward Taylor's late seventeenth- and early eighteenth-century poems contain alchemical metaphores:

> This is the Heavenly Alkahest that brings
> Lean Soul t' ore thrive Pharao's fattest Ware.[9]

Christ is compared to a still in

> Thy Humane Frame, my Glorious Lord, I spy,
> A Golden Still with Heavenly Choice drugs filld;
> Thy Holy Love, the Glowing heate whereby,
> The Spirit of Grace is graciously distilld.
> Thy Mouth the Neck through which these spirits still.
> Thy Soul thy Violl make, and therewith fill.[10]

Taylor wrote two separate stanzas in which he compared man to an alembic, an alchemist's still. The first was a verse of glowing praise, but the second was a verse of almost Swiftian revulsion for the human body, though again tempered by praise for the soul.

6. Walsh, *Education of the Founding Fathers*, p. 20.
7. Franklin, *Papers*, VII: 349.
8. *Ibid.*, p. 353.
9. Taylor, "Preparatory Meditations," 2nd Series, no. 68 [B], 19-20.
10. *Ibid.*, 1st Series, no. 7, 1-6.

For when the Objects of thy Joy impress
  Their shining influences on my heart.
My Soule seems as Alembick doth possess
  Love stilld into rich Spirits by thy Art.
And all my pipes, were they ten thousand would
Drop Spirits of Love on thee, more rich than gold.[11]

The other stanza had a very different tone:

Natures Alembrick 't is, Its true: that stills
  The Noblest Spirits terrene fruits possess,
Yet, oh! the Relicks in the Caldron will
  Proove all things else, Guts, Garbage, Rotteness.
And all its pipes but Sincks of nasty ware
That foule Earths face, and do defile the aire.[12]

Taylor was interested in minerals. He had made a condensation of John Webster's *Metallography,* and he was clearly acquainted with some of the chemical processes that accompanied alchemy. There exists, however, no evidence that Taylor had any direct contact with alchemy, other than its defense in Webster's *Metallography,* and certainly no evidence that Taylor was involved in actual alchemical experiments.[13] Other colonists, including his grandson, Ezra Stiles, were more deeply involved.

Ezra Stiles was apparently one of a number of men in late eighteenth- and early nineteenth-century New England who were interested in alchemy. He himself does not appear to have actually attempted any alchemical experiments, and at times unconvincingly denied that he was interested in alchemy; but he was in fact quite interested, and his *Diary* furnishes us with most of the information we have concerning late eighteenth-century New England alchemists.[14]

11. *Ibid.,* no. 48, 25-30.
12. *Ibid.,* 2nd Series, no. 75, 19-24.
13. For details concerning his abridgment of Webster's *Metallography,* see Taylor, *Poems,* pp. 508-9.
14. Except where additional citations are given, for my study of this group of New England alchemists I have relied upon Ronald Sterne Wilkinson, "New England's Last Alchemists," *Ambix,* X (October 1962): 128-38.

One of these alchemists was Samuel Danford (Harvard 1715), who became Massachusetts' chief justice and one-time president of the Governor's Council. He corresponded with Benjamin Franklin about the use of the philosopher's stone as a panacea and source of eternal life. On Danford's death, Stiles noted that "he was deeply studied in the writings of the Adepts, believed the Philosophers Stone a Reality and perhaps for Chemical knowledge might have passed among the Chemists for a [Baal Shem]." ("Baal Shem" was a cabalistic term, meaning one who could work wonders by using the true name of God.)[15] Danford's son, Samuel Danford, Jr., may also have been interested in alchemy for a limited period of time, although in 1812 he donated hs father's alchemical texts to the Boston Athenaeum.

Rabbi Tobiah Bar Jehudah of Poland once told Stiles that he had witnessed the transmutation of base metals into gold, but that unfortunately "it was folly to persue it," for it required more gold to prepare the transformation than resulted from it.[16]

Other alchemists known to Stiles included the Reverend Samuel West, Aeneas Munson (who showed Stiles some "fixed mercury"), and Dr. Ebenezer Cahoon (who showed him some "alchemical silver").[17]

While considering the phenomena of monetary inflation, Stiles came upon a curious historical problem which he thought might have been caused by alchemy. Not only had the value of specie in general declined since the discovery of America, but the value of silver in particular had declined relative to that of gold. At one time, ten ounces of silver had been the equivalent of one ounce of gold, but now it took sixteen ounces of silver to buy one ounce of gold. This decline in the relative value of silver was due to the greater proportion of silver relative to gold found in the mines of America. But why should the American mines have a different ratio of gold to silver than had previously existed in the rest of the world? "May we not suppose that the nat. proport. of the Mines of both are alike in all Regions?" Thus did Stiles reason; therefore his

15. George L. Kittredge, "Dr. Robert Child the Remonstrant," *Transactions of the Colonial Society of Massachusetts,* XI (March 1919): 139n. For "Baal Shem" see Gershom G. Scholem, *On the Kabbalah and Its Symbolism,* trans. by Ralph Manheim (New York: Schocken Books, 1969), p. 200.

16. Ezra Stiles, "Literary Diary," MS, Yale University, Nov. 23, 1773.

17. Stiles, *Literary Diary,* III: 348, 471.

problem was to determine why there had previously existed in the world
an unnaturally high ratio of gold to silver, which imbalance had reduced
the relative value of gold compared to that of silver. He suggested that

> the Chinese & Japanese abound with Adepts who, it is said, have
> augmented the Gold. They were dispersed thro' Europe as well as
> Asia & Egypt, & made the general Ratio 1 to 10. Perhaps an Exam.
> of the Peruvian Registers would shew the natural Quantity 1 to 20.

He neatly combined an understanding of the inverse relationship between
quantity and value with a belief in alchemy, explaining that with the
discovery of America and the opening of direct trade with the Orient, "if
the Adepts have increased the Gold in Europe, while also the Amer.
Mines have augmented both Gold & Silver, there will be a double Cause
for the Depreciation of Money in Europe so as to be but one seventh of its
Value 200 y. ago." [18]

Ezra Stiles's acquaintances were not the only practicing alchemists in
the colonies. Another was William Gerard De Brahm, a German. He had
been an engineering officer in the army of Emperor Charles VII, but after
converting to Protestantism in the late 1740s he had led a party of
immigrants to Bethany, Georgia, in 1751. By the 1760s he had been
appointed surveyor general of East Florida and surveyor general of the
Southern District, the latter appointment lasting until the Revolution
terminated the position. During the Revolution, De Brahm was held
captive for a time by the patriots in South Carolina, and then expelled to
France for refusing to abjure his allegiance to the king. After some
traveling he finally settled in the 1790s in Philadelphia, where he wrote
several difficult mystical-philosophical tracts, and there he eventually died
in 1799.

De Brahm sent the Latin text of his major alchemical work, "Hercules
ex Rore Rosatus," to Lord Dartmouth in 1769. In a later letter to Lord
Dartmouth, De Brahm explained that he had worked on it since 1743,
following in his father's footsteps. De Brahm claimed that by utilizing
authorities, whose dates ranged from 1413 to 1744, as well as his own
experiments, he had succeeded in learning "Treasurers of Nature" which

---

18. *Ibid.,* II: 179-80.

had hitherto been hidden as "so many Hieroglyphics, Enigmatics, Allegorys, and Metaphysical Metamorphoses, that one without a divine inspiration or manuduction of a faithful pious instructor, and Master in true philosophy may rather undertake to Searge [Search?] for a needle in a Bottel of Hay."

His alchemical studies were laid aside when he became surveyor general (or at least so he was careful to explain to Lord Dartmouth, his superior), but he later decided to incorporate its fruits into his unpublished "General Survey of the Southern District of North America." This work was written in the early 1770s, while De Brahm was in London to answer charges which had risen out of a complex and bitter dispute with Governor James Grant of East Forida, and in 1773 he had personally presented it to the king. Before presenting it, however, he had asked the advice of Lord Dartmouth and, presumably upon receiving a negative response, had omitted the alchemical appendix from the presentation copy. It may be found, however, in an otherwise almost identical copy of the "Survey" preserved at Harvard University.[19]

The appendix consisted of five parts. The first was a rambling introduction which alleged to explain the origin of the text. De Brahm claimed to have known the one man in America who knew the secret of the panacea, and to have learned the secret from him. He had written it down on parchment in 1763 (the copy sent to Lord Dartmouth was dated 1763 on its title page) and now, to prevent its being lost, was recopying it into the "Survey."

The second part of the appendix was the actual Latin alchemical text, now entitled, "Hercules Ex Rore sub Flora Corona." Next came a

19. For biographical data I have relied primarily upon the introduction to William Gerard De Brahm, *De Brahm's Report of the General Survey in the Southern District of North America,* ed. and introduced by Louis De Vorsey, Jr. (Columbia, S.C.: University of South Carolina Press, 1971), and De Brahm to Lord Dartmouth, May 25, 1773, MS, Dartmouth Manuscripts, Stafford County Record Office, England. The MS alchemical text, dated 1763 but sent November 1769, is also preserved in the Dartmouth Papers. I wish to acknowledge the permission of the Earl of Dartmouth for my use of the Dartmouth Manuscripts.

See also the *Dictionary of American Biography* and Charles L. Mowat, "That 'Odd Being' De Brahm," *Florida Historical Quarterly,* XX (April 1942): 323-45.

shorter English explanation of the Latin text. De Brahm noted that it was more than a simple translation, it was an explanation of the hidden meaning of the original text. As the most elaborate eighteenth-century colonial alchemical text extant, it is well worth sampling.

> 2. You therefore, who are faithfully, diligently and patiently enquiring into the wonderful Virtues of Nature! to you I address myself, and advise you to collect for this Operation spagerically a grand Vessel as much as three Philosophical Weightes, then prepare three Athanors, each capacious to hold three Pounds; in each of these Athanors put one pound of the Vessel, with two Pounds of the Chaos (favorite Subject) N.B. each Pound of the Vessel is equal in measure to two Pounds of Chaos.
>
> 3. In each Athanor gently and with great judgment generate a particular Earth, as per instance, in the first Athanor produce a Mecurial Earth of a two-fold Nature, in the above Fable [Latin text] called by the Names Sosias and Mercurius: The Earth is obtained by Sublimation, Precipitation, Circulation, Digestion, and Calcenation. In the second Athanor is made an imflammable (phlogistic) Earth of two different Natures, named Amphitryon and Jupiter, Which are kindled by Precipitation, Calcenation, Circulation, Digestion & Filtration. And in the third Athanor is formed a vitresible Earth, also of a double Nature mentioned above by the Names Alcemena and Juno, which is produced by Circulation, Digestion, Filtration, and Congelation.

To aid those planning to use his text, he thoughtfully pointed out the fact that the earths, the vessels, and the athanors came "from the favorite Subject (Chaos)." Unfortunately, it was never quite clear where Chaos was to be found.[20]

20. "Chaos" was a standard alchemical term here used for primeval matter, the source of all the elements. Wolfgang Schneider, *Lexikon Alchemistisch-Pharmazeutischer Symbole* (Weinheim, Germany: Verlag Chemie. GmbH., 1962), p. 70, and Gino Testi, *Dizionario Di Alchimia e Di Chimica Antiquaria* (Rome: Casa Editrice Mediterranea, 1950), "Caos."

For a discussion of primal matter see Willard, *A Compleat Body of Divinity,* pp. 113-16.

After the earths were properly prepared and mixed,

> Alcemena will bring forth her Son Hercules, which means that the
> Light of Nature in Disguise by help of the Mercurial Earth will
> penetrate through the Sulphur of Nature and impregnate the
> Vitresible Earth, which saturated in that Sal enixum whose Virtue
> entitles it to be a Panacea, not volatile, but able to sustain the same
> degree of Fire with a fluid Metal, nor solid, but adapted to mix with
> any Vegetable Juice for the greatest Benefit of Human Nature.

De Brahm did in fact thus attempt to explain his allegorical Latin text,
but it is unlikely if anyone not already initiated into the secrets of alchemy
could have benefited from his explanation. It is worth noting that the goal
(as in Samuel Danford's correspondence with Franklin) was not gold but
the universal cure, the panacea. This panacea was probably the "admirable salt" which he would later offer as a cure for George III's madness.[21] If
one considers not only purely alchemical efforts but also such episodes as
John Tennent's snake root and George Berkeley's tar water, it will appear
that the search for some form of a panacea was rather widespread in the
eighteenth century.

The fourth part of the appendix was a diagram of De Brahm's newly
invented "Copper Athanor," a copy of which was also sent to Lord
Darthmouth in 1773.[22] The fifth and last section consisted of a rather
mystical essay, "Of Religion." Here De Brahm explained that "the
elements and all sublunary Beings were created first to improve themselves and come to their Perfection, in which they were to nurse and serve
Man . . . ," while man's role was "to receive and return the incomparable
Emanation of Divine Love." [23]

Although the only formal alchemical text in the eighteenth-century

21. De Brahm, *Report of the General Survey,* p. 56.

22. De Brahm to Lord Dartmouth, May 25, 1773, MS, Dartmouth Manuscripts, Stafford County Record Office, England.

23. The appendix is found in William Gerard De Brahm, "Survey of East
Florida, Carolina, Georgia, &c.," MS, Houghton Library, Harvard University,
pp. 343-68. Unfortunately, as the recently published edition of the *General
Survey* was prepared from the English manuscript, it does not contain the
appendix. By permission of the Harvard College Library.

colonies was that by De Brahm, the commonplace book of John Paschall was rich in alchemical lore. It contained, among other items of interest, notes on philosophical alchemy (i.e., the purification and spiritual transformation of an individual), on Paracelsus's description of alkahest (the universal solvent), a formula for the philosopher's stone, and a recipe for extracting silver and gold from any stone or mineral. The latter required the melting and precipitation, reiterated when necessary, of a quarter of an ounce of gold, two drams of silver, eight ounces of copper, and eight ounces of regular iron (?). Such formulas well merited Paschall's description of the earth as "this Sublunary Kitchen of the elements." [24]

William Hooker Smith, a New Yorker whose account of witchcraft has already been referred to, seems to have dabbled in alchemy. He told of a dream he had had in which he was informed that he would soon become rich. "I could not Se how That could com unless I Should Have Luck in making the Philosophers Stone . . . ." Considering the rest of Smith's "Remarkable Acurances," there is little doubt that he was in fact searching for the secret of the philosopher's stone, without any luck. [25]

Other indications of an eighteenth-century colonial interest in alchemy include a "Liber de Alchemia" in the 1766 catalogue of the New York City Library, notes on one or more alchemy books copied by Benjamin Stockbridge in the first third of the century, and a marginal note defending alchemy written into a copy of William Jones's *Physiological Disquisitions* which had formerly belonged to the New York Society Library. [26]

24. John Paschall, Commonplace Book (1729-31), MS, Historical Society of Pennsylvania. The existence of this alchemical material was first noted in George Edward Bates, Jr., "The Emergence of a Modern Mind in Colonial America, 1700-1760," (unpublished Ph.D. dissertation, University of Illinois at Urbana-Champaign, 1970), pp. 165-66.

25. William Hooker Smith, "Remarkable Acurances," MS, New York Public Library.

26. New York City Library, *A Catalogue of the Library Belonging to the Corporation of the City of New York* (New York: Holt, 1766), p. 20; Benjamin Stockbridge, "Account Book and Notes in Alchemy 1705-1730," MSS, Massachusetts Historical Society; and William Jones, *Physiological Disquisitions; or, Discourses on the Natural Philosophy of the Elements* (London: J. Rivington and Sons, 1781), p. xiii. The latter is currently in the Science Division of the New York Public Library.

Alchemy in eighteenth-century America, as earlier, appears to have been an esoteric science, practiced by only a few, although its language was probably recognizable by many. We do have just enough information to know that the two traditional goals of alchemy, the transmutation of precious metals and the creation of the panacea, were still being actively pursued, and even the mystical philosophical alchemy was not unknown.

# 5

## The Fascinating Rattlesnake

*It is generally believed that they charm birds, rabbits, squirrels and other animals, and by stedfastly looking at them possess them with infatuation; be the cause what it may, the miserable creatures undoubtedly strive by every possible means to escape, but alas! their endeavours are in vain, they at last loose the power of resistance and flitter or move slowly, but reluctantly towards the yawning jaws of their devourers, and creep into their mouths or lay down and suffer themselves to be taken and swallowed.*

—William Bartram, *Travels* (1791)

### I

There was one segment of the supernaturalism of seventeenth-century England which, by and large, did not successfully cross the Atlantic. Nonhuman creatures with supernatural power—elves, fairies, and dwarfs—did not accompany witches and cunning men to the New World. Perhaps the fact that they were often linked with specific geographic features kept them from being transported. Perhaps it seemed incongruous that creatures accustomed to the placid English countryside should reside in the howling American wilderness! [1] However, within

1. For fairies in seventeenth-century England, see Thomas, *Religion and the Decline of Magic*, pp. 606-14; Lewis, *The Discarded Image*, pp. 122-38; K. M. Briggs, *The Anatomy of Puck: An Examination of Fairy Beliefs Among Shakespeare's Contemporaries and Successors* (London: Routledge and Kegan Paul, 1959); Burton, *The Anatomy of Melancholy*, pt. 1, sec. 2, memb. 1, subs. 2.

three-quarters of a century, America had developed its own nonhuman inhabitant with supernatural powers—the rattlesnake. This native son of the New World was soon endowed with its own version of the "evil eye," and was said to work its charms on man and beast alike. The development of this belief is of special interest because it was indigenous. Unlike other colonial occult beliefs, it developed in the colonies themselves from a variety of sources, some from the Old World but some from the New. It easily survived debates in eighteenth-century natural history circles, in both the colonies and abroad, and indeed survives as a viable belief in the twentieth century.[2]

## II

The belief appears to have developed in the second half of the seventeenth century. Prior to that, the continued absence of any mention of this power of the rattlesnake, even in writings in which it would have been most appropriate, indicates that the belief was not current throughout most of the century. One such opportunity had arisen in 1632 with the publication of George Sandys's translation of and commentary on Ovid's *Metamorphoses*. Sandys had certainly been well situated to learn of the development of any such belief among the Virginians. In the early 1620s he had been the resident treasurer of the colony, and he had interested himself in the collection of Virginia curiosities. Even after leaving the colony he had remained in close contact with it through his land holdings and his position on the subcommittee of the Privy Council which supervised Virginia affairs. The most famous result of his stay in Virginia was, of course, his translation of Ovid's *Metamorphoses*. He published it on his return from Virginia, and, more valuable for our purposes, in 1632 he published the translation with an elaborate commentary. The commen-

---

2. For instances of this belief in the nineteenth and twentieth centuries, see Lloyd N. Jeffrey, "Snake Yarns of the West and Southwest," *Western Folklore,* XIV (October 1955): 251; "The Rattlesnake & Its Congeners," *Harper's New Monthly Magazine,* X (March 1855): 479-80; Calvin Claudel, "Tales from San Diego," *California Folklore Quarterly,* II (April 1943): 117-18; Laurence M. Klauber, *Rattlesnakes: Their Habits, Life Histories, and Influence on Mankind* (Berkeley and Los Angeles: published for the Zoological Society of San Diego by the University of California Press, 1956), II: 1222-23.

tary used various illustrations from Sandys's readings on and experiences in the New World. It mentioned opposums, frogs, Florida hermaphrodites, and West Indian cannibals; yet Sandys made no mention of the rattlesnake and its power of fascination, despite several passages in Ovid where such a comment would have been most apposite.[3]

> With that, the Serpent his blew head extends;
> And suffering ayer with horrid hisses rends.
> The water from them [the Tyrians] fell: their colour fled:
> Who all, astonished, shook with sudden dread.[4]

> With twice foure birds: these, and their dam (which now
> Flutter'd about her young) the greedy snake
> At length deuour'd.[5]

Sandys was not the only one to omit such opportunities. A midseventeenth-century display of rattlesnakes in England brought no mention of the power of fascination,[6] and even in the 1670s John Josselyn, who "loved a good story," made no mention of it when discussing rattlesnakes.[7] Not only did many seventeenth-century accounts of the rattle-

---

3. Richard Beale Davis, *George Sandys, Poet-Adventurer: A Study in Anglo-American Culture in the Seventeenth Century* (London: The Bodley Head, 1955); *idem,* "America in George Sandys' 'Ovid,' " *William and Mary Quarterly,* 3rd Series, IV (July 1947): 297-304.

4. Ovid, *Ovid's Metamorphosis Englished, Mythologiz'd, and Represented in Figures,* trans. and notes by George Sandys (Oxford: John Kichfield, 1632), p. 82. For a modern translation see Ovid, *Metamorphoses,* trans. by Frank Justus Miller, Loeb Classical Library, (Cambridge: Harvard University Press, 1951), iii. 37-40.

5. Ovid, *Metamorphosis,* trans. by George Sandys, p. 399. Other potential occasions for a discussion of rattlesnake fascination were the legend of Medusa and a collection of snake stories, *ibid.,* pp. 147-49, 169, 319.

6. John Evelyn, *The Diary of John Evelyn,* ed. by E. S. De Beer (Oxford: Clarendon Press, 1955), Sept. 19, 1657.

7. John Josselyn, "An Account of Two Voyages to New-England," *Massachusetts Historical Society Collections,* 3rd Series, III (1833): 277-78; *idem, New-England Rarities Discovered* (London: G. Widdowes, 1672), pp. 38-39; Stearns, *Science in the British Colonies of America,* p. 140.

snake not mention the power of fascination,[8] but, as we shall see, many Renaissance and seventeenth-century works discussed fascination without mentioning rattlesnakes.

The first statement concerning rattlesnake fascination seems to have been published in 1672. John Lederer, while exploring western Virginia, reported that the Indians had told him that rattlesnakes caught squirrels

> by fixing their eye steadfastly upon them; the horrour of which strikes such an affrightment into the little beast, that he has no power to hinder himself from tumbling down into the jaws of his enemy, who takes in all his sustenance without chewing, his teeth serving him only to offend withal. But I rather believe what I have heard from others, that these Serpents climb the trees, and surprise their prey in the nest.[9]

This passage contains several interesting points. Its attribution of this belief to the Indians will be discussed in more detail below. Its denial of the reality of the power of fascination, although somewhat unusual especially for a traveler's account, was not a rare occurrence. The concept of rattlesnake fascination never achieved unchallenged acceptance, although it rapidly became and remained a widespread belief. Moreover, the belief had perhaps not yet achieved its definitive eighteenth-century form. Lederer left it unclear as to whether fascination was thought to have stemmed from some innate power of the serpent's eye or from the prey's fear of the snake. In addition, neither of the words which soon became near obligatory, "charm" and "fascination," were used. Once the eighteenth-century stereotype was fully formed, an account of the rattlesnake

---

8. Peter Lindeström, *Geographia Americae with an Account of the Delaware Indians Based on Surveys and Notes Made in 1654-1656*, trans. from the manuscript by Amandus Johnson (Philadelphia: The Swedish Colonial Society, 1925), p. 240; Thomas Morton, *New England Canaan,* in Peter Force *Tracts,* II: 56; William Wood, *New Englands Prospect* (New York: Burt Franklin, 1967), pp. 49-51; John Clayton, "A Letter from Mr. John Clayton . . . to the Royal Society, May 12, 1688," Peter Force *Tracts,* III: 38-45.

9. John Lederer, *The Discoveries of John Lederer,* ed. and with notes by William P. Cumming (Charlottesville, Va.: University of Virginia Press, 1958), pp. 15-16.

which omitted the occult language and explained fascination as due to the natural fear of the prey would be seen as an attempt to explain away the phenomenon rather than merely to describe it.

Lederer was followed in 1687, perhaps in part copied, by an account of Carolina rattlesnakes in Richard Blome's *The Present State of His Majesties Isles and Territories in America.* The only significant difference between the two was that Blome did not deny the reality of rattlesnake fascination.[10] By 1709 English readers had an eyewitness account of this phenomenon.

They have the Power, or Art (I know not what to call it) to charm Squirrels, Hares, Partridges, or any such things, in such a manner, that they run directly into their Mouths. This I have seen by a Squirrel and one of these Rattle-Snakes; and other Snakes have, in some measure, the same Power.[11]

John Lawson's last point, that other snakes shared this power, soon became the settled convention that blacksnakes as well as rattlesnakes possessed this ability.

Accounts of this power of fascination soon reached the one group in England which naturally would have been most interested in it, the Royal Society. In 1714 the Society received but did not print a description of the rattlesnake by Thomas Walduck, which, the Society disapprovingly noted, "gave too much credit to the ill-grounded reports of the Vulgar." [12] A more favorable reaction was given to a lengthy letter on a variety of subjects, including rattlesnake fascination, by Cotton Mather, F.R.S. An abstract of the letter was printed in the 1714 *Philosophical Transactions.*[13]

10. Richard Blome, *The Present State of His Majesties Isles and Territories in America* (London: H. Clark, 1687), p. 161.

11. John Lawson, *A New Voyage to Carolina,* ed. and introduced by Hugh Talmage Lefler (Chapel Hill: University of North Carolina Press, 1967), p. 134. Also see p. 138 for a drawing of a rattlesnake charming a squirrel out of a tree.

12. James R. Masterson, "Colonial Rattlesnake Lore, 1714," *Zoologica,* XXIII (July 1938): 213-16; Stearns, *Science in the British Colonies of America,* pp. 354-55.

13. Cotton Mather, "An Extract of Several Letters from Cotton Mather, D.D. to John Woodward, M.D. and Richard Waller, Esq.," *Philosophical Transactions,* XXIX (January-March 1714): 62-71.

A fuller description of this phenomenon was printed in a 1723 account by Paul Dudley, another colonial Fellow of the Royal Society. Dudley was "abundantly satisfied from many Witnesses, both *English* and *Indian*, that a Rattlesnake will charm both Squirrels and Birds from a Tree into his Mouth." [14]

By this time, simple descriptions of fascination by rattlesnakes and blacksnakes were becoming commonplace, often following an established stereotype. The snake stared at a squirrel or a bird in a tree. The prey sounded its protest, looked unhappy, moved about in circles, but eventually descended into the snake's jaws. However, more often than not, this pattern was broken by the observer, driven by a hatred of snakes, who either killed the serpent or distracted its attention by poking it with a stick. Once the serpent's concentration was broken, the charm was broken, and the prey escaped, apparently uninjured by the entire affair. [15]

There was, however, one major variation, or rather addition, to this pattern. Sometimes the victim was not a small beast sought for food but man himself. As a harbinger of this last development, Paul Dudley reported of the rattlesnake that "The Eye of this Creature has something so singular and terrible, that there is no looking stedfastly on him; one is apt, almost, to think they are possest by some Demon." [16] Colonel Byrd of Virginia reported that ogling a rattlesnake caused him to perceive "a sickness at my stomach." This, together with John Bartram's report of people who "were so overcome when the Snake had fixed his Eyes upon them; that they were presently seized with such a feebleness & Langour all over them, that they were ready to drop down," helped convince Byrd's and Bartram's mutual English scientific correspondent, Peter Collinson, that rattlesnakes could indeed charm men. [17]

14. Paul Dudley, "An Account of the Rattlesnake," *Philosophical Transactions*, XXXII (March-April 1723): 292-95.

15. The best guides to the contemporary literature on the topic are James R. Masterson, "Traveler's Tales of Colonial Natural History," *Journal of American Folklore*, LIX (April-June 1946): 178-80; Benjamin Smith Barton, *A Memoir Concerning the Fascinating Faculty Which Has Been Ascribed to the Rattle-Snake and Other American Serpents* (Philadelphia: for the author by Henry Sweitzer, 1796); Klauber, *Rattlesnakes*, II: 1188-1224.

16. Dudley, "An Account of the Rattlesnake," p. 292.

17. William Darlington, *Memorials*, p. 102; Letter from John Bartram to Peter Collinson, Penn., Feb. 27, 1727/28 [1737/38], History of Science Material, I

There exist numerous descriptions of such occurrences, some by the victims themselves. In the 1730s Christopher Witt, Joseph Breintnall, and John Bartram sent such accounts to Peter Collinson, and in 1765 a number of similar tales were printed in *The Gentleman's Magazine* as "Remarkable and Authentic Instances of the Fascinating Power of the RATTLESNAKE over Men and Other Animals, with some other curious particulars, communicated by Mr. Peter Collinson, from a Letter of a Correspondent at Philadelphia." [18]

Another wave of such tales appeared in the second edition of Samuel Williams's *The Natural and Civil History of Vermont*. Williams, former Hollis Professor of Mathematics and Natural History at Harvard, had concluded his discussion of fascination, in the first edition of his book, by commenting that it required "more accurate observations, and a more philosophical investigation." [19] The result was a flood of letters in 1795, describing various encounters with fascination by serpents. Williams was convinced by his correspondents, and printed a selection of their accounts in an appendix to the second edition of his book.[20]

Several of these accounts are especially interesting for the descriptions they furnish of the mental state of an individual in the process of being

---

(microfilm), American Philosophical Society. All the material in this series was taken from the Royal Society.

The date Feb. 27, 1727/28, for the Bartram letter was apparently an error in transcription. The letter appears to be part of a general correspondence concerning rattlesnakes which occurred in the 1730s, and it contains a marginal note that it was read at the Royal Society on Dec. 21, 1738. Stearns also dates this letter Feb. 27, 1737/38. Stearns, *Science in the British Colonies of America,* p. 581n.

18. Letter from Joseph Breintnall to Peter Collinson, Philadelphia, Nov. 3, 1735; Letter from John Bartram to Peter Collinson, Penn., Feb. 27, 1727/28 [1737/38]; Letter from Christopher Witt to Peter Collinson, Germantown, Nov. 11, 1735. American Philosophical Society, History of Science Material, I.

J.B. [John Bartram ?], "Remarkable and Authentic Instances of the Fascinating Power of the Rattlesnake . . . ," *The Gentleman's Magazine,* XXXV (November 1765): 511-14.

19. Samuel Williams, *The Natural and Civil History of Vermont* (Walpole, N.H.: Isaiah Thomas and David Carlisle, 1794), p. 129, and (2nd ed.; Burlington, Vt.: Samuel Mills, 1809), I: 156.

20. *Ibid.* (2nd ed.), pp. 483-93.

fascinated by a serpent. In one nightmarish account, a boy was charmed
by a blacksnake which

> raised his head with a quick motion, and the lad says, that at that
> instant there appeared something to flash in his eyes, which he could
> compare to nothing more similar, than the rays of light thrown from
> a glass or mirror when turned, in the sun shine; he said it dazzled his
> eyes, at the same time the colours appeared very beautiful, and were
> in large rings, circles, or rolls, and it seemed to be dark to him every
> where else, and his head began to be dizzy, much like being over
> swift water. He then says, he thought he would go from the snake;
> and as it was dark every where but in the circle, he was fearful of
> treading any where else; and as they still grew in less circumference,
> he could still see where to step; but as the dizzyness in his head still
> increased, and he tried to call to his comrade for help, but could not
> speak, it then appeared to him as though he was in a vortex or
> whirlpool, and that every turn brought him nearer the centre.

The boy escaped only when his comrade killed the snake, but he was "in a
melancholy, stupid situation for some days after." [21] Indeed, some after-
effects were quite common.

In contrast to the befuddlement and horror of the first boy was the
experience of another youth who was fascinated by a rattlesnake. He was
looking at the serpent

> when the most vivid and lively colours that imagination can paint,
> and far beyond the powers of the pencil to imitate, among which
> yellow was the most predominant, and the whole drawn into a
> bewitching variety of gay and pleasing forms, were presented to my
> eyes; at the same time, my ears were enchanted with the most
> rapturous strains of music, wild, lively, complicated and harmonious,
> in the highest degree melodious, captivating and enchanting, far
> beyond any thing I ever heard before or since, and indeed far
> exceeding what my imagination in any other situation could have
> conceived. I felt myself irresistibly drawn towards the hated reptile;
> and as I had been often used to seeing and killing rattle snakes, and

21. *Ibid.*, pp. 486-87.

my senses were so absorbed by the gay vision and rapturous music, I was not for some time apprehensive of much danger; but suddenly recollecting what I had heard the Indians relate (but what I had never before believed) of the fascinating power of these serpents, I turned with horror from the dangerous scene, but it was not without the most violent efforts that I was able to extricate myself. All the exertions I could make, with my whole strength, were hardly sufficient to carry me from the scene of the horrid, yet pleasing enchantment; and while I forcibly dragged off my body, my head seemed to be irresistibly drawn to the enchanter, by an invisible power. And I fully believe, that in a few moments longer it would have been wholly out of my power to make an exertion sufficient to get away.[22]

Nor was this instance of fascination by glamour unique. Others, too, were "fascinated" and "charmed" by serpents in all senses of the words. Brientnall reported that often, when another person broke the serpent's spell, the rescued victims were ungrateful and "very angry at being forced from beautiful Sights which had strangely delighted them . . . ." [23]

Most instances of fascination, however, were not so vivid. The victim either had no memory of what had occurred or had merely felt weak and unable to turn away. There were other possibilities also. The Swedish naturalist Pehr (Peter) Kalm stared at a rattlesnake but found it unable to fascinate him.[24] Finally, completing all possibilities, a follower of Chris-

22. *Ibid.*, p. 487. This description, which clearly hinted that fascination was accomplished through the overstimulation of the imagination, brings to mind Michel Foucault's statement that the eighteenth century conceived of madness as accepting and acting upon the images of the imagination. Michel Foucault, *Madness and Civilization: A History of Insanity in the Age of Reason,* trans. by Richard Howard (New York: Pantheon Books, 1965), pp. 93-94.

23. Letter from Joseph Breintnall to Peter Collinson, Philadelphia, Nov. 3, 1735, American Philosophical Society, History of Science Material, I. See also Masterson, "Traveler's Tales of Colonial Natural History," pp. 179-80.

24. Peter Kalm, "Pehr Kalm's Account of the North American Rattlesnake and the Medicines Used in the Treatment of Its Sting," trans. by Esther Louise Larsen, *The American Midlands Naturalist,* LVII (April 1957): 508.

topher Witt tested one of Witt's theories; by staring at a rattlesnake he was able to turn the tables on it and fascinate the serpent.[25]

These often firsthand accounts of humans fascinated by snakes were awkward facts for the opponents of fascination to deal with; to a great extent they simply ignored them in their discussions of fascination. Some of these stories no doubt should be ignored as mere fabrications, deliberate tall tales, lies to gain attention, etc. (Apparently in an attempt to neutralize such a reaction in advance, Williams was careful to give a character reference for each of his correspondents.[26]) But in other instances the victims may indeed have been "fascinated." Not, needless to say, by any power of a snake, but by their own mind working from the firm belief that the serpent did indeed have such a power.

It is possible that the wide range of reactions to fascination, from longing to horror to blankness, may reflect the different types of personalities susceptible to the suggestion of fascination. However, no one appeared to have detected any pattern in the selection of victims, with the exception of Christopher Witt. And his diagnosis, that only women were subject to fascination, "for which I think a very good reason might be given in Divinity," was contradicted by many other reports, and was no doubt less the result of either his observations in natural history or in divinity than of his misogyny.[27]

Coincidence too, no doubt, played a role in some accounts of fascination. It may well explain the case of a woman who suddenly felt ill and only afterward discovered a rattlesnake near her; after it was killed she recovered, but only "by degrees."[28]

It is also worth noting that in the eighteenth century no one was reported bitten while fascinated by a rattlesnake.[29] If the victim did not

25. Letter from Christopher Witt to Peter Collinson, Germantown, Nov. 11, 1735, American Philosophical Society, History of Science Material, I.

26. Williams, *The Natural and Civil History of Vermont* (2nd ed.), I: 488.

27. Letter from Christopher Witt to Peter Collinson, Germantown, Nov. 11, 1735, American Philosophical Society, History of Science Material, I. For a hint of his misogyny, see Darlington, *Memorials*, p. 252.

28. Letter from Christopher Witt to Peter Collinson, Germantown, Nov. 11, 1735, American Philosophical Society, History of Science Material, I.

29. But for a nineteenth-century Romantic tale with a different outcome, see Whittier, *Legends of New England*, pp. 27-36.

have a companion nearby to rescue him, he would always, somehow, manage to break the charm and escape on his own.

## III

With description of fascination came attempted explanations and scientific disputations. Although descriptions of fascination had reached the Royal Society by 1714, there was no significant scientific discussion of it there until the 1730s.[30] In 1734 Hans Sloane, president of both the Royal Society and the College of Physicians, published in *Philosophical Transactions* an explanation of this phenomenon. He argued that instances of small birds and animals being allegedly fascinated could be best explained by assuming the beasts had been bitten earlier and escaped from the snake, only to stagger about and collapse from the effect of the venom.[31] This article apparently inspired Peter Collinson to inquire of his colonial correspondents concerning this question.[32] Collinson was cautious, and at first somewhat skeptical, and warned Bartram that

30. Scientific interest in snakes and especially rattlesnakes was not limited to the power of fascination. Articles in the *Philosophical Transactions* discussed the rattlesnake's anatomy, venom, and cures for its bite. See Edward Tyson, *"Vipera Caudi-Sona Americana,* or the Anatomy of a Rattlesnake," *Philosophical Transactions,* XIII (February 1682/83): 25-46 [58]; Hans Sloane, "The Anatomy of the Poisonous Apparatus of a Rattle-Snake," *Philosophical Transactions,* XXXV (January-March, 1728): 377-81; Hall, "An Account of Some Experiments on the Effects of the Poison of the Rattle-Snake," *Philosophical Transactions,* XXXV (July-September 1727), 309-15.

31. Hans Sloane, "Conjectures on the Charming or Fascinating Power Attributed to the Rattle-Snake," *Philosophical Transactions,* XXXVIII (July-August 1734): 321-31. Sloane supported his opinion with a lengthly quotation from Robert Beverley's description of fascination. This description had indeed probably been made from a previously bitten beast. See Klauber, *Rattlesnakes,* II, 1199.

32. Darlington, *Memorials,* pp. 81-82. Kearsley wrote to Collinson because he had heard that Collinson was interested in information about rattlesnakes. John Kearsley to Peter Collinson, Philadelphia, Nov. 18, 1735, American Philosophical Society, History of Science Material, I. Breintnall noted in a letter to Collinson that "You have also sent those Conjectures [Sloane's] on rattlesnakes

The hearsay of others can't be depended on. The common and long-received opinion of *charming*, is so riveted in people's imagination, that unless they will divest themselves of it, they may not easily distinguish to the contrary.[33]

The replies Collinson received were mixed. Breintnall, Bartram, Witt, and Byrd agreed that rattlesnakes did have the power of fascination. Dr. John Kearsley and Randolph Isham disagreed.[34] The apparent weight of the evidence, with many specific and circumstantial cases cited, was sufficient to convince Collinson that this power did in fact exist; a position he publicly reaffirmed in 1765 with the publication of a letter which described many such cases.[35]

The Sloane article was but one of many attempts to explain the phenomenon. Most often, as with Sloane, the explanation was made by an opponent of the theory of fascination who was forced to accept the apparently incontrovertible facts but attempted to give them a rational explanation. Often the supporters of fascination (that is, of the belief that the observed facts were the result of some hidden power of the serpent's eye) did not bother to attempt an explanation, but merely stated what they had observed or been told. Believers in the concept of fascination found explanations difficult and rather embarrassing, for such explana-

---

to several other Persons; requesting more Observations on this Creature." Joseph Breintnall to Peter Collinson, Philadelphia, Nov. 3, 1735, American Philosophical Society, History of Science Material, I.

33. Darlington, *Memorials*, pp. 81-82.

34. Joseph Breintnall to Peter Collinson, Philadelphia, Nov. 3, 1735; John Bartram to Peter Collinson, Penn., Feb. 27, 1727/28 [1737/38]; Christopher Witt to Peter Collinson, Germantown, Nov. 11, 1735, and Sept. 27, 1736; John Kearsley to Peter Collinson, Philadelphia, Nov. 18, 1735, and March 21, 1736/37; Randolph Isham to Peter Collinson, April 22, 1737. All these letters are in the American Philosophical Society, History of Science Material, I.

William Byrd's reply is mentioned in a letter from Collinson to Bartram, which is printed in Darlington, *Memorials*, p. 102. Kearsley's letter was printed in part in [John] Kearsley, "Extract of a Letter From Dr. Kearsley to Mr. P. Collinson; dated Philadelphia, Nov. 18, 1735," *The Gentleman's Magazine*, XXXVI (February 1766): 73-76.

35. Darlington, *Memorials*, p. 102; J.B., "Remarkable and Authentic Instances," 511-514.

tions tended toward either occultism or theories which, though acceptable by the physical science of the day, violated all that was known about the physiology of the eye.

Not at all surprisingly, the only person involved in the scientific discussion who favored an occult explanation of fascination was Christopher Witt. He drew the obvious parallel which most believers carefully avoided.

> Seeing that this fascinating Power of the Snake cannot be denied, why may it not be also allow'd in some malicious wicked old women who, not having the fear of God before their Eyes, give themselves over to Spite, Envy and Revenge: whereby the the Spirit of the old Serpent becomes powerfull in them. I could write a pretty large Volume upon this subject, of my own Experiences, many of which Examples would, I believe, put to Silence, if not convince the greatest Athiest. But I spare them as not being needfull in this place. . . .[36]

The only others who explicitly connected fascination with witchcraft and the evil eye were the opponents of the concept of fascination. They, of course, urged the relationship in order to discredit fascination. Sir Hans Sloane had already warned:

> These Opinions are the greatest Support of a common Notion, that several chronical wasting Diseases, and such Disorders of the Nerves as are not easily accounted for, not only in Men, but in Cattle, are believed to be the Effects of an evil Eye of old malicious Woman, &c. thought to be Witches and Sorcerers, or assisted by the Devil.[37]

Benjamin Smith Barton, in a later dispute over fascination, also hinted at this objection when he warned that one who believed in fascination would find grounds to

36. Christopher Witt to Peter Collinson, Germantown, Nov. 11, 1735, American Philosophical Society, History of Science Material, I.

37. Sloane, "Conjectures on the Charming or Fascinating Power," p. 321.

suppose, that the property belongs to other beings, besides the serpents; and he will, perhaps imagine that it forms a part of a more extensive plan, the effects of which, he will assert, are prominent, and unequivocal, though its ways, he will confess, are incomprehensible to mortal minds.[38]

A more common explanation advanced by believers in fascination was that "all purpose problem-solver" of eighteenth-century science—effluvia. Breintnall suggested that rattlesnakes "have the Power; and use it, of darting from their Eyes some harmful Effluviums, subtile as the Rays of Light, which thro' our Opticks find quick Admission to the Brain." [39] John Bartram considered the most likely explanation of fascination to be that "there proceeds such subtile Emanations from the Eyes of this Creature beyond which we can comprehend." [40] By the early nineteenth century no better explanation was yet available, and Samuel Williams rhetorically asked:

Can there be any subtile effluvia, poisonous exhalation, or stupifying virus, emitted by the eye of the serpent, and received by that of the enchanted animal, equal to, and producing the uncommon effects which have been mentioned. This seems contrary to all the other appearances of animal nature; and yet the phenomena seem to indicate such a physical kind of operation.[41]

As Williams's last sentence indicated, there was a problem with this explanation. By the eighteenth century, vision was understood to be the result of light striking the eye. The eye was a passive receiver of external stimuli, and thus any theory which required the eye to emit a particle or ray was most upsetting, because it was not in conformity with current theories of vision and optical physiology.

Before leaving the supporters of the concept of fascination, it should be

38. Barton, *A Memoir,* pp. 69-70.
' 39. Joseph Breintnall to Peter Collinson, Philadelphia, Nov. 3, 1735, American Philosophical Society, History of Science Material, I.
40. John Bartram to Peter Collinson, Penn., Feb. 27, 1727/28 [1737/38], American Philosophical Society, History of Science Material, I.
41. Williams, *The Natural and Civil History of Vermont* (2nd ed.), I: 491.

noted that both Breintnall and Bartram were willing to propose explanations which were not in accord with the concept of fascination by some hidden power of the serpent's eye. They suggested the possiblity that the color and shape of the serpent was the cause of fascination, and Breintnall even proposed that this theory be tested by using pictures and wax images of serpents.[42] In general, it appears that most supporters of the belief in fascination were not especially fond of the idea. Some may have found its occult and archaic tendencies slightly embarrassing, but the apparent evidence in its favor was too overwhelming and could not be satisfactorily explained by any other theory.

Opponents of this theory, however, did come up with many such proposals. The object of their theories was to explain the numerous observations of small animals running into the serpent's jaws, but without attributing to the serpent's eye some incomprehensible, active, attractive power. These theories argued that the prey merely accidentally passed near a snake,[43] or the prey was overcome by the odor of the snake,[44] or the prey was overcome by fear on seeing the snake,[45] or the prey was attracted by the rattlesnake's rattle.[46] Sloane's suggestion, that fascination was merely the effect of a previous bite, also remained popular.[47] But none of these theories gained general acceptance; perhaps because many of them failed to explain critical and generally accepted facts, such as blacksnakes also possessing this power, or the immediate recovery of the

---

42. Joseph Breintnall to Peter Collinson, Philadelphia, Nov. 3, 1735, and John Bartram to Peter Collinson, Penn., Feb. 27, 1727/28 [1737/38], American Philosophical Society, History of Science Material, I.

43. Peter Kalm, *Peter Kalm's Travels in North America: The English Version of 1770*, trans. by John Reinhold Forster, ed. by Adolph B. Benson (New York: Dover Publications, Inc., 1964), I: 293.

44. Kalm, "Pehr Kalm's Account," p. 508; Barton, *A Memoir*, pp. 28-39.

45. Kearsley, "Extract of a Letter," p. 73.

46. Barton, *A Memoir*, pp. 46-49; [Johann Friedrich] Blumenbach, "On the Fascinating Power of the Rattle-Snake, With Some Remarks on Dr. Barton's Memoir on That Subject," *The Philosophical Magazine*, II (December 1798): 251-56.

47. Kalm, "Pehr Kalm's Account," pp. 507-8; John Kearsley to Peter Collinson, Philadelphia, Nov. 18, 1735, American Philosophical Society, History of Science Material, I; "Snake, rattle," Chambers's *Cyclopedia*, 1768.

prey once the serpent's attention was distracted, or the ability of serpents to fascinate human beings.

The most extensive discussion of fascination and its literature is found in a 1796 treatise by Benjamin Smith Barton, *A Memoir Concerning the Fascinating Faculty Which Has been Ascribed to the Rattle-Snake and other American Serpents.* In this seventy-page work, Barton dismissed out of hand the reality of fascination, and then analyzed and dismissed the various explanations given by others to account for the phenomenon. Barton's own explanation was based upon the observation that the only birds involved in instances of fascination were ground- or low-nesting birds. From this he argued that fascination was merely the efforts made by birds and small animals to drive snakes from their nests, and that on occasion, but not too often, the beasts may have run too close to the snake and been caught.[48] He dismissed the entire problem of the fascination of humans by simply noting that "snakes are supposed, by some foolish people, to have the power of charming even children."[49]

This treatise, and the ensuing dispute, well illustrate the international extent of interest in this colonial belief. Barton himself had used English translations of books by the Swedish naturalists Peter Kalm and Carl Linnaeus, de la Cèpéde's *Histoire Naturelle des Serpents,* and Johann Friedrich Blumenbach's *Handbuch der Naturgeschichte.*[50] Barton's *Memoir* was translated into German,[51] where it was answered in 1798 by Blumenbach, a professor at the University of Göttingen whose *Handbuch* is said to have "ushered in a new era in natural history." Blumenbach's reply, which defended his theory that rattlesnake fascination was caused by the snake's rattle, was first printed in *Voigt's Magazin für den neuesten Zustand der Naturkunde,* and later excerpted in a British journal, *The*

---

48. Barton, *A Memoir,* pp. 49-63. For some earlier statements of this theory, see Kearsley, "Extract of a Letter," p. 73; Randolph Isham to Peter Collinson, April 22, 1737, American Philosophical Society, History of Science Material, I; Kalm, *Travels in North America,* translator's note, I., 168n.

49. Barton, *A Memoir,* p. 65.

50. *Ibid.,* pp. 9-10, 21-25, 28-31, 46-49.

51. The *Deutscher Gesamtkatalog* lists it as *Abhandlungen über die vermeinte Zauberkraft der Klapperschlange und anderer amerikanischen Schlangen.* Übers. mit e Einl. v. erl. Anm. versehen von E. A. W. v. Zimmermann (Leipzig: Reinicke & Hinrichs, 1798).

*Philosophical Magazine,* where it was read by Barton. The article had chided Barton for not using Kalm's Swedish writings on the rattlesnake, and, in addition, pointed out several accounts of fascination in Latin America.[52] Barton replied to Blumenbach in the form of a lengthy open letter to Professor Zimmermann, who had translated Barton's earlier treatise.[53] This letter, however, was not translated into German, at least not as a separate pamphlet.

The trans-Atlantic interest in this phenomenon had been highlighted earlier by a passage from Michaëlis's article in the 1785 *Göttingen Magazin,* which, in effect, foreshadowed Barton's theory. "One of my friends, Mr. David Colden, at Flushing, an amateur of natural history, and son of Governor Colden, whose services to science is so well known, assured me that he has several times seen birds fascinated by snakes, but always found the nest of the bird either with eggs or young ones in the neighbourhood, which made the spectators give up the idea of fascination."[54]

Despite these scientific disputes, the concept of fascination, sometimes qualified by the warning that not everyone believed in it, continued to reach the general public. It was found in such popular works as Oliver Goldsmith's *A History of the Earth* and Jedidiah Morse's *American Geography,* and, as we have already seen, as a popular belief it continued into the twentieth century.[55]

## IV

How did the belief in fascination by rattlesnake arise? What were its origins? It is not always possible to answer such questions, but it does

52. Blumenbach, "On the Fascinating Power of the Rattle-Snake," pp. 251-52. For Johann Friedrich Blumenbach see Charles Coulston Gillispie, ed., *Dictionary of Scientific Biography* (New York: Charles Scribner's Sons, 1970—).

53. [Benjamin Smith Barton], *Supplement to a Memoir Concerning the Fascinating Faculty Which Has Been Ascribed to the Rattle-Snake and Other American Serpents* [Philadelphia, 1800].

54. Blumenbach, "On the Fascinating Power of the Rattle-Snake," pp. 255. Michaëlis, however, had rejected this theory himself.

55. Oliver Goldsmith, *An History of the Earth, and Animated Nature* (Philadelphia: Mathew Carey, 1795), IV: 124-25, and Jedidiah Morse, *The American Universal Geography* (3rd ed.; Boston: Thomas & Andrews, 1796), I: 219-20.

appear to have had at least four distinguishable roots. Contributions to this belief were made by the widespread belief in the evil eye, by Neoplatonic beliefs concerning "fascination," by certain characteristics of the snakes themselves, and by Indian legends.

Of the evil eye little need be said. The parallel was obvious, and we have already seen it used. The existence of the belief in the evil eye in the seventeenth century meant that if a person was confronted by the theory of fascination by serpents, he was not really faced with a totally new concept. He already knew of the malevolent powers which could reside in an eye; he had merely to transfer this belief to a serpent, instead of creating it *de novo*. Although by the eighteenth century the belief in rattlesnake fascination had reached a level where it provided additional support for the concept of the evil eye, as in Chambers's *Cyclopedia* where it was cited as one of the proofs which made it past dispute "that the eye has some very considerable powers . . . ," [56] in the seventeenth century it was undoubtedly the other way around.

On a higher intellectual plain, the same function was performed by Renaissance Neoplatonism with its theory of fascination. This theory indeed included and explained the evil eye; but belief in that concept had developed independent of such theorizing, and many believers in it had little or no interest in Neoplatonic theories. [57] Rattlesnake fascination, however, was spread by books; and no doubt it was originated, at least in part, by well-educated men who certainly would have been familiar with this widespread strain of European thought.

Renaissance Neoplatonism explained that both the evil eye and certain forms of love were the result of spirits projected from the eye. Such spirits (as C. S. Lewis has warned us) had nothing to do with "spirits" in the sense of a ghost or a supernatural entity. Rather, they were thought to be natural constituents of the body, highly rarefied substances produced from the blood which served as the intermediary between the material body and the immaterial soul. [58] They carried out the necessary interplay

56. "Witchcraft," Chambers's *Cyclopedia*, 1768. In the 5th ed., 1741-43, possibly by error, this ability was attributed to a toad.

57. This point about the independence of popular belief from Neoplatonic theory is made in Thomas, *Religion and the Decline of Magic*, p. 228.

58. Lewis, *The Discarded Image*, pp. 165-69.

between body and soul; they created "That subtile knot, which makes us man." [59]

An early and full explication of this theory was to be found in the major Renaissance work on love, Marsiglio Ficino's *Commentary on Plato's Symposium*. In the chapter "Earthly Love Is a Certain Bewitchment," which was meant as a simple statement of fact rather than as a figure of speech, Ficino presented a physiological explanation of love and fascination. The heat of the heart, he explained, generated spirits from the blood, and this spirit "sends rays like itself through the eyes as though through glass windows." Such a ray "draws with itself a spiritual vapor, and the vapor draws with it the blood. . . ." This explained how a person with bloodshot or bleary eyes caused others to become so afflicted; and it also explained the "fact," noted by Aristotle, that menstruating women "often by their own gaze soil their mirrors with bloody drops." Such a ray, darting between two people, carried out a spiritual transfusion which, as Ficino carefully described, could result in "love."

> Put before your eyes, I pray Phaedrus the Myrrhinusian and that Theban who was captivated by love for him, the orator Lysias. Lysias stares open-mouthed at the face of Phaedrus. Phaedrus sends into the eyes of Lysias the sparks of his own eyes, and with the sparks sends along a spirit. The light of Phaedrus is easily joined by the light of Lysias, and the spirit also easily joins his spirit. The vapor of this sort springing from the heart of Phaedrus immediately seeks the heart of Lysias. By the hardness of this heart it is made denser and returns to its former state, as the blood of Phaedrus, so that the blood of Phaedrus is now in the heart of Lysias, a truly remarkable phenomenon.
>
> Hence each immediately cries out. Lysias to Phaedrus: "Phaedrus, my heart, dearest body." Phaedrus, to Lysias: "O my spirit, my blood, Lysias." Phaedrus pursues Lysias because his heart seeks its own humor. Lysias pursues Phaedrus because the sanguine humor desires its own proper vessel, seeks its own seat. But Lysias pursues Phaedrus more ardently, for it is easier for the heart to live without a small part of its humor than for the humor to live without

59. John Donne, "The Extasie," l. 65.

its own heart. A river is more dependent upon its source than the source on the river. Therefore an iron, receiving the influence of a loadstone, is drawn towards this stone, but does not attract it, so Lysias pursues Phaedrus more than Phaedrus, Lysias.[60]

But spirits projected from the eye also could have other effects. Gian Francesco Pico had acknowledged, "if some strong desire leads to these spirits being emitted, they may produce an external effect; concupiscence may produce a seminal emission and hence a child, or anger may result in fascination (evil eye) and hence a disease." [61]

Montaigne, in "Of the Force of Imagination," explained that the external effects of the imagination were transmitted through the eye. Therefore, he explained, legend held that some Scythian women could kill with only a look, while tortoises and "Estriges" could hatch eggs with only a look, "a signe they have some ejaculative vertue." Witches "are said to have offensive and harme-working eies." Precursors of the fascinating rattlesnake appeared in his tale of a cat and a bird who stared at each other until the bird fell at the cat's feet, "either drunken by his owne strong imagination, or drawne by some attractive power of the Cat"; and his tale of a falconer who drew his birds back to earth "with the only force of his looke." [62]

Nor was this theme lacking in English authors. Most famous, no doubt, is John Donne's *Extasie*, but there are others. Joseph Glanvill, in his influential *Saducismus Triumphatus*, argued:

> So that I am apt to think there may be a *power* of *real fascination* in the *Witches eyes* and *imagination*, by which for the most part she acts

60. Marsilio Ficino, *Marsilio Ficino's Commentary on Plato's Symposium*, ed. and trans. by Sears Reynolds Jayne, *University of Missouri Studies*, XIX (1944): 221-24 (7th speech, chap. IV). For the influence of the *Commentary* in England, see Ernst Cassirer, *The Platonic Renaissance in England*, trans. by James P. Pettegrove (Austin, Tex.: University of Texas Press, 1953), p. 111.

61. D. P. Walker, *Spiritual and Demonic Magic: From Ficino to Campanella* (Leiden: E. J. Brill, 1958), pp. 149-50. The passage quoted was a paraphrase by Walker.

62. Michael Montaigne, *The Essays of Michael Lord of Montaigne*, trans. by John Florio and introduction by Desmond MacCarthy (New York: E. P. Dutton & Co., Inc., 1928), I: 101-03.

upon *tender* bodies. *Nescio quis teneros occulus.— —*For the *pestilential spirits* being darted by a *spightful and vigorous imagination* from the *eye*, and meeting with *those* that are *weak* and *passive* in the bodies which they enter, will not fail to infect them with a *noxious quality* that makes *dangerous* and *strange alternations* in the person invaded by this *poisonous influence:* which way of acting by subtile and *invisible instruments*, is *ordinary* and *familiar* in all natural *efficiencies.* And 'tis now past question, that *nature* for the most part acts by *subtile streams* and *aporrhoea's* of *minute particles*, which pass from one body to another.[63]

Even Reginald Scot, the famous opponent of witchcraft beliefs, although noting that there were certain common reports which he could not "admit, without some doubts, difficulties and exceptions, yet will I give free libertie to others to beleeve them, if they list; for that they doo not directlie oppugne my purpose." They did not "oppugne" his purpose because, under the theory we have been discussing, they would be considered as purely natural events, unconnected with demons or supernatural beliefs of any kind. Some of these reports concerned old women who no longer naturally purged their blood each month. Such women might harm others; for their eye beams enter other individuals and then reconvert back to blood, "which bloud disagreeing with the nature of the bewitched partie, infeebleth the rest of his bodie, and maketh him sicke: the contagion wherof so long continueth, as the distempered bloud hath force in the members." The effect of the evil eye was, in essence, ascribed to a mismatched blood transfusion, given via the eyes.

Scot explained that other forms of fascination had other results. "For if the fascination or witchcraft be brought to passe or provoked by the desire, by the wishing and coveting of any beautiful shape or favor, the venome is strained through the eies, though it be from a far, and the imagination of a beautifull form resteth in the hart of the lover, and kindleth the fier wherewith it is afflicted." Moreover, citing John Baptista Porta Neapolitanus, Scot explained that the cockatrice took the life, and

63. Joseph Glanvill, "Some Considerations About Witchcraft. In a Letter to Robert Hunt, Esq.," *Saducismus Triumphatus* (London: J. Collins, 1681), p. 23.

the wolf the voice, of those they met, by poisoning the air with the venom of the spirits projected from their eyes.[64]

Robert Burton, in *The Anatomy of Melancholy*, citing as was his wont a profusion of authorities but especially "Ficinus," repeated the theory that love was a species of fascination effected through the eyes. He did note an objection to this theory, but easily dismissed it. "I know, they that hold that sight goes inward, will make a doubt of this; but Ficinus proves it from blear-eyes, that by sight alone, make others blear-eyed: and it is more than manifest, that the vapour of the corrupt blood doth get in together with the rays, and so by the contagion the spectators' eyes are infected." He confirmed this belief with a variety of stories, including the basilisk and the bloody mirror; and had the book been written some eighty or one hundred years later, it might well have included the "fascinating rattlesnake." [65]

By that time, however, the objection might well have given him more difficulty. It was decisive for Charles Morton who explained that vision was "(not as it seems to be) by Extramission or Sending forth Rayes, or Spirits from the Eye to the Object; . . . But by Introreception (or re-ceiving inwards) of Lightson rayes, Sent Originally (as from Luminous Bodyes) or Reflected (as from all others) into the Eye." As Morton pointed out, this tended to discredit the "Conceit of Fascination (or Witch-Craft) by Looking upon with an Evill Eye. . . ." [66]

Although some of those involved in the Salem witchcraft scare might have already come to this conclusion, Thomas Brattle stated that the judges tested the accused witches by having them touch the afflicted children to cure them, on the theory that the "venemous and malignant particles, that were ejected from the eye, do, by this means, return to the

64. Scot, *The Discoverie of Witchcraft*, pp. 398-400.

65. Burton, *The Anatomy of Melancholy*, pt. 3, sect. 2, memb. 2, subs. 2.

66. Morton, *Compendium Physicae*, p. 161. See also Increase Mather's rebuttal of the evil eye in virtually the same language as Morton used. "*Sennertus* has discovered the Superstition of these Fancies; Sight does not proceed from an Emission of Rays from the Eye, but by a reception of the visible Species; and if it be (as Philosophers conclude) an innocent Action and not an Emission of the Optick Spirits, so that sight as such, does receive from the Object, and not act upon it, the Notion of Fascination by the Eye is unphilosophical: . . ." Increase Mather, *Cases of Conscience Concerning Evil Spirits Personating Men*, in Cotton Mather, *The Wonders of the Invisible World* (Ann Arbor, Mich.: University Microfilms, 1969), p. 261.

body whence they came, and so leave the afflicted person pure and whole." [67]

The concept of fascination also appears in the works of a colonial Neoplatonic poet, Edward Taylor. It is the basis of an image which is intermittently found in his "Preparatory Meditations," God emitting Grace from His eyes into the recipient's soul. At times it is found subordinated to other images:

> Thy Pidgen Eyes dart piercing, beames on Love.
>     Thy Cherry Cheeks sends Charms out to Loves Coast.
> Thy Lilly Lips drop myrrh. . . .[68]

Most often, however, it is the guiding image of the poem.

> Lord let thy Golden Beams pierce through mine Eye
>     And leave therein an Heavenly Light to glaze
> My Soule with glorious Grace all o're, whereby
>     I may have Sight, and Grace in mee may blaze.
>     Lord ting my Candle at thy Burning Rayse,
>     To give a gracious Glory to thy Prayse.
>
> Thou Lightning Eye, let some bright Beames of thine
>     Stick in my Soul, to light and liven it:
> Light, Life, and Glory, things that are Divine;
>     I shall be grac'd withall for glory fit.
>     My Heart then stufft with Grace, Light, Life, and Glee
>     I'le sacrifice in Flames of Love to thee.[69]
>
> Lord let these Charming Glancing Eyes of thine
>     Glance on my Souls bright Eye its amorous beams
> To fetch as upon golden Ladders fine
>     My Heart and Love to thee in Hottest Steams.
>     Which bosom'd in thy brightest beauty cleare
>     Shall tune the glances of thy Eyes Sweet Deare.[70]

67. Morton, *Compendium Physicae*, p. 161n, and Burr, *Narratives of the Witchcraft Cases*, p. 171.

68. Edward Taylor, "Meditations," 2nd Series, no. 121, 7-9.

69. *Ibid.*, 1st Series, no. 16, 25-36.

70. *Ibid.*, 2nd Series, no. 119, 25-30.

Then let the Beams of my Souls eye ev'n meet
  The brightsome Beams of thy blesst Eye my Lord,
And in their meeting let them sweetly greet
  And back return laden as each affords.
  Mine then return'd well loaded with thine flame
  Shall tune my harp to sing thy glories fame.

My Soul then quickend by thy beames brought in
  By my Souls Eye beams and glaz'd be thereby
With glorious Grace that will mee make more sing
  Thy praises my Lord, then shall thou have more joy.
  My Soul strung with thy grace as golden Wier,
  Will by its musick Raise thy joy the Higher.[71]

One of Taylor's poems even discussed this in relation to a serpent, not a rattlesnake but the brass serpent raised by Moses. It is possible that this poem was influenced by the belief in rattlesnake fascination; but it is equally possible that the poem developed independent from that belief, although from the same Renaissance theory of fascination.

This Brazen Serpent is a Doctors Shop.
  On ev'ry Shelfe's a Sovereign remedy.
The Serpents Flesh the Sovereign Salve is got
  Against the Serpents bite, gaind by the eye.
  The Eyebeames agents are that forth do bring
  The Sovereign Counter poison, and let't in.[72]

Although the basilisk and cockatrice were mentioned in some Renaissance discussions of fascination, they did not appear to have had any direct influence in the development of rattlesnake fascination. Probably by the late seventeenth century it was too late for these fabulous beasts to be taken very seriously. However, in the eighteenth century one man, the German-born surveyor general of the Southern District, chose to show his awareness of the analogy by calling rattlesnakes, "Basilisks." [73]

71. *Ibid.*, no. 136, 37-48.
72. *Ibid.*, no. 61, 31-36.
73. William Gerard de Brahm, *Report of the General Survey*, p. 227.

A rather more surprising omission was the failure of anyone to mention Plotinus' own account of fascination by a serpent; an account which was quite similar to some of the colonial experiences. "A human being fascinated by a snake has neither perception nor sensation of what is happening; he knows only after he has been caught, and his highest mind is never caught." [74]

By the first few decades of the eighteenth century, the time when scientific explanations of rattlesnake fascination were first attempted, this Neoplatonic doctrine of fascination was already obsolete. The arguments used by Ficino and Burton were no longer tenable. The heart was now a pump rather than a source of heat used to generate spirits; the doctrine of spirits was itself in decay and undergoing change; most important, the eye was now a passive receiver of light rather than an active emitter. The only person to mention this by then obsolete doctrine in connection with rattlesnake fascination was Christopher Witt. He simply noted that the theory of rattlesnake fascination as the result of "beams of sight meeting each other in a direct line . . ." was disproved by the fact that a woman had been fascinated without ever seeing a snake. [75] This would tend to indicate that a theory of rattlesnake fascination directly based on Renaissance fascination had at one time been current. It is also worth noting that Witt did not deny that rattlesnake fascination depended upon "beams of sight"; he only denied that the beams of the snake and the victim must meet. Witt's belief, proved as far as he was concerned, that a man could fascinate a snake, required that the power of fascination could not be derived from something unique to the serpent's eye. This fact, together with Witt's continued belief in the evil eye and his general air of being a continuation of the seventeenth century, make it at least possible that Witt himself used some variation of Renaissance fascination to explain rattlesnake fascination.

Although the Renaissance theory of fascination was obsolete, the most popular explanation of rattlesnake fascination in the eighteenth century, effluvia emitted from the serpent's eye, was obviously a modification of the earlier theory. It was, however, in terms of the science of its own day,

74. Plotinus, *The Enneads,* trans. by Stephen MacKenna (4th ed. revised; London: Faber and Faber Limited, 1969), IV. 4. 40.

75. Christopher Witt to Peter Collinson, Germantown, Nov. 11, 1735, American Philosophical Society, History of Science Material, I.

less satisfactory than the Renaissance theory had been in its day. The basic problem, that the eye would be acting contrary to its known nature, continued. Spirits had been a commonplace of Renaissance medical theory; the specific effluvia ejected from the eye was of an unknown nature and had to be hypothesized just for this theory. The mode by which the spirits worked within the body of the one fascinated was fully explained, at least as fully as Renaissance biology explained anything; the mode of operation of the effluvia was unknown, although there were perhaps some vague hints that it influenced the imagination. In short, the Renaissance theory of fascination was quite satisfactory, as long as its theoretical basis was not undermined; but the eighteenth-century theory of rattlesnake fascination via effluvia really never had a theoretical basis, and was never well integrated into the rest of eighteenth-century science. As a result, it was never very satisfactory even to its supporters, but as the best explanation available of carefully observed facts, it continued to be used.[76]

Another root of the belief in rattlesnake fascination may be found in the "natural history" of the rattlesnake. A number of possible interactions between the rattlesnake and its prey gave rise to the observed facts which were the foundations and continuing proof of this belief. Many of the explanations of these facts by eighteenth-century opponents of this belief were in fact partially correct. Some animals could indeed have collapsed after being previously bitten by a rattlesnake; others perhaps were caught after being fatally attracted by the serpent's colors; even the most unlikely of all the theories, that birds and small animals were caught while attempting to drive snakes from their nests, may have occurred. Witness the recorded instance of a rabbit stomping a rattlesnake that was devouring its young. Probably most frequent were instances of birds decoying snakes from their nests.[77] It is important to realize that many eyewitnesses to this latter phenomenon left the scene before the presumed capture, or else distracted the snake. Thus they often assumed that they had seen an instance of fascination that would inevitably result in the

76. There were occasional attempts to elaborate on the theory. Thus Chambers's *Cyclopedia* suggested that the "nervous juice" played the role previously assigned to spirits. "Witchcraft," 5th ed. But there never developed anything as elaborate or comprehensive as the Renaissance synthesis.

77. Klauber, *Rattlesnakes,* II: 1048, 1221.

capture of the prey; whereas, had they remained to watch the incident conclude undisturbed, they would have seen the bird escape and the fascination fail.

The fourth root from which the belief in rattlesnake fascination stemmed was Indian beliefs. There was, however, some dispute as to what the Indians actually believed. John Lederer, the first man to report upon the fascinating powers of the rattlesnake, explicitly stated that the Indians told him about it.[78] So too, in the eighteenth century, a Moravian missionary to the Delaware Indians stated that both Indians and white men believed in this power.[79] However, many others who attributed this belief to the Indians may have had little actual contact with them, and their attribution may reflect no more than the general assumption that the Indians had known about it.

There were others, moreover, who argued that this was *not* a native Indian belief. Barton so argued, and noted that William Bartram, the naturalist, a believer in fascination and a man who had traveled among the Indians, had informed him that none of the Indians he had met had held this belief.[80] So too, a friend of Barton's had asked many Indians if they believed in it, but all had denied it.[81] This friend, John Gottlieb Ernestus Heckewelder, a Moravian missionary to the western Pennsylvania Indians, had collected a miscellany of information from "intelligent Indians" which included accounts of how rattlesnakes hunt but ignored the theory of fascination.[82]

The available evidence on Indian lore does not indicate that the Indians believed that rattlesnakes captured their prey through the power of fascination. There is, instead, substantial evidence that many Indians believed in certain mythical serpents—not the common everyday variety of rattlesnake or blacksnake which one could find in the woods—which possessed a power very similar to that of fascination.

78. Lederer, *The Discoveries of John Lederer,* pp. 15-16.

79. David Zeisberger, "David Zeisberger's History of the Northern American Indians," edited by Archer Butler Hulbert and William Nathaniel Schwarze, *Ohio Archaeological and Historical Publications,* XIX (1910): 72.

80. Barton, *A Memoir,* p. 14, and *idem, Supplement to a Memoir,* pp. 33-34.

81. [Barton], *Supplement to a Memoir,* pp. 30-32.

82. John Heckewelder, "Further Communications Collected Last Summer From Intellligent Indians," n.d., MSS, American Philosophical Society.

James Adair told of an Indian myth about a valley in which were found "some bright old inhabitants, or rattle snakes, of a more enormous size than is mentioned in history," each of which had a dazzling carbuncle in its forehead. Being too huge to capture their prey in a normal manner, "no living creature moves within the reach of their sight, but they can draw it to them; . . . as they cannot support themselves by their speed, or cunning to spring from ambuscade, it is needful they should have the bewitching craft of their eyes and forked tongues." [83] A variant of this tale, told by nineteenth-century Cherokee Indians, spoke of a huge horned serpent with a crystalline gem in its forehead. Any man who attempted to hunt it would be so dazzled by the light of the gem that he would run toward the serpent and be unable to escape from it. [84] In 1714 Thomas Walduck mentioned "a vulgar Opinion [whether among Indians or colonists is not stated] that there is a king among the Snakes, in whose head is a Carbuncle that shines in the night with wonderfull Lustre. . . ." [85] A Delaware Indian, Pemaholend, when questioned about fascination, stated that the white men had probably taken this belief from an old Indian tradition which had given a single rattlesnake, now long dead, this power. [86] The Creek Indians spoke of a mythological horned serpent which did not harm men but which did draw game animals such as deer into the water to be devoured. [87] Another Creek belief, which held that one who killed a rattlesnake would in turn be killed by other rattlesnakes, described the unfortunate snake slayer as "dazed at the sight of their glistening eyes and darting tongues." [88]

83. James Adair, *Adair's History of the American Indians*, ed. by Samuel Cole Williams (New York: Argonaut Press Ltd., 1966), p. 250. See a discussion of this report in James Mooney, "Myths of the Cherokee," *Nineteenth Annual Report of the Bureau of American Ethnology* (1897-98), pt. I, pp. 456-461, 542.

84. Mooney, "Myths of the Cherokee," pp. 297-98, 542.

85. Masterson, "Colonial Rattlesnake Lore, 1714," p. 214.

86. [Barton], *Supplement to a Memoir*, pp. 31-32.

87. John R. Swanton, "Religious Beliefs and Medical Practices of the Creek Indians," United States Bureau of American Ethnology: *Annual Report*, XLII (1924-25): 494.

88. Mooney, "Myths of the Cherokee," p. 294. See also William Bartram, *The Travels of William Bartram*, ed. by Francis Harper (New Haven: Yale University Press, 1958), pp. 164-66; John Heckewelder, "An Account of the History, Manners, and Customs, of the Indian Nations, Who Once Inhabited

Elements of this belief can perhaps be seen in the Iroquois legend about a man who was about to kill a two-headed snake, but "charmed by the swaying heads and their bright eyes glistening in the sun, his fears were forgotten. . . ." [89] So, too, a New England Algonquin legend told of a woman who fell in love with Atosis the Serpent while he was in human form. "One day while the woman cut away the ice, she saw in the water a bright pair of large eyes looking steadily at her. They charmed her so that she could not move." Eventually, it was said, she gave birth to black-snakes! [90]

Actually, rattlesnake fascination offers a very rare example of the interaction of European and Indian beliefs in forming a new colonial belief. The development of this belief, in turn, illustrates the limited but successful adaptation of an essentially seventeenth-century concept to meet eighteenth-century science. The colonists entered the New World with a firm set of both popular and learned beliefs concerning the power of the eye to create strange and often harmful effects in others. The Indians had a set of legends about mythological serpents who had somewhat analogous powers derived from their eyes, or tongues, or gems in their head. Upon contact, the colonists apparently developed their own new set of beliefs in which this power was commonly exercised by certain real serpents; however, in accord with European beliefs, this power was now based solely in the eye.

Indeed, it was probably no coincidence that the first report of this belief came from John Lederer; for Lederer was an early explorer in western Virginia, and the earliest reports of this belief did in fact come from the interior of Virginia and Carolina.[91] That is, they came from the territory

---

Pennsylvania and the Neighbouring States," *Transactions of the Historical & Literary Committee of the American Philosophical Society,* I (1819): 245; Vernon Kinietz, "Delaware Culture Chronology," *Prehistory Research Series,* III (April 1946-June 1960): 100.

89. Harriet Maxwell Converse, *Myths and Legends of the New York State Iroquois,* New York State Museum Bulletin 125 (New York State Museum, 1908), p. 112.

90. Charles G. Leland, *The Algonquin Legends of New England* (Boston: Houghton, Mifflin and Company, 1884). pp. 278-80.

91. Lederer, *The Discoveries of John Lederer,* pp. 15-16; Blome, *The Present State,* p. 161. For a brief account of Lederer's explorations, see Richard L.

inhabited and influenced by the Creek and Cherokee Indians, Indians from whom have come some of the best-preserved tales of mythological serpents with the power of fascination.

How did the Indian belief about certain mythological serpents come to be transformed into a belief about all rattlesnakes and blacksnakes? Perhaps the Indian legends were simply misunderstood or mistranslated. It was certainly possible that an Indian warning against slaying rattlesnakes lest others avenge it and leave one "dazed at the sight of their glistening eyes and darting tongue" could be misunderstood as implying that all rattlesnakes commonly used this power. Furthermore, any such misunderstandings would have been reinforced by incorrect interpretations of the actions of rattlesnakes and their prey.

It is uncertain when the blacksnake became associated with this belief. Conceivably the blacksnake was associated with this belief from its origin, as the Atosis myth may indicate, but the blacksnake was not mentioned in the earliest accounts of this belief. Perhaps it was simply added later because it was another large and impressive snake, and was undoubtedly the one with which the colonists were most familiar. Indeed, some colonists seem to have treated the blacksnake as a semidomesticated animal, useful as a vermin exterminator.[92]

However formed, the belief appears to have solidified quickly. There seem to have been no significant differences between accounts of fascination written in the first half of the eighteenth century and those dating from the very end of the century. Some of the latter accounts are more graphic and are visibly filled with awe; however, this is almost certainly the result of a change in literary styles, from Augustan Neoclassicism to Romanticism, rather than a change in the belief itself.

---

Morton, *Colonial Virginia* (Chapel Hill: published for the Virginia Historical Society by the University of North Carolina Press, 1960), I: 201-2.

See also Hans Sloane's attribution of this belief to "curious and credible Authors, who have given us Accounts of *Virginia, Carolina,* and the neighbouring Countries. . . ." Sloane, "Conjectures on the Charming or Fascinating Power," p. 321.

92. John Bartram to Peter Collinson, Penn., Feb. 27, 1727/28 [1737/38], American Philosophical Society, History of Science Material, I; Mark Catesby, *The Natural History of Carolina, Florida, and the Bahama Islands* (London: C. Marsh, 1754), II: 48.

Not surprisingly, Romanticism was the more effective, and affective, tool for describing fascination.

However, as we have seen, the belief did face challenges in the eighteenth century. As knowledge of it spread to England and Europe in general, some naturalists denied its validity; as Neoplatonism was replaced by atomism and mechanistic theories, and as the eye was recognized to be only a passive receiver of light, fascination lost its theoretical basis. This loss was probably of little concern to those many colonists who were uninterested in problems of theory, and who, at any rate, most likely explained fascination by an analogy with the evil eye. But for colonists active in natural history, involved as they were with the Royal Society and European scientists, this was a real problem. They discussed and attempted to explain rattlesnake fascination as eighteenth-century naturalists. To them the collapse of a scientific theory which could explain fascination was an insoluable problem, forcing many of them to deny that "fascination" actually occurred. Some attempted to explain it in terms acceptable to eighteenth-century science by little more than a change in terminology, by speaking of effluvia instead of spirits. But, as we have seen, this was not fully satisfactory, and in any case the mainstay of this belief in the eighteenth century was probably observation rather than theory. Numerous observations of snakes and their prey acting in a manner which appeared to confirm fascination were undoubtedly a major reason for the continued existence of this piece of colonial folklore, despite the collapse of the Renaissance theory on which it was in part based.

Part Two


The Natural World

# 6

## The Old Heavens and the New

*Philosophers of spreading Fame are found,*
*Who by th' Attraction of the Orbs around*
*Would move the Earth, and make its Course obey*
*The Sun's and Moon's inevitable Sway.*
*Some from the Pressures and impelling Force*
*Of Heav'nly Bodies would derive its Course:*
*Whilst in the dark and difficult Dispute*
*All are by turns confuted and confute.*
*Each can subvert th' Opponent's Scheme, but none*
*Has Strength of Reason to support his own*
—Titan Leeds, *The American Almanack for . . . 1736* [1]

### I

Although the eighteenth century has been proudly called "The New-tonian Epoch in the American Colonies," [2] little attempt has been made to evaluate the various challenges which Newton and, to a lesser extent, Copernicus received in eighteenth-century America. It was undoubtedly true that the overwhelming majority of colonists, at least those who cared

1. The quotation was taken from Richard Blackmore, *Creation.* See the 1806 Philadelphia edition printed by Robert Johnson, p. 90.
2. Frederick E. Brasch, "The Newtonian Epoch in the American Colonies (1680-1763)," *Proceedings of the American Antiquarian Society,* N.S., IL (October 1939): 314-32.

170

about such things, came to believe in the Copernican-Newtonian universe[3]; nevertheless it faced some challenges from both the "Old Science" and heterodox theories of the eighteenth century itself.

No aspect of the Renaissance world picture had been more sophisticated, more fully elaborated, than its picture of the heavens—its astronomy. Yet it was just this aspect of Renaissance science which suffered total collapse as Ptolemaic and Aristotelian astronomy and physics were replaced by Copernican and Newtonian science. Indeed, by 1659 the Copernican system was well established at Harvard, and was being promulgated throughout the region by Cambridge almanacs.[4] By the end of the seventeenth century it was also being disseminated by almanacs in the middle colonies.[5] Despite this, however, Yale retained the Ptolemaic system well into the eighteenth century. Through 1717 it was still being taught at Yale, where it was "as much believed as the Scriptures," and was displaced only with the appointment of new tutors interested in the New Learning, which had just reached Yale.[6]

Many who had learned the old system were not easily, if ever, converted to the new. In 1714 Samuel Sewall had noted in his *Diary* that Cotton Mather had preached an excellent sermon. The only fault Sewall found with it was that Mather "spake of the Sun being in the centre of our System. I think it inconvenient to assert such Problems."[7] The poet Edward Taylor (1642?-1729) was also representative of those who brought a seventeenth-century education into the eighteenth century. Although his poems were rarely intended to be scientific works, they often used metaphysical conceits derived from the Old Science. Taylor's elegy for Samuel Hooker declared:

3. I am using such terms, as they are often used, to designate the final system rather than the beliefs of the individual. Thus "Copernicanism" refers not only to a heliocentric solar system but also to eliptical orbits and an infinite universe.

4. Samuel Eliot Morison, *Harvard College in the Seventeenth Century* (Cambridge: Harvard University Press, 1936): I, 216-19.

5. See Daniel Leeds, *An Almanack and Ephemerides for . . . 1693* ([Philadelphia]: William Bradford). There are no extant almanacs for the southern colonies until well into the eighteenth century.

6. Samuel Johnson, *Works,* I: 8-9.

7. Samuel Sewall, *Diary,* in *Collections of the Massachusetts Historical Society,* 5th Series, VII: 31.

And though his Epicycle was but small
His shining Beams did fly to lighten all.[8]

Perhaps the most pervasive influence of Renaissance astronomy upon Taylor was the term "crystal." Sometimes it was used to denote purity and incorruptibility, as when he wrote:

If I thy Valley, thou its Lilly bee
    My Heart shall be thy Chrystall looking Glass.[9]

The resurrected body, he said,

Is raised up anew and made all bright
And Christalized; all top full of delight.[10]

The blood of the Lord's Supper was metaphorically described as

This Liquor brew'd, thy sparkling Art Divine.
    Lord, in thy Chrystall Vessells did up tun,
(Thine Ordinances,) which all Earth o're shine
    Set in thy rich Wine Cellars out to run.
    Lord, make thy Butlar draw, and fill with speed
    My Beaker full: for this is drink indeed.[11]

This use of the word "chrystall" was undoubtedly derived from the Ptolemaic universe, where the planets and stars were on crystalline spheres composed of the incorruptible quintessence. The most common use of this word in Taylor was specifically in this astronomical context. "Chrystall" comes very close to being a stock epithet for the heavens.

8. Taylor, "An Elegy upon the Death of that Holy and Reverend Man of God, Mr. Samuel Hooker," 31-32. This poem was undated but probably written shortly after Hooker's death in 1697.

9. *Ibid.*, "Meditations," Second Series, no. 132 (1716), 31-32.

10. *Ibid.*, "A Fig for Thee Oh! Death," 43-44 (1720s). The unusual substitution of "Christalized" for "Chrystalized" probably was a pun which indicated that the body was both made of crystal and risen in Christ.

11. *Ibid.*, "Meditations," First Series, no. 10, (1684), 19-24.

> Methinks I spy Almight holding in
>> His hand the Chrystall Sky and Sun in't bright.[12]

> Thy Lower House, this World well garnished
>> With richest Furniture of Ev'ry kinde
> Of Creatures of each Colour varnished
>> Most glorious, a Silver Box of Winde.
> The Crystall Skies pinkt with Sun, Moon, and Stars
> Are made its Battlements on azure Spars.[13]

Even Taylor's "Valedictory" poems, written in the 1720s, which more than any other were intended as accurate descriptions of the world he was soon to leave, described the Ptolemaic heavens:

> You Starry Choristers at Boe peep Play,
> With in your Chrystall sockets down do dart
> Your Influence on my Cask of clay.[14]

One unique variation on this theme made it clear that Taylor was perfectly aware of the technical use of crystal in astronomy: "Nay, th' heavenly Orbs all Quintessenced clear."[15]

It has been argued that Taylor's didactic poem, *Gods Determinations,* utilized the Copernican system. "The Cambridge Platonists considered the new spatial astronomy a fresh support for biblical and Platonic revelations; and since Taylor's 'Preface' to *Gods Determinations* suggests a spatial astronomy, and his second ascension lyric substitutes the music of the atoms for the music of the spheres, one can assume that his science was relatively up-to-date and that his ladder, unlike Milton's, was Copernican."[16]

12. *Ibid.,* Second Series, no. 68 [A], (1705), 1-2.

13. *Ibid.,* no. 93 (1709), 13-18.

14. Thomas M. Davis, "Edward Taylor's 'Valedictory Poems,'" *Early American Literature,* VII (Spring 1972): 42. Successive redactions of the poem left the phrase "Chrystall sockets" unaltered.

15. Taylor, *Poems,* "Meditations," Second Series, no. 51 (1702), 9.

16. Willie T. Weathers, "Edward Taylor and the Cambridge Platonists," *American Literature,* XXVI (March 1954): 23.

This argument does not appear to be correct. The Ptolemaic universe was, after all, as spatial as the Copernican. The purpose of Taylor's second ascension lyric, "Our Insufficiency to Praise God suitable, for his Mercy," was not to substitute the music of the atoms for those of the spheres. Rather, by making each atom into a world, it magnified the numbers of men in the universe until they became numberless; yet even so their songs of praise would be "unfit within thine Eares to ting." [17]

Even if the ascension lyrics do include a progress from planet to planet, the order of the planets—moon, Mercury, Venus, Sol, Mars, Jupiter, and Saturn[18]—is that of the Ptolemaic rather than the Copernican solar system. In fact, it is the same route that Dante had followed in *Paradiso*.

As late as 1743 a no more than lukewarm acceptance of Copernicanism can be seen in an aside by Nathanael Appleton (Harvard 1712). "The *Sun* . . . , is very regular in its Motions, . . . Or, if we consider the earth to move instead of the Sun, which is the prevailing Opinion, it comes to the same Thing, . . ." [19] However, it seems safe to assume that by the end of the second or third decade of the eighteenth century, the Copernican system had almost completely triumphed.

So too, Newtonian physics had displaced earlier formulations. Prior to the acceptance of Newton, at least two different theories of gravity had been taught in New England. One of these was discussed, or rather defined, in some detail, in Samuel Johnson's "A Synopsis of Natural Philosophy or Physics."

Q 78 Which are the secondary qualities arising from the primary?
[The primary qualities were heat, cold, moistness, and dryness.]
A They are: (1) Density is a quality arising from cold, according to which the parts subjected immediately cling together and are drawn together.
(2) Rarity is a quality arising from heat having the parts thinned out and not really in contact.

17. Taylor, *Poems,* pp. 451-53.
18. Weathers, "Edward Taylor and the Cambridge Platonists," pp. 23-24.
19. Nathanael Appleton, *Faithful Ministers of Christ* (Boston: Rogers & Fowle for Eliot, 1743), p. 37.

(3) Weight is a quality arising from cold and from the matter's weighing down and blunting the form, on account of which things are bent downwards.

(4) Lightness is a quality commonly arising from heat and from the form's lifting and thinning out the matter whereby things hold their course.[20]

This explanation apparently depended upon the old Scholastic distinction between form and matter. Johnson saw matter as naturally tending downward to the earth, while forms naturally tended upward to the heavens. Heat and cold altered the amount of matter in an object (i.e., what we would today describe as a change in its density), and thus determined whether the tendency of the form would predominate, sending the object upward, or whether the tendency of the matter would send it downward.

At Harvard another explanation was favored. Morton's *Compendium* briefly discussed the above theory but then went on to describe the theory of "latter phylosophers who assert that all bodyes are heavy or tending to the center of the Globe to which they belong. . . ."[21] A casual reading might assume this to be a statement of the Newtonian concept of gravity, but this was not so. Rather, it reflected an adaptation which Aristotelian physics had undergone under the influence of the new astronomy. Originally it had been thought that each element had its natural place in the universe to which it tended: earth down to the earth, fire upward to the heavens. This geocentric physics was no longer viable after the collapse of the Ptolemaic universe. Fire could no longer naturally belong in the heavens, for the heavens were now no different from the earth. Each planet was now but a sphere of matter. Therefore, it was felt, all parts of the earth belonged to the earth, and all parts of the moon belonged to the moon, and so forth. All matter belonged to some specific orb, and would naturally tend to seek its own orb if displaced. Thus each orb had its own

20. Johnson, *Works*, II: 47-49. See also II: 45, where angels are described as having "the least of matter and most of form, hence they are very light, and invisible to us."

21. Morton, *Compendium Physicae*, pp. 39-40.

"gravity," which attracted only its own matter. Gravity was not yet the bond of the universe.[22]

This doctrine apparently remained intact at Harvard until the *Compendium* was superseded in 1728 by the arrival of Isaac Greenwood at the college. As late as 1723, when President Leverett was teaching science from a modified copy of the *Compendium*, this doctrine was still upheld: "Gravity is chiefly from cold, & Causeth Bodies to descend; & Levity is Chiefly from Heat & Causeth Bodies to Ascend: But it is no way allowed by Latter Philosophers who assert that all Bodies are heavy or tending to the Center of the Globe to which they belong." [23] Newtonian gravity apparently reached Harvard only with the arrival of Isaac Greenwood. It is interesting to note in this connection that apparently although Harvard accepted Copernicanism well before Yale, Newtonianism reached Yale first, in the second decade of the eighteenth century.

A curious allusion to this aspect of Scholastic physics may well be found in a mideighteenth-century colonial play by Thomas Godfrey, *The Prince of Parthia,* in which the younger brother of the heir to the throne is consolingly told that the reason his older brother was born first was that

> I must think that of superior mould
> Your soul was form'd, fit for a heav'nly state,
> And left reluctant its sublime abode,
> And painfully obey'd the dread command,
> When Jove's controuling fate forc'd it below.
> His soul was earthly, and downward mov'd
> Swift as to the center of attraction.[24]

Another relic of the old physics was the term "sublunary." In Scholastic physics, only the sphere below the moon, namely, the earth, was composed of the four elements and therefore subject to change and corruption. From this had developed the use of the word "sublunary" to

22. A. Rupert Hall, *The Scientific Revolution, 1500-1800: The Formation of the Modern Scientific Attitude* (2nd ed.; Boston: Beacon Press, 1966), pp. 259-60.

23. Varney, "Manuscript Exercises," chap. 6.

24. Thomas Godfrey, *The Prince of Parthia,* in *Representative American Plays,* ed. by Arthur Hobson Quinn (7th ed.; New York: Appleton-Century-Crofts, Inc., 1956), p. 10.

denote the transitoriness, changeability, and ultimate decay of all things on earth. At one time a statement of physical fact (of profound moral and philosophical import), it continued to be used through the eighteenth century as a mere figure of speech. Instances of its use ranged from Nathaniel Ames gnomic comment, "Time's Parent of all Sublunary Things," [25] to the parallel arguments against political inaction by John Adams and the American educator Samuel Johnson. As the latter once wrote:

> His next reason is "No Charter ought to be obtained, because it may be altered." The gentleman, when he conjured up this reason, unhappily forgot that all sublunary things were subject to change and decay; . . . .[26]

John Adams reacted to claims that titles were empty and meaningless when one died by noting that so were fame, liberty, and freedom. Yet, "Shall laws and governments, which regulate sublunary things, be neglected because they appear baubles at the hour of death?" [27]

## II

Although the Ptolemaic-Aristotelian universe was collapsing in the colonies by the early eighteenth century, its replacement did not go entirely without challenge. There were several attempts to complete or to contradict Newton by explaining the force of gravity. The most influential of these efforts was made by the self-educated Englishman, John Hutchinson. Using the theory (perfectly valid in itself) that the Masoretic vowel points were not part of the original system of written Hebrew, Hutchinson's exercise in biblical exegesis would seem to have been Old Testament. He argued that the Bible, if properly understood, offered a complete system of science. The sun gave forth light which cohered into spirit and which finally, at its furthest extent from the sun, solidified into gross spirit or air and fell back into the sun. It was this circulation,

25. Ames, *The Almanacks of Nathaniel Ames,* p. 110.

26. Johnson, *Works,* IV: 202.

27. John Adams, *The Works of John Adams,* ed. by Charles Francis Adams (Boston: Charles C. Little and James Brown, 1851), VI: 242.

according to Hutchinson, which accounted for the movements of the planets and most of the other phenomena in nature.

With its analogies to the Trinity and explanations involving angels, Hutchinson's exercise in biblical exegesis would seem to have been totally opposed to the main currents of eighteenth-century thought. Yet his theory (promulgated in such books as *Moses' Principia, Moses Sine Principia, Treatise of Power, Glory or Gravity,* and *Glory Mechanical)* had considerable influence even in England.[28] In 1739 John Wesley drew up a list of readings for an academy he had founded. The list included Newton's *Principia* as part of the curriculum for the second year, and Hutchinson's *Works* for the third year. Wesley was ambivalent; he never fully accepted the theories of Hutchinson yet was greatly impressed by the latter's criticism of Newton.[29]

Other British supporters of Hutchinson included George Watson, Fellow of the University College at Oxford; George Horne, president of Magdalen College and future bishop of Norwich; and Duncan Forbes, a noted Scottish jurist.[30] A similar theory, though lacking the biblical exegesis, was produced by William Jones, described by the *Dictionary of National Biography* as "one of the most prominent churchmen of his day," who was apparently considered by almost everyone but himself to be a Hutchinsonian. His theory was even used extensively in place of Newton's in the third through the seventh editions of the *Encyclopaedia Britannica* (1788-1842).[31]

28. Descriptions of his theory can be found in Arthur Hughes, "Science in English Encyclopedias, 1704-1875," *Annals of Science,* VII (December 1951): 365-66; Robert E. Schofield, *Mechanism and Materialism: British Natural Philosophy in An Age of Reason* (Princeton, N.J.: Princeton University Press, 1970), pp. 122-28; Samuel Miller, *A Brief Retrospect of the Eighteenth Century* (London: J. Johnson, 1805), I: 15-19, 379-81. This work had first been published in New York, in 1803.

29. Robert E. Schofield, "John Wesley and Science in 18th Century England," *Isis,* XLIV (December 1953): 331-40.

30. Hughes, "Science in English Encyclopedias," p. 366, and Theodore Hornberger, "Samuel Johnson of Yale and King's College: A Note on the Relation of Science and Religion in Provincial America," *New England Quarterly,* VIII (September 1935): 393-94.

31. Hughes, "Science in English Encyclopedias," pp. 366-68, and Schofield, *Mechanism,* pp. 124-33.

Hutchinsonianism also traveled to the colonies. Its most noteworthy, in fact its only identifiable convert there, was the Anglican minister and educator Samuel Johnson, who first became interested in it through a secondhand account he read in the 1740s. By the 1750s he had read not only John Hutchinson, whom he faulted only for his obscure and difficult style of writing and his bad temper, but also some of the lesser supporters of Hutchinson's theories such as George Horne. Johnson was so en-amored by Hutchinson's system of divinity and science that he resolved "to induce as many as I can to study the Hebrew Scriptures to understand his writings." Indeed, he even attempted to obtain George Horne to serve as vice president of King's College, but Archbishop Secker vetoed that suggestion because, ironically, he felt that Horne was too tinged by Hutchinsonian philosophy and Hebrew, "both of which I take to be groundless." One wonders what Johnson thought as he read this reply. Johnson also attempted to introduce the Hutchinsonian system to friends and acquaintances as disparate as East Apthorp (Anglican rector of Christ Church in Cambridge, Massachusetts), Thomas Clap (Congregationalist minister and president of Yale), and Cadwallader Colden (Scotch-Irish-born lieutenant governor of New York and a prominent colonial scien-tist)—but all in vain.[32]

Nevertheless, it seems probable that other colonists knew of the sys-tem even if they were not converted to it. An early nineteenth-century survey of the preceding century was to state that Hutchinson and his followers "occupy a considerable space in the scientific history of the eighteenth century," and to rank him first among the opponents of Newton, even ahead of Leibnitz.[33] Modern scientists will not agree with this ranking, but it clearly reflected the impact which Hutchinson had had on the eighteenth century.

Samuel Johnson's support of Hutchinsonianism deserves further study. He explained it thus in his Autobiography, speaking of himself in the third person:

32. Johnson, *Works,* II: 291, 338, 339-40, 341-44; IV: 60, 71; Cadwallader Colden, *The Letters and Papers of Cadwallader Colden* (in *New-York Historical Society Collections,* L-LVI, LXVII-LXVIII), III: 163; Hornberger, "Samuel Johnson of Yale," pp. 393-95.

33. Miller, *A Brief Retrospect,* I: 15. For Leibnitz see *Ibid.,* pp. 19-20.

He especially re-examined with particular care the several conclusions he had gone into in all the former stages of his life and read over again with much pleasure most of the best books he had formerly read, twenty, thirty or forty, and even fifty years before, and especially several of the best tracts of some of the ancient fathers and philosophers and some of the best moderns who had endeavored to make the study of nature subservient to religion. In this interim Mr. Horne of Oxford sent the Dr. a present of Mr. William Jones' *Principles of Natural Philosophy* with many experiments incontestably proving Mr. Hutchinson's Scripture philosophy, and he shows plainly by many passages from the ancients that this was indeed the original and most ancient system. With this the Dr. was vastly delighted, as also with Mr. Spearman's *Search after Philosophy and Theology.* It is remarkable that Bishop Berkeley in Ireland, Mr. Hutchinson in England, and Abbe Pluch in France, the greatest men of the age, without any communication with each other should at the same time though by different media come into the same conclusion, namely that the Holy Scriptures teach the only true system of natural philosophy as well as the only true religion, and that Mr. Franklin in America should at the same time without any design by his electrical experiments greatly confirm it.[34]

A sharp modern assessment of this statement has been made by Theodore Hornberger:

This linking of Berkeley and Franklin with an anti-scientific fanatic and a second-rate French savant is the achievement of a mind sadly lacking in perspective and warped by a determination that science must be subverted to orthodoxy, whatever the cost. As Johnson's editor observes, his efforts to reunite the realms of science and religion are at once pathetic and absurd. . . .
. . . As professor Schneider says, it was a far cry from accepting the Berkeleian transformation of nature to explaining the mysteries of the Trinity and the angelic hierarchy, and so Johnson turned to the vague reasoning and stout orthodoxy of the Hutchinsonians. His whole intellectual career illustrates the fact that provincial America was at one and the same time close to and isolated from the ideas of

34. Johnson, *Works,* I: 45. "Abbé Pluch" was probably Noël Antoine Pluche.

contemporary Europe. To Johnson came in great number and with astonishing speed the books which resulted from some of the most significant movements of the time, both religious and scientific. He, at least, however, was too isolated to sift them properly or to achieve the perspective necessary to solve rationally the problems which they raised.[35]

Even Johnson's friend and first biographer, Thomas Bradbury Chandler, could say no more about this statement by Johnson than to call it a "curious observation."[36]

Nevertheless, despite this understandable scorn, Johnson's statement can and should be better understood, for it was part of a small but significant conservative religious reaction to eighteenth-century science. Much of the surprise and scorn that Johnson's statement draws today is due to the shock that results from the realization that a follower of George Berkeley (one of the most if not the most distinguished English philosophers of the eighteenth century) became a convert to the nonsense of John Hutchinson. Yet, as Johnson made clear, he did not consider himself to be moving from one philosophy to another, but rather, believed that they had important points in common.

At first it may appear impossible to link the author of the *Principles of Human Understanding* with the author of *Moses' Principia;* but the key to the linkage is that Johnson simply knew a fact which commentators on Berkeley sometimes ignore, that his final work was not the *Principles, De Motu,* or the *Alciphron* but *Siris: A Chain of Philosophical Reflections and Inquiries.* Whether it should be considered the capstone of Berkeley's philosophical career or an aberration to be ignored is not our problem,[37] but what is clear is that Johnson apparently took it very seriously indeed.[38]

35. Hornberger, "Samuel Johnson of Yale," pp. 396-97.

36. Thomas Bradbury Chandler, *The Life of Samuel Johnson* (London: C. and J. Rivington, 1824), p. 116.

37. See Berkeley, *Works,* V: introduction; John Wild, *George Berkeley: A Study of His Life and Philosophy* (Cambridge: Harvard University Press, 1936), pp. 422-79 and *passim;* J. D. Marbott, "The Place of God in Berkeley's Philosophy," in *Locke and Berkeley: A Collection of Critical Essays,* ed. by C. B. Martin and D. M. Armstrong (Garden City, N.Y.: Anchor Books, Doubleday & Company, Inc., 1968), p. 377.

38. He discussed *Siris* with Cadwallader Colden. See Colden, *Papers,* III: 206.

The most obvious link between the two works was "fire." For Hutchinson, fire was the starting point for his explanations of the workings of the universe. So too, as Berkeley moved upward along his chain of philosophical reflections from the curative powers of tar water to ultimate causes, he found that the source of tar water's virtue and effectiveness was pure aetherial fire:

> This aether or pure invisible fire, the most subtle and elastic of all bodies, seems to pervade and expand itself throughout the whole universe. If air be the immediate agent or instrument in natural things, it is the pure invisible fire that is the first natural mover or spring from whence the air derives its power (Sects. 139, 149, 151). This mightly agent is everywhere at hand, ready to break forth into action, if not restrained and governed with the greatest wisdom. Being always restless and in motion, it actuates and enlivens the whole visible mass, is equally fitted to produce and to destroy, distinguishes the various stages of nature, and keeps up the perpetual round of generations and corruptions, pregnant with forms which it constantly sends forth and resorbs. So quick in its motions, so subtile and penetrating in its nature, so extensive in its effects, it seemeth no other than the vegetative soul or vital spirit of the world.[39]

Fire, too, was what linked Benjamin Franklin to the others. Franklin's theory of electricity included a subtle, all-enveloping sea of electrical fluid which could very easily be identified with the "aetherial fire" of Berkeley and Hutchinson. Franklin himself did not make this connection, but, as Johnson pointed out, his work could very easily be taken as confirming a key element in their theories. Franklin did write:

> Common fire is in all bodies, more or less, as well as electrical fire. Perhaps they may be different modifications of the same element; or they may be different elements. The latter is by some suspected.[40]

39. Berkeley, *Works*, V, sec. 152. See secs. 152-219.

40. Benjamin Franklin, *Experiments and Observations on Electricity, Made at Philadelphia in America* (4th ed.; London: David Henry, 1769), p. 50. Schofield notes that Franklin dropped this tentative identification after 1750, but he never actually repudiated it. Schofield, *Mechanism and Materialism*, p. 172.

In a passage in some ways reminiscent of Berkeley's explanation of how tar water received its curative powers, Franklin noted:

> I have been rather inclined to think that the fluid *fire*, as well as the fluid *air*, is attracted by plants in their growth, and becomes consolidated with the other materials of which they are formed. . . .[41]

Whether or not Franklin's electricity should be identified with "fire," there is much in his scientific writings which could be used to justify claims of the existence of some form of a universal all-penetrating "fire" pervading the universe.

Berkeley and Hutchinson were also in agreement on a far more basic point. Both were attempting to counter the growing autonomy of natural science and to place in its stead religion, not only for salvation and moral behavior but also as the guide to the physical universe. In *Siris* an elusive and hierarchical relationship exists between the physical universe and the spiritual world. Each step in the explanation of any natural phenomenon leads one up along the chain of connections until one leaves the physical universe for the spiritual reality which activates it.

Berkeley starts out in *Siris* with a single mundane fact: the effectiveness of tar water in curing diseases. He discusses the chemical reasons for its effectiveness, and then moves on to inquire how the pine trees received this power. It is obtained, he argues, from the air, and the air in turn must have received it from the solar fire.

> Whatever perspires, corrupts, or exhales, impregnates the air, which, being acted upon by the solar fire, produceth within itself all sorts of chemical operations, dispensing again those salts and spirits in new generations, which it had received from putrifications.[42]

> If air be the immediate agent or instrument in natural things, it is the pure invisible fire that is the first natural mover or spring from whence the air derives its power.[43]

---

41. Franklin, *Experiments and Observations*, p. 346.
42. Berkeley, *Works*, V, sec. 137.
43. *Ibid.*, sec. 152.

This aetherial fire is the central unifying agent in *Siris*. It serves as a bridge between the material and the immaterial worlds; it is animated by the Soul, that is, by God, and in turn activates the entire material universe. We have already seen Berkeley describe it as the "vegetative soul or vital spirit of the world"; and, like the spirits in a human being binding the soul to the body, fire (the soul or spirit of the visible world) connects the matter of the universe with the spiritual reality and power of the Godhead.

> A divine Agent doth by His virtue permeate and govern the elementary fire or light (Sects. 157, 172), which serves as an animal spirit to enliven and actuate the whole mass, and all the members of this visible world.[44]

> Air-vessels are by later experiments allowed to be found in all plants and animals. And air may in some sort not improperly be said to be the carrier or vehicle of the soul, inasmuch as it is the vehicle of fire, which is the spirit immediately moved and animated by the soul (Sects. 163, 171).[45]

> Both Stoics and Platonics held the world to be alive, though sometimes it be mentioned as a sentient animal, sometimes as a plant or vegetable. But in this, notwithstanding what hath been surmised by some learned men, there seems to be no atheism. For, so long as the world is supposed to be quickened by elementary fire or spirit, which is itself animated by soul and directed by understanding, it follows that all parts thereof originally depend upon, and may be reduced unto, the same indivisible stem or principle, to wit, a Supreme Mind—which is the concurrent doctrine of Pythagoreans, Platonics, and Stoics.[46]

The "soul" and "understanding" in the last passage are to be understood as the second and third hypostasis of the Neoplatonic Trinity. For Berkeley, as for all Christian Neoplatonists, these were identified with the

44. *Ibid.,* sec. 291.
45. *Ibid.,* sec. 280.
46. *Ibid.,* sec. 276.

Second and Third Persons of the Christian Trinity. And, in fact, the final passages of *Siris* dealt directly with the Trinity, and carefully analyzed the relationship between the Christian and Neoplatonic concepts.[47]

The Trinity was indeed the preordained conclusion of *Siris*. It explained the tar-water phenomenon because the explanation of all phenomena in the universe was ultimately the Trinity. Everything occurred through the influence of the aetherial fire, and this aetherial fire itself existed only because it was animated and directed by God. All that occurred, occurred only through the power of God.

Nor was this a mechanical chain of causation. The relationship of God, fire, air, and animals was not a mechanistic one; it was not one gear turning another. Rather, it was an organic flow, for all nature existed as a unity without any chasm or break in its continuity and it was all permeated by a spiritual essence whose origin was God and which activated the entire physical universe.

> There is no chasm in nature, but a Chain or Scale of beings rising by gentle uninterrupted gradations from the lowest to the highest, each nature being informed and perfected by the participation of a higher. As air becomes igneous, so the purest fire becomes animal, and the animal soul becomes intellectual: which is to be understood not of the change of one nature into another, but of the connexions of different natures, each lower nature being, according to these philosophers, as it were a receptable or subject for the next above it to reside and act in.[48]

Samuel Johnson could hardly have been surprised when reading *Siris* to find that Berkeley's theme was that any analysis of the material world must lead to God. By the 1720s Johnson had already understood from his readings of Berkeley's earlier books that matter had no power to act, and therefore that the study of any physical phenomenon must lead one to God:

> For in the next place, to be a little particular; if we essay to examine the make and texture of any of the bodies about us, though we are

47. *Ibid.*, secs. 351ff.
48. *Ibid.*, sec. 274.

presently lost in impenetrable mysteries, yet the further we extend our search, the more we discern of the presence and agency of this almighty mind. If we take a body and break, or file, or any way dissolve it, we find it consists of a combination of numberless extremely fine and minute particles which strongly cleave together. But how? Not by any force of their own. If we take up a stone, and let it go, it immediately falls to the ground again, but why downwards, rather than upwards? It has no principle of activity in it or counsel to direct itself. Some invisible cause, there must therefore be, of this strong tendency of the parts of bodies one to another, and of the bodies themselves to the earth, visibly exerting itself in these effects.

This cause does not act mechanically, for all the laws of mechanism suppose it. It does not act on, nor according to, the surfaces of bodies, but penetrates their dimensions, and every where equally pervades all things. These effects therefore, being immechanical, the cause of them must be immaterial; and there evidently appearing in them all a plain design and tendency towards some aim and end, the cause of them must always act by counsel; whenever therefore we see these and the like effects, even all the productions of nature, we may be as evidently certain of the presence and agency of a most wise and powerful spiritual being, as we can of the presence of man, when we hear him speak, and see him walk.[49]

Johnson followed this with an attempt to prove the existence of God from the great complexity and order in which matter is arranged. That is a typical argument of natural theology, but the passage which we have just read was not simple natural theology, it was pure Berkeleyanism. Natural theology argued that the great complexity and order in which matter is found, the existence of complex constructs such as animals and man, prove the existence of God; Johnson, influenced by Berkeley, was able to argue that the very existence of matter proved the existence of God. One does not need a complex living animal to prove that the designer God exists; the ability of a shapeless stone to hold itself together is sufficient proof.

49. Johnson, *Works*, II: 257-58.

John Hutchinson had sought the goal of supremacy of religion over science by a rather different route. Instead of finding the reality and activating power of nature as something which flowed out of the God-head, as Berkeley had done, he took the Bible and set it up as a complete system of science. The subservience of science to religion was not organic, not based on the very nature of things, but rather, on authority and revelation. Perhaps the sharpest distinction between *Siris* and Hutchinson's writings was that Hutchinson placed a very definite gap between God and physical universe. Our very names for God and our understanding of Him, according to Hutchinson, came from analogies with the workings of the physical universe, workings clearly set forth in the Bible, but there was a clear separation between God and the universe:

> [the universe] which the first Heathens knew to be a Machine composed of Three Parts, yet took it for their God; and to which, the later Heathens, from whom we have our Language, gave the Attributes of [eternal], Infinite, all Eye, all Hand, &c. In Scripture God claims the Machine, and all the Attributes the Heathens then gave to it, to himself, and we borrow those words to convey Ideas of the Personality: . . .[50]

The three parts of the universe, fire, spirit, and air, were created by God and must not be confused with Him.[51] Yet they are our source of knowledge about His names and attributes. In fact, they are types of the Divinity.[52]

How can one account for the popularity which Hutchinson's *Works* achieved in the eighteenth century? Berkeley was a far more brilliant man, and *Siris* is much more interesting and better written than anything done by Hutchinson; yet Hutchinson's *Works* were more influential than *Siris*. Hutchinson did in fact have several advantages. One was his biblicism. There already existed difficulties in reconciling the Bible, so central to British Protestantism, with the latest scientific theories, especially in

50. John Hutchinson, *The Philosophical and Theological Works*, ed. by Roberts Spearman and Julius Bate (3rd ed.; London: J. Hodges, 1748), II: 25.

51. *Ibid.*, p. 31.

52. See especially *ibid.*, III: 181.

the field of geology.[53] A theory which not only restored the repute of the Bible but made it the fountainhead of all science, no matter how distorted in fact its interpretation of the Bible was, had a far greater claim to popularity among the devout than did Berkeley's Neoplatonic analysis of nature and old philosophies, no matter how learnedly it was written.

Hutchinson's second advantage was that he treated the universe like a machine; indeed, he often used that very word to describe the universe. It was this aspect of Hutchinson's thought that a modern scholar was describing when he wrote, "Its roots are not primitive and Semitic, but sophisticated and French. The hands may have been those of Esau, but the voice was that of Descartes."[54] The late seventeenth and eighteenth centuries favored explanations of nature couched in mechanistic terms. Indeed, a difficulty Newton's theory of gravity had originally faced was that its action at a distance, without any physical or mechanical explanation of how it worked, smacked to many people of occultism.[55] William Jones, the reluctant Hutchinsonian, gave voice to this position in his *Physiological Disquisitions:*

> In short, wherever distant bodies are found to effect each another, there is always something to mediate, whether we see it or not; and where this mediation is no farther to be traced, there philosophy ends, and the fictions of imagination begin; which are all of equal value, whatever name you call them by, be it sympathy, antipathy, attraction, repulsion, cohesion, elasticity, antiperistasis, or any other, ancient or modern. Nothing is intelligible but the action of matter upon matter; . . .[56]

53. Andrew Dickson White, *A History of the Warfare of Science with Theology* (New York: Dover Publications, Inc., 1960): I, 209-48; Ernst Cassirer, *The Philosophy of the Enlightenment,* trans. by Fritz C. A. Koelln and James P. Pettegrove (Boston: Beacon Press, 1965), pp. 48-49.

54. Schofield, *Mechanism,* p. 122.

55. Alexander Koyré, *Newtonian Studies* (Cambridge: Harvard University Press, 1965), pp. 115-63; I. Bernard Cohen, *Franklin and Newton: An Inquiry into Speculative Newtonian Experimental Science and Franklin's Work in Electricity as an Example Thereof* (Philadelphia: American Philosophical Society, 1956), pp. 98-103, 107, 145-46.

56. William Jones, *Physiological Disquisitions,* p. 49.

Hutchinson, in the spirit of the seventeenth-century system-makers, had devised an elaborate mechanistic explanation of the universe. The circulation of light, spirit, and air was somehow more "real" and less "occult" to his followers than the indescribable force of gravity acting in some unknown manner over distances. Hutchinson had attempted and succeeded, if only for a limited time, in combining two phases of eighteenth-century thought—religion and mechanism[57]—into a makeshift alternative to Newton himself.

Other would-be scientists and philosophers, without any religious motivation, also tried to formulate a mechanistic system of gravity to replace, or rather to explain and complete, the Newtonian theory of gravity. A colonial representative of this school of thought was Cadwallader Colden, lieutenant governor of New York and a well-known botanist.

Colden's theory held that there were three types of matter: resisting, moving, and elastic. Ordinary matter combined the first two qualities; aether was the elastic matter. A piece of common matter, such as a planet, would be pushed on all sides by the aether. As long as the pressure from all sides was equal it would have no effect on the common matter. However, if the pressure became unbalanced, the matter would be pushed in the direction of the least pressure. According to Colden, the pressure of the aether was reduced when the aether was between two bodies, such as the earth and the sun, and therefore the two bodies would be pushed together. Thus did Colden explain the force of gravity mechanically. Colden also felt it necessary that there be a counterbalancing force to prevent the planets from falling into the sun, and he argued that this counterbalancing force was the light of the sun.

This theory seems to have left Colden's colonial friends totally nonplussed. It at first received a mixed reaction in England, but was soon demolished in a paper by Leonhart Euler read before the Royal Society, which explained that the supposed variation in the pressure of the aether was "absolutely contrary to the first principles of Hydrostaticks."[58]

57. For a discussion of the role of mechanism in eighteenth-century thought, see Schofield, *Mechanism*.

58. Brooke Hindle, "Cadwallader Colden's Extension of the Newtonian Principles," 3rd Series, *William and Mary Quarterly*, XIII (October 1956): 459-75, and Cadwallader Colden, *An Explication of the First Causes of Action in Matter, and of the Cause of Gravity* (New York: James Parker, 1745).

The last eighteenth-century American cosmologist was James Bowdoin, governor of Massachusetts and first president of the American Academy of Arts and Sciences. In 1785 Bowdoin argued that there were orbs of matter about each solar system and about groups of solar systems, although he vehemently, and correctly, stated that he was not returning to the Ptolemaic system. The orbs acted to reflect most of the sun's light back to the sun, so preventing it from losing its matter and decaying. Lenses in the orb permitted the transmittal of a certain proportion of light to other stars, in a perpetual interchange of light. The orbs about groups of stars provided a gravitational counterbalance to the stars themselves, and kept them from gravitating together into one huge mass.

After discussing observations which he thought tended to uphold his theory, Bowdoin turned to the Bible in a manner reminiscent of Hutchinson. He knew no Hebrew, but he attempted to prove his theory with a philological analysis of the Old Testament, and suggested that a translation and study of those portions of the Scriptures which related to "the constitution and economy of nature" could "lead to discoveries, of which, at present, we can form no idea." [59]

### III

Colonial resistance to the Copernican-Newtonian universe thus stemmed from three separate sources. One was simply cultural lag. It took time for new ideas to reach the New World, and it took time for new ideas to be accepted. For those who had learned the old science but were no longer very interested in science, it was perhaps as satisfying and certainly easier to continue accepting the old ideas. But this type of resistance, passive and unaggressive as it was, died out early in the century as the colonies imported books and men to teach them the new science.

The second source of opposition was a conservative religious reaction

59. James Bowdoin, "Observations on Light, and the Waste of Matter in the Sun and Fixt Stars, . . . ," "Observations Tending to Prove, by Phaenomena and Scripture, the Existence of an Orb, . . . ," *Memoirs of the American Academy of Arts and Sciences,* I (1785): 195-207, 208-33. See also Hindle, *The Pursuit of Science,* p. 333.

against the growing claims of natural science. There had already existed, especially in England, by the later seventeenth century, a dispute between religion and science concerning the relationship of new geological discoveries to the biblical accounts of creation and the flood. John Hutchinson, in effect, had led a counterattack against the most prestigious of all the achievements of the new science, Newton's theory of gravity, and he, for a time, had made some headway. Nor was it surprising to see Samuel Johnson supporting him in America. As a disciple of George Berkeley, Johnson had always been in opposition to Newtonianism as a description of basic reality.[60] He greatly respected Newton's "Experiments & the mathematical Reasonings, but in merely physical Conjectures or metaphysical matters it is no wonder if he should Sometimes be mistaken, (with relation to which it is that he has been faulted chiefly by Berkely & Hutchinson,) nor is it to be wondered at if they also in their turn be Sometimes mistaken; tho' I confess I can't but think Bp Berkely is one of the first men of his age." [61]

Johnson thus had not changed his allegiance; he had merely added an ally, albeit a dubious one. Perhaps the greatest damage to Johnson's reputation from his Hutchinsonianism should not be to his reputation as a philosopher but to his repute as a Hebraicist.

The third source was the continuing dissatisfaction with the concept of action at a distance. It had inspired various elaborate mechanistic attempts to explain how gravity worked, including Colden's attempt in America.

Although eighteenth-century America was undoubtedly Newtonian and Copernican, one should not totally ignore the fact that Ptolemaic and Aristotelian science lingered on and that even in the eighteenth century itself challenges to Newton appeared and gained some success.

60. Johnson had recognized quite early the opposition between Berkeleyanism and Newtonianism. That was his first comment in his first letter to Berkeley. Johnson, *Works*, II: 264. For Berkeley's reply, see *ibid.*, p. 271.

61. Colden, *Letters and Papers*, III: 206.

# 7

## The Old Earth Decays

*When in Six Days the Elements,*
*    Extracted were from* Chaos,
*And each its Simple Quality,*
*God did on them impose.*
*The Light, the Air, the Earth and Sea,*
*Their Order well receiv[e]d,*
*Alternate Parent each of each,*
*Begat and eke unceiv'd*
*—A Brief Essay on the Number Seven,* 1735

The old heavens, although structured into complex orbs and epicycles, were made out of the uniform and incorruptible quintessence. The old earth, on the other hand, presented one with a bewildering melange of differing substances. The four qualities—hot, cold, moist, and dry—united in differing combinations to form the four elements—fire, air, water, and earth—and the four humors—choler or yellow bile, melancholy or black bile, blood, and phlegm. In the human body these were joined by the three spirits—natural, vital, and animal. Moreover, living beings also contained a soul, of which there were again three varieties—vegetable, animal, and rational. The latter, it is true, would one day leave the earth for an infinitely better or infinitely worse abode; but while a man was alive his soul was an integral component of the old earth. Beliefs about each of these components of a once unified world picture traced their own paths as the picture slowly decayed in the eighteenth century.

I

The old Renaissance doctrines of the four qualities and the four elements were being taught at Yale early in the eighteenth century, complete and unchallenged although tinged by atomism. Samuel Johnson wrote in 1714:

826. Perishable nature is either elementary atoms or what is composed of elements.

827. Elementary atoms are the perishable natures out of which elements and compounds are made, and into which they are at last resolved.

828. Atoms are the smallest of all physical things, and the first of all natural things.

829. Elements have qualities and species.

830. The qualities are hot and cold, humidity and dryness.

831. Heat is the quality of an element making it hot, drawing together the homogeneous and segregating the heterogeneous.

832. Cold is the quality making cold, drawing together the homogeneous and not segregating the heterogeneous.

833. Humidity is the moist quality, with it gone (it is) difficult to hold together.

834. Dryness is the drying out quality, with it gone it is easy to hold together.

835. An element is hotter or colder.

836. The hotter are fire and air.

837. Fire is the hottest element and dry.

838. Air is the wettest element and hot.

839. The colder are water and earth.

840. Water is the coldest element and wet.

841. Earth is the driest element and cold.[1]

A further admixture of seventeenth-century atomism, moreover, is found in the appendix of this work. There, atoms of fire are described as fast moving and sharply pointed; atoms of air as fast moving, smooth, and

1. Johnson, *Works,* II: 143. See also *ibid.,* pp. 47-53.

slippery; atoms of water as quiescent, smooth, slippery, and "stickish"; and atoms of earth as totally quiescent, but craggy and pointed.[2]

Unlike some other aspects of the "old science," the elements did not disappear from Johnson's later writings, although his tendency to stress logic, metaphysics, and ethics naturally reduced their importance. His "Revised Encyclopedia" of 1716 briefly listed a series of sciences together with their subject matter, including "The elements for the subject of stoichology."[3] Many years later, in 1771, his final revision of his earlier attempts to organize all human knowledge still had a place, under physics, for "the elements, fire, air, water and earth: . . ."[4]

At Harvard, Morton's *Compendium* presented a more complex situation. It appears to have not been difficult to define the term "element." It was "a simple body made or composed of Elementary matter and Form" which "are not resolvable into any former bodyes that are Specifically distinct from themselves." But how many elements were there? That was a more difficult question. The Cartesians said three; the atomists said one, Aristotle said four; and the chemists said five. After stating these divergent views, however, Morton himself proceeded with an essentially Scholastic analysis of the four elements, although with additions and modifications from more modern scholarship.[5] On another related issue, however, he tentatively decided "to allow Cartesian Subtile matter, than the Atomists intersperced vacuityes, to Solve the Doctrine of Locall motion."[6]

This uncertainty over the proper number and types of the elements appeared in many serious discussions of the issue. Chambers's *Cyclopedia* noted the great confusion about what was an element, and appeared to

---

2. *Ibid.*, p. 186.

3. *Ibid.*, p. 213. "Stoichology," derived from the Greek words for *element* and *study of,* may have been a neologism by Samuel Johnson. The *Oxford English Dictionary* cites the first recorded use of "stoicheiology" as not occurring until over a century later.

4. *Ibid.*, p. 354. See also *ibid.*, pp. 366, 431.

5. Morton, *Compendium Physicae*, pp. 36-53.

6. *Ibid.*, p. 210. Local motion seems simply to have meant the movement of an object from one place to another. It would be distinguished from motion such as that found in waves where the impulse is transmitted from object to object but the object remains in the same location.

give a major role to fire.[7] Isaac Watts (whose textbooks in various fields, especially logic, were widely used in the colonies) tended toward the five elements of the chemists—spirit, salt, sulphur, water, and earth—but noted that there was disagreement over this issue.[8] Another influential textbook, *Rohault's System of Natural Philosophy,* which Ezra Stiles noted had once been "a philosophical Bible in the Universities," also discussed this problem. This must have been an odd book to use because its Cartesian text, written by Jacques Rohault, was frequently directly contradicted by its notes, written by its Latin translator, the early Newtonian, Samuel Clarke. Thus the text of the Cartesian Rohault rejected the four elements of the Aristotelians and the five elements of the chemists, and argued instead that there were but three elements—irregular particles, particles becoming round, and round particles. But this, in turn, was rejected in Samuel Clarke's Newtonian notes, which argued for the atomist's position that all matter was composed of round unchangeable atoms.[9] Somewhat later, Joseph Black, the distinguished Scottish chemist and professor of medicine at the University of Glasgow, where many colonists studied, continued to argue for the four elements, despite some difficulties. He then proceeded to teach chemistry on the basis of divisions between salts, earths, inflammables, metals, and water.[10]

Benjamin Rush, the famous American doctor, forthrightly explained that the best way to organize chemistry would be by the elements. He then discussed several theories about the elements, but disproved them all. He argued that earth, air, and water were not elements; and that while

7. Chambers, *Cyclopedia* (5th ed.), "Elements."

8. Isaac Watts, *Logick: or, the Right Use of Reason in the Enquiry After Truth* (16th ed.; Philadelphia: Thomas Dobson, 1789), p. 26. For the popularity of Watts's *Logick,* see Robert Middlekauff, *Ancients and Axioms: Secondary Education in Eighteenth-Century New England* (New Haven: Yale University Press, 1963), p. 91.

9. [Jacques] Rohault, *Rohault's System of Natural Philosophy Illustrated with Dr. Samuel Clarke's Notes Taken Mostly Out of Sir Issac Newton's Philosophy,* trans. by John Clarke (London: James Knapton, 1723), I: 105-17. For the history of *Rouhault's System,* see Michael A. Hoskin, " 'Mining all Within' Clarke's Notes to Rohault's *Traité de Physique,* " *The Thomist,* XXIV (April to October 1961): 353-63. Stiles, *Literary Diary,* I: 556.

10. Joseph Black, MS, "Lectures on Chemistry," notes of C. Dilloyes, I: 127-31 (Historical Society of Pennsylvania).

fire was, we know little about it. His conclusion concerning the state of contemporary knowledge of the elements would appear to have admirably summarized the problem. "But as we are ignorant of the Number, as well as the nature of these Elementary Principles, we cannot pretend to treat of them separately." [11]

Generally speaking, however, the Aristotelian four elements seem to have remained standard throughout the eighteenth century. They appeared in both scientific works and casual literary allusions. An English play popular in the colonies, George Farquhar's *The Beaux-Stratagem*, asks us to

> View all the works of Providence below,
> The fire, the water, earth, and air, we know,
> All in one plant agree to make it grow.[12]

A popular English textbook for children used as one of its phrases, "Air, one of the Elements." [13] The American radical Ethan Allen once explained "that earth, water, fire and air, in their various compositions subserve us. . . ." [14] The Federalist John Adams argued that

> Animal life is a chemical process, and is carried on by unceasing motion. Our bodies and minds, like the heavens, the earth, and the sea, like all animal, vegetable, and mineral nature, like the elements of earth, air, fire, and water, are continually changing.[15]

The *Independent Reflector*, the New York triumvirate's magazine, noted that for medical training "the Qualities of Air, Fire, Water and Earth,

11. Benjamin Rush, MS, "A Course of Lectures on the Theory and Practice of Chemistry," pp. 253-55 (College of Physicians of Philadelphia).

12. George Farquhar, *The Beaux-Stratagem*, in *Restoration Plays*, introduction by Edmund Grosse (New York: E. P. Dutton & Co., Inc., 1932), III: iii. For the popularity of this play in the colonies see Hugh F. Rankin, *The Theater in Colonial America* (Chapel Hill: University of North Carolina Press, 1960), p. 192.

13. Quoted in Monica Kiefer, *American Children through Their Books, 1700-1835* (Philadelphia: University of Pennsylvania Press, 1948), p. 123.

14. Ethan Allen, *Reason the Only Oracle of Man* (Bennington, Vt.: Haswell & Russell, 1784), p. 33.

15. John Adams, *Works*, VI: 395.

in all their Quantities and Modifications, must be sagaciously investigated."[16]

Even Thomas Jefferson used the Aristotelian formulation of the four elements while disputing Buffon's claim that animals naturally degenerated in the New World. "It is by the assistance of *heat* and *moisture* that vegetables are elaborated from the elements of earth, air, water, and fire," Jefferson claimed. He went on to speak of the four qualities which underlay the four elements, even to the use of the technical term "contraries." "Here then a race of animals [oxen], and one of the largest too, has been increased in its dimensions by *cold* and *moisture,* in direct opposition to the hypothesis, which supposes that these two circumstances diminish animal bulk, and that it is their contraries *heat* and *dryness* which enlarge it."[17]

Ezra Stiles, in a letter to Benjamin Franklin in 1757, speculated on the number and nature of the elements, but within an essentially Aristotelian framework.

> Perhaps there are many Elements, or Kinds of Fluids, in our System, besides Water, Fire, Air, Light [he suggested cold as a separate element]. . . . May not the *volatile Salts,* Sulphur and the several Sorts of *Aromatics* . . . be so many different Elements? . . . If *Salts* must be supposed sharp pointed; mayn't *Fire* with the same propriety?[18]

The appendix to Jared Eliot's *Essays on Field Husbandry* in 1761 contained the following speculations based on the four elements:

> There have been great Disputes whether Fire, Air, Earth or Water, is separately the Principles of Vegetation, and the Disputes have been carried on by Men of great Integrity. For my own Part, there is no Doubt with me, but they unite in promoting the Growth of Plants; but I am apt to think that Water is the chief Cause. . . .[19]

---

16. William Livingston, [William Smith, and John Morin Scott], *The Independent Reflector,* ed. by Milton Klein (Cambridge: Harvard University Press, 1963), p. 137.

17. Thomas Jefferson, *Notes on the State of Virginia,* ed. by William Peden (Chapel Hill: University of North Carolina Press, 1955), p. 48.

18. Franklin, *Papers,* VII: 242.

19. Jared Eliot, *Essays Upon Field-Husbandry in New-England,* p. 162.

A Yale student noted in 1762 that President Thomas Clap "made a Disputation Concerning fier," and his opinion was that fire was an element which was present in all bodies.[20]

We have already seen Benjamin Franklin discuss electricity as an element, similar to some ways yet distinct from the element of fire. This undoubtedly became standard in Philadelphia electrical circles, and thus it is not surprising to find Ebenezer Kinnersly explaining that electricity "is a distinct Element from those heretofore known & nam'd, even from that call'd Fire, will appear from several remarkable Properties." [21]

Although the term "element" was not used, a similar pattern of postulating a new and unique substance to explain a previously unexplainable phenomenon was found among colonial students of magnetism. William Gilbert's classical study of magnetism, which had stated that electrical phenomena were caused by material effluvia, had explained magnetism in Scholastic terminology as the result of form not matter, and in one famous passage had described magnetism as the soul of the world.[22] Eighteenth-century colonial students of magnetism, however, ignored Gilbert's Scholastic and Neoplatonic explanations, and instead pursued material ones. Franklin conjectured, in an obvious parallel to his theory of electricity, that magnetism was the result of changes in the denstiy of a magnetic fluid.[23] James Madison, president of the College of William and Mary, eliminated the problem of action at a distance by assuming that magnetic attraction was communicated by means of particles of iron in the air, each of which became magnetized in turn.[24] John Page suggested that

20. Peter Pratt, MS, "Diary," p. 101, Yale University Manuscripts and Archives Division, Sterling Memorial Library.

21. E[benezer] Kinnersly, MS, "A Course of Experiments on the Newly Discover'd Electrical Fire," pp. 12-13 (Historical Society of Pennsylvania). For further comments by Franklin see his *Papers*, VII: 183, 184-90; Franklin, *Experiments and Observations on Electricity, passim;* see also Schofield, *Mechanism*, p. 172.

22. William Gilbert, *On the Lodestone and Magnetic Bodies and on the Great Magnet the Earth*, trans. by P. Fleury Mottelay, vol. 28 of *Great Books of the Western World* (Chicago: Encyclopaedia Britannica, Inc., 1952), bk. II, chaps. ii-iv; bk. V, chap. 12.

23. B. Franklin, "Conjectures Concerning the Formation of the Earth, &c.," *Transactions of the American Philosophical Society*, III (1793): 1-5.

24. James Madison, "Experiments Upon Magnetism," *ibid.*, IV (1799): 323-28.

magnetism "is only a species of electricity, whose *matter* is as yet not discovered by human sight. . . .[25] David Rittenhouse was perhaps slightly more receptive that most to the theory that the magnetic force was capable of acting at a distance, but he too explained that iron could be magnetized because it had certain magnetic particles within it.[26] Even Cotton Mather, writing a half-century earlier, spoke of effluvia circulating between the two poles of the magnet, although he spent considerably more space glorifying man's ignorance of how a magnet worked as a proof that man could never fully comprehend the infinite God.[27]

Thus we find that the doctrine of the four elements continued to be important in eighteenth-century America. Of the field of chemistry, we are told that prior to Lavoisier, it consisted of a "chaotic legacy in which were jumbled the Greek doctrine of elements, old Stoic vestiges of fire and flux, Paracelsian principles of salt, sulphur, and mercury; alchemistical distillations and purifications, mineralogical and metallurgical lore, and the proliferating laboratory discoveries of his own time." [28] In this complex, the doctrine of the four elements maintained its existence, but without being especially important or fruitful. Outside chemistry, however, the old classical doctrine of the four elements seems to have maintained its vitality.

It was what an educated man who was not a devotee of contemporary chemistry was perhaps most likely to think of as the "building blocks" of the world. Probably its most fruitful application was in Franklin's theory of electricity, in which the elemental fluid electricity appears to have been developed, in part, as a parallel to elemental fire. And this in turn may have been only a part of a broader cultural stress on the role of fire. As we have already seen, this was the basis of several cosmologies of the period, for example, Berkeley's *Siris* and Hutchinson's elaborate theories; and even Colden had depended upon the rays of the sun to play a key role in his theory of the universe. Thus, despite Donne's fear that the "new

25. John Page, "To David Rittenhouse," *ibid.,* II (1786): 173-74.

26. David Rittenhouse, "An Account of Some Experiments on Magnetism," *ibid.,* pp. 178-81.

27. Cotton Mather, *The Christian Philosopher,* pp. 108, 111-14.

28. Charles Coulston Gillispie, *The Edge of Objectivity: An Essay in the History of Scientific Ideas* (Princeton, N.J.: Princeton University Press, 1960), pp. 212-13.

Philosophy calls all in doubt/The Element of fire is quite put out"; [29] the element of fire continued to play a major role in the speculative thought of the eighteenth century.

## II

The underlying condition of disease had long been viewed as a morbid state of the humors (blood, bile and so on). These were said to be impure or out of place; or again, were thought to be present in excessive or in deficient amounts. If excessive, the illness could be treated by depletion (bleeding, purging, sweating); if deficient, the patient could be aided by restoring the humor through diet and drugs. This humoral doctrine continued to be held by many practitioners throughout the eighteenth and into the nineteenth century. [30]

The doctrine of the four humors received only passing mention in the encyclopedias of Samuel Johnson, probably because they largely ignored the entire field of medicine. Some of the terminology of the humoral theory, however, was briefly used in a discussion of the elements. "Simple [temperament] is where one quality is dominated by another, as choleric, sanguine, phlegmatic, melancholic." [31] Moreover, in one portion of the "Encyclopedia of Philosophy," Johnson described the human body as a container for the humors and the animal spirits. [32]

Other works scattered throughout the century clearly state, or assume, the classical doctrine of the four humors. Nicholas Culpeper of course did so, [33] as did the popular pseudonymous *Works* of Aristotle. [34] The 1712 *Husband-man's Guide* warned that the first thing one should know about purging is "The humor which aboundeth." [35] In 1718 the similarly named *Husbandman's Magazine* noted that "The Spleen is the seat of Mel-

29. John Donne, "An Anatomie of the World: The First Anniversary," ll. 205-6.

30. Richard Harrison Shryock, *Medicine and Society in America, 1660-1860* (New York: New York University Press, 1960), pp. 50-51.

31. Johnson, *Works,* II: 143.

32. *Ibid.,* p. 151.

33. Culpeper, "An Astrologo Physical Discourse," in *Pharmacopoeia Londinensis.*

34. Aristotle [pseud.], *The Problems of Aristotle,* in *Works,* p. 49.

35. *The Husband-man's Guide,* pp. 29-30.

ancholy." [36] Titan Leeds's *Almanack* for 1732 asserted that summer "was assimulated into *Fire* in the Elements, *Choler* in the Humours, and unto *Mankind* in Human Race," while autumn's humor was melancholy and winter's was phlegm.[37]

Some authors even gave dietary advice based upon the humors and their qualities. In 1766 Thomas Bond explained that mineral water was useful because it would "counteract the Summers Sune, dilute a thick putrid Bile (the instrument of Mischief in all Hot Climates). . . ." [38] A 1769 Virginia almanac advised in verse (perhaps not very seriously):

> In summer heat, when choler hath dominion,
> Cool meats, and moist, are best in my opinion;
> The fall is like the spring, but endeth colder,
> With wine and spice the winter may be bolder.[39]

William Byrd II appears to have followed the humoral theory. He explained the virtue of ginseng by arguing that it "dissolves all the phlegmatic and viscous humors, that are apt to obstruct the Narrow channels of the Nerves." [40] More interesting was a rather odd passage in his *A Progress to the Mines:*

> I retired to a very clean lodging in another house and took my bark, but was forced to take it in water, by reason a light-fingered damsel had ransacked my baggage and drunk up my brandy. This unhappy girl, it seems, is a baronet's daughter; but her complexion, being red-haired, inclined her so much to lewdness that her father sent her, under the care of the virtuous Mr. Cheep, to seek her fortune on this side of the globe.[41]

36. John Smith, *The Husbandman's Magazine,* p. 63.

37. Titan Leeds, *The American Almanack for . . . 1732* (New York: William Bradford).

38. Carl Bridenbaugh, "Dr. Thomas Bond's Essay on the Utility of Clinical Lectures," *Journal of the History of Medicine and Allied Sciences,* II (Winter 1947): 18.

39. T. T. Philomath [pseud.], *The Virginia Almanack for . . . 1769* (Williamsburg, Va.: Purdie & Dixon).

40. William Byrd, *History of the Dividing Line,* in *The Prose Works,* ed. by Louis B. Wright (Cambridge: Harvard University Press, 1966), p. 292.

41. Byrd, *A Progress to the Mines,* in *Prose Works,* p. 248.

By complexion he meant not merely her coloration but her temperament, the mixture of her humors. She was lewd not because she was red-headed, but she was both lewd and red-headed because she had a too sanguine temperament: an overabundance of the humor blood.

It is often difficult to be certain if an author is in fact following the humoral theory. A mere mention is no more than proof that he was familiar with it, not that he followed it. Thus, little can be deduced from the following comment from Henry Flynt's "Common Place Book": "The antients say that black choler—& other bad humours gathered about the Spleen & Liver. . . ." [42] This difficulty of course exists in all aspects of the study of the old science during the Enlightenment, but an even more misleading problem exists in the study of the humoral theory. Much of its language was taken over by other physiological theories, and thus even the serious use of the terms traditionally connected with the humoral theory may not necessarily indicate an acceptance and use of that theory.

The word "humor" itself had two possible meanings. It could specifically relate to one of the "four humors," but it could also be used in a much more general sense. Chambers's *Cyclopedia* explained that the moderns do not accept the ancient classification of the humors. Instead, "HUMOUR, in medicine, is applied to any juice, or fluid part of the body, as the chyle, blood, milk, fat, serum. . . ." [43] Hermann Boerhaave had found various humors within the blood.[44] Morton's *Compendium*, describing the eye, spoke of watery, crystalline, and vitreous humors.[45]

So too, use of the traditional temperaments and complexions cannot be taken as a certain indication of the classical humoral theory. Thomas Robie had copied into his commonplace book "Observations taken from Dr. Pitcarn's Element of Physic." It at first would appear to be no more than a variant upon the classical theory. Instead of the traditional four temperaments, one for each humor, it had only three: bilious, melancholy,

42. Henry Flynt, MS, "Common Place Book," [1712-1724], p. 86 (Massachusetts Historical Society).

43. Chambers, *Cyclopedia* (5th ed.), "Humour."

44. Lester S. King, *The Medical World of the 18th Century* (Chicago: University of Chicago Press, 1958), pp. 66-67.

45. Morton, *Compendium Physicae*, pp. 153-54. The 1720s copies merely state that humors are a part of the eye, but they do not cite the specific types of humors found there. See Cabot, MS, "Commonplace Book," chap. 23.

and pituitous; however, the major feature of this theory appears to have been the great stress placed upon the velocity of the blood as the decisive factor, and thus it must be considered one of the new mechanistic theories rather than a continuation of the old humoral theory.[46]

Jonathan Elmer, founding member and later president of the Medical Society of New Jersey, and a student of John Morgan's at the College and Academy of Philadelphia, also used, in the late eighteenth century, a theory which sounded like, but was not, the old humoral theory. He used the traditional temperaments, but accounted for them not by the mixture of the humors but by the status of the body's solids and fluids. A sanguine temperament was the result of lax solids and a high proportion of fluids, while a melancholy temperament had more rigid solids and a lesser proportion of fluids.[47]

From another and more basic perspective however, the essential principles and major manifestations of the humoral theory can be seen as dominating many of the newer theories of the eighteenth century. The basic principle of the humoral theory was equilibrium and homeostasis. As long as the body maintained a proper balance of the four humors, it would be well. Medical treatment of most ailments consisted of attempts to restore the proper balance by eliminating excess or corrupt humors through bleeding, blistering, vomiting, etc. Equilibrium was health and its disruption was disease, and the function of a doctor was to restore health by restoring the equilibrium. Or, as Benjamin Grosvenor had put it:

> Philosophers and physicians both run mightily upon the Notion of a *Balance* of Humours, the due *Temperament* of all the Qualities, a Sort of Geometry in our Composition, which is destroyed by a Redundancy or Defect in any of the particular Parts.[48]

46. Thomas Robie, MS, "Commonplace Book" (Massachusetts Historical Society).

47. Jonathan Elmer, MS, "A Compleat System of the Materia Medica," pp. 50-60 (College of Physicians of Philadelphia). For some comments on Jonathan Elmer, see Maurice Bear Gordon, *AEsculapius Comes to the Colonies: The Story of the Early Days of Medicine in the Thirteen Original Colonies* (Ventnor, N.J.: Ventnor Publishers, Inc., 1949), pp. 360, 364-66.

48. B[enjamin] Grosvenor, *Health. An Essay on its Nature, Value, Uncertainty, Preservation and Best Improvement* (Boston: D. & J. Kneeland, 1761), p. 3.

Although today one can still define health as an equilibrium, one normally thinks of doctors as restoring the equilibrium or health by removing the cause of the imbalance, for example, curing an infection, while in the Renaissance a doctor would act directly upon the equilibrium and ignore the reason why it went out of balance. Thus the modern medical procedure which comes as close as any to this Renaissance conception of restoring the balance, giving insulin to a diabetic, is today never considered to be a true cure because it merely restores the balance without removing the basic cause of the imbalance. This is not to deny that systematic treatments are used today or that specific cures were not used earlier, although mercury for syphilis and jesuit bark for malaria just about exhausted the specific cures of the older pharmacy, but the overall philosophical orientations differ.

Many of the new medical theories of the eighteenth century appear to have been equilibrium theories, just as the humoral theory had been. William Cullen of Edinburgh, a teacher of many colonial doctors, and Benjamin Rush of Philadelphia both expounded theories in which sickness was due to an abnormal change in the nervous force and vascular tone of the body.[49] The role of the physician was to return the body to normal. Rush argued that the equilibrium depended upon the stimuli the individual received, for all bodily functions, even thought itself, he said, "are all the effects of stimuli acting upon the organs of sense and motion." [50]

This theory, he claimed:

2. ... discovers to us the true means of promoting health and longevity, by proportioning the number and force of stimuli to the age, climate, situation, habits and temperament of the human body.
  3. It leads us to a knowledge of the causes of all diseases. These consist in excessive, or preternatural excitement in the whole, or a part of the human body, accompanied *generally* with irregular motions, and induced by natural, or artificial stimuli. The latter have

49. Richard H. Shryock, "Empiricism versus Rationalism in American Medicine, 1650-1950," *Proceedings of the American Antiquarian Society*, LXXIX (April 1969): 109-10; King, *The Medical World of the 18th Century*, 139-50.
  50. Benjamin Rush, *The Selected Writings of Benjamin Rush*, ed. by Dagobert D. Runes (New York: Philosophical Library, 1947), p. 137.

been called very properly by Mr. Hunter *irritants.* The occasional absence of motion in acute diseases is the effect only of the excess of impetus in their remote causes.

4. It discovers to us that the cure of all diseases depends simply upon the abstraction of stimuli from the whole, or from a part of the body, when the motions excited by them, are in excess; and in the increase in their number and force, when motions are of a moderate nature. For the former purpose, we employ a class of medicines known by the name of sedatives. For the latter, we make use of stimulants. Under these two extensive heads, are included all the numerous articles of the Materia Medica.[51]

If the old underlying philosophy often remained unchanged in the eighteenth century, so too, and much more obviously, did the remedies. Bleeding and other forms of purging remained among the most popular cures throughout the eighteenth century, not only in the well-known excesses of Benjamin Rush but also in popular theory and practice. It perhaps mattered little whether the theory behind the practice was to restore the proper balance of the humors or the tension of the blood vessels; the new medical theories of the eighteenth century appear to have added or subtracted very little from the prevaling curative procedures. As Morton noted in an afterthought, "All this of temperament complexions, and their Consequents is by moderns Solved by the Matters Variety, in the Particles, Figure, Motion, or Rest, etc.: but however the thing be solved the Use of it is the same." [52]

## III

The Renasissance doctrine of the three spirits also continued into the eighteenth century. It, of course, appeared in the writings of Nicholas Culpeper, and Samuel Johnson noted as late as 1714 that "the beating of the pulse is the alternate contracting and expanding of the animal spirits in the heart and arteries." [53] Although Johnson no doubt soon learned to

51. *Ibid.,* p. 177.
52. Morton, *Compendium Physicae,* p. 80.
53. Culpeper, "An Astrologo Physical Discourse," in *Pharmacopoeia Londinensis;* Johnson, *Works,* II: 155.

attribute the pulse to the blood rather than to the animal spirits, he still at times continued to treat the spirits as the link between body and mind. "As such is the law of union between our souls and bodies, that upon our being affected or disaffected towards any object, we are sensible of certain commotions and perturbations in our blood and spirits, corresponding and in proportion to those pleasing or displeasing apprehensions." [54] Perhaps this was no more than a slip into conventional language, for earlier in the *Noetica* Johnson had carefully avoided such terms in explaining perception and action, and instead (as befitted a disciple of Berkeley) had treated it as the result of divine fiat:

> And accordingly I apprehend that the union between our souls and bodies, during our present state, consists in nothing else but this law of our nature, which is the will and perpetual fiat of that infinite Parent Mind . . . , *viz.* that our bodies should be thus acted by our minds, and that our minds should thus perceive and act by the organs of our bodies, and under such limitations as in fact we find ourselves to be attended with. [55]

As Johnson was unwilling at this point to deny the existence of the body, this arbitrary mind-body linkage was a necessary preliminary for the Berkeleyan interpretation of perception which followed. Shortly afterward he attempted still another explanation of the mind-body linkage; this one utilized "a fine etherial machine or vehicle" which he claimed was fully compatible with his Berkeleyan beliefs. [56]

Robert Hunter, an early eighteenth-century governor of New York, once alluded to the belief that insanity was the result of a disorder of the animal spirits. In his clever 1714 political satire on New York politics, *Androboros*, one of the characters, Tom of Bedlam, explained why he had become the clerk of the Senate: "I found in my reading, That Man was composed of three parts, *Body, Soul,* and *Spirit,* and that the two first were entirely ingross'd by two Societys [doctors and clergy], so I Resolv'd to Exercize my poor Talent upon the Infirmitys of the last, not with any

---

54. Johnson, *Works,* II: 418.
55. *Ibid.,* p. 373. See also Chandler, *The Life of Samuel Johnson,* pp. 44-45.
56. Johnson, *Works,* I: 266.

hopes or intentions to Cure them, but as others do, meerly to raise my self a Maintenance out of them. . . ." [57]

Cotton Mather used this same concept in his description of insanity:

A dismal Spectacle! Where in the Animal Spirits inflamed, form raging, or shatter'd Ideas in the Brain, and raise in a confused Manner, those that have been formerly there; and perhaps . . . from thence . . . proceeds often an extraordinary Strength in the Limbs, with Patience of Cold, and other Inconveniences. . . . [58]

Morton's *Compendium* commonly used the word "spirit" as we do today, to signify a nonphysical body, that is, a soul. But it also explained that "Matter Volatilized, and put in motion, is Somtimes Equivocally cal'd Spirits as the form or Life of Vegitables, and those Steams cal'd natural, Vital, and Animal Spirits in the bodyes of men and beasts." [59] Motion was explained as the result of an influx of spirits from the brain through the nerves into a muscle. This caused the muscle to swell up and bulge in the center, thereby causing the ends of the muscle to contract. As one end of the muscle was attached to a movable bone, the bone moved when the muscle contracted.[60] Thus these spirits were still the bridge between mind and body, but as "volatalized" matter which could only equivocally be called "spirit," it appeared to have lost its role as the conceptual link between matter and soul.

This, however, was not so. Morton listed five categories of spirits, exclusive of God:

1.  Spirits unrelated to matter—angels.
2.  Spirits related to matter but not necessarily forever—human souls.

57. Laurence H. Leder, "Robert Hunter's *Androboros,*" *New York Public Library Bulletin,* LXVIII (March 1964): 165. It includes the text of this very rare play.

58. Quoted in Eric T. Carlson and Meribeth M. Simpson, "Models of the Nervous System in Eighteenth Century Psychiatry," *Bulletin of the History of Medicine,* XLIII (March-April 1969): 103. My overall picture of eighteenth-century theories about nerves comes from this article.

59. Morton, *Compendium Physicae,* p. 189. Omitted in the 1720s copies.

60. *Ibid.,* p. 187.

3.  Spirits which are necessarily related to matter and which vanish when they are separated—souls of beasts.
4.  Volatized matter—natural, vital, and animal spirits.
5.  Matter "fixed and quiescent" with nothing of spirit about it.

The existence of volatized matter was important to Morton, for "thus the Order of things, and harmony of the World appear, without that great Gapp [between] Spirituall, and bodyly Substance." [61] The idea of the continuum was still very strong in Morton; and spirits, even if now defined as volatized matter, still played their traditional role as the conceptual link between the immaterial and the material worlds.

The belief that sleep was the result of a deficiency of spirits is found scattered throughout the eighteenth century. Morton thought that sleep was caused "by the Steams of food and blood ascending into the brain, by whose coldness they are Said to be condensed into moysture which obstructs the passages of the Spirits that they cannot freely permeate to the Organs of Sens." [62] As late as 1762, while upholding the affirmative in a Yale disputation on "Whether a Person can commit a sin when he is asleep," Manasseh Cutler found it necessary to use spirits to explain exactly what sleep was:

> And as Sleep is said to consist in a Scarcity of Spirits; which occasion that the orifices or pores of the Nerves of the Brain, whereby the spirits used to flow in the nerves, being no longer kept open by the frequency of spirits, shut up of themselves, and as this want of animal spirits in the humane Body can have no affect on the Mind the Body's Leiying thus motionless does not in the Lest hinder the Opperation of the Mind. . . .[63]

So too, Jonathan Elmer's late eighteenth-century manuscript "Praxis Medica" explained "Coma or Drowsiness by the secretion of the Spirits

61. *Ibid.,* p. 189. Omitted in the 1720s copies. This discussion of the different varieties of spirits was a digression in the midst of a chapter on locomotion, and it was simply omitted in these later shorter versions.

62. *Ibid.,* p. 194.

63. Manasseh Cutler, "A Common-Place-Book," 1762 (typescript, Beinecke Rare Book and Manuscript Library, Yale University), pp. 47-48.

being impeded, & is cured by Blisters &c." [64] Neither such a diagnosis nor such a cure would have been at all out of place at the end of the sixteenth century.

A somewhat different description of the effect of spirits on the brain was presented by another Yale disputant in 1763, who was willing to argue that "Authorities affirm that the clearness of humane conception and reflection depend very much on the smallness of the Capillary & Arterie that pass through the Brain fild with blood, animal spirits &c." Here, however, the problem was purely mechanical, for if the blood vessels were too large they would disturb the brain. The same disputant also made the more orthodox statement that the soul, located in the brain, learns of "the State of the Body by the Disposition of animal Spirits to which it seems more peculiarly to be united. . . ." [65]

Perhaps even more important than the continued traditional use was the role played by the spirits as a starting point for speculation about the workings of the nerves. At times "spirit" was merely redefined in a manner more consistent with atomism and a purely materialistic science (which of course could and did coexist with a firm belief in God and orthodox religion). Such were Morton's spirits of volatized matter.

Many authorities, such as the very influential Boerhaave, spoke of a "nervous fluid," a fluid in the nerves which carried messages to and from the brain. [66] Health would depend upon the proper quality, quantity, and flow of the nervous fluid—an obvious parallel and derivation from the earlier concern about the proper flow of the spirits. [67] William Shippen of

64. Jonathan Elmer, "Praxis Medica," MS, p. 12 (College of Physicians of Philadelphia).

65. John Tyler, "Whether all the Souls of the Human Race were Created Equal" and "Whether the Soul of Man is active in Receiving its Ideas," in "Book of Forensick Desputes," MS, Students Declamations Collection, Yale University Archives, Yale University Library.

66. The discovery of neurosecretions has shown that the nervous system's activities are not exclusively electric and that the theory of fluids flowing through nerves has a certain validity to it. Needless to say, the modern theories are considerably different from those of the eighteenth century and are not directly derived from them. See Chandler McC. Brooks, *et al., Humors, Hormones, and Neurosecretions* (State University of New York, 1962), chaps. 5-8.

67. Carlson, "Models of the Nervous System," pp. 105-7.

Philadelphia, who thought that the mode of operation of the nerves was "not known nor is it likely to be known," explained in a lecture the position of the advocates of nervous fluid. Nerves

> are hollow & carry a fine fluid. From the similarity of Brain to Kidneys, some suppose it to be glandular, & that being a large Secretary Mass, it must Secrete a large quantity of fluid which must have one large or a great number of small outlets, and that the Nerves are these outlets, or the Excretory Ducts of the Brain.[68]

This theory must also have been discussed at Harvard around the 1770s, since several master's theses dealt with it. In 1770 it was argued that nervous fluid exists. In 1769 a master's candidate had denied that the nervous fluid should be called "animal spirits," but in 1781 this thesis was defended.[69] The author of the essay *Health,* Benjamin Grosvenor, also believed that the nervous fluid and animal spirits were identical, but admitted that what it was, was unknown. "We know as little (it seems) of that Volatile Fluid, commonly called the *Animal Spirits,* designed to put that Fibre [muscle] in Motion." [70]

Another popular theory, which perhaps owed something to the doctrine of spirits but more to Newtonian speculation, held that nervous messages were transmitted by vibrations of the aether in the nerves.[71]

The pattern was quite similar to that which we have already seen with the humors. While medical thought remained in flux and confusion, the old concepts continued to be viable, and at the same time strongly influenced some of the newer theories of the eighteenth century.

## IV

The belief that there existed three different classes of souls—vegetable, animal, and rational—also entered the eighteenth century, although it

68. William Shippen, "Anatomical Lectures," MS, College of Physicians of Philadelphia.
69. Young, "Master's Degree in Harvard College," p. 134.
70. Grosvenor, *Health,* p. 70.
71. Carlson, "Models of the Nervous System," pp. 108-11.

soon dropped from sight.[72] It was extensively, if at first somewhat inaccurately, reviewed in Johnson's "Encyclopedia of Philosophy" of 1714.

901. The soul is the member which is the elementary spirit, which is the principle of those operations.

902. An animated being is furnished with one (or several) souls.

903. Single [souled] are the plants (or stars).

904. A plant is an animated being furnished with a single soul, *viz.*, the vegetative.

905. The vegetative soul is the elemental spirit which is the principle of the vegetative operations.

906. Its operations or faculties are appetite, attraction, retention, digestion, nutrition, growth, excretion, and procreation. . . .

918. So far one-souled beings; there follow beings furnished with several souls, as an animal. An animal is accordingly an animated being furnished with several souls, *viz.*, the vegetative, motive, and sensitive. . . .

944. . . . The sensitive soul is the elemental spirit which is the principle of sensation, appetite and motion.

945. Its faculties are, therefore, these three.

946. Sense is the faculty of the sensative soul by which the animal senses single objects. . . .

966. An animals appetite is the faculty by which it seeks good and avoids evil.

967. The motive of an animal is the faculty by which its animal spirits are excited.

968. And is an emotion, locomotion, respiration, or the beating of the pulse. . . .

971. The emotion of approval is whatever agrees with pleasure. This motion of the spirits comes from the heart. . . .

991. Now the species; animals are brutes or men.

---

72. This Scholastic doctrine has, however, continued to be used in at least some Catholic schools until the midtwentieth century. See Raymond J. Anable, S.J., *Philosophical Psychology: A Text for Undergraduates* (New York: Fordham University Press, 1941).

992. A brute is an animal only sentient or irrational, whose principal soul is the sensitive. . . .

995. Man is a rational animal, or one whose principal soul is the rational soul.

996. His properties are speech, or his system of mental symbols by articulate sound; his ability to laugh, or his sign of joy; weeping, or his sign of grief.[73]

These lines require some detailed analysis. The passage which Johnson first placed in parentheses in line 902 (and later crossed out) indicate that he was at first uncertain as to whether a being could actually have several distinct souls, or whether the "higher" souls incorporated the faculties of the "lower" souls. He obviously rechecked his authorities and found that all beings could have only a single soul. He forgot, however, to correct line 918, which stated that animals have several souls. This line had an additional error in its assertion that the three types of souls were "the vegetative, motive, and sensitive." The three types of souls should have been listed as the vegetative, sensitive, and rational; the motive was, as Johnson himself indicated in lines 944 and 967-68, only a power or faculty of the sensitive soul.

This interpretation of Johnson's position on multiple souls is further verified by a sermon which Johnson preached in 1716, in which he was obviously reacting to his own previous error:

By the soul of man I mean his rational spirit, the principle of his rational actions. Some have thought that there are three distinct souls in man, the vegetable, the sensitive, besides the rational, but I know no absurdity in thinking that all the vital, but especially sensitive actions owe their original to the rational soul.[74]

The three types of souls were also very important in Morton's *Compendium*. They served as the organizing principle for Morton's entire discussion of animate beings or, as we would call it, biology, apparently

---

73. Johnson, *Works*, II: 147-155. The passages in parentheses in lines 902-3, and also lines 915-17, were originally placed in parentheses by Johnson, who then later crossed them out.

74. *Ibid.*, III: 338-39.

using Aristotle's *De Anima* as a model.[75] Chapter 19 of the *Compendium* defined the three types of souls and discussed the first faculty or power of the vegetative soul, the digestive faculty. Chapters 20 and 21 discussed the vegetative soul's other faculties, the growing and procreative powers. Chapters 22 through 29 discussed the various faculties of the sensitive soul. They included the five external senses of sight, hearing, smell, touch, and taste; the three internal senses of common sense, phantasy, and memory; the power of locomotion; and a discussion of sleep. Finally, chapter 30 briefly discussed the different types of beasts, and then moved on to man and the rational soul. It briefly discussed the faculties of reason and will as well as the secondary characteristics of passion, but the faculties of the rational soul received short shrift because they belonged to the science of pneumatics rather than physics.

Such an analysis of the three souls soon became obsolete, although the traditional faculties of the rational soul did not. A series of mideighteenth-century disputations were held at Yale on such topics as whether the soul always thinks and whether or not brutes think. Relevant arguments could have been generated from that aspect of the doctrine of the three souls which held that only the rational soul thinks, but this possibility was ignored. The disputants in fact often identified the soul with thought, ignoring the functions once assigned to the vegetative and sensitive souls. They either argued that as the soul was thought it must think, or that a distinction should be made between the action of thinking and the substance or agent that thought. In either case, the three types of souls were wholly ignored here, as well as in the other writings of the last seven decades of the eighteenth century.[76]

75. Morton, *Compendium Physicae,* p. 126n.

76. Daniel N. Brinsmade, "Book of Disputes," MS, pp. 21-25; Tyler, "Whether Beasts Think," in "Book of Forensick Desputes August 9, 1763," MS; Anon., "Book of Disputations," in Box, "Declamations," in Folder "unidentified papers of the Stiles Period," MS, pp. 7-11; Joseph Camp, "Logic Notebook," MS, Jan. 22, 1764, July 24, 1764; Justus Forward, "His Book," in Box 1, Folder 3 of the Justus Forward Collection, MS, July 20, 1752, July 27, 1752; Peter Pratt, "Diary," MS, 1760-62, p. 20. All the above are in Manuscripts and Archives, Stirling Memorial Library, Yale University.

Ezra Stiles, "Whether Beasts Have a Rational Soul," "Notebook 1744-45," and Cutler, "A Common-Place-Book," pp. 46-48, Beinecke Rare Book and Manuscript Library, Yale University.

The science of pneumatology also lost favor about this time. Actually, the early eighteenth century knew of two sciences called by this name. One was the study of air and air pressure,[77] but the one which we are interested in was the study of rational souls. Samuel Johnson defined this science in the *Elementa Philosophica* as "the doctrine of spirits or created intelligences; and here we begin with our own souls, their powers and operations, both perceptive and active: and thence we proceed to other intelligencies whether good or bad: [and by analogy we rise to consider God which is the subject of theology.]"[78] Morton's *Compendium,* as we have seen, largely ignored the rational soul because it was the subject of "pneumaticks," and therefore it did not belong in a *Compendium Physicae.*[79] At Harvard, master's theses argued affirmatively in 1688, 1709, and 1715 that pneumatics was a science "distinct" from metaphysics and theology.[80]

Despite this early interest, the science of pneumatics seems to have disappeared from the colonial scene by the 1720s, with the notable exception of Samuel Johnson. Until the 1730s Johnson maintained that

77. I. Bernard Cohen, *Some Early Tools of American Science: An Account of the Early Scientific Instruments and Mineralogical and Biological Collections in Harvard University* (New York: Russell & Russell, 1950), pp. 33, 35, 36.

78. Johnson, *Works,* II: 355-56.

79. Morton, *Compendium Physicae,* p. 199. "Pneumaticks" does not appear in the 1720s copies. These versions, however, did state that the soul could be considered under two categories, as a form or as a being, and that only when it was considered as the form of the body was it a part of physics. Varney and the anonymous 1729 version of Morton's *Compendium Physicae* did not state what science dealt with the soul as a being, but Cabot's copy (chap. 30) stated that it belonged under "Metaphysics."

80. Young, "Master's Degree in Harvard College," p. 129. This has been confused with the other science of pneumatics, the study of the air, but it was clearly the study of souls which required differentiation from metaphysics and theology. I. Bernard Cohen, "The Beginning of Chemical Instruction in America: A Brief Account of the Teaching of Chemistry at Harvard Prior to 1800," *Chymia:* III (1950), 31-32. See also Morton's comment that souls "have been formerly handled in the Speciall part of metaphysics: but of late they are referred (with good reason) to a Distinct Science, Cal'd pneumaticks or [the] doctrine of Spirits, as Physicks is of bodyes." Morton, *Compendium Physicae,* p. 198. Not in 1720s copies and obviously rejected in Cabot's 1723-24 copy.

pneumatics was a subdivision of physics.[81] From about 1744 on he continued to list pneumatics as a distinct subject, but now it was listed as a subdivision of moral theology.[82] As a Berkeleyan, Johnson had to consider the science of the soul as a subject of major importance for the nature of the universe, as well as for both ethics and the nature of God (i.e., theology). The other colonial writers, however, seem to have been able to ignore this subject. Perhaps the virtual identification of the soul with thought made it possible to subsume the study of the nature of the soul under the study of logic.

A second line of analysis existed somewhat more persistently in eighteenth-century thought. This line of analysis recognized only two types of souls, those of men and those of unintelligent entities. Often only the former was called a soul, while the latter was often called a "spirit." This spirit, however, was not the same as the natural, vital, and animal spirits; it performed the organizing and controlling functions of the vegetative and sensitive souls, and often lacked the rather physical and mechanical characteristics of the natural, vital, and animal spirits. The terminology of this second line of analysis, however, was vague, confusing, and often idiosyncratic.

The fullest development of this theory in eighteenth-century America is found in Cotton Mather's unpublished "Angel of Bethesda," written in the early 1720s. The spirit, which Mather called the "Nishmath-Chajim," was held to be of a middle nature between the rational soul and the corporal body, and was the means by which they communicated. Some of Mather's statements described the "Nishmath-Chajim" in terms which would have been appropriate for the natural, vital, and animal spirits. It was "a sort of Luminous Air which is of a Middle Nature, betwixt spirituous and corporeous." It was an *"Ethereal Spirit, elaborated out of the purest Part of the Blood, and changed into the substance of a very subtil Air; . . ."* But to a greater extent it resembled the vegetative and sensitive souls. It had "marvellous Faculties; which yet all of them short of those Powers, which enable the Rational Soul, to penetrate into the Causes of Things; to do curious and exquisite Things in mathematical Science; and above all, to act upon a principle of Love to GOD, and with the Views of Another World." If the "Nishmath-Chajim" was not the rational soul, it

81. Johnson, *Works*, II: 199, 213, 311.
82. Johnson, *Works:* II, 318, 321, 323, 355-56.

was what sees, hears, feels, gives motion to all parts of the body, performs the acts of generation, "and performs the several Digestions in the Body."

> The Nishmath-Chajim is much like the Soul which animates the Brutal World; even that Spirit of the Beast, which goeth downward unto the Earth; but is by the Hand of the Glorious Creator impraegnated with a Capacity and Inclination for those Actions, which are necessary for the Praeservation of themselves, and the Propogation of their Species. The Nidification of Birds, the Mellification of Bees, and a thousand such Things, how surprising Works done in the Brutal World without any rational Projection for them! And Hence, there are also many Actions done by us, that have a Tendency to our Safety and Welfare, which are not the Effects of any rational Projection; but such as we do by what we call, a meer Instinct of Nature, fall into. The sucking Infant, yea, and the nursing Mother, too, do very needful and proper Things, without consulting of Reason for the doing of them.
>
> It is a Thing, which who can observe without Astonishment? In every other Machin, if anything be out of Order, it will remain so till some Hand from abroad shall rectify it; it can do nothing for itself. But the Humane Body is a Machin, wherein, if anything be out of Order, presently the whole Engine, as under an Alarum, is awakened for the helping of what is amiss, and other Parts of the Engine strangely putt themselves out of their Way that they may send in Help unto it. Whence can this proceed but from a *Nishmath-Chajim* in us, with such Faculties and such Tendencies from God imprinted on it?

The "Nishmath-Chajim" also explained witchcraft, possession, the impact of a mother's imagination on her unborn child, and after death it served as the vehicle of the rational soul and accounted "for Apparitions of the Dead; the Spectres, which are called Spirits and Phantasms, in our Gospel." [83]

---

83. Otho T. Beall and Richard H. Shryock, *Cotton Mather: First Significant Figure in American Medicine* (Baltimore, Johns Hopkins University Press, 1954), chap. 5 of Cotton Mather's "Angel of Bethesda."

Samuel Johnson was apparently thinking along similar lines when in 1756 he explained to his son:

> strictly speaking there is no such thing as any separate state of the soul, but that, as it is immediately, and indissolubly united with a fine etherial machine or vehicle, by which it is united with and animates and actuates this gross animal body now, while it continues in good order; so when that is ruined by sickness and death, the soul goes off still united with its vehicle by which, though it escapes our present gross senses, souls may still be as sensible to each other and as capable of conversing with one another as we are now.[84]

In 1760 an unnamed friend of Alexander Garden was making a careful distinction between the *animus* and the *spiritus* or *anima*. The former was said to be the same as the rational soul, and belonged to a higher class than the latter, the *spiritus* or *anima*, which was common to both beasts and men and was "the breath, life, *spiritus*, *anima*, or animal life; . . ."[85] Benjamin Waterhouse, professor of physic at Harvard from 1783 to 1812 and of natural history at the College of Rhode Island from 1784 to 1786, continued this tradition at the end of the century. "Man is a being composed of *body*, *spirit*, and *mind;* or *Corpus, Vis Actuosa, et Mens.*" An involuntary function of the body, such as nourishment, "depends upon a principle which some call *Vis Actuosa*, others *Impetum Faciens*, others *Archaeus.*"[86] Some such similar schema probably was the basis for a 1758 Harvard master's thesis which affirmed that the spirit of man was distinct from his soul.[87]

It is quite clear that Mather's "Nishmath-Chajim," Johnson's "etherial machine," Garden's friend's "*spiritus* or *anima*," and Waterhouse's *"Vis*

84. Johnson, *Works*, I: 266-67.

85. James Edward Smith, *A Selection of the Correspondence of Linnaeus and Other Naturalists* (London: Longman, Hurst, Rees, Orme, and Brown, 1821), I: 491; see also I: 448, 454-56.

86. Benjamin Waterhouse, *Heads of a Course of Lectures Intended as an Introduction to Natural History* (Providence, R.I.: Wheeler [ca. 1794]), and Benjamin Waterhouse, *A Synopsis of a Course of Lectures on the Theory and Practice of Medicine* (Boston: Adams and Nourse, 1786), p. 15.

87. Young, "Master's Degree in Harvard College," p. 129.

*Actuosa,*" "*Impetum Faciens,*" or "*Archaeus*" were all the same entity and derived from the same belief. It seems equally certain that the belief they were derived from was the "plastic nature," "substantial soul," or "*archei*" of the Cambridge Neoplatonists.[88] These had been seventeenth-century attempts to restore a vitalist and integrated interpretation of nature in the place of the new mechanistic and atomistic interpretations.[89] It has been argued that these beliefs were obsolete in England by the start of the eighteenth century (although later revived by Berkeley in *Siris,* and thus passed on to Samuel Coleridge),[90] but it is clear that these beliefs maintained some vitality in the colonies throughout the eighteenth century.

88. For the use of this concept in Neoplatonism see William B. Hunter, "The Seventeenth Century Doctrine of Plastic Nature," *Harvard Theological Review,* XLIII (July 1950); Robert A. Greene, "Henry More and Robert Boyle on the Spirit of Nature," *Journal of the History of Ideas,* XXIII (October-December 1962); J. E. Saveson, "Differing Reactions to Descartes Among the Cambridge Platonists," *Journal of the History of Ideas,* XXI (October-December 1960). For Henry More's use of *archei,* see Greene, p. 454.

89. Cassirer, *The Platonic Renaissance in England,* chap. 5.

90. Hunter, "The Seventeenth Century Doctrine of Plastic Nature," pp. 210-13.

# 8

## The Chain of Being

*Vast chain of being, which from God began,*
*Natures etherial, human, angel, man*
*Beast, bird, fish, insect! what no eye can see,*
*No glass can reach! from Infinite to thee [man],*
*From thee to Nothing!—On superior powers*
*Were we to press, inferior might on ours:*
*Or in the full creation leave a void,*
*Where, one step broken, the great scale's destroyed:*
*From Nature's chain whatever link you strike,*
*Tenth or ten thousandth, breaks the chain alike.*

—Alexander Pope, *An Essay on Man*

## I

"The great chain of being" was a commonplace of eighteenth-century thought. Its best-known expression in English was, of course, that by Alexander Pope in his famous *Essay on Man.* Pope was extremely popular in the colonies, and his poems, especially the *Essay on Man,* were often quoted,[1] but belief in this concept was too widespread to be attributed to any one source. The colonists found the concept set forth by many of

1. Agnes Marie Sibley, *Alexander Pope's Prestige in America, 1725-1835* (New York: King's Crown Press, 1949), chap. I.

their favorite English authors, including John Locke, Joseph Addison, James Thompson, and Edward Young.[2]

Nor were the colonists entirely dependent upon outside sources for statements of the principles of the chain of being. Cotton Mather's *Christian Philosopher* included a full statement of this concept.

> There is a *Scale of Nature*, wherein we pass regularly and pro-
> portionably from a *Stone* to a *Man*, the Faculties of the Creatures in
> their *various Classes* growing still brighter and brighter, and more
> capacious, till we arrive to those noble ones which are found in the
> *Soul* of MAN; and yet MAN is, as one well expresses it, *but the
> Equator of the Universe.*
>
> It is a just View which Dr. *Grew* had of *the World*, when he came
> to this Determination: "As there are several Orders of *animated
> Body* before we come to *Intellect*, so it must needs be that there are
> several Orders of *imbodied Intellect* before we come to pure Mind."
>
> It is likely that the transition from *Human* to *perfect* MIND is
> made by a *gradual Ascent*; there may be *Angels* whose Faculties may
> be as much superior to *ours*, as ours may be to those of a *Snail* or a
> *Worm*. [This idea later became immortalized in Pope's famous lines
> about superior beings who "showed a NEWTON as we show an
> Ape."]
>
> By and by we may arrive to *Minds* divested of all *Body*, excellent
> *Minds*, which may enjoy the Knowledge of Things by a more
> *immediate Intuition*, as well as without any inclination to any *moral
> evil*.[3]

Virtually paraphrased by Benjamin Franklin in 1728 were Mather's second and third paragraphs. Franklin's "Articles of Belief and Acts of Religion" included: "For I believe that Man is not the most perfect Being but One, rather that as there are many Degrees of Beings his Inferiors, so

2. For a discussion of English sources of the chain of being, see Arthur Stuart Pitt, "The Sources, Significance, and Date of Franklin's 'An Arabian Tale,'" *Publications of the Modern Language Association of America*, LVII (May 1942): 158-64.

3. Mather, *The Christian Philosopher*, pp. 292-93. For Pope on Newton, see *Essay on Man*, epistle II, 34.

there are many Degrees of Being superior to him."[4] Much later, Franklin again stated the theme of the chain of being in his "Arabian Tale." When questioning the existence of evil, which he could not comprehend by reason, Albumazar was told to contemplate

> the scale of beings, from an elephant down to an oyster. Thou seest a gradual diminution of faculties and powers, so small in each step that the difference is scarce perceptible. There is no gap, but the gradation is complete. Men in general do not know, but thou knowest, that in ascending from an elephant to the infinitely Great, Good, and Wise, there is also a long gradation of beings, who possess powers and faculties of which thou canst yet have no conception.[5]

Thus Franklin hinted at the answer of the optimists to the perennial problem of evil, namely, if the universe were truly understood (which limited man was incapable of doing) it would be seen that evil did not exist.

This tale seems to have been a reaffirmation of a part of one of Franklin's earliest works, *A Dissertation on Liberty and Necessity, Pleasure and Pain.* With a youthful arrogance which he was later to lose, he had then not only proclaimed that "Evil *doth not exist,*" but attempted to prove it. He had deduced from the axiomatic assumptions that God was all-good, all-wise, and all-powerful, the fact that evil *could not* exist.[6] This probably

4. Franklin, *Papers,* I: 102.

5. Benjamin Franklin, *The Writings of Benjamin Franklin,* ed. by Albert Henry Smyth (New York: Haskell House Publishers, Ltd., 1970), X: 123.

6. Later in life, Franklin regarded this essay as an "Erratum." However, it appears that what he was recanting was not the denial that evil existed, but, rather, the deduction which he made from that supposition—that virtue and vice were meaningless distinctions. Instead he came to believe "that tho' certain Actions might not be bad *because* they were forbidden . . . yet probably the Actions might be forbidden *because* they were bad for us, or commanded *because* they were beneficial to us, in their own Natures, all the Circumstances of things considered." As the last phrase indicates, Franklin still denied that there existed anything which in and of itself could be called evil, but admitted that there were things which were usually harmful to man. Benjamin Franklin, *Autobiography,* ed. by Leonard W. Labaree *et al.* (New Haven: Yale University Press, 1964), pp. 96, 115.

was still the basic reasoning which lay behind the "Arabian Tale." Indeed, even the specific argument used in the "Arabian Tale," that man's faculties were too weak to comprehend the universe properly, was more than hinted at in the *Dissertation*. The *Dissertation*'s title-page motto, taken from Dryden, read:

> Whatever is, is in its Causes just
> Since all Things are by Fate; but purblind Man
> Sees but a part o' th' Chain, the nearest Link,
> His Eyes not carrying to the equal Beam
> That poises all above.[7]

As a young man, Franklin was not yet ready to apply this to himself, but by the time he wrote the "Arabian Tale" he seems to have been willing to include himself among "purblind Man."

Franklin was not the only colonist to include the chain of being in his credo. Ezra Stiles included in this 1752 creed, "I believe the Moral World is composed of Intelligences, of various Orders, succeeding in a most beautiful Gradation in the Scale of Being, from infinite to nothing." [8] And Samuel Johnson, in his *Elementa Philosophica* (but not in his purely religious creeds), stated:

> I cannot reasonably doubt but there are others of various orders above me, which may probably have other and nobler senses than those five narrow inlets that I am acquainted with, and confined to, and far greater and nobler abilities, both of understanding and activity, than I am furnished with. Such I can easily conceive to be possible; and, from the various gradations in perfection of being, in the several tribes below me, it is very probable there may be the like gradations in several tribes of beings above me.[9]

A contributor to the American Philosophical Society made use of the chain of being to justify "useless" scientific curiosity. "All the works of nature are linked the one to the other and form a whole, in the immensity

7. Franklin, *Papers*, I: 55-71.
8. Morgan, *Gentle Puritan*, p. 69.
9. Johnson, *Works*, II: 458.

of which we only perceive some points which appear to us detached, because those which unite them are concealed from us." Therefore all knowledge about nature is of value, for "that which appears futile, should be grasped like the others, and in possessing ourselves of it we should be assured that we have hold of a chain, the precious links of which will be discovered by time." [10]

## II

> As those who unripe veins in mines explore,
> On the rich bed again the warm turf lay,
> Till time digests the yet imperfect ore
> And know it will be gold another day.[11]

The concept of the chain of being served as a means of giving a structure to nature. Nature did not consist of a jumble of disorganized and unrelated species; it was an array of interlinked and carefully ordered entities. By using the chain of being, man was able to place any entity in its proper place, and determine its relationship to all other beings. Therefore, many implications and uses of the chain of being are found not in general discussions of the theory, but rather, in its application, explicitly or implicitly, to specific links in the chain.

The lowest link in the chain was inanimate matter, stones and minerals. There were a variety of traditional theories still current in the eighteenth century concerning their origin. The most venerable theory was that derived from Aristotle, which combined Aristotle's belief in the mutability of the four elements with the theory, stated by Aristotle in *Meteorologica,* that the heat of the sun raised two exhalations which, if trapped in the bowels of the earth, form metals and fossils.

A second theory, which was an elaboration upon the first, was that

---

10. D'Aboville, "Two Hearts Found in One Partridge," *Transactions of the American Philosophical Society,* II (1786): 330-35. See also Thomas Sprat, *History of the Royal Society,* quoted in Greenleaf, *Order, Empiricism and Politics,* pp. 107-8.

11. Dryden, quoted in John Arthos, *The Language of Natural Description in Eighteenth-Century Poetry* (Ann Arbor, Mich.: The University of Michigan Press, 1949), p. 302.

typical of the alchemists. This theory identified the two exhalations of Aristotle with sulphur and mercury; not, indeed, common sulphur and mercury, but the philosopher's sulphur and mercury. A third basic constituent of minerals was added to alchemical theory by Paracelsus—salt. There were, of course, many elaborate variations upon these ideas, and naturally the possiblity of altering the nature of a mineral by altering its constituents was stressed.

A third theory, first clearly stated in the sixteenth century by Georgius Agricola, held that minerals were created when a certain *succus lapidifus* or "lapidifying juice," in the earth, evaporated. The residue it left behind became minerals.

A fourth theory, popular in the sixteenth and seventeenth centuries and given renewed influence in the second half of the seventeenth by Joseph Pitton de Tournefort, held that stones and minerals literally grew from seed. There was thus no essential difference between the generation of minerals, plants, and animals: all grew from seeds. This theory, like all other theories, of course had numerous variations, as each author added his own touch. Some versions required the heat of the earth for the seeds to develop; other versions spoke of a *vis plastica*.

A fifth theory, which was surprisingly weak in the eighteenth century when one considers its obvious attractions, held that God had simply created the minerals during the creation.

In all but the last theory, heat was often believed to be of great importance in the creation of minerals. Some versions stressed the fire at the center of the earth, while others added the occult influences of the planets and other heavenly bodies. Quite common was the belief that the heat of the sun was necessary for metals to develop fully. The most fully developed and hence most perfect metal was, of course, gold, and it was often assumed that precious metals and gems could best be found in tropical regions, where the sun was at its hottest. The precious metals and gems seem to have been visualized as tropical fruits ripening under the hot tropical sun until they were ready for the plucking.[12]

---

12. Frank Dawson Adams, *The Birth and Development of the Geological Sciences* (Baltimore: The Williams & Wilkins Company, 1938), pp. 78-94, 277-307; Arthos, *The Language of Natural Description in Eighteenth-Century Poetry,* pp. 300-6; Edgar Hill Duncan, "The Natural History of Metals and Minerals in the Universe of Milton's *Paradise Lost,"* *Osiris,* XI (1954): 386-421; Stearns, *Science in the British Colonies of America,* pp. 9-13.

This belief explains the otherwise rather curious assumption of William Byrd that he would find gold and silver mines in his travels, because he was in the same latitude as gold- and silver-bearing regions elsewhere in the world, such as Portugal, Thrace, "Pactolus in Lesser Asia," the African Gold Coast, New Mexico, and Santa Barbara. If precious metals were formed by the sun, it was natural to expect precious metals to be found at about the same degrees of latitude around the world, since each degree received the same amount of solar influence (excluding such factors as clouds) along its entire circumference.[13]

All theories, again excepting that of direct creation by God, held that minerals, in some sense, developed and grew. Moreover, the gestation period of minerals generally appeared to be calculated not in geological eons but in periods comparable to those of animal and plant life. This in itself tended to bridge the gap between the animate and inanimate worlds. It also lent itself to the formation of popular analogies between plant and mineral life.

There were other ways in which various of these theories fitted in with the chain of being. Both the Aristotelian exhalation and the alchemical mercury-sulphur-salt theories considered such minerals as iron, copper, silver, and gold not to be specific and differentiated substances. Rather, they were thought of as points on a continuum that stretched from lead to gold. Under the proper circumstances, whether by the influence of heavenly bodies on the metals in the earth or by efforts of an alchemist in his laboratory, metals could be moved from one point on the continuum to a higher point. Iron was not a distinct substance; it was merely imperfect gold. There were no gaps, no unbridgeable differences, between a dull stone and a nugget of gold.

The theory that minerals and stones grew from seeds could also utilize the continuum, as they not only would grow in size but also might ripen into richer metals or precious gems. Even more important, this theory bridged the gap between the organic and inorganic worlds. Indeed, it virtually eliminated the distinction. Both organic creatures and inorganic substances grew from seeds, and perhaps both grew under the influence of the Neoplatonic plastic spirit. In this most vitalistic of all theories,

13. William Byrd, *Histories of the Dividing Line Betwixt Virginia and North Carolina*, ed. by Percy G. Adams and William K. Boyd (New York: Dover Publications, Inc., 1967), pp. 192, 240, 242.

mineral growth was not merely analogous to plant growth; it was identical to it.

Such theories, at times clearcut but often blurring into one another, were common in eighteenth-century America. At the start of the century, Samuel Willard explained that minerals "were at first made in the Earth, and its womb was then impregnated, and made fruitful of them, which are continually generated by Influence of the Sun, on the Places naturally adapted for them." [14] In about 1706 Edward Taylor wrote:

> Herein doth lie the Path of Natures race
> She runneth ore from goal to goale apace . . .
> Her darksom root bears melancholy Rocks,
> Breeds Stones, Lead, Churlish iron in their plots.
> Her brighter Spirits with good warmth refinde
> Through her rich Calender breed richer kinde
> And so hath Silver bright and Gold more fine
> And sparkling Gems that mock the Sun and 'ts Shine.
> Her Spirit that ascen'd the florid Bough
> Of Vegetation over do allow
> Our Eyes a Paradise of spekld Spots. [15]

Later in the poem, sensible and rational creatures are also discussed; each—minerals, vegetation, animals, and men—being a part of the same hierarchical continuum, the great chain of being.

These theories of growing minerals were available to the colonists throughout the eighteenth century from a variety of British sources. Chambers's *Cyclopedia* noted that "Some attribute the formation of *minerals* to the action of the sun without. . . ," but referred the reader to its article on stones where it devoted over a column to Tournefort's theory that stones grew from seeds and were nourished by juices brought up by their roots. Considerably less space was given to the theory that all stones had solidified out of a liquid. [16]

Benjamin Martin's *Philosophical Grammer,* first published in 1735 and frequently reprinted, treated the issue in question-and-answer form.

---

14. Willard, *A Compleat Body of Divinity,* p. 117.

15. Donald E. Stanford, "The Great Bones of Claverack, New York, 1705," *New York History,* XL (January 1959): 56-57.

16. Chambers, *Cyclopedia* (7th ed.), "Minerals," "Stones." See also "Metal."

Do Minerals, Metals, Stones, &c. grow in the Earth?

Undoubtedly: Yea, it is well known that divers Mines, when emptied of Stone, Metal, &c. have, after a while, recruited again. Also divers stony, sparry Isicles, and other stalactical Substances, may be daily seen engendered from the Exudations of some petrifying Juices out of the rocky Earth in great Caves; . . .[17]

William Derham assumed that vegetables and minerals were similar in their requirements when he noted, in 1715, that some strata of the earth are "for the Service of the vegetable Kingdom; some for the Generation and Nourishment of Minerals and Metals; . . ." [18] He continued with this assumption when he noted that absolute darkness would result in "great inconveniences" for "Vegetables, Minerals, and every other such part of the Creation. . . ." [19]

Students of Charles Alston, lecturer in botany and materia medica at Edinburgh until his death in 1760, heard a full but somewhat agnostic account of the theory that minerals grew like plants.

The principal arguments for the vegetation or rather growing of minerals are taken ($\alpha$) from the position and figure of the metalic veins; ($\beta$) the form in which gold or silver are often found, as of hairs, herbs, trees, &c. ($\gamma$) the real growth of lead, tin, iron which is strongly asserted by Agricola. . . . But whether the growing of minerals, if real, is more analogous to cristalisation or accretion, than to nutrition, let others determine.[20]

17. Benjamin Martin, *The Philosophical Grammer* (7th ed.; London: J & F Rivington, 1769), p. 257. For its use as a textbook at Yale, see John C. Schwab, "The Yale College Curriculum, 1701-1901," *Educational Review*, XXII (June 1901): 4-5.

18. William Derham, *Astro-Theology: Or, A Demonstration of the Being and Attributes of God From a Survey of the Heavens* (7th ed.: London: W. Innys and R. Manby, 1738), p. 133. See also William Derham, *Physico-Theology: Or, a Demonstration of the Being and Attributes of God, From His Works of Creation* (Glasgow, Scotland: Robert Urie, 1758), p. 99n.

19. Derham, *Astro-Theology*, p. 179.

20. Charles Alston, *Lectures on the Materia Medica* (London: Edward & Charles Dilly, 1770), I: 23.

Students of Joseph Black, at the University of Glasgow, would have heard him speak about both the role of heat in producing minerals and about mineral's "growth & Nourishment." [21] These organic metaphores, continually used, were perhaps as influential as the detailed theories themselves in linking the mineral and vegetable kingdoms.

In the colonies, at Harvard, Morton's *Compendium* taught the alchemist's theory of the generation of minerals. "METTAL (they say) is a perfect Mixt body generated in the Veins of the Earth out of Sulphur ( ♄ ) and Mercury ( ☿ ) or Quicksilver by vertue of the heavens and Elements. . . ." [22] Morton pointed out, however, the fact that "Men are not well agreed whether to call them degrees or Kinds," that is, whether each metal was a specific substance, or whether each was just a point upon the continuum on which all metals were ordered. But after noting this conflict, he discussed only the opinion of "The Chymists [who] say that all mettals are Speciffically the Same, only there are two great principles of constitution ( ♄ ) [sulphur] which hath more of Earth, and ( ☿ ) [mercury] more congenial to water, and according to the Various Combynations of those in Quantity and Quality, and their different purity, and Concretion, give the Various differences which we call Kinds of Mettal." [23]

The so-called middle minerals, such as salt, sulphur, mercury, and antimony, were described by Morton as "a Sort of Imperfect Metall or Mineral juyces, contributing to the constitution of Mettalls; . . ." [24] For the origins of stones, however, Morton was eclectic, and argued that stones were formed by a mechanical crystallization from a mineral-bearing fluid, a variation of Agricola's theory. [25]

Morton laid stress upon the difference between the way plants grew and the way minerals grew. When discussing vegetative growth, Morton explained that stones grew by "Accression . . . which is by Juxtaposition; or Vicinity of convertible matters; whereas this is by Inward reception, and (Even in Plants) as it use[th] to be said to vitall applycation of the

21. Joseph Black, "Lectures on Chemistry," MS notes by C. Dilloyes, I: 91, 126 (Historical Society of Pennsylvania).

22. Morton, *Compendium Physicae,* p. 117.

23. *Ibid.,* pp. 118-19.

24. *Ibid.,* p. 125.

25. *Ibid.,* pp. 113-14.

Nutriment; . . ." [26] That is, a stone grew by adding additional matter to its exterior, but a plant grew by ingesting matter different from itself and converting that matter into its own substance. Or, in the Scholastic language which Morton sometimes used, "it partially Introduceth its own form in the matter" it is digesting.[27]

It is probable that the doctrine of the three souls (which, as we have seen, Morton used as the framework for his discussion of all organic beings) strongly mitigated against treating minerals as being too similar to plants. Minerals and stones lacked the vegetative soul; therefore, as organic growth and nutrition were powers of the vegetative soul, minerals could not possess these powers. With the collapse of the doctrine of the three souls, however, one difficulty disappeared, and this may help to account for the growth in popularity of Tournefort's seed theory at the end of the seventeenth century and in the eighteenth. Whatever the causes, it surely increased in popularity at Harvard, where in 1767 a master's thesis affirmatively answered the question, "are all bodies (metals and stones not excepted) produced from seed?" [28]

Indeed, the middle and latter portions of the eighteenth century exhibited at least as strong a belief as had the earlier period in the theory that minerals grew just like plants. William Livingston of New York in 1747 praised the sun for its role in producing roses and forests, and added

> Deep in teeming earth, the rip'ning ore
> Confesses thy consolidating power.[29]

If "consolidating" is a somewhat mechanical expression, "rip'ning" is not, and the juxtaposition of images clearly gave the passage an organic implication. As late as 1799 Thomas Jefferson spoke of "the thousands and thousands of instances of the renovative power constantly exercised by nature for the reproduction of all her subjects, animal, vegetable, and mineral." [30]

26. *Ibid.*, p. 134.
27. *Ibid.*, pp. 126-27.
28. Young, "Subjects for Master's Degree in Harvard College," p. 131.
29. William Livingston, *Philosophic Solitude* (New York: James Parker, 1747), ll. 183-84.
30. Thomas Jefferson, "A Memoir on the Discovery of Certain Bones of a Quadruped of the Clawed Kind in the Western Part of Virginia," *Transactions of the American Philosophical Society*, IV (1799): 256.

A full discussion of the growing of mineral ore, specifically iron ore, is found in an 1804 essay by James Thacher on iron mining and manufacturing in Plymouth, Massachusetts. There, iron ore was found in ponds, and after it was mined it took about twenty-five years to regrow.[31] Indeed, to aid its regrowth, after removal of the bog ore

> the workmen are careful to cover the cavity with loose earth, leaves, bushes, and other rubbish, calculating upon another growth in ten or fifteen years; not infrequently, however, this expectation is realized in seven years, and it may be remarked, as a curious fact in natural history, that in the short period of four or five years, these vegetable substances, even branches of trees, suffer a complete transition to a metallick state. Does not this indicate an analogy between mettalick and organick substances?" [32]

> [As we have seen at the head of this section, Dryden described the same practice in England many years earlier.]

This happy result, however, did not always occur, and Dr. Thacher duly noted that after one formerly productive pond was mined out, its "growth [being] remarkably slow, very little ore has been produced from it for twenty five years past." [33] Indeed, like any plant, the iron ore needed water to grow, and "diverting the course of the water subverts the production of ore no less effectively than vegetation is destroyed by depriving the stamina of its nutriment." [34]

Not only did this growing iron ore illustrate the analogies between the mineral and vegetable kingdoms; it also demonstrated the continuum that existed within the mineral kingdom.

> By investigating their internal texture, the process of metallisation from earthly and stoney substances appears to be clearly demonstrated. In one fragment the stone, or original substance, is found

31. James Thacher, "Observations Upon the Natural Production of Iron Ores," *Collections of the Massachusetts Historical Society,* 1st Series, IX: 254.

32. *Ibid.,* pp. 256-57.

33. *Ibid.,* p. 255.

34. *Ibid.,* p. 256.

just assuming the metallick character, another exhibits the process in a more advanced state resembling mouldering wood, and in the third the stone or earthly substance is obliterated and the process perfected; . . .[35]

## III

There is, as it were, a certain chain of created beings, according to which they seem all to have been formed, and one thing differs so little from some other, that if we hit upon the right method we shall scarcely find any limits between them. This no one can so well observe as he who is acquainted with the greatest number of species. Does not everyone perceive that there is a vast difference between a stone and a monkey? But if all the intermediate beings were set to view in order, it would be difficult to find the limits between them. The polypus [hydra] and the sea-moss join the vegetable and animal kingdoms together, for the plants called Confervae [algae] and the animals called Sertularia [marine polyzoa and hydroids] are not easy to distinguish. The corals connect the animal, vegetable, and the fossil worlds.[36]

The concept of the chain of being also had important implications for the overall structure of the organic world. Thus Benjamin Waterhouse used the concept as the organizing principle for his late eighteenth-century lectures on nature.

What led some philosophers to believe that all nature was animated. The imperceptible translations of inert matter to organized—from a vegetating body to the lowest order of animals.

Of the Zoophytes, or that class of beings which connects, animated and insensible nature.

35. *Ibid.,* p. 255.

36. Carl Linnaeus, quoted in Philip C. Ritterbush, *Overtures to Biology: The Speculations of Eighteenth-Century Naturalists* (New Haven: Yale University Press, 1964), p. 113.

On the SCALE OF BEINGS

The Universe a system whose very essence consists in *subordination.*

SYSTEMA NATURAE of *Linnaeus* briefly explained.

A connection between all ranks and orders by subordinate degrees necessary towards sustaining the magnificent fabric of the world. Wide distinctions made in the *dignity* and *perfections* of animals, little or none in their happiness. Concerning the various degrees of perfection, beauty, strength and understanding.[37]

Waterhouse clearly appears to have adopted the optimistic position of many eighteenth-century advocates of the chain of being. He felt that the lesser links in the chain had no grounds for complaining that they were not different from what they were, for all were equal in happiness; and the very distinction between higher and lower forms of existence was what made the universe beautiful and perfect. If all were as beautiful as butterflies, as strong as elephants, or as knowledgeable as angels, the universe would be less perfect because possible modes of existence would not be fulfilled.[38]

At times, specific creatures were found which were felt to exemplify the interrelatedness of all creatures in the chain of being. To Alexander Garden, the South Carolina doctor and botanist after whom Linnaeus named the gardenia, the toad-fish [*Gadus tau*] was "a fish that connects two classes together, and is probably the most distinguishable, middle, or connecting, link in the scale."[39] To Cadwallader Colden (as to Linnaeus and others) the polypus (which actually was a sedentary animal) was "a notable instance of the Chain between Vegetables & Animals & which probably extends through the Whole Creation from the lowest degree of Vegetation in Minerals to the most perfect animal."[40]

37. Benjamin Waterhouse, *A Synopsis of a Course of Lectures, on the Theory and Practice of Medicine* (Boston: Adams and Nourse, 1786), pp. 12-13.

38. See Lovejoy, *The Great Chain of Being,* pp. 214-17.

39. James Edward Smith, *A Selection of the Correspondence of Linnaeus and Other Naturalists,* I: 314, 305.

40. Colden, *The Letters and Papers of Cadwallader Colden,* III: 45. For a discussion of the eighteenth-century reaction to the theory of zoophytes and the discovery of the polypus, see Ritterbush, *Overtures to Biology,* pp. 122-141.

The very concept of a perfect and eternal chain of being made it seem inconceivable to many that any creature could ever have become extinct. Thus, Thomas Jefferson felt certain that the mammoth [41] still existed someplace, for

> Such is the oeconomy of nature, that no instance can be produced of her having permitted any one race of her animals to become extinct; of her having formed any link in her great work so weak as to be broken. To add to this, the traditionary testimony of the Indians, that this animal still exists in the northern and western parts of America, would be adding the light of a taper to that of the meridian sun.[42]

Jefferson, at least on this one issue, preferred metaphysical logic to human evidence. A decade later he reaffirmed his belief in the chain of being, and showed why it was so necessary for him to believe it eternal, when he argued that the "megalonyx," the fossil remains of a great sloth which Jefferson incorrectly identified as a large carnivore, could not be extinct. "For if one link in nature's chain might be lost, another and another might be lost, till this whole system of things should evanish by piece-meal; . . ." [43]

There did develop in the eighteenth century, however, a current of thought which opposed this static chain of being. This countercurrent was generated as part of the eighteenth century's interest in theories of a changing and developing earth and in the origins and nature of fossils of unknown and presumably extinct animals. This acceptance of the possibility of change, even of evolutionary development, did not necessarily refute the concept of a chain of being. Instead, to accommodate the

41. Although Jefferson consistently called them mammoths, they were in fact mastodons. Both mammoth and mastodon fossils are found in North America and for a time there was confusion over the two. See George Gaylord Simpson, "The Beginnings of Vertebrate Paleontology in North America," *Proceedings of the American Philosophical Society*, LXXXVI (September 1942): 142-51.

42. Jefferson, *Notes on Virginia*, pp. 53-54.

43. Jefferson, "A Memoir on the Discovery of Certain Bones," pp. 255-56. For a discussion of Jefferson and the megalonyx, see Edwin T. Martin, *Thomas Jefferson: Scientist* (New York: Henry Schuman, Inc., 1952), pp. 107-11.

possibility of change and development, what has been called the "temporalization of the chain of being" occurred.

The traditional chain of being was customarily conceived of as eternally existing and immutable in time, but the temporalized chain of being was seen as developing in time. The traditional concept held that everything which could exist did exist; therefore everything which would exist must always have existed and must always continue to exist. Even after being reconciled with traditional Christian beliefs, this meant that every species which ever existed must have continued to be in existence from the end of the days of creation to the Last Judgment, in other words, for virtually all time though not for all eternity. The temporalized chain of being, on the other hand, while agreeing that all which could exist would exist, did not demand that they all exist at the same time. Just as not all animals had to be in existence in any one specific geographical region, so they did not all have to be in existence at any one specific time. Some species might exist in one era and others in another, with no one era containing the complete chain of being; but, when viewed from the standpoint of eternity, the complete chain of being would be seen as existing.[44]

This evolutionary chain of being permitted Nicholas Collins to argue in 1799: "The analogy so visible in the order of Divine Providence makes it very probable that a rude earth and barbareous men had congenial animals; and that some of these became extinct in the course of moral and physical improvement." This statement demonstrates the typical bias toward evolution that resulted from the temporalization of the chain of being. It was used in this instance, however, to explain why dragons were no longer to be found on earth.[45]

44. For the scientific developments, see John C. Greene, *The Death of Adam: Evolution and Its Impact on Western Thought* (Ames, Iowa: The Iowa State University Press, 1959), *passim* and especially chaps. III and IV. It should also be noted that the theories of growing and ripening minerals would have fitted very well into this framework.

For the change in the concept of the chain of being, see Lovejoy, *The Great Chain of Being*, chap. IX.

45. Nicholas Collins, "Philological View of Some Very Ancient Words in Several Languages," *Transactions of the American Philosophical Society*, IV (1799): 506-7.

More popular than the argument from analogy was the assumption that extinction of a species probably occurred only because of the needs of mankind and through the intervention of man. Thus John Filson, the early historian of Kentucky, managed with great difficulty to reconcile the extinction of the mammoth with his belief in the chain of being.

> Can then so great a link have perished from the chain of nature? Happy we that it has. How formidable an enemy to the human species, an animal as large as the elephant, the tyrant of the forests, perhaps the devourer of man! Nations, such as Indians, must have been in perpetual alarm. The animosities among the various tribes must have been suspended till the common enemy, who threatened the very existence of all, should be exterpated. To this circumstance we are probably indebted for a fact, which is perhaps singular in its kind, the extinction of a whole race of animals from the system of nature.[46]

In 1801 James G. Graham pondered over the reason "why Providence should have destroyed an animal or species it once thought proper to create. . . . If, however, they were voracious, it must appear happy for the human race that they are extinct, by whatever means." [47] In 1799 George Turner had had "no hesitation in believing, that they [fossils] belonged to some link in the chain of animal creation, which, like those of the Mammoth, has long been lost." He admitted that he thus differed with Jefferson but simply dismissed "the benevolent persuasion, that no link in the chain of creation will ever be suffered to perish. . . ." But he too suggested that the "Mammoth may have been at once the terror of the forest and of man!—And may not the human race have made the extirpation of this terrific disturber a common cause?" [48]

46. John Filson, *The Discovery, Settlement, and Present State of Kentucke* (Wilmington: John Adams, 1784), p. 36.

47. James G. Graham, "Further Account of Fossil Bones in Orange and Ulster [N.Y.] Counties," *Medical Repository and Review of American Publications*, IV (1801): 214.

48. George Turner, "Memoir on the Extraneous Fossils, Denominated Mammoth Bones," *Transactions of the American Philosophical Society*, IV (1799): 510-18.

Not all were willing to accept this thesis. A 1786 contributor to *The Columbian Magazine,* after quoting the English anatomist William Hunter to the same effect, exploded in defense of the traditional position.

> This sentence, I apprehend, conveys an idea injurious to the Deity; who, at the creation, wanted neither foresight to discover how detrimental so powerful an enemy must prove to the human, as well as animal race, or benevolence to prevent the evil, without requiring or depending on experience. I believe our globe, and every part and particle thereof, came out of the hand of its creator as perfect as he intended it should be, and will continue in exactly the same state (as to its inhabitants at least) till its final dissolution. Particular species of animals may become extinct in some places, as wolves in the British Islands, but I cannot see any reason to suppose any, the minutest animalcule, even inferior to those discoverable by the microscope, has been, or ever will be, annihilated, before this heaven and earth are done away.[49]

Despite such opposition, the reality of extinction was accepted by the nineteenth century. Rembrandt Peale noted in 1803 that "formerly it was as unphilosophical and impious to say that any thing ceased to exist which had been created, as it is now to say the reverse. . . ." [50] Nevertheless, throughout almost all of the eighteenth century the position of Jefferson, the belief in a static and full chain of being, was dominant. Thus the principle of plentitude led one of Benjamin Franklin's correspondents, who argued that "we find all Nature crowded with life," to explain correctly in 1753 that the phosphorescence which was sometimes seen at sea was the product of the many small animals which lived there.[51]

Nor were phosphorescent creatures the only strange form of life found in the sea. The principle of plentitude, that everything which could exist did exist, combined with the obscurity of the ocean depths and the

49. "Description of Bones, &c. found near the River Ohio," *The Columbian Magazine or Monthly Miscellany,* I (November 1786): 106.

50. Rembrandt Peale, *An Historical Disquisition on the Mammoth* (London: printed for E. Lawrence by C. Mercier, 1803), p. 75. See also the discussion in Daniel J. Boorstin, *The Lost World of Thomas Jefferson* (Boston: Beacon Press, 1960), pp. 255-56n9.

51. Franklin, *Experiments and Observations on Electricity,* p. 275.

common habit of reasoning by analogy, led to the assumption that much of life on earth was duplicated at sea. In other words, the eighteenth century believed in mermaids! [52] After all, men could read Locke's statement of the chain of being (made in support of the proposition that there exist many species of angels), and learn that

> There are fishes that have wings, and are not strangers to the airy region: and there are some birds that are inhabitants of the water, whose blood is cold as fishes, and their flesh so like in taste that the scrupulous are allowed them on fish-days. There are animals so near of kin to birds and beasts that they are in the middle between both: amphibious animals link the terrestrial and aquatic together; seals live at land and sea, and porpoises have the warm blood and entrails of a hog; not to mention what is confidently reported of mermaids, or sea-men. [53]

Cotton Mather reported in 1716 that several fishermen had seen a Triton with a human top and a fish bottom. [54] *The American Magazine or Monthly Chronicle for the British Colonies,* a colonial journal which frequently printed mathematical and scientific essays, in 1757 gave a favorable summary of a portion of a recent English translation of Erich Pontoppidan's *A Natural History of Norway.* Pontoppidan had written about mermaids, but *The American Magazine,* preferring the unique status of man to the principle of plentitude, noted that the very existence of mermaids

> is even doubted by many sensible people, on account of the fabulous relations concerning them. On this subject, indeed, the pride of man has urged with some degree of plausibility, that tho' there may be a pretty general resemblance and analogy between terrestrial and sea-animals, yet man, who is more expressly and immediately the Image of his *Maker,* is exempt from this resemblance both of his figure and his faculties.

52. See Lovejoy, *The Great Chain of Being,* p. 366.

53. John Locke, *An Essay Concerning Human Understanding,* III, vi, 12.

54. Kittredge, "Cotton Mather's Scientific Communications to the Royal Society," pp. 38-39.

Fortunately for man's pride, Pontoppidan was willing to call his creatures "sea apes" instead of "mermaids," and in that case the reviewer was willing to agree that the existence of "such an animal is all he contends for; and of this he has given many convincing proofs, founded on the testimony of some hundreds of persons of undoubted credit and veracity. . . ." Indeed, of one such account of a merman and a sea-calf found together dead on a rock, the reviewer ignored his earlier scruples and sagely commented, "*Indeed, it is analogous enough, to think that a* Seaman *should covet a repast* of Sea-veal." [55]

*The New-England Courant* devoted virtually all of its front page one day in 1726 to a translation of an encounter with a merman off the coast of Brest. The creature was described in detail:

> The Monster is about eight Feet long: His Skin is brown and tawny, without any Scales: All his Motions are like those of Men, the Eyes of a proportionable Size, a little Mouth, a large and flat Nose, very white Teeth, black Hair, the Chin covered with a mossy beard, a sort of Whisker under the Nose, the Ears like those of Men, Fins between the Fingers of his Hands and Feet, like those of Ducks. In a word, he is like a well shaped Man.[56]

The *Virginia Gazette* reported a similar capture at Exeter, England, about a decade later.[57] In 1762 an almanac reported the capture of a mermaid in the Netherlands. She had long black hair, a human face, "Breasts and Belly to her Navel were perfect," and she had the tail of a fish.[58]

Aquatic parallels to man were only an anomaly in the chain of being. Man was usually conceived as having his own very special place in the chain. He was the highest of animals but the lowest of intellectual beings. He was the middle link in the chain of being which connected the material and intellectual worlds. According to Pope's famous lines, man was

55. *American Magazine or Monthly Chronicle for the British Colonies,* I (October 1757): 29.

56. *The New-England Courant,* April 16-April 23, 1726.

57. *Virginia Gazette,* April 21-April 28, 1738.

58. Abraham Weatherwise [pseud.], *Father Abraham's Almanack . . .* for . . . 1762 (Philadelphia: Dunlap).

> Placed on this isthmus of a middle state,
> A being darkly wise, and rudely great:
> With too much knowledge for the Sceptic side,
> With too much weakness for the Stoic's pride,
> He hangs between; in doubt to act, or rest,
> In doubt to deem himself a God, or Beast;
> In doubt his Mind or Body to prefer.[59]

The colonists agreed, and called man the *"Equator of the Universe,"* [60] "the Link uniting Divinity and Matter," [61] and a being "in a gradation but a little lower than the angelic world." [62]

Not only did the chain of being determine man's place in nature, it still was occasionally used to order human society and government. Even in the eighteenth century, the traditional correspondences were still made between human society and other links in the chain of being, such as a well-ordered beehive.[63] An equally traditional comparison was also made between the human body and the state, the body politic, which comparison served to point up the necessity for each member of the society to carry out his appointed task, just as each member of the body carried out its assigned functions:

> All who understand the Nature of *Society,* see a manifest Analogy between a *natural Body,* and a *Body politic.* Now if the natural Body be supposed in Danger of perishing; and the Hands refused to administer proper Nourishment, or the Stomack to receive and concoct it, when administered: If the Eyes and Feet are on contrary Sides of the Question, the former refusing to direct, and the latter to

59. Pope, *Essay on Man,* epistle II, 3-9.

60. Mather, *The Christian Philosopher,* 293.

61. [Robert Dodsley], *The Oeconomy of Human Life. Part the Second.* (3rd ed.; Philadelphia: Franklin & Hall, 1752), p. 5. This English work was frequently reprinted in the colonies.

62. Richard Ely, *Christ's Minister* (New Haven: Thomas & Samuel Green, 1774), p. 3.

63. *The American Magazine and Historical Chronicle,* III (May 1746): 232, and Lawrence A. Cremin, *American Education: The Colonial Experience, 1607-1783* (New York: Harper & Row, 1970), p. 346.

move;—is it not certain, that such recusant Members do not only hurt their respective Opponents, [sic] but the whole Body? [64]

The *Health,* the *Vigour,* and the *Beauty* of the *Body Politick,* like that of the natural Body, depends on the Proportion, Connection, and mutual subserviency of the several Members. [65]

In the eighteenth century such a metaphor or an analogy was not merely a literary form but an accepted mode of reasoning, albeit not the most conclusive. [66]

It is interesting to note that John Adams also used the chain of being for purposes of political and social theory. In several instances he quoted some of the most famous lines of Pope and Shakespeare about the need for man, both as an individual and as a species, to remain in his "proper place" in the hierarchical chain of being:

> Order is Heaven's first law; and, this confess'd,
> Some are, and must be, greater than the rest;
> More rich, more wise; but who infers from hence,
> That such are happier, shocks all common sense. [67]

Adams made it quite clear, in his "Discourses on Davila" (1790), that human society was bound by the same chain of being which controlled the rest of nature.

64. Samuel Finley, *The Curse of Meroz* (1757), quoted in Alan Heimert, *Religion and the American Mind: From the Great Awakening to the Revolution* (Cambridge: Harvard University Press, 1966), p. 332.

65. John Callender, *A Sermon Pearch'd at the Ordination of Mr. Jeremiah Condy* (Boston: Kneeland & Green, 1739), pp. 20-21.

66. Bert E. Bradley, Jr., "The *Invento* of John Ward," *Speech Monographs,* XXVI (March 1959): 60-61, and Wilbur Samuel Howell, "The Declaration of Independence and Eighteenth-Century Logic," *William and Mary Quarterly,* 3rd Series, XVIII (October 1961): 473.

67. John Adams, *Works,* VI: 264. See also *ibid.,* pp. 265-66, 517.

Nature, which has established in the universe a chain of being and universal order, descending from archangels to microscopic animalcules, has ordained that no two objects shall be perfectly alike, and no two creatures perfectly equal. Although, among men, all are subject by nature to *equal laws* of morality, and in society have a right to *equal laws* for their government, yet no two men are perfectly equal in person, property, understanding, activity, and virtue, or even can be made so by any power less than that which created them; and whenever it becomes disputable, between two individuals or families, which is superior, a fermentation commences, which disturbs the order of all things until it is settled, and each one knows his place in the opinion of the public.[68]

Although the traditional political implications of the chain of being were conservative, it could also be used in support of more radical positions. A modern interpreter of the political thought of Thomas Jefferson and Tom Paine has argued that they used the concept of the chain of being to support a belief in the equality of all men. "Since each species was a single link in the Creator's chain, to show that all men were members of the same species would be the most striking possible confirmation of the indestructible equality of men." [69]

A complete analysis of the role of the chain of being in eighteenth-century political thought is, however, the subject for future study, relating it perhaps to the persistence of other older political theories such as

68. *Ibid.,* pp. 285-86. The objective reality which Adams attributed to the chain of being is further exemplified by a footnote which Adams appended to this passage, in which he refuted an objection to the concept. "This is not a chain of being from God to nothing; *ergo,* not liable to Dr. Johnson's criticism, nor to the reviewer's." Samuel Johnson, the great English lexicographer, had criticized the concept of the chain of being because "the highest Being not infinite must be, as has been often observed, at an infinite Distance below Infinity. . . ." For this, and other objections of Johnson which Adams did not answer, see Lovejoy, *The Great Chain of Being,* pp. 253-54.

69. Daniel J. Boorstin, *The Lost World of Thomas Jefferson* (Boston: Beacon Press, 1960), pp. 61-62. For John Milton's use of both this and the traditional interpretation of the political implications of the chain of being, see C. S. Lewis, *A Preface to Paradise Lost* (New York: Oxford University Press, 1961), pp. 73-81.

passive obedience,[70] the divine right of kings,[71] the binding nature of oaths,[72] the role of the church as a support for the state,[73] and the political uses of the Fifth Commandment and of Romans 13:1-7.[74]

## IV

> Are these bright Luminaries hung on high
> Only to please with twinkling Rays our Eye?
> Or may we rather count each *Star* a *Sun*,
> Round which *full peopled Worlds* their Courses run? [75]

If man was the middle link in the chain of being, what was above him? The most obvious answer, the answer implied by "in gradation but a little

70. Leonard Woods Labaree, *Conservatism in Early American History* (New York: New York University Press, 1948), pp. 74, 152; Stiles, *Literary Diary,* I: 489-90; Samuel Seabury, *St. Peter's Exhortation* (New York: H. Gaine [1777]), pp. 11-12; Oberholzer, *Delinquent Saints,* pp. 223-25.

71. Kaledin, "The Mind of John Leverett," pp. 280-81; Godfrey, *The Prince of Parthia,* p. 36; Winthrop Sargent, *The Loyalist Poetry of the Revolution* (Philadelphia: Collins, 1857), p. 65; Charles Inglis, *The Duty of Honouring the King, Explained and Recommended: In a Sermon, Preached . . . On Sunday, January 30, 1780* (New York: Hugh Gaine, 1780). I would like to thank Professor Leslie F. S. Upton of the University of British Columbia for pointing out the Inglis sermon to me. In addition, there is of course a fairly extensive literature on Jonathan Boucher.

72. Labaree, *Conservatism in Early American History,* p. 147; *The Nature and Importance of Oaths and Juries* (New York: Ja. Parker, 1747), *passim;* Donald George Smith, "Eighteenth Century American Preaching—A Historical Survey" (unpublished doctor of theology dissertation, Northern Baptist Theological Seminary, 1956), p. 248.

73. Johnson, *Works,* I: 300, 359.

74. *The New-England Primer,* ed. by Paul Leicester Ford (New York: Dodd, Mead, and Company, 1897), pp. 119-20; *Brooklyn-Hall Super-Extra Gazette,* June 8, 1782 (a copy can be found in the Long Island Historical Society); Durward T. Stokes, "Different Concepts of Government in the Sermons of Two Eighteenth Century Clergymen," *Historical Magazine of the Protestant Episcopal Church,* XL (March 1971): 83-86; *The Nature and Importance of Oaths and Juries,* p. 22.

75. J. A. Leo Lemay, "Richard Lewis and Augustan American Poetry," *Publications of the Modern Language Association of America,* LXXXIII (March

lower than the angelic world," was the angelic hierarchy. However, to many people in the eighteenth century this was only a partial truth. The eighteenth century believed in angels, but it was also fully prepared to believe in embodied beings from other planets, who might be far superior to man.

The eighteenth-century universe was more than merely Copernican. It was an infinite universe, with stars scattered throughout. The stars were themselves suns surrounded by planets, and these planets, for many, had to be inhabited by intelligent beings.

This belief, or rather, complex of beliefs, was not the direct result of Copernicus. It had been hinted at by Nicholas Cusanus in the fifteenth century, and was at times accepted by men opposed to Copernicus, and vice versa. One of its strongest early advocates was the Renaissance magus Giordano Bruno. It had been supported by Descartes, by the English Neoplatonist Henry More, and had been widely popularized by Bernard Le Bouvier de Fontenelle's famous 1686 work, *On the Plurality of Worlds*.

This theory was of course unsupported by observation, but the eighteenth century saw many cogent arguments on its behalf. Reasons for accepting it included a simple analogy between the earth and the other planets, the assumption that an infinite God would have an infinite creation, and the argument that as God would create nothing in vain, the stars must have planets and the planets inhabitants. There was also the argument from the principle of plentitude that as these planets and inhabitants could exist, they presumably must exist. As Richard Blackmore's *Creation* argued:

> When we on faithful nature's care reflect,
> And her exhaustless energy respect, . . .
> We may pronounce each orb sustains a race
> Of living things adapted to the place. . . .

---

1968): 87. This poem, "A Journey from *Patapsco* to *Annapolis*, April 4, 1730," was printed in the 1730s in a number of colonial newspapers as well as in several English journals including *The Gentleman's Magazine* and *The London Magazine*. *Ibid.*, p. 85.

> Were all the stars, those beauteous realms of light,
> At distance only hung to shine by night,
> And with their twinkling beams to please our sight? . . .
> Are all those glorious empires made in vain? [76]

There was, especially at first, some resistance to this idea. Morton's *Compendium* thought it unlikely that there were other inhabited solar systems.[77] Others may have had doubts, also. Manassah Cutler in the 1760s agreed that God could have placed inhabitants on ten thousand additional worlds, but doubted that He had done so.[78] Nathaniel Dominy did not deny the possibility of other inhabited planets, but, possibly following the Cartesian Rohault's *System of Natural Philosophy,*[79] Dominy did deny the validity of these arguments based on analogy and the chain of being when he noted in a discussion of logic that "we could neither Condemn as false or assert as true that there are in the universe many inhabitants more than mankind and that some planets are the residence of happier and others of more unhappy natives." [80]

Nevertheless, belief in this doctrine soon became widespread. At Harvard, by the 1740s at the latest, it was taught that the other planets were inhabited, for otherwise they would have been created in vain.[81] In 1752, when Justus Forward of Yale was assigned the negative in a disputation over "Whether the Planets are inhabited," the best he could come up with was a series of verbal quibbles such as denying that "wanderers" (the original Greek meaning of planet) were inhabited and

76. See Lovejoy, *The Great Chain of Being,* chap. IV. For the passage from Blackmore see *ibid.,* p. 136.

77. Morton, *Compendium Physicae,* p. 208.

78. Manasseh Cutler, "A Common-Place-Book," 1762 (typescript copy, Beinecke Rare Book and Manuscript Library, Yale University), pp. 70-71.

79. See Rohault, *Rohault's System of Natural Philosophy,* II: 78-79. See also *ibid.,* p. 4.

80. Nathaniel Dominy, "Commonplace Book" (undated eighteenth-century MS, Queens Borough Public Library, Long Island Division), p. 17.

81. Isaac Watts, *The First Principles of Geography and Astronomy,* vol. VIII of *The Works of the Rev. Isaac Watts* (Leeds: Edward Baines, 1813), pp. 268-69. For its use at Harvard, see Louis Franklin Snow, *The College Curriculum in the United States* (privately printed, 1907), p. 47.

denying that the heathen Gods (i.e., Mercury, Venus, Mars, etc.) could be inhabited.[82] David Rittenhouse, the colonies' foremost astronomer, argued that although feared by some to be opposed to Christianity, "the doctrine of a plurality of worlds, is inseparable from the principles of Astronomy . . . ," and added the hope that at least some of the inhabitants of other planets were as yet unfallen.[83] Ezra Stiles was careful to include in the moral world not only unbodied beings (angels) but also "those inhabitants of this earth & the planetary starry universe, all bodied beings, capable of *morals.* "[84] Samuel Johnson, in a sermon which he periodically preached on the creation, citing William Whiston's *Theory of the Earth,* explained that

> By the beginning here we are not to understand the first beginning of all existence and duration, for doubtless there was long before this world which we are concerned in, a vast number of creatures. Innumerable other globes with their inhabitants there might be with whom we have nothing to do, and which therefore Moses was not at all concerned to give an account of.[85]

Other ministers who dealt with the existence of other inhabited worlds ignored the problems it raised in the interpretation of Genesis, and instead considered their inhabitants' role in relationship to grace and salvation. William Prior, an Englishman whose sermon was reprinted in Boston in 1748, noted that Christ's love "is *Grace* which, I make no Doubt, raiseth the Admiration of more Worlds than our's."[86] William

82. Justus Forward, "His Book," MS, Box 1, Folder 3, Justus Forward Collection, Manuscripts and Archives, Sterling Memorial Library, Yale University. For this belief at Yale in the 1780s, see Stiles, *Literary Diary,* II: 418; III: 98, 144; and Dyan Troop Hinckley, "Diary" 1784-85, MS (Yale Manuscripts and Archives, Sterling Memorial Library, Yale University), Dec. 20, 1784.

83. David Rittenhouse, *An Oration* (Philadelphia: John Dunlap, 1775), p. 19.

84. Ezra Stiles, "The Universe or Moral View of the Intellectual World and the Analogy of Nature," MS, Beinecke Rare Book and Manuscript Library, Yale University.

85. Johnson, *Works,* III: 423-24; William Whiston, *New Theory of the Earth* (6th ed.; London: J. Whiston and B. White, 1755), pp. 4-5.

86. William Prior, *A Charge Delivered . . . at Bridgeport, in Dorset* (3rd ed.; Boston: J. Bushell and J. Green for D. Gookin, 1748), p. 55.

Hobby had elaborated on this theme in 1746, and used it to portray an optimistic picture of the universe. After discussing the many men who would undoubtedly be damned, he attempted to redeem the dark picture he had painted.

> . . . that you may not think me void of Charity, I venture to say with Regard to the intelligent Creation in general, there appears to me Ground of Hope and Belief, that the greater Part of them will be happy in the Enjoyment of God, rather than miserable in the want of this Enjoyment. It doth not appear to me becoming the King of Glory, the God whose Name is Love, to exercise his severer beyond his milder & benign Attributes, and so bind down the greater Part of his Subjects in the Chains of eternal Darkness. But what have we to do here with the Intelligencies of other Worlds, with Respect to whom perhaps and probably, all the Inhabitants of this bear but a small Proportion.[87]

It is doubtful if this reflection did much to console those inhabitants of this world who were doomed to damnation!

An unusual variation on this theme was made by the young Benjamin Franklin, who conceived

> that the INFINITE has created many Beings or Gods, vastly superior to Man, who can better conceive his Perfections than we, and return him a more rational and glorious Praise. As among Men, the Praise of the Ignorant or of Children, is not regarded by the ingenious Painter or Architect, who is rather honour'd and pleas'd with the Approbation of Wise men and Artists.
>
> It may be that these created Gods, are immortal, or it may be that after many Ages, they are changed, and Others supply their Places.
>
> Howbeit, I conceive that each of these is exceedingly wise, and good, and very powerful; and that Each has made for himself one

87. William Hobby, *Self-Examination* (Boston: Kneeland & Green, 1746), pp. 159-60.

glorious Sun, attended with a beautiful and admirable System of Planets.[88]

There was, however, relatively little imagination displayed in colonial discussions of nonhuman intelligent beings. Benjamin West did write in one of his many almanacs that one

> Who there [Saturn] inhabits must have other pow'ers
> Juices, and veins and senses, and life than ours.

and

> Strange and amazing must the diff'rence be,
> 'Twixt this dull planet and bright Mercury;
> Yet reason says, nor can we doubt at all,
> Millions of beings dwell on either ball
> With constitutions fitted for that spot.
> Where Providence, all-wise, has fix'd their lot.[89]

Such speculation was rare, however, in colonial America. That other planets and their inhabitants existed was generally accepted and seen as another reason why God the creator should be praised; [90] but there was little echo in colonial America of such flights of fancy as Voltaire's tale of a visit to earth by inhabitants of Saturn and Sirius, the latter visitor having nearly a thousand different senses,[91] or Imanuel Kant's theory that the further away a planet was from its sun, the more highly advanced its inhabitants would be.[92]

88. Franklin, *Papers,* I: 102-3. The origin of this concept has been variously traced to Newton and to the influence of Plato. See I. Bernard Cohen, *Franklin and Newton,* p. 209, and I. Woodbridge Riley, *American Philosophy: The Early Schools* (New York: Dodd, Mead & Co., 1907), pp. 249-54.

89. Benjamin West, *Bickerstaff's Boston Almanack for . . . 1778* (Danvers, Mass.: Russell).

90. See Darlington, *Memorials,* p. 399, and James Bowdoin, "A Philosophical Discourse," *Memoirs of the American Academy of Arts and Sciences,* I (1785): 20.

91. Voltaire, *Micromegas,* in *Candide, Zadig and Selected Stories,* ed. by Donald M. Frame (Bloomington, Ind.: Indiana University Press, 1961).

92. See Lovejoy, *The Great Chain of Being,* pp. 193-94.

## V

It is a Thing beyond all Questions, That among *Rational Beings,* there are some which are *Invisible* to Humane sight; *Spirits* belonging to an Heavenly World, who are called ANGELS. . . .[93]

The highest links in the chain of being, the most perfect created beings, were the angelic and demonic hierarchies. Yes, devils too, for in the natural though not in the moral order of things, devils, being angels gone wrong, were far superior to man.[94] Probably all even remotely orthodox Christians believed in angels and devils. In 1774 Philip Fithian was so furious at the impious statements of a man who swore there was no devil, that he left the room.[95] Angels and devils were traditional elements of Christian belief.

However, belief is one thing, interest and study another. Only in the early years of the eighteenth century was the study of angels, called angelology, still a living science. Samuel Johnson discussed angels in his "Synopsis of Natural History."

(1) They were all created in the beginning at the same time and immediately. (2) They are not pure forms but are really composed of matter and form. (3) They are most fine, spiritual, light and pure. (4) All have one common nature. (5) They have the least of matter and the most of form, hence they are very light, and invisible to us. (6) They are able to contract themselves (but not to a point) and to expand (but not infinitely); hence assume different shapes.[96]

Perhaps the most interesting point that Johnson made was his claim that angels are composed of both form and matter. What the matter

93. Cotton Mather, *Coelestinus* (Boston: Kneeland for Belknap, 1723), pt. I: 12.

94. Hobby, *Self-Examination,* p. 165, and Ebenezer Thayer, *Ministers of the Gospel* (Boston: Garrish, 1727), pp. 13-14.

95. Philip Vickers Fithian, *Journal and Letters of Philip Vickers Fithian,* ed. by Hunter Dickinson Farish (Princeton: Princeton University Press, 1943), p. 194.

96. Johnson, *Works,* II: 45.

consisted of is not clear. In a previous passage Johnson had stated that angels did not "dwell in a body composed of elements." [97] Probably, therefore, their matter was composed of the fifth element, the incorruptible quintessence.

This belief that angels were composed of matter was not unique to Johnson or to Yale. A series of masters' theses at Harvard also affirmed this belief, but, although this thesis appeared five times between 1680 and 1703, it never reappeared after the latter date.[98] Samuel Willard's description of angelic matter, probably first delivered in the early 1700s, was very similar to a description of the quintessence. The matter of angels was finer than elements of normal matter and was not subject to change or corruption. It was the same as the substance of the third heaven, where the saints would dwell. Probably only the fact that Willard had already rejected the Ptolemaic system kept him from identifying the substance of angels with the substance of the crystalline spheres.[99] Even Thomas Robie, who believed angels "to be pure Spiritual Substances [disengaged?] from matter," noted, probably shortly before 1714, that "Some of the Antient [?] have covered the angels . . . with fine Subtle celestial body as Tertellian [,] Agustine [,] Basil [,] Cyril [,] Alex. [,] &c." [100]

The most famous application of this theory is in Milton's *Paradise Lost,* where angels eat food and wear armor into battle for protection. This was neither figurative speech nor sheer invention by Milton. As C. S. Lewis has shown, the Renaissance, under the influence of the "Platonic theology," and unlike both medieval Scholastic and modern beliefs, believed that all souls including angels were corporal. Apparently this became the standard position of English and American Puritanism by the midseventeenth century.[101]

The decline of interest in angelology can be traced in the Mather family. Increase Mather's 1696 teatise, *Angelographia,* was primarily a devotional work. It was not concerned with such abstract questions as the

97. *Ibid.*

98. Young, "Subjects for Master's Degree in Harvard College," p. 146.

99. Willard, *A Compleat Body of Divinity,* pp. 52-53, 111-12, 115.

100. Henry Flynt, "Common Place Book" [1712-24], MS (Massachusetts Historical Society), p. 31.

101. Lewis, *A Preface to Paradise Lost,* pp. 108-13, and Morison, *Harvard College in the Seventeenth Century,* I: 256-57.

nature of angels or their modes of understanding, but rather, with their relationship to human faith and salvation. Increase Mather did not despise the more abstract problems, however. He simply felt that these were of no use for the lay audience he wished to address, and he felt moreover that they were already fully discussed in books easily available to the scholars of New England. When the question of the corporality or spirituality of angels arose, he merely noted, "Whether they have not *Vehicles* of a more Spiritual Nature, than the Bodies of other Creatures, is a Philosophical Question, not proper here Discussed." [102]

By 1723 Cotton Mather, Increase Mather's son, had taken a very different attitude toward such learning. It was not merely useless for a lay audience; it was of no use whatsoever. The only thing we can and do know about angels is what the Bible tells us; all other speculation is in vain.[103]

Although belief in angels continued throughout the century, there was less interest in them. Such comments as there were, were largely limited to the existence of a hierarchy, of orders and ranks, amongst the angels. Both Mathers had agreed that "THERE is an Incomparable *Order* among the Angels of our GOD. It is not for us to say, What the *Order* is: . . ." [104] Whereas Increase Mather carefully cited Colossians to prove the existence of a hierarchy of thrones, dominions, principalities, and powers together with angels and archangels, Cotton Mather was satisfied simply to affirm the existence of an order among angels, and later to casually mention archangels.[105]

In 1747 a Harvard master's thesis had argued that there were distinct orders and offices among angels.[106] In 1747 Charles Chauncey, alluding to

---

102. Increase Mather, *Angelographia* (Boston: B. Green & F. Allen for Samuel Phillips, 1696), "To the Reader," p. 11. For a discussion of Increase Mather and angels, and the decline of interest in angelology, see Robert Middlekauff, *The Mathers: Three Generations of Puritan Intellectuals, 1596-1728* (New York: Oxford University Press, 1971), pp. 175-77.

103. Cotton Mather, *Coelestinus*, pt. I, pp. 24-26, pt. II, pp. 91-92.

104. *Ibid.*, pt. I, p. 14, and Increase Mather, *Angelographia*, pp. 15-16.

105. Cotton Mather, *Coelestinus*, pt. II, p. 92, and Increase Mather *Angelographia*, p. 17.

106. Young, "Subjects for Master's Degree in Harvard College," p. 150. In 1714 it had been affirmed that there was "an order of rank among demons." *Ibid.*, p. 147.

the need for order among men, pointed out that even "among the inhabitants of the upper world, there seems to be a difference of *order*, as well as species; which the scripture intimates, by speaking of them in the various stile of *thrones, dominions, principalities, powers, archangels,* and *angels.*"[107] Perhaps the minimal continuing interest in angelic hierarchies was due to the conservative political implications of the existence of due order and hierarchy even among the spotless and unfallen angels.[108]

There was, however, one exception to the general lack of interest in angels. The ever inquisitive Ezra Stiles became enthralled by angels and the details of their celestial hierarchy. His interest was stimulated in 1772 when he received from London a two-volume folio of Dionysius the Areopagite. Here he first learned of the ordering of angels into three groups of threes.[109] The first and highest triad consisted of the seraphim, cherubim, and thrones. Next came the dominations, virtues, and powers. The last triad included the principalities, archangels, and angels.[110] Stiles (as no doubt many before him) accidentally introduced a variation when he listed the second triad as powers, dominions, and authorities.[111]

Stiles was soon calling Dionysius "a truly divine & sublime Writer," and frequently included him in his daily studies.[112] He fully accepted the traditional belief concerning the origin of Dionysius's celestial hierarchy. "The number, names & arrangement of these Dionysius the Areopagite received from the mouth of St. Paul."[113] This venerable tradition, so

107. Charles Chauncy, *Civil Magistrates* (Boston: by order of the Honorable House of Representatives, 1747), p. 8.

108. See Alan Edward Heimert, "American Oratory: From the Great Awakening to the Election of Jefferson" (unpublished Ph.D. dissertation, Harvard University, 1960), pp. 197-98, and also Greenleaf, *Order, Empiricism, and Politics,* chap. II and *passim.*

109. Stiles, *Literary Diary,* I: 225; III: 470.

110. C. A. Patrides, "Renaissance Thought on the Celestial Hierarchy: The Decline of a Tradition," *Journal of the History of Ideas,* XX (April 1959): 160.

111. Stiles, "Literary Diary," MS, July 21, 1792. Stiles's substitution of "Authorities" for "Virtues" was not unusual. See Gustav Davidson, *A Dictionary of Angels* (New York: The Free Press, 1967), "Authorities." Stiles erred, however, by inserting powers as the first order of the second triad instead of placing it as the third order of that triad.

112. Stiles, *Literary Diary,* I: 299, 369, 374, 476, III: 76, 128, 152, 399, 561.

113. *Ibid.,* III: 470.

influential in the Middle Ages, had already come under sharp attack in the sixteenth and seventeenth centuries.[114] Both Increase and Cotton Mather, adhering to an already established English Protestant position, had explicitly labeled these works false and counterfeit.[115] Stiles, however, remained unconvinced by such criticism, and happily maintained the tradition which gave these works a status barely short of canonical.[116]

Stiles's interest in angels was reinforced by his study of the cabala. His original interest in the cabala had been unconnected with angelic hierarchies. Instead he had been attempting to find evidences of early Jewish trinitarian beliefs.[117] In 1772 he recieved a copy of the classic twelfth-century Hebrew cabalistic work, the *Zohar*.[118] He received lessons in its interpretation from a visiting rabbi, Moses the son of David of Apta, Poland, who also gave him an additional guide in the form of *The Book of the Gate of the Zohar*.[119] This was apparently an introductory cabalistic text, consisting of "Illustrations upon each of the X holy Names, or the X Saphirot." Nor was this discussion at all unusual for Stiles. He had once recorded that he had met with five rabbis at various times, and of the five he had discussed the cabala with at least four.[120]

Stiles's use of the *Zohar* was very similar to his treatment of the works

114. Patrides, "Renaissance Thought on the Celestial Hierarchy," pp. 155-66, and C. A. Patrides, "Renaissance Views on the 'Vnconfused Orders Angellick,' " *Journal of the History of Ideas,* XXIII (April-June 1962): 265-67.

115. Increase Mather, *Angelographia*, p. 16; Cotton Mather, *Coelestinus*, pt. I, pp. 14, 26; Patrides, "Renaissance Thought on the Celestial Hierarchy," pp. 162-64.

116. Stiles, *Literary Diary*, III: 470; MSS Diary, June 11, 1777.

117. *Ibid.*, I: 7. See also Moore, "Ezra Stiles' Studies in the Cabala," *Proceedings of the Massachusetts Historical Society,* LI (March 1918): 298; Joseph Leon Blau, *The Christian Interpretation of the Cabala in the Renaissance* (Port Washington, N.Y.: Kennikat Press, 1965), *passim.*

118. Stiles, *Literary Diary*, I: 298. For the *Zohar,* see Gershom G. Scholem, *Major Trends in Jewish Mysticism* (New York: Schocken Books, 1967), pp. 156-243.

119. Stiles, *Literary Diary,* I: 299, 302, and Stiles, "Literary Diary," MS, Nov. 9 and 23, 1772.

120. Stiles, *Literary Diary,* III: 77-78. His conversation with Moses Bar David has been discussed in the text. For some conversations between Stiles and his friend Rabbi Carigal, see *ibid.*, I: 357-58, 398. On June 21, 1773 they discussed

of Dionysius the Areopagite. He noted that Dionysius had "the same sublime Mysteries as the Zohar." [121] He made the *Zohar* a part of his daily readings.[122] Just as he had denied attacks upon the antiquity and authority of the works of Dionysius the Areopagite, so too he unquestionably accepted the tradition that the *Zohar* was a second-century creation.[123] In both he found a Neoplatonic doctrine of emanations from God. In the one, they were the nine orders of angels; in the other, the ten Sephiroth. His reconciliation of the two authorities, and their impact upon his thought, can best be examined in a study of Stiles's "emblems of the universe."

The first of these emblems was conceived of in 1766, put on paper in either 1770 or 1771, and included in a portrait of Stiles which was painted by Samuel King in August 1771. Stiles described the emblem and its symbolic meanings in detail. It

> is an Emblem of the Universe or intellectual World. It is as it were one sheet of Omniscience. In a central Glory is the name [Yahweh in Hebrew] surrounded with white Spots on a Field of azure, from each Spot ascend three hair Lines denoting the Tendencies of Minds to Deity & Communion with the Trinity in the divine Light; these Spots denote *(Innocency,)* a Spirit, a World, Clusters or Systems of

---

metempsychosis, which had a significant role in postsixteenth-century cabalistic thought. Stiles, *ibid.,* 388; Scholem, *Jewish Mysticism,* pp. 280-84.

For Rabbi Tobiah Ben Jehudah, whom Stiles called "a great *Cabbalist,*" and for Rabbi Bosquila, whom Stiles disapprovingly noted was versed in only the Bible and the cabala but not the Talmud, see Stiles, *Literary Diary,* I: 422, 443. Stiles had met his fifth rabbi, Rabbi Samuel, prior to the development of Stiles's interest in the cabala. It is worth noting, however, that Rabbi Samuel had been educated at Safed, once famous as a center of cabalistic learning. *Ibid.,* I: 594; III: 77n.

Stiles's apparent lack of further contacts with itinerant rabbis after 1775, other than correspondence with Rabbi Carigal, reflects not a decline of interest on Stiles's part but, rather, the disruptive effects of the American Revolution, followed by Stiles's removal from the cosmopolitan town of Newport.

121. *Ibid.,* I: 302, and Stiles, "Literary Diary," MS, Nov. 9, 1772. See also Scholem, *Jewish Mysticism,* pp. 354n, 394-95n.

122. Stiles, *Literary Diary,* I: 329, 555.

123. Moore, "Ezra Stiles' Studies in the Cabala," p. 297.

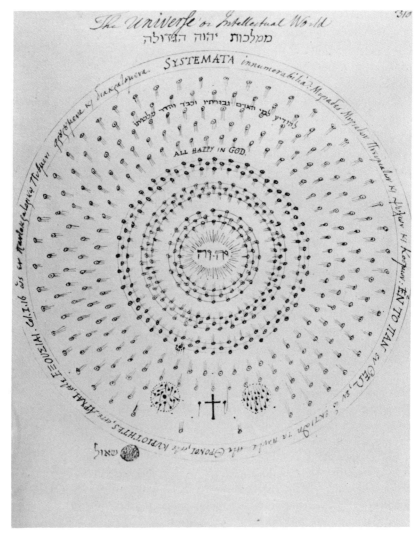

*Fig. 2.* Ezra Stiles's emblem of the universe, from his MS "Literary Diary," July 21, 1792.

Worlds, & their Tendencies to the eternal central yet universal omnipresent Light. This world is represented by a Cluster of Minds whose central Tendencies are turned off from Gd to Earth, self & created good—and also in a state of Redemption. Intervening is the Crucifixion of Christ between two Thieves—both Tendencies going off, but one turning back to the Light. Denotes also a converted & an unconverted Man.

At a little Distance on the Left hand is a black Spot—the Receptacle of fallen Angels & the finally wicked. And as we know only of two Worlds (out of infinite Myriads) that have revolted; so this is big eno' to contain all those, if none were saved. And the collection of moral Evil & Misery, in comparison with the moral Perfection & Happiness of the immense Universe, is but a small Spot & as nothing in proportion. . . . So that under this small minutesimal Exception of the Misery of all the fallen Angels & even most of the Posterity of Adam, when we consider what is held forth in the Description of Coloss. i, 16, of Principalities, Dominions &c. innumerable grand assemblages of Intelligence, we may say ALL HAPPY IN GOD.[124]

Almost immediately thereafter, Stiles began his studies in the cabala and the works of Dionysius the Areopagite, and as a result he redrew his emblem of the universe (see Fig. 2). Yahweh, in Hebrew, is still in the center of the emblem, but now it is surrounded by "3 ternaries of Nine concentric Circles, denoting the nine orders of Angels about the Throne, or the angelic Hierarchy at the Head of the Universe; which, with the Deity in Supremacy, may be the Ten Saphirot of the Hebrew Caballists." This in turn is surrounded by dots representing planets inhabited by embodied souls. Both the planets and the angels still have the triple thread pointing toward the center, that is, God. Toward the bottom of the emblem is a cross flanked by two dots which, as in the earlier emblem, symbolize the crucifixion of Christ with the two thieves. The condemned thief is on the left; the thief who has been saved is on the right. They can be distinguished by their threads, for those of the condemned one point

124. Stiles, *Literary Diary*, I: 132; Stiles, "Literary Diary," MS, July 23, 1792; Edmund S. Morgan, *The Gentle Puritan: A Life of Ezra Stiles, 1727-1795* (New Haven: Yale University Press, 1962), frontispiece.

away from the center, while those of the saved start to point away and then bend back and point toward the center.

Flanking the cross are two circles, representing the earth, filled with dots. To the left of the cross is "This lapsed World," where the threads on the dots are disorganized and point in all directions. To the right is the earth "glorified," with all the threads pointing toward God. Finally, at the lower left, outside the universe proper, is sheol, or hell. In this emblem, Stiles is again optimistically assuming that only men and fallen angels, among all the myriad intelligences of the universe, were to be damned, and that the remainder of the universe was "All Happy in God."[125]

Stiles essayed a third emblem of the universe immediately after completing his second. This one was similar to the second, except that the planets of the embodied intelligences were much fewer and less impressive. He preferred the second emblem, however, and stated that it "now comprehends all my Ideas of the Universe." [126]

In this emblem Stiles combined three separate areas of belief. The first included such traditional Christian beliefs, still current in the eighteenth century, as the Trinity and hell. These concepts were found in his first emblem, created before his study of Dionysius the Areopagite and the cabala. The second set of beliefs, also found in his first emblem, concerned an infinite universe of inhabited solar systems. This again was a commonplace of eighteenth-century thought.

The third set of beliefs was of an elaborate angelic hierarchy. This was novel. It was not found in Stiles's first emblem, whose only acknowledgement of angels was hell for the fallen angels. The dots in the first emblem clearly represented planets not angels, and had no specific order. In his second emblem the angels now had a recognized place next to God and a distinct threefold structure derived from Dionysius the Areopagite, while the worlds of inhabited beings were displaced to the periphery, and their inhabitants now took their rightful place in the chain of being, just beneath the angels.

Just as the necessity to use sources foreign to eighteenth-century colonial thought, such as Dionysius the Areopagite, in order to organize the angelic realm, indicates the poverty of eighteenth-century angelology, so too the overall primitiveness and crudity of Stiles's symbolism points up

125. Stiles, "Literary Diary," MS, July 21, 1792.
126. *Ibid.*

the iconographic poverty of the Puritanism of the time. It is crude because Stiles himself was forced to invent virtually all his symbolism; he had no rich tradition to rely upon.

Stiles was also isolated in his interest in the cabala, for there were few others in the colonies involved with it. Although most of the rabbis whom Stiles met were students of the cabala, they were all merely visiting the colonies. In fact, mainland colonial Jewry never had a settled rabbi. There were a few signs of interest in the cabala among the colonial Jewish population. A number of colonial Jews, including Judah Monis, originally from Italy, who taught Hebrew at Harvard after being converted to Christianity, were familiar with the cabala; [127] and at least one religious practice followed by colonial Jews—reading from the Bible and the Mishnah all Shabuot night—was derived from the cabalists.[128] But for colonial Jewry in general, according to a distinguished modern historian of early American Jewry, mystical movements such as Hasidism and the cabala had little influence.[129]

The rest of the colonists displayed little more interest. There is no evidence that Monis ever taught any aspect of the cabala to his students at Harvard. Most of them clearly never evinced sufficient interest or knowledge of Hebrew to reach such an esoteric level.[130] Monis may, however, have been a source for tutor Henry Flynt's notes in his "Common Place Book" on the cabala, in which he discussed such cabalistic concepts as the ten sephiroth, Adam Kadmon (Primordial Man), and the belief that God created the universe to express His nature.[131] Other than this, the only signs of any interest in or knowledge of the cabala come from such items as a book on the cabala worth one shilling in the 1732 estate of Richard Hickman,[132] some passages by John Leverett indicating

127. Jacob R. Marcus, *The Colonial American Jew, 1492-1776* (Detroit: Wayne State University Press, 1970), II: 1075, 1081, 1083, 1097-98, 1102.

128. *Ibid.*, 980.

129. *Ibid.*, 860, 962.

130. *Ibid.*, 1096-1102; Lee M. Friedman, "Judah Monis, First Instructor in Hebrew at Harvard University," *Publications of the American Jewish Historical Society*, no. 22 (1914): 15; Morison, *Three Centuries of Harvard, 1636-1936*, pp. 57-58.

131. Henry Flynt, "Common Place Book," MS (Massachusetts Historical Society), pp. 29-31.

132. *William and Mary Quarterly*, 1st Series, III (April 1895): 250.

a belief that the Hebrew names for things have a deep significance and hidden meaning,[133] and an article on the "political cabala" in a 1733 issue of Peter Zenger's *New-York Weekly Journal.* The latter was an attack on Governor Cosby, slightly veiled as a historical analysis of the problems which had befallen New York whenever she had had governors whose names began with the letter *c.*[134] This article of course had no real interest in the cabala, but it did presumably indicate a general public awareness that the cabala placed great significance in the letters of the alphabet.

## VI

Despite the occasional use of the ordered universe to justify an ordered human society, despite the occasional use of the human body as an analogy for the body politic, despite the use of the argument from analogy to support the reality of "mermaids," despite even the arguments of such men as Jefferson that no link in nature's chain could ever be lost, the chain of being in the eighteenth century differed substantially from that held earlier in the Renaissance. With the "temporalization of the chain of being" and the eighteenth century's great interest in fossils of apparently extinct species, the older, static concept of the chain of being even started to take on evolutionary overtones.

Still other changes in the concept were now even more fully accepted. For example, the chain of being in the Renaissance had been as much concerned with establishing "proper order" in human society as it had been in ordering nature. The common assertion that the lion was the "king of the beasts" had not been, in essence, a biological statement at all, but rather, a reflection of what was the norm for human political structure. This reflection was taken as an independent truth—and then was used to justify the existing norm as being in conformity with nature!

In the American colonies by the eighteenth century such a political usage of the chain of being had become secondary, rare, perhaps even archaic. The primary purpose and use of the chain was now to "order" nature itself. This ordering, done by the great taxonomists, culminating in the work of Linnaeus, was now more clear, more detailed, and more

133. Arthur Daniel Kaledin, "The Mind of John Leverett" (unpublished Ph.D. dissertation, Harvard University, 1965), p. 120.
134. *The New-York Weekly Journal,* Dec. 24, 1733.

firmly structured in the eighteenth century than at any time before. The place of the human species in the chain of being was still of course very important (most colonists still believed that man was at the midpoint of the chain),[135] but the hierarchical structure of human politics and society was no longer a major concern of the chain.

The web of occult relationships which had characterized the chain of being in the seventeenth century was almost entirely absent in the eighteenth. It was now only a "law of nature," and not a tool to be used in manipulating and controlling nature. The chain of being in eighteenth-century America could be described as Neoclassical and perhaps even "Whiggish." It was now firmly ordered and structured, but no longer entailed a "Tory" political theory, and occult phenomena no longer played a role in it.

135. For a discussion of the place of man in relationship to other primates, see Greene, *The Death of Adam,* pp. 175-99.

Part Three


The Elizabethan World Picture in Decay

# 9

## The Elizabethan World Picture in Decay

*Yet the early Renaissance left a heritage that remained effective at least down to the end of the eighteenth century. . . .*

—Kristeller, *Renaissance Thought*

## I

The late seventeenth and early eighteenth centuries saw the gradual disintegration of the "Elizabethan world picture" in the American colonies. It no longer existed as a gestalt, as a unified set of interlocking and mutually supporting ideas. A person who believed in one aspect of it did not necessarily, or even probably, believe in the rest. One could believe in the elements, but not necessarily believe in spirits or humors. One could believe in the chain of being, but have no interest in the celestial hierarchy or the nature of angels. One could believe in astrology, but totally reject the Ptolemaic universe.

But even though the Elizabethan world picture had fallen apart, it had not entirely disappeared. Some of its ideas and concepts continued into the eighteenth century with unabated vigor, others suffered a loss of influence and prestige, while some did disappear. Each concept now had its own independent history.

Interestingly enough, the occult arts, although in decline, were far from the hardest hit. The extent to which astrology declined is somewhat uncertain simply because astrology's exact status in seventeenth-century America is rather unclear. Judging from the scanty literature on the

262

subject, unfortunately limited almost entirely to New England, astrology was popular in the seventeenth century. Judicial astrology, as always, was under attack; but despite this attack the almanacs printed at Cambridge continued to include prognostications, and many of the respected compilations of knowledge used by the New Englanders contained astrological concepts.[1]

Although astrology continued to be used in the eighteenth century, signs of decline were evident. The zodiac man, useful for venesection, remained a standard feature of most almanacs, but more detailed astrological-medical texts were limited to the first two decades of the century and to reprints of older works. Almanac prognostications also continued, most conspicuously in the popular and well-written almanacs of Nathaniel Ames, but by the last quarter of the eighteenth century had virtually disappeared. Probably this sharp decline in almanac prognostications accounted for the publication in the 1790s of a remarkably dull broadside prognostication by John Nobles, "Astrologer and Doctor." It was enlivened only by its apparent claim to be "Published according to Act of Congress," which however merely referred to the federal copyright law.[2]

Some other aspects of astrology seem to have maintained their popularity. Especially important was "planting by the signs," which continued to be an important aspect of American rural culture well past the eighteenth century.

Although astrology thus survived the Enlightenment, it survived only as almanac astrology and folklore. It did not have the influence or the widespread general acceptance that it had had in Renaissance Europe. Colonial textbooks of the eighteenth century did not accept the reality of astrology. The growing interest in judicial astrology evidenced by the seventeenth-century Cambridge almanacs had become a declining interest in the eighteenth century. Symbolic of the change were the rejections of astrology around 1701 by Jacob Taylor, who became one of its most persistent colonial critics, and probably around 1720 by William Parsons,

1. Hall, "Renaissance Science," pp. 131-35, and Edward Eggleston, *The Transit of Civilization: From England to America in the Seventeenth Century* (Boston: Beacon Press, 1959), pp. 4-5, 36-37n.

2. John Nobles, *These are the Predictions of John Nobles, Astrologer and Doctor . . . for . . . 1794* ([Boston?]: 1793).

later a founding member of the Junto and the American Philosophical Society. Parsons, Franklin explained, had acquired "a considerable Share of Mathematics, which he first studied with a View to Astrology that he afterwards laught at." [3]

The decline of astrology, however, seems to have been less drastic than might have been expected. This was probably because even in the early seventeenth century there had been a strong Puritan opposition, whereas in the eighteenth century the astrological traditions did remain stronger in England, and thus presumably also in America, than anywhere else in the Western World. [4]

The history of witchcraft beliefs in eighteenth-century America tended to parallel that of astrology. Many still believed in it, but it no longer had universal acceptance or significance, nor was it given official recognition by the civil authorities after the third decade of the century. Witchcraft, and magic of all kinds, existed only as a folk belief, albeit a widespread one. This belief, however, had one support that the occult arts, and Renaissance sciences in general, lacked—strong religious support. As long as the Bible was read as affirming the reality of witchcraft, only the truly "Enlightened," only those willing to reject the inspired status of the Bible, could categorically deny with ease the theoretical validity of witchcraft beliefs.

Rattlesnake fascination was, of course, a rather special situation. Unlike the occult arts, belief in it had only developed in the late seventeenth and early eighteenth centuries, out of a variety of sources, many of them occult, and it reached its full development only in the eighteenth century. In that century it survived various attacks and attempted explanations and even survives today as a popular belief, although no longer as a tenable scientific theory. It should be noted, however, that even in the eighteenth

---

3. Jacob Taylor, *An Almanack . . . for . . . 1746;* Franklin, *Autobiography,* pp. 117, 293.

4. For Puritan opposition to astrology, see Thomas, *Religion and the Decline of Magic,* pp. 367-78. For astrology in eighteenth-century England, see William D. Stahlman, "Astrology in Colonial America: An Extended Query," *William and Mary Quarterly,* 3rd Series, XIII (October 1956): 557, and Ellic Howe, *Astrology: A Recent History Including the Untold Story of Its Role in World War II* (New York: Walker and Company, 1967), p. 21.

century the occult elements in this belief were an embarrassment to many naturalists who still believed in it.

Alchemy, which was both an occult art and an ancester of chemistry, also survived. A number of studies, although again restricted to New England, indicate the existence of a fairly active interest in alchemy in seventeenth-century America. These alchemists included John Winthrop, Jr., governor of Connecticut among his other manifold interests; Robert Child, the Presbyterian Remonstrant; Jonathan Brewster, son of William Brewster of Plymouth; and George Starkey, a Bermudan educated at Harvard. As was customary in both the seventeenth and eighteenth centuries, alchemy remained an esoteric art, perhaps interesting to many but practiced by few.

Seventeenth-century alchemists, with perhaps the exception of John Winthrop, Jr., do not appear to have been more distinguished or reputable than such eighteenth-century alchemists and followers of alchemy as William Gerard De Brahm, Samuel Danford, and Ezra Stiles. Both centuries had alchemists who were persons of substance and reputation. A noticeable difference, however, is that the seventeenth-century alchemists included figures of significance in the history of European alchemy, which the eighteenth-century alchemists were not. The "findings" of the eighteenth-century colonial alchemists appear to have gone unrecorded or to have been buried in unread manuscripts, and so to have influenced no one. This, of course, probably reflects less upon the ability of the eighteen-century alchemists than upon the general decay of alchemy in that period.[5]

A number of interesting features can be detected in the histories of

5. For seventeenth-century colonial alchemy, see Kittredge, "Robert Child the Remonstrant," pp. 123-46; G. H. Turnbull, "George Stirk, Philosopher by Fire," *Publications of the Colonial Society of Massachusetts,* XXXVIII (1947-51): 219-51; *idem,* "Robert Child," *Publications of the Colonial Society of Massachusetts,* XXXVIII (1947-51): 21-53; Ronald Sterne Wilkinson, "The Alchemical Library of John Winthrop, Jr. (1606-1676) and His Descendants in Colonial America," *Ambix,* XI (February 1963): 33-51, and XIII (October 1966): 139-86; *idem,* "George Starkey, Physician and Alchemist," *Ambix,* XI (October 1963): 121-52; *idem,* "The Problem of the Identity of Eirenaeus Philalethes," *Ambix,* XII (February 1964): 24-43; Robert C. Black, III, *The Younger John Winthrop* (New York: Columbia University Press, 1966), 155-57.

several of the occult arts. In both astrology and witchcraft beliefs the same bifurcation developed. Learned and scholarly elements disappeared much more thoroughly than did simpler folk beliefs. In witchcraft, the "witches' sabbath," the "pact with the devil," and demonic possession, all scholarly imports foreign to English folk tradition, disappeared. The elaborate bookish magic of the Renaissance appears to have never really taken root in the colonies. It seems not to have been transplanted from England, and even the German sectarians who introduced it soon disappeared as an organized community. But such traditional English beliefs as the witch's familiar and the malevolent witch, working evil without any elaborate paraphernalia or ceremony, continued to be widely accepted. Even the divining rod, which was used in rather elaborate ceremonies, seems to have been traditional among German and English miners.[6]

So too, in astrology, almanac prognostications declined, and individual horoscopes seem always to have been rather rare, whereas simple folk beliefs concerning the significance of the signs and moon's phase for medicine and agriculture continued to maintain a high degree of vitality.

Another interesting feature was the attempt, frequently rather feeble, for the occult arts to become reconciled with the findings of contemporary science. This tendency was most apparent in the explanations of rattlesnake fascination, probably because it was the only occult phenomenon to attract much attention from eighteenth-century scientists and naturalists. This tendency was seen even in alchemy, where De Brahm attempted to use the then popular phlogiston theory, of which he was a follower.[7] In astrology, the Copernican system was generally accepted, several attempts were made to explain the influence of the planets by the particles or effluvium they emitted, and Jared Eliot attempted to explain the influence of the moon on plants by the force of gravity. Only witchcraft appears to have remained completely impervious to any attempt at modernization.

## II

Renaissance science frequently proved less durable in the Age of the Enlightenment than did Renaissance occultism. A number of important

6. Vogt, *Water Witching, U.S.A.*, p. 19.
7. De Brahm, *Report of the General Survey*, pp. 80, 105, 156; *idem*, "Survey of East Florida," MS, Harvard University, p. 354.

concepts—the Ptolemaic universe; pre-Newtonian descriptions of gravity; the careful distinction between natural, vital, and animal spirits; pneumatics; and angelology—all these had died out by the first few decades of the eighteenth century.

Ptolemy had been replaced by Copernicus. Pre-Newtonian gravity had been replaced by Newtonian gravity. The belief in the three spirits had been upset by the discovery of the circulation of the blood. The impact of Harvey's discovery can be seen in the fact that little was heard in the eighteenth century about natural spirits, which had been thought to flow through the veins, or about vital spirits, which had been thought to flow through the arteries. On the other hand, animal spirits, which had been thought to flow through the nerves, and therefore were unaffected by the acceptance of the circulation of the blood, continued to be spoken of in the eighteenth century. The reasons for the decay of pneumatics and angelology, the sciences of souls, are more obscure. Perhaps in part they were absorbed by logic; perhaps eighteenth-century scientific interest had simply turned away from all aspects of the "invisible world."

A less than total decline is seen in some other aspects of Renaissance science. Belief in the four elements, the four humors, and animal spirits continued, although with less authority. They had once been unquestioned elements of the natural world; they were now isolated and challenged beliefs. They may even have served as the inspiration or model for several eighteenth-century scientific theories: for example, the humors were a probable source for the concepts of equilibrium and balance so important in much eighteenth-century medical thought, and animal spirits served as a basis for speculation about the workings of the nerves.

A continuing aspect of Renaissance thought was the chain of being. This was used to give an overall structure and organization to nature, and was even appealed to as scientific theory for answers to specific problems: for example, was it possible for an entire species to become extinct? Correspondences or analogies were made between different segments of the chain of being, with the implicit assumption that what held true for one segment would hold true for the other. This tendency manifested itself in beliefs about stones which grew like plants, sea creatures which paralleled land animals, and the assumption that the chain of being rose as far above man as it fell beneath him.

As we have seen, even the political implications of the chain of being continued to be fruitful as late as the writings of John Adams, although it had much less overall significance than it had had in the seventeenth century.

## III

One aspect of the intellectual life of the eighteenth century in colonial America which requires further study is the continued influence of Neo-platonism. We have already seen that it influenced Edward Taylor, played an important role in the development of the belief of rattlesnake fascination, and had served as the source of the aetherial spirit, *Nishmath-Chajim*, *spiritus*, *Vis Actuosa*, *Impetum Faciens*, or *Archeus*, of various eighteenth-century colonial thinkers. The chain of being was also, of course, to a great extent, a Neoplatonic concept.[8]

Additional evidences of influence of Platonism and Neoplatonism in eighteenth-century thought include Samuel Johnson's early doubts about Berkeleyanism, which doubts were clearly derived from orthodox Neo-platonism, and the role of the Cambridge Neoplatonists in the formation of Jonathan Edwards's philosophy.[9] Furthermore, the Neoplatonic concept of plastic power can be found in the writings of Morton, Leverett, and Cotton Mather.[10]

Henry More's *Enchiridon Ethicum*, which has been described as "the principal ethical writing" of the Cambridge Neoplatonists, was the ethics textbook at Harvard and Yale in the 1720s. The ethics of the Cambridge Neoplatonists also strongly influenced the colonies indirectly, by their influence on Shaftesbury and thus on the Scottish common-sense philosophy, so popular in the latter half of the century.[11]

Nor were the works of the Cambridge Neoplatonist the only channel

8. Lovejoy, *The Great Chain of Being,* chap. II, especially pp. 61ff.

9. Johnson, *Works,* II: 266-68, and Emily Stipes Watts, "Jonathan Edwards and the Cambridge Platonists" (unpublished Ph.D dissertation, University of Illinois, 1963).

10. Morton, *Compendium Physicae,* p. 136; John Leverett, President Leverett's Exposition of Scripture, 1708-1724, MSS, Harvard University Archives, bk. 19, p. 3r; Beall, *Cotton Mather,* p. 139; Cotton Mather, *The Christian Philosopher,* p. 125. But see *ibid.,* p. 87, for his rejection of it.

11. Cassirer, *The Platonic Renaissance in England,* p. 160 and chap. VI; Benjamin Rand, "Philosophical Instruction in Harvard University from 1636-1900," *The Harvard Graduates' Magazine,* XXXVII (September 1928): 36-37; G. Stan-

by which Platonic thought could reach the colonies. It had always been an important element in Christian thought, including early Puritanism, and, in addition, the works of Plato and of the Italian Neoplatonists were available to the colonists.[12]

A proper evaluation of the influence of Platonism may be necessary not only for understanding important eighteenth-century currents of thought, but also for understanding such later developments as Transcendentalism.[13]

## IV

Another important area for further investigation is the extent to which such vestigial remains of the Renaissance world view were to be found not only in colonial America but in Enlightenment Europe as well. There are indeed indications that what we have seen in America did also continue to exist in the rest of the Western world. Astrology appears to have been most prevalent in the eighteenth century in England and America, but strong traces of it are found on the Continent as well. Almanacs in Switzerland, Spain, Germany, Belgium, the Netherlands, and France contained either astrological prognostications, horoscopes for the four seasons, or the zodiac man.[14] Astrologers and other forms of fortune-

---

ley Hall, "On the History of American College Textbooks and Teaching in Logic, Ethics, Psychology and Allied Subjects," *Proceedings of the American Antiquarian Society,* N.S., IX (April 1894): 144; Anna Haddow, *Political Science in American Colleges and Universities, 1636-1900* (New York: Appleton-Century Company, 1939), p. 21.

12. Paul Oskar Kristeller, "The European Significance of Florentine Platonism," *Medieval and Renaissance Studies,* 3 (Chapel Hill: University of North Carolina Press, 1968): 229n.

13. See Octavius Brooks Frothingham, *Transcendentalism in New England: A History* (New York: Harper & Brothers, 1959), pp. 107-8. Also suggestive is Perry Miller, "From Edwards to Emerson," *Errand into the Wilderness* (New York: Harper & Row, 1964), pp. 184-203.

For studies of colonial Platonism, see Herbert W. Schneider, *A History of American Philosophy* (New York: Columbia University Press, 1946), pp. 1-32, and Clarence Gohdes, "Aspects of Idealism in Early New England," *The Philosophical Review,* XXXIX (November 1930): 537-55.

14. Antoine Souci, *Almanach Historique Nommé La Messager Boiteux . . .* (Bern: 1779); Marc Henrioud, "Les Astrologues de Combremont-Le-Petit et Leur

tellers were found in late eighteenth-century Paris, and, as we have already seen, even the *Encyclopédie* adopted Chambers's *Cyclopedia*'s version of Boyle's defense of natural astrology.[15]

Scattered incidents of witchcraft are also found throughout Enlightenment Europe. The last execution of an individual for witchcraft occurred in France in 1745, in Germany in 1775, in Scotland in 1727, in Switzerland in 1782, in Poland in 1793, and in Spain in 1781.[16] Many other incidents involving the belief in witchcraft, sometimes resulting in death by mob action, are found throughout eighteenth-century Europe.[17]

In England, the Royal Society, as late as the 1780s, investigated (and disproved) an alleged transmutation of base metal into gold.[18] In France, as a twentieth-century monograph has argued, all the occult arts with the possible exception of astrology flourished during the eighteenth century.[19]

---

Almanachs (1697-1838)," *Revue Historique Vaudoise,* XXI (March 1913): 71; (June 1913): 218-21; (August 1913): 225-29; Geronymo Cortes [pseud.], *El Non Plus Ultra: Del Lunario, Y Pronostico Perpetuo, Y General . . .* (Barcelona, 1713); *Ephemeris Eclesiastica, Astronomica-Ethico-Politica, Ad Annum Salutis Natae MDCCXI* (Salisburg); A. Warzée, "Recherches Bibliographiques Sur Les Almanachs Belges," *Bulletin du Bibliophile Belge,* VIII (1851): 267, 425, 427-28, 458; Wickersheimer, "La Médecine Astrologique," p. 21; *Ephemerides des Mouvements Celestes Pour Les Anneés 1735, Jusqu'en 1775* (Paris: Jacques Collombat, 1734), pp. 30, 86; John Grand-Carteret, *Les Almanachs Français* (Paris, 1896), items 90, 488, 1076.

15. Robert Darnton, *Mesmerism and the End of the Enlightenment in France* (Cambridge: Harvard University Press, 1968), pp. 33-34.

16. See Rossell Hope Robbins, *The Encyclopedia of Witchcraft and Demonology* (New York: Crown Publishers, Inc., 1959), p. 551, and Kittredge, *Witchcraft in Old and New England,* p. 370.

17. Kittredge, *Witchcraft in Old and New England,* pp. 361-62, 369-70; Montague Summers, *The Geography of Witchcraft* (New York: University Books, 1958), pp. 167-70, 246-50, 437-42, 503-18; Hole, *Witchcraft in England,* pp. 195-215.

18. E. J. Holmyard, *Alchemy* (Baltimore: Penguin Books, Inc., 1968), pp. 267-70.

19. Constantin Bila, *La Croyance A La Magie Au XVIII^e Siècle En France* (Paris: Librairie J. Gamber, 1925). For astrology see pp. 89-90, but also see pp. 76, 55-56.

The same continuation of Renaissance thought appears to hold true also for scientific theories. Both Copernican astronomy and Newtonian physics faced far greater opposition in parts of Europe than they ever faced in America,[20] while the Hutchinsonianism which Samuel Johnson had adopted was English in origin and had influential supporters abroad. The concept of the chain of being was certainly as important in England and Europe as it was in America. Even American medical and chemical theories were usually only copies or adaptations of English or European theories, whose archaic features they thus shared.

Viewed in this framework, the significance of this study is not limited to American history but extends to the history of the Enlightenment. Hopefully, it will join current studies on eighteenth-century popular culture and be joined by further studies on eighteenth-century occultism to create a fuller and more rounded picture of the Age of the Enlightenment.

---

For a specialized study in the belief and use of elemental spirits—sylphes, undines, salamanders, and gnomes—see P. Vernière, "Au Aspect de l'irrationnel au XVIIIème siècle: Le Démonologie et Son Exploitation littéraire," *Studies in Eighteenth-Century Culture,* vol. II: *Irrationalism in the Eighteenth Century,* Harold E. Pagliaro, ed. (Cleveland: The Press of Case Western Reserve University, 1972), pp. 289-302.

Two studies of occultism in France raise certain difficulties, however: Darnton, *Mesmerism and the End of the Enlightenment in France,* and Auguste Viatte, *Les Sources Occultes du Romantisme: Illuminisme—Théosophie, 1770-1820* (Paris: Librairie Ancienne Honore Champion, 1928). Both deal with what they clearly see as a post-Enlightenment development in late eighteenth-century France. These works point up the danger of treating any late eighteenth-century occultism as a direct continuation of seventeenth-century thought. They also, however, make little effort to determine whether any such continuity actually existed, and thus point up the necessity for further studies of occultism as a continuing phase of the eighteenth century.

20. Dorothy Stimson, *The Gradual Acceptance of the Copernican Theory of the Universe* (New York, 1917); Pierre Brunet, *L'Introduction Des Théories de Newton En France Au XVIIIe Siècle* (Paris: Librairie Scientifique Albert Blanchard, 1931).

# Bibliography

## Primary Sources

### Manuscripts Consulted

American Philosophical Society. Film History of Science, No. 1, and miscellaneous letters.

American Philosophical Society Library. Heckelwelder, John. "Further Communications Collected Last Summer From Intelligient Indians." n.d.

College of Physicians of Philadelphia. Various notebooks on medicine and chemistry.

Dartmouth College. Eleazar Wheelock to Stephen Williams, Aug. 18, 1737.

Harvard University. Various student commonplace books, John Leverett Papers, William Gerard De Brahm, "Survey of East Florida, Carolina, Georgia, &c," and miscellaneous MSS.

Historical Society of Pennsylvania. Various commonplace books and notebooks, Thomas Mifflin's "Abridgment of Metaphysics," Ebenezer Kinnersly, "A Course of Experiments in the Newly Discover'd Electrical Fire," and miscellaneous MSS.

Massachusetts Historical Society. Various commonplace books, Benjamin Stockbridge's "Account Book and Notes on Alchemy," William Brattle's "A Compendium of Logick."

New York Public Library. John Coppock and others' commonplace book and William Hooker Smith's "Remarkable Acurances."

Queens Borough Public Library. Nathaniel Dominy's "Common-Place Book."

Stafford County Record Office, England. Dartmouth Papers.

Yale University. Ezra Stiles Papers and various student diaries, commonplace books, and notebooks from the Diaries Misc. Collection.

### Periodicals

*The American Magazine and Historical Chronicle,* III (1746).
*American Magazine or Monthly Chronicle for the British Colonies,* I (1757-58).
*Boston Weekly Magazine,* I (1802).
*Brooklyn-Hall Super-Extra Gazette,* June 8, 1782.

*Memoirs of the American Academy of Arts and Sciences,* I-III (1783-1809).
*The New York Weekly Journal,* Dec. 24, 1733.
*The Pennsylvania Magazine or, American Monthly Museum.*
*Philosophical Transactions,* I-LXX (1665-1780).
*Port Folio,* February 1803.
*The Virginia Gazette.*

### Almanacs Used

Aguecheek, Andrew [pseud.]. *The Universal American Almanack . . . for . . . 1762.* Philadelphia: Bradford and Steuart.

Ames, Nathaniel. *The Almanacks of Nathaniel Ames, 1726-1755.* Ed. by Samuel Briggs. Cleveland: Short & Forman, 1891.

[Andrews, William.] *Poor Will's Almanack for . . . 1778.* Philadelphia: Joseph Crukshank.

Andrews, William. *Remarkable News from the Stars: Or, An Ephemeris for . . . 1738.* London: A. Wilde.

Coley, Henry. *Merlinus Anglicus Junior: Or the Starry Messenger, for . . . 1738.* London: J. Read.

Cortes, Geronymo [pseud.]. *El Non Plus Ultra: Del Lunario, Y Prognostico Perpetuo, Y General. . . .* Barcelona, 1713.

Daboll, Nathan. *The New-England Almanack . . . for . . . 1794.* New London: Green.

Eddy, John. *An Astronomical Diary, or, an Almanack for . . . 1761.* Boston: Edes & Gill.

*Ephemerides des Mouvements Celestes Pour Les Année 1735, Jusqu'en 1775.* Paris: Jacques Cullombat, 1734.

*Ephemeris Eclesiastica, Astronomica-Ethico-Politica, Ad Annum Salutis Natae MDCCXI.* Salisburg.

Fox, Thomas. *The Wilmington Almanack . . . for . . . 1762.* Wilmington: Adams.

Freebetter, Edmund [Nathan Daboll]. *The New-England Almanack . . . for . . . 1778.* New London: T. Green.

Hutchins, John Nathan. *Hutchins Improved: Being an Almanack . . . for . . . 1761.* New York: Gaine.

Jerman, John. *The American Almanack for . . . 1743.* Philadelphia: Bradford.

———. *The American Almanack for . . . 1746.* Philadelphia: Bradford.

*The Kalendar & Compost of Shepherds.* Ed. by G. C. Heseltine. London: Peter Davies, 1931.

Leeds, Daniel. *An Almanack and Ephemerides for . . . 1693.* [Philadelphia]: William Bradford.

———. *An Almanack for . . . 1700.* New York: William Bradford.

———. *The American Almanack . . . for 1713.* New York: Bradford.

Leeds, Felix. *The American Almanack for . . . 1730.* New York: Wm. Bradford.

Leeds, Titan. *The American Almanack for . . . 1722.* Philadelphia: Andrew Bradford.

———. *The American Almanack for . . . 1730.* Philadelphia: Nearegress & Arnot.

———. *The American Almanack for . . . 1731.* New York: William Bradford, and Philadelphia: Andrew Bradford.

———. *The American Almanack for . . . 1732.* New York: Wm. Bradford, and Philadelphia: Andrew Bradford.

———. *The American Almanack for . . . 1733.* New York and Philadelphia: William Bradford.

———. *The American Almanack for . . . 1735.* Philadelphia: Andrew Bradford.

———. *The American Almanack for . . . 1736.* Philadelphia: Andrew Bradford.

———. *The American Almanack for . . . 1737.* Philadelphia: Bradford.

———. *The American Almanack for . . . 1738.* Philadelphia: Bradford.

———. *The American Almanack for . . . 1739.* Philadelphia: Bradford.

———. *The American Almanack for . . . 1740.* 2nd ed., Philadelphia: Bradford.

———. *The American Almanack for . . . 1741.* Philadelphia: Bradford.

———. *The American Almanack for . . . 1742.* Philadelphia: Andrew Bradford.

———. [pseud.]. *The American Almanack for . . . 1743.* Philadelphia: Bradford.

———. [pseud.]. *The American Almanack for . . . 1744.* Philadelphia: Warner & Bradford.

———. [pseud.]. *The American Almanack for . . . 1745.* Philadelphia: Bradford.

———. [psued.]. *The American Almanack for . . . 1746.* Philadelphia: Cornelia Bradford.

———. *The Genuine Leeds Almanack for . . . 1730.* Philadelphia: Harry.

———. *The Genuine Leeds Almanack for . . . 1734.* Philadelphia: Bradford.

Low, Nathaniel. *An Astronomical Diary, or an Almanack for . . . 1762.* Boston: Kneeland.

———. *An Astronomical Diary: or Almanack for . . . 1772.* Boston: Kneeland & Adams.

Moore, Francis. *Vox Stellarum: Or, A Loyal Almanach for . . . 1738.* London: Samuel Idle.

More, Roger [pseud.]. *The American Country Almanack, for . . . 1761.* New York: James Parker, and Company.

More, Thomas [pseud.]. *The New York Pocket Almanack for . . . 1761.* New York: Gaine.

——— [pseud.]. *Poor Thomas Improved: Being More's Country Almanack for . . . 1761.* New York: Weyman.

——— [pseud.]. *Poor Tom Revived: Being More's Almanack, for 1770.* Charles Town, S.C.: Grouch.

*The Pennsylvania Pocket Almanack for . . . 1761.* Philadelphia: W. Bradford.

Philomath, T. T. [pseud.]. *The Virginia Almanack for . . . 1769.* Williamsburg: Purdie & Dixon.

Poor Robin [pseud.]. *The Rhode-Island Almanack, for . . . 1728.* Newport: Franklin.

*Poor Robin's Spare Hours . . . for 1758.* Philadelphia: Bradford. [As the title page was missing, the title was taken from an advertisement.]

Rittenhouse, David. *The Virginia Almanack for . . . 1777.* Williamsburg: Dixon & Hunter.

Robie, Thomas. *An Almanack . . . for . . . 1712.* Boston: Bartholomew Green.

Saunders, R. [pseud.]. *A Pocket Almanack for . . . 1761.* Philadelphia: R. Franklin & D. Hall.

——— [pseud.]. *Poor Richard Improved . . . an Almanack . . . for . . . 1762.* Philadelphia: Franklin and Hall.

Sharp, Anthony [David Rittenhouse]. *The Lancaster Almanack for . . . 1778 . . . .* Lancaster: Bailey.

Souci, Antoine. *Almanach Historique Nommé Le Messager Boiteux . . . MDCCLXXIX.* Bern.

Stafford, Joseph. *An Almanack for . . . 1740.* Boston: T. Flees.

———. *The Rhode-Island Almanack for . . . 1738.* Newport: The Widow Franklin.

Taylor, Jacob [pseud?]. *An Almanack . . . for . . . 1740.* Philadelphia: Bradford.

——— [pseud?]. *An Almanack . . . for . . . 1741.* Philadelphia: Bradford.

Taylor, Jacob [pseud?]. *An Almanack . . . for . . . 1743.* Philadelphia: Isaiah Warner.

——— [pseud?]. *An Almanack . . . for . . . 1745.* Philadelphia: Bradford.

——— [pseud?]. *An Almanack . . . for . . . 1746.* Philadelphia: W. Bradford.

——— [pseud?]. *A Compleat Ephemeris . . . for 1726.* Philadelphia: Keimer.

——— [pseud?]. *Pennsilvania* [sic], 1740. *An Almanack . . . for . . . 1740.* Philadelphia: Andrew Bradford.

Tobler, John. *The Pennsilvania* [sic] *Town and Country-Man's Almanack for . . . 1764.* Germantown: G. Sower.

———. *The Pennsylvania Town and Country-Man's Almanack, for . . . 1761.* Germantown: Sower for Fussel, Marshall, and Zone.

———. *The South-Carolina and Georgia Almanack, for . . . 1764.* Savannah: James Johnston.

Trueman, Timothy [pseud.] *New Jersey. The Burlington Almanack for . . . 1775.* Burlington, N.J.: Collins.

*The Virginia Almanack for . . . 1751.* Williamsburg: Hunter.

Warner, John. *Warner's Almanack . . . for . . . 1742.* Williamsburg: Wm. Pares.

Weatherwise, Abraham [pseud.]. *Father Abraham's Almanac . . . Fitted for the Latitude of Rhode-Island, for . . . 1762.* Philadelphia: Dunlap.

[West, Benjamin]. *Bickerstaff's Boston Almanack, for . . . 1775.* Boston: Mills & Hicks.

West, Benjamin. *Bickerstaff's Boston Almanack, for . . . 1778.* Danvers: Russell.

———. *Bickerstaff's Boston Almanack, for . . . 1779.* Danvers: Russell.

[West, Benjamin]. *Brickerstaff's New-England Almanack, for . . . 1776.* Norwich: Robertson & Trumbull.

———. *Bickerstaff's New-England Almanack, for . . . 1777.* Norwich: John Trumbull.

———. *Bickerstaff's New-England Almanack, for . . . 1778.* Norwich: J. Trumbull.

———. *Bickerstaff's New-York Almanack, for . . . 1778.* Norwich: Trumbull for Loudon at Fishkill.

West, Benjamin. *The New-England Almanack . . . for . . . 1778.* Providence: Carton.

Wreg, Theophilus [pseud.]. *The Virginia Almanack for . . . 1761.* Williamsburg: William Hunter.

———. *The Virginia Almanack, for . . . 1762.* Williamsburg: Royle.

Wreg, Theophilus [Theophilus Grew]. *The Virginia Almanack for . . . 1764.* Williamsburg: Joseph Royle.

———. *The Virginia Almanack for . . . 1766.* Williamsburg: Purdie.

### Other Primary Sources

*An Abridgement of the Laws in Force and Use in Her Majesty's Plantations.* London: J. Nicholson, 1704.

*Acts of the General Assembly of . . . New-Jersey from . . . 1702, to . . . 1776.* Burlington, N.J.: Isaac Collins, 1776.

*Acts of the Privy Council of England. Colonial Series.* Hereford: printed for His Majesty's Stationery Office of the Hereford Times Co., Ltd., 1910.

Adair, James. *Adair's History of the American Indians.* Ed. by Samuel Cole Williams. New York: Argonaut Press, Ltd., 1966.

Adams, Abigail. *New Letters of Abigail, 1788-1801.* Ed. by Steward Mitchell. Boston: Houghton Mifflin Company, 1947.

Adams, John. *The Adams Papers.* Ed. by L. H. Butterfield. *Adams Family Correspondence.* Vols I-II. Cambridge: Harvard University Press, 1963. *Diary and Autobiography of John Adams.* Vols. I-IV. Cambridge: Harvard University Press, 1961. *The Earliest Diary of John Adams.* Cambridge: Harvard University Press, 1966.

——. *The Legal Papers of John Adams.* Ed. by L. Kinvin Wroth and Hiller B. Zobel. Vols. I-III. Cambridge: Harvard UniversityPress, 1965.

——. *The Works of John Adams.* Ed. by Charles Francis Adams. Boston: Charles G. Little and James Brow, 1850-56.

Adams, John, and Rush, Benjamin. *The Spur of Fame: Dialogues of John Adams and Benjamin Rush, 1805-1813.* Ed. by Douglass Adair and John A. Schultz. San Marino, Calif.: Huntington Library, 1966.

Addison, Joseph. *The Miscellaneous Works of Joseph Addison.* Ed. by A. C. Guthkelch. London: G. Bell and Sons Ltd., 1914.

Addison, Joseph, and Steele, Richard. *Selections from The Tatler and The Spectator.* Ed. by Robert J. Allen. New York: Holt, Rinehart & Winston, 1957.

Agricola, Georgius. *De Re Metallica.* Trans. by H. C. Hoover and L. H. Hoover. London: The Mining Magazine, 1912.

Allan, Ethan. *Reason the Only Oracle of Man.* Bennington, Vt.: Haswell & Russell, 1784.

Alston, Charles. *Lectures on the Materia Medica* . . . . London: Edward & Charles Dilly, 1770.

Appleton, Nathanael. *Faithful Ministers of Christ.* Boston: Rogers & Fowle for Eliot, 1743.

*Archives of the State of New Jersey.* First Series, Vol. XI. Paterson, N.J.: The Press Printing and Publishing Co., 1894.

Aristotle. *Meteorologica.* Trans. by H. D. P. Lee. The Loeb Classical Library. Cambridge: Harvard University Press, 1952.

Aristotle [pseud.]. *Aristotle's Master-Piece Completed. New York: Company of Flying Stationers, 1798.*

———. *The Works of Aristotle the Famous Philosopher in Four Parts. Containing: His Complete Master-Piece* . . . . *His Experienced Midwife* . . . . *His Book of Problems* . . . . *His Last Legacy* . . . . A New Edition. Philadelphia: printed for the Booksellers, 1798.

Ashton, John, ed. *Chap-Books of the Eighteenth Century.* London: Chatto and Windus, 1882.

Barton, Andrew [Thomas Forrest?]. *The Disappointment; or, the Force of Credulity. A New American Comic-Opera of Two Acts.* New York: William Goddard, 1767.

Barton, Benjamin Smith. *Fragments of the Natural History of Pennsylvania.* Philadelphia: Way & Groff, 1799.

———. *A Memoir Concerning the Fascinating Faculty Which Has Been Ascribed to the Rattle-Snake and Other American Serpents.* Philadelphia: for the author by Henry Sweitzer, 1796. Also printed in *Transactions of the American Philosophical Society,* IV (1799): 74-113.

[Barton, Benjamin Smith.]. *Supplement to a Memoir Concerning the Fascinating Faculty Which Has Been Ascribed to the Rattle-Snake and Other American Serpents.* [Philadelphia: n.p., 1800].

B., J. [John Bartram?]. "Remarkable and Authentic Instances of the Fascinating Power of the Rattlesnake . . . ." *The Gentleman's Magazine,* XXXV (November 1765): 511-14.

Bartram, William. *The Travels of William Bartram.* Ed. by Francis Harper. New Haven: Yale University Press, 1958.

Beauvois, de. "Memoir on Amphibia: Serpents." *Transactions of the American Philosophical Society,* IV (1799): 362-81.

Belknap, Jeremy. *The Belknap Papers. Collections of the Massachusetts Historical Society,* 5th Series, vols. II-III.

Berkeley, George. *The Works of George Berkeley, Bishop of Cloyne.* Ed. by A. A. Luce and T. E. Jessop. New York: Thomas Nelson and Sons Ltd., 1948-57.

Beveridge, William. *Private Thoughts.* [Boston?: n.p., 1730?].

Blackmore, Richard. *Creation.* Philadelphia: Robert Johnson, 1806.

Blackstone, William. *Commentaries on the Laws of England.* Philadelphia: Robert Bell, 1771-72.

Blome, Richard. *The Present State of His Majesties Isles and Territories in America.* London: H. Clark, 1687.

Blumenbach. "On the Fascinating Power of the Rattle-Snake, With Some Remarks on Dr. Barton's Memoir on That Subject." *The Philosophical Magazine,* II (December 1798): 251-56.

Boswell, James. *Boswell's Life of Johnson Together with Boswell's Journal of a Tour of the Hebrides and Johnson's Diary of a Journal into North Wales.* Edited by George Birkbeck Hill and revised by L. F. Powell. Oxford: Clarendon Press, 1964.

Bradstreet, Anne. *The Works of Anne Bradstreet.* Ed. by Jeannine Hensley. Cambridge: Harvard University Press, 1967.

Brahm, William Gerard De. *De Brahm's Report of the General Survey in the Southern District of North America.* Ed. by Louis De Vorsey, Jr. Columbia, S.C.: University of South Carolina Press, 1971.

*A Brief Essay on the Number Seven.* Newport: printed for the author, 1735.

Buchan, William. *Domestic Medicine or the Family Physician.* Philadelphia: John Dunlap for R. Aitken, 1772.

Burn, [Richard]. *An Abridgment of Burn's Justice of the Peace and Parish Officers.* Abridged by J. Greenleaf. Boston: Joseph Greenleaf, 1773.

Burr, George Lincoln, ed. *Narratives of the Witchcraft Cases, 1648-1706.* New York: Barnes and Noble, Inc., 1968.

Burton, Robert. *The Anatomy of Melancholy.* Ed. by Floyd Dell and Paul Jordan-Smith. New York: Tudor Publishing Co., 1927.

Byrd, William. *Another Secret Diary of William Byrd of Westover For the Years 1739-1741.* Ed. by Maude H. Woodfin. Decoded by Marion Tinling. Richmond, Va.: The Dietz Press, 1942.

———. *Histories of the Dividing Line Betwixt Virginia and North Carolina.* Introduced by Percy G. Adams and William K. Boyd. New York: Dover Publications, Inc., 1967.

———. "Letters of William Byrd, 2nd, of Westover, Va." *Virginia Magazine of History and Biography,* IX (January 1902): 225-51.

———. *The London Diary (1717-1721) and Other Writings.* Ed. by Louis B. Wright and Marion Tinling. New York: Oxford University Press, 1958.

———. *The Prose Works.* Ed. by Louis B. Wright. Cambridge: Harvard University Press, 1966.

Callender, John. *A Sermon Preach'd at the Ordination of Mr. Jeremiah Condy.* Boston: Kneeland & Green, 1739.

Calvin, Jean [John]. *An Admonicion Against Astrology Iudiciall.* Trans. by G. G. London: R. Hall, [1561].

Calvin, John [Jean]. *Commentaries on the First Book of Moses Called Genesis.* Vol. I. Grand Rapids, Mich.: Wm. B. Eerdmans Publishing Company, n.d.

Carter, Landon. *The Diary of Colonel Landon Carter of Sabine Hall, 1752-1778.* Ed. by Jack P. Greene. Charlottesville, Va.: University Press of Virginia, 1965.

Catesby, Mark. *The Natural History of Carolina, Florida, and the Bahama Islands.* London: C. Marsh 1754.

Chambers, Ephraim. *Cyclopedia: or an Universal Dictionary of Arts and Sciences.* 5th ed. (1741–43), and 7th ed. (1751–52).

———. *Cyclopedia: or an Universal Dictionary of Arts and Sciences.* Supplemented and improved by Abraham Rees. (1786).

Chandler, Allen D., ed. *Statutes, Colonial and Revolutionary, 1768-1773.* Vol. XIX, Part I of *The Colonial Records of the State of Georgia.*

———. *Statutes, Colonial and Revolutionary, 1774–1805.* Vol. XIX, Part II of *The Colonial Records of the State of Georgia.*

———. *Statutes Enacted by the Royal Legislature of Georgia From Its First Session in 1754 to 1768.* Vol. XVII of *The Colonial Records of the State of Georgia.*

Chandler, Thomas Bradbury. *The Life of Samuel Johnson.* London: C. and J. Rivington, 1824.

Charles, R. H. *The Apocrypha and Pseudoepigrapha of the Old Testament in English.* Oxford: Clarendon Press, 1968.

*The Charter and General Laws of the Colony and Province of Massachusetts Bay.* Boston: T. B. Wait and Co., 1814.

*The Charter Granted by His Majesty Charles II to the Colony of Rhode-Island and Providence Plantations, in America.* New Port: James Franklin, 1730.

*The Charter Granted by His Majesty King Charles II.* Newport: Widow Franklin, 1744.

*The Charter, Granted by His Majesty, King Charles II to the Governor and Company of the English Colony of Rhode-Island and Providence-Plantations in New-England in America.* Newport: Samuel Hall, 1767.

Chauncy, Charles. *Civil Magistrates.* Boston: by order of the Honorable House of Representatives, 1747.

Colden, Cadwallader. *An Explication of the First Causes of Action in Matter, and of the Cause of Gravity.* New York: James Parker, 1745.

———. *The Letters and Papers of Cadwallader Colden.* Vols. L-LVI and LXVII-LXVIII of the *Collections of the New-York Historical Society.*

Collins, Nicholas. "Philological Views of Some Very Ancient Words in Several Languages." *Transactions of the American Philosophical Society,* IV(1799): 476-509.

*The Colonial Laws of New York.* Albany: James B. Lyon, 1894.

*Conductor Generalis, or, a Guide for Justices of the Peace* . . . . [New York, 1711].

*Conductor Generalis: or the Office, Duty and Authority of Justices of the Peace, High-Sheriffs, Under-Sheriffs* . . . . Philadelphia: Andrew Bradford, 1722.

*Conductor Generalis* . . . . 2nd ed. Philadelphia: B. Franklin & D. Hall, 1749.

*Conductor Generalis* . . . . 2nd ed. New York: J. Parker, 1749.

Cooper, Thomas, ed. *The Statutes at Large of South Carolina.* Columbia, S.C.: A. S. Johnson, 1836-39.

*Copy of the Order for Repealing of Several Acts.* Boston: printed by Order of the Honorable the Lieutenant Governor and Council; by Bartholemew Green, and John Allen, 1697.

Cox, Thomas. *Catalogue of Books.* Boston: T. Cox, [1734].

Cradock, Thomas. "Thomas Cradock's Sermon on the Governance of Maryland's Established Church." Ed. and intro. by David Curtis Skaggs. *William and Mary Quarterly,* 3rd Series, XXVII (October 1970): 630-53.

Cullen, William. *First Lines of the Practice of Physic.* Worcester, Mass.: Isaiah Thomas, 1790.

Culpeper, [Nicholas]. *Culpeper's English Family Physician or Medical Herbal Enlarged.* London: W. Locke, 1792.

Culpeper, Nicholas. *A Directory for Midwives.* London: C. Hitch, 1762.

———. *The English Physician Enlarged.* London: S. Ballard, 1765.

———. *Pharmacopoeia Londinensis: or the London Dispensatory.* Boston: Nicholas Boone, 1720.

D'Aboville. "Two Hearts Found in One Partridge." *Proceedings of the American Philosophical Society,* II (1786): 330-35.

Dalton, Michael. *The Covntrey Justice.* London: 1618.

———. *The Country Justice.* In the Savoy: E. and R. Nutt, and R. Gosling, 1727.

———. *The Country Justice.* London: H. Lintot, 1742.

Darlington, William, ed. *Memorials of John Bartram and Humphry Marshall.* Philadelphia: Lindsay & Blakiston, 1849.

Davies, Samuel. *Collected Poems of Samuel Davies, 1723-1761.* Ed. by Richard Beale Davis. Gainesville, Fla.: Scholars' Facsimiles & Reprints, 1968.

Davis, James. *The Office and Authority of a Justice of Peace.* Newbern, N.C.: James Davis, 1774.

Deane, Samuel. *NewEngland* [sic] *Farmer, or Georgic Dictionary.* 2nd ed. Worcester, Mass.: Isaiah Thomas, 1797.

Defoe, Daniel. *A System of Magick; or, a History of the Black Art.* London: J. Roberts, 1727.

Derham, William. *Astro-Theology: Or, a Demonstration of the Being and Attributes of God From a Survey of the Heavens.* 7th ed. London: W. Innys and R. Manby, 1738.

———. *Physico-Theology: Or, a Demonstration of the Being and Attributes of God From His Works of Creation.* Glasgow, Scotland: Robert Urie, 1758.

"Description of Bones, &c. Found Near the River Ohio." *The Columbian Magazine or Monthly Miscellany,* I (November, 1786): 103-7.

Diderot and D'Alembert. *Encyclopédie, ou Dictionnaire Raisonné Des Sciences, Des Arts et Des Métiers.* New York: Readex Microprint Corporation, 1969.

Drake, Samuel G. *Annals of Witchcraft in New England and Elsewhere in the United States.* New York: Benjamin Blom, 1959.

Eliot, Jared. *Essays Upon Field-Husbandry in New-England.* Boston: Edes and Gill, 1760 [1761].

Erra Pater [pseud.]. *The Book of Knowledge Treating of the Wisdom of the Ancients in Four Parts.* Made English by W. Lilly. Portsmouth, N.H.: Charles Peirce, 1795.

Evelyn, John. *The Diary of John Evelyn.* Ed. by E. S. De Beer. Oxford: Clarendon Press, 1955.

Farquhar, George. *The Beaux-Stratagem.* In *Restoration Plays.* Introduction by Edmund Grosse. New York: E. P. Dutton & Co. Inc., 1932.

———. *The Recruiting Officer.* Lincoln, Neb.: University of Nebraska Press, 1965.

Ficino, Marsilio. "Marsilio Ficino's Commentary on Plato's *Symposium.*" Ed. and trans. by Sears Reynolds Jayne. *University of Missouri Studies,* XIX (1944).

Filson, John. *The Discovery, Settlement, and Present State of Kentucke.* Wilmington, Del.: James Adams, 1784.

Fithian, Philip Vickers. *Journal and Letters of Philip Vickers Fithian.* Ed. by Hunter Dickinson Farish. Princeton, N.J.: Princeton University Press, 1943.

Force, Peter, ed. *Tracts.* New York: Peter Smith, 1947.

Franklin, Benjamin (1650-1727). "Commonplace Book of Benjamin Franklin." Ed. by Appleton P. C. Griffin. *Transactions of the Colonial Society of Massachusetts,* X (January 1906): 190-205.

Franklin, Benjamin (1706-90). *Autobiography.* Ed. by Leonard W. Labaree and others. New Haven: Yale University Press, 1964.

———. *Experiments and Observations on Electricity, Made at Philadelphia in America.* 4th ed. London: David Henry, 1769.

———. *The Papers of Benjamin Franklin.* Ed. by Leonard W. Labaree. New Haven: Yale University Press, 1960- .

———. *The Political Thought of Benjamin Franklin.* Ed. by Ralph Ketcham. New York: Bobbs-Merrill Company, Inc., 1965.

———. *The Writings of Benjamin Franklin.* Ed. by Albert Henry Smyth. New York: Haskell House Publications, Ltd., 1970.

Frothingham, Octavius Brooks. *Transcendentalism in New England: A History.* New York: Harper & Brothers, 1959.

Gadbury, John. *Nauticum Astrologicum: or, the Astrological Seaman.* London: George Sawbridge, 1710.

Gatchel, Samuel. *The Signs of the Times.* Danvers, Mass.: E. Russell, 1781.

Gilbert, William. *On the Lodestone and Magnetic Bodies and on the Great Magnet the Earth.* Trans. by P. Fleury Mottelay. Vol. 28 of *Great Books of the Western World.* Chicago: Encyclopaedia Britannica, Inc., 1952.

Glanvill, Joseph. *Saducismus Triumphatus.* London: J. Collins, 1681.

Godfrey, Thomas. *The Court of Fancy: A Poem.* Philadelphia: William Dunlap, 1762.

———. *Juvenile Poems on Various Subjects.* Philadelphia: Henry Miller, 1765.

———. *The Prince of Parthia.* In *Representative American Plays.* Ed. by Arthur Hobson Quinn. 7th ed. New York: Appleton-Century-Crofts, Inc., 1957.

Goldsmith, Oliver. *A History of the Earth, and Animated Nature.* Philadelphia: Mathew Carey, 1795.

[Gordon, Thomas and Trenchard, John.]. *The Independent Whig.* Philadelphia: S. Keimer, 1724.

Graham, James G. "Further Accounts of Fossil Bones in Orange and Ulster Counties." *Medical Repository and Review of American Publications,* IV (1801): 213-14.

Greenwood, Isaac. *An Experimental Course of Mechanical Philosophy.* Boston: n.p., 1726.

———. *A Philosophical Discourse Concerning the Mutability and Changes of the Material World.* Boston: S. Gerrish, 1731.

Grosvenor, B[enjamin]. *Health. An Essay on Its Nature, Value, Uncertainty, Preservation and Best Improvement.* 3rd. ed. Boston: D. & J. Kneeland, 1761.

Hale, John. *A Modest Inquiry Into the Nature of Witchcraft.* Boston: Kneeland and Adams, 1771.

Harrower, John. "Diary of John Harrower, 1773-1776." *American Historical Review,* VI (October 1900): 65-107.

Harvard College. *Pietas et Gratulatio.* Boston: J. Green & J. Russell, 1761.

Heckewelder, John. "An Account of the History, Manners, and Customs of the Indian Nations, Who Once Inhabited Pennsylvania and the Neighboring States." *Transactions of the Historical & Literary Committee of the American Philosophical Society,* I (1819): 1-348.

Hobby, William. *Self-Examination.* Boston: Kneeland & Green, 1746.

Hunter, Robert. *Androboros.* Monoropolis [New York], 1714.

———. "Robert Hunter's Androboros." Ed. by Lawrence A. Leder. *New York Public Library Bulletin,* LXVIII (March 1964): 153-90.

*The Husband-man's Guide.* 2nd ed. Enlarged. Boston: Elea Phillips, 1712.

Hutchinson, John. *The Philosophical and Theological Works.* Ed. by Robert Spearman & Julius Bate. London: various publishers, 1749-76.

Hutchinson, Thomas. *The History of the Colony and Province of Massachusetts-Bay.* New York: Kraus Reprint Co., 1970.

Inglis, Charles. *The Duty of Honoring the King.* New York: Hugh Gaine, 1780.

[Jacob, Giles]. *Every Man His Own Lawyer.* 7th ed. New York: Hugh Gaine, 1768.

Jefferson, Thomas. *A Jeffersonian Profile as Revealed in His Letters.* Ed. by Saul K. Padover. New York: The John Day Company, 1956.

———. "A Memoir on the Discovery of Certain Bones of a Quadruped of the Clawed Kind in the Western Part of Virginia." *Transactions of the American Philosophical Society,* IV (1799): 246-60.

———. *Notes on the State of Virginia.* Ed. by William Peden. Chapel Hill: University of North Carolina Press, 1955.

———. *The Papers of Thomas Jefferson.* Ed. by Julian P. Boyd. Princeton: Princeton University Press, 1950- .

Jenks, Samuel. "Journal of Captain Jenks." *Proceedings of the Massachusetts Historical Society,* 2nd Series, V (1889-90): 352-91.

Johnson, Samuel. *Samuel Johnson, President of Kings College: His Career and Writings.* Ed. by Herbert and Carol Schneider. New York: Columbia University Press, 1929.

Johnson, William. *The Papers of Sir William Johnson.* Albany: University of the State of New York, 1921-65.

Jones, Hugh. *The Present State of Virginia.* Chapel Hill: University of North Carolina Press, 1956.

Jones, William. *Physiological Disquisitions: or, Discourses on the Natural Philosophy of the Elements.* London: J. Rivington, and Sons, 1781.

Josselyn, John. "An Account of Two Voyages to New-England." *Collections of the Massachusetts Historical Society,* 3rd Series, III: 211-354.

———. *New-England Rarities Discovered.* London: G. Widdowes, 1672.

Kalm, Pehr [Peter]. "Pehr Kalm's Account of the North American Rattle Snake and the Medicine Used in the Treatment of the Sting." Trans. by Esther Louise Larsen. *The American Midlands Naturalist,* LVII (April 1957): 502-11.

———. *Peter Kalm's Travels in North America: The English Version of 1770.* Trans. by John Reinhold Foster. Ed. by Adolph B. Benson. N.Y.: Dover Publications, Inc., 1964.

Kearsley, [John]. "Extract of a Letter From Dr. Kearsley to Mr. P. Collinson: Dated Philadelphia, Nov. 18, 1735." *The Gentleman's Magazine,* XXXVI (February 1766): 73-76.

Kendall, Edward Augustus. *Travels Through the Northern Parts of the United States in the Years 1807 and 1808.* New York: I. Riley, 1809.

Kennedy, John. *A Scriptural Account of the Uncommon Darkness That Happened . . . May 19, 1780.* [Boston, 1800].

*Laws of Maryland.* Annapolis, Md.: Jonas Green, 1765.

*Laws of New-York, From the Year 1691, to 1751, Inclusive.* New York: James Parker, 1752.

*Law[s] of New-York From the 11th Nov. 1752, to 22nd May 1762.* New York: William Weyman, 1762.

*Laws of the Commonwealth of Pennsylvania.* Vol. I. Philadelphia: Hall and Sellers, 1797.

*Laws of the State of Delaware.* Newcastle, Del.: Samuel and John Adams, 1797.

Lawson, John. *A New Voyage to Carolina.* Ed. by Hugh Talmage Lefler. Chapel Hill: University of North Carolina Press, 1967.

Lederer, John. *The Discoveries of John Lederer.* Ed. by William P. Cumming. Charlottesville, Va.: University of Virginia Press, 1958.

Le Jau, Francis. *The Carolina Chronicle of Dr. Francis Le Jau, 1706-1717.* Ed. by Frank J. Klingberg. Berkeley and Los Angeles: University of California Press, 1956.

Levin, David. *What Happened at Salem?* 2nd ed. New York: Harcourt Brace & World, Inc., 1960.

Lindeström, Peter. *Geographia Americae With an Account of the Delaware Indians Based on Surveys and Notes Made in 1654-1656.* Trans. from the manuscript by Amandus Johnson. Philadelphia: The Swedish Colonial Society, 1925.

Livingston, William [Smith, William and Scott, John Morton]. *The Independent Reflector.* Ed. by Milton Klein. Cambridge: Harvard University Press, 1963.

Livingston, William. *Philosophical Solitudes.* New York: James Parker, 1747.

Locke, John. *An Essay Concerning Human Understanding.* Ed. by Alexander Cambell Fraser. New York: Dover Publications, Inc., 1959.

Markham, J. [Gervase], G. Jefferies, and Discreet Indians. *The Citizen and Countryman's Experienced Farrier.* Baltimore: Somes, 1797.

Martin, Benjamin. *The Philosophical Grammer.* 7th ed. London: J. & F. Rivington, 1749.

Mather, Cotton. *The Christian Philosopher: A Collection of the Best Discoveries in Nature With Religious Improvements.* London: Eman. Matthews, 1721.

———. *Coelestinus.* Boston: Kneeland for Belknap, 1723.

———. *Manuductio Ad Ministerium: Directions for a Candidate of the Ministry.* [New York?]: Columbia University Press for Facsimile Text Society, 1938.

———. *The Wonders of the Invisible World.* Ann Arbor, Mich.: University Microfilms, 1969.

Mather, Increase. *Angelographia.* Boston: B. Green & F. Allen for Samuel Phillips, 1696.

———. *Several Sermons.* Boston: B. Green for B. Eliot, 1715.

Mead, Richard. *A Treatise Concerning the Influence of the Sun and Moon Upon the Human Body.* London: J. Brindley, 1748.

Mein, John. *A Catalog of Curious and Valuable Books.* [Boston]: Mein, [1766?].

———. *A Catalogue of Mein's Circulating Library.* Boston: [Mein], 1765.

Miller, Samuel. *A Brief Retrospect of the Eighteenth Century.* London: J. Johnson, 1805.

[Minor, Jehu]. *Catechism, Physico-Medicum.* Hartford, Conn.: Watson & Goodwin, [1778].

Montaigne, Michael. *The Essays of Michael Lord of Montaigne.* Trans. by John Florio. Introduced by Desmond MacCarthy. New York: E. P. Dutton & Co. Inc., 1928.

Morse, Jedidiah. *The American Universal Geography.* 3rd. ed. Part I. Boston: Thomas & Andrews, 1796.

Morton, Charles. *Compendium Physicae.* Vol. XXXIII of the *Collections of the Colonial Society of Massachusetts.*

*A Most Unaccountable Relation of One Miss Sarah Green.* N.p.: n.p. 1762.

*The Nature and Importance of Oaths and Juries.* New York: Ja. Parker, 1747.

*A New and True Relation, of a Little Girl in the Country of Hartford, at Salmon-Brook in Simsbury Who Acted in a Strange Manner, Supposed to be Bewitch'd, on March 1763.* Boston, 1766.

*The New England Primer.* Ed. by Paul Leicester Ford. New York: Dodd, Mead and Company, 1897.

[New York City]. *A Catalogue of the Library Belonging to the Corporation of the City of New-York.* New York: Holt, 1766.

Nobles, John. *These are the Predictions of John Nobles, Astrologer and Doctor . . . for . . . 1794.* Boston, [1793?].

"Observations on the Influence of the Moon on Climate and the Annual Economy." *Medical Repository and Review of American Publications,* IV ([1801] 2nd ed.; 1808): 285-90.

Ovid. *Metamorphoses.* Trans. by Frank Justus Miller. Loeb Classical Library. Cambridge: Harvard University Press, 1951.

———. *Ovid's Metamorphosis Englished, Mythologiz'd, and Represented in Figures.* Trans. and annotated by George Sandys. Oxford: John Lichfield, 1632.

Parker, George, ed. *Eland's Tutor to Astrology: or Astrology Made Easy.* 10th ed. London: printed for G. Conyers, 1704.

Parker, James. *Conductor Generalis.* Woodbridge, N.J.: Parker for Hall, 1764.

Peale, Rembrandt. *An Historical Disquisition on the Mammoth.* London: printed for E. Lawrence by C. Mercier, 1803.

*Pennsylvania Archives.* 8th Series, vol. V.

Philanthropos [pseud.]. *The Universal Peace-Maker.* Philadelphia: Anthony Ambruster, 1764.

Plotinus. *The Enneads.* Trans. by Stephen MacKenna. 4th ed. revised. London: Faber and Faber Limited, 1969.

Powers, Peter. *Jesus Christ the True King.* Newbury-Port, Mass.: John Mycall, 1778.

Prior, William. *A Charge Delivered . . . at Bridport, in Dorset, Sept. 26, 1738.* 3rd ed. Boston: J. Bushell and J. Green for D. Gookin, 1748.

*The Public Laws of the State of South-Carolina.* Philadelphia: Aitken and Son, 1790.

Raleigh, Walter. *The History of the World. The Works of Sir Walter Ralegh* [sic] *Kt.* New York: Burt Franklin, n.d.

Rittenhouse, David. *An Oration.* Philadelphia: John Dunlap, 1775.

[Rogers, Ransford.]. "The Morris-Town Ghost Deliniated." *A Collection of Essays on a Variety of Subjects in Prose and Verse.* Newark, N.J.: John Woods, 1797.

Rohault, [Jacques]. *Rohault's System of Natural Philosophy Illustrated with Dr. Samuel Clarke's Notes Taken Mostly Out of Sir Isaac Newton's Philosophy.* Trans. by John Clarke. London: James Knapton, 1723.

Rush, Benjamin. *Letters of Benjamin Rush.* Ed. by L. H. Butterfield. Princeton, N.J.: Princeton University Press, 1951.

———. *The Selected Writings of Benjamin Rush.* Ed. by Dagobert D. Runes. New York: Philosophical Library, 1947.

Sargent, Winthrop, ed. *The Loyalist Poetry of the Revolution.* Philadelphia: Collins, 1857.

Scot, Reginald, *The Discoverie of Witchcraft.* Introduced by Hugh Ross Williamson. Carbondale, Ill.: Southern Illinois University Press, 1964.

Seabury, Samuel. *St. Peter's Exhortation.* New York: H. Gaine, [1777].

Sewall, Samuel. *Diary. Collections of the Massachusetts Historical Society,* 5th series, vols. V-VII.

Simpson, William. *The Practical Justice of the Peace . . . of His Majesty's Province of South-Caroline.* Charlestown. Robert Wells, 1761.

Smith, James Edward, ed. *A Selection of the Correspondence of Linnaeus and Other Naturalists.* London: Longman, Hurst, Rees, Orme, and Brown, 1821.

[Smith, John] J. S. *The Husbandman's Magazine.* Boston: Allen for Boone, 1718.

Starke, Richard. *The Office and Authority of a Justice of Peace.* Williamsburg: Alexander Purdie and John Dixon, 1774.

Stiles, Ezra. *The Literary Diary of Ezra Stiles.* Ed. by Franklin Bowditch Dexter. New York: Charles Scribner's Sons, 1901.

Swift, Jonathan. *Satires and Personal Writings of Jonathan Swift.* Ed. by William Alfred Eddy. London: Oxford University Press, 1965.

*The Table* [to the laws of 1767]. [Newport]: Southwick, 1768.

Taylor, Edward. *The Poems of Edward Taylor.* Ed. by Donald E. Stanford. New Haven: Yale University Press, 1968.

———.*The Poetical Works of Edward Taylor.* Ed. by Thomas H. Johnston. New York: Rockland Editions, 1939.

Thacher, James. "Observations Upon the Natural Production of Iron Ores." *Collections of the Massachusetts Historical Society,* 1st series, vol. IX: 253-68.

Thomson, James. *The Complete Poetical Works of James Thomson.* Ed. by J. Logie Robertson. New York: Oxford University Press, 1951.

[Turell, E.] E. T. "Detection of Witchcraft." *Collections of the Massachusetts Historical Society,* 2nd series, X: 6-22.

Turner, George. "Memoir on the Extraneous Fossils Denominated Mammoth Bones." *Transactions of the American Philosophical Society,* IV (1799): 510-18.

Virgil. *Georgics. Works.* Trans. by H. Rushton. Loeb Classical Library. Cambridge: Harvard University Press, 1950.

———. *The Georgics of Virgil.* Trans. by John Dryden. N.Y.: Cheshire House, 1931.

Voltaire. *Candide, Zadig and Selected Stories.* Ed. by Donald M. Frame. Bloomington, Ind.: Indiana University Press, 1961.

*A Warning Piece. A Poetical Thought.* [Boston, 1780].

Waterhouse, Benjamin. *Heads of a Course of Lectures.* Providence, R.I.: Wheeler, [1788?].

———. *Heads of a Course of Lectures Intended as an Introduction to Natural History.* [Providence, R. I.: Wheeler, ca. 1794].

———. *A Synopsis of a Course of Lectures on the Theory and Practice of Medicine.* Boston: Adams and Nourse, 1786.

Watts, Isaac. *Geography and Astronomy. The Works of the Rev. Isaac Watts.* Leeds: Edward Baines, 1813.

———. *Logick: or, the Right Use of Reason in the Enquiry After Truth.* 16th ed. Philadelphia: Thomas Dobson, 1789.

Webb, George. *The Office and Authority of a Justice of the Peace.* Williamsburg: William Parks, 1736.

Webster, John. *Metallographia: Or: An History of Metals.* London: A. C. for Walter Kettilby, 1671.

Wesley, John. *The Journal of the Rev. John Wesley.* Ed. by Nehemiah Curnock. London: Charles H. Kelly, 1909-16.

Whiston, William. *New Theory of the Earth.* 6th ed. London: J. Whiston and B. White, 1755.

Willard, Samuel. *A Compleat Body of Divinity.* Boston: B. Green and S. Kneeland, 1726.

Williams, Samuel. *The Natural and Civil History of Vermont.* Walpole, N.H.: Isaiah Thomas and David Carlisle, 1794.

———. *The Natural and Civil History of Vermont.* 2nd ed. enlarged. Burlington, Vt.: Samuel Mills, 1809.

Winslow, Ola Elizabeth, ed. *American Broadside Verse.* New Haven: Yale University Press, 1930.

Wood, William. *New England's Prospects.* New York: Burt Franklin, 1967.

Zeisberger, David. "David Zeisberger's History of the Northern American Indians." Ed. and trans. by Arthur Butler Hulbert and William Nathaniel Schwarze. *Ohio Archeological and Historical Publications,* XIX (1910).

## Secondary Sources

Adams, Frank Dawson. *The Birth and Development of the Geological Sciences.* Baltimore: The Williams and Wilkins Company, 1938.

Adams, George C. S. "Rattlesnake Eye." *Southern Folklore Quarterly,* II (March 1938): 37-38.

Adams, James Truslow. *Provincial Society, 1690-1763.* New York: The Macmillan Co., 1927.

Allen, Don Cameron. *The Star-Crossed Renaissance: The Quarrel About Astrology and Its Influence in England.* New York: Octagon Books, Inc., 1966.

Allen, Neal. "A Maine Witch." *Old-Time New England,* LXI (Winter 1971): 75-81.

Altschule, Mark D. "The Pneuma Concept of the Soul." *Journal of the History of the Behavioral Sciences,* I (October 1965): 314-20.

Andrews, Charles M. *Colonial Folkways.* New Haven: Yale University Press, 1919.

Arthos, John. *The Language of Natural Description in Eighteenth-Century Poetry.* Ann Arbor, Mich.: The University of Michigan Press, 1949.

Ashton, John. *The Devil in Britain and America.* N.p.: Ward and Downey, 1896.

Aston, Margaret E. "The Fiery Trigon Conjunction: An Elizabethan Astrological Prediction." *Isis,* LXI (Summer 1970): 159-87.

Aurand, A. Monroe. *Little Known Facts About the Ritual of the Jews and the Esoteric Folklore of the Pennsylvania-Germans.* Harrisburg, Pa.: The Aurand Press, 1939.

Bailyn, Bernard. *Education in the Forming of American Society: Needs and Opportunities for Study.* Chapel Hill: University of North Carolina Press, 1960.

Baldwin, Alice M. *The New England Clergy and the American Revolution.* New York: Frederick Unger Publishing Co., 1965.

Barber, John. *Historical Collections of the State of New Jersey.* Newark, N.J.: Benjamin Olds, [1852].

Barker, Charles A. *American Convictions: Cycles of Public Thought, 1600-1850.* Philadelphia: J. B. Lippincott Company, 1970.

Barnes, Gertrude. "Superstitions and Maxims From Dutchess County, New York." *The Journal of American Folk-Lore,* XXXVI (January-March 1923): 16-22.

Baroja, Julio Caro. *The World of the Witches.* Trans. by O. N. V. Glendinning. Chicago: University of Chicago Press, 1964.

Bates, George Edward, Jr. "The Emergence of a Modern Mind in Colonial America, 1700-1760." Unpublished Ph.D. dissertation, University of Illinois at Urbana-Champaign, 1970.

Baughman, Ernest W. *Type and Motif Index of the Folktales of England and North America.* The Hague: Mauton & Co., 1966.

Beall, Otho T., Jr. "*Aristotle's Master Piece* in America: A Landmark in the Folklore of Medicine." *William and Mary Quarterly,* 3rd Series, XX (April 1963): 207-22.

——— and Shryock, Richard H. *Cotton Mather: First Significant Figure in American Medicine.* Baltimore: Johns Hopkins University Press, 1954.

Beardsley, E. Edwards. *Life and Correspondence of Samuel Johnson, D.D.* New York: Hurd and Houghton, 1874.

———. *Life and Times of William Samuel Johnson.* New York: Hurd and Houghton, 1876.

Beck, H. P. "Herpetological Lore From the Black Ridge." *Midwest Folklore,* II (Fall 1952): 141-50.

Bedini, Silvio A. *The Life of Benjamin Banneker.* New York: Charles Scribner's Sons, 1972.

Bell, Charles H. *History of the Town of Exeter, New Hampshire.* Exeter: [Press of J. E. Farwell & Co., Boston], 1888.

Bell, Whitfield J., Jr. *Early American Science: Needs and Opportunities for Study.* Williamsburg: Institute of Early American History and Culture, 1955.

———. "Medical Practice in Colonial America." *Bulletin of the History of Medicine,* XXXI (September-October 1957): 442-53.

———. "Medical Students and Their Examiners in Eighteenth Century America." *Transactions and Studies of the College of Physicians of Philadelphia,* 4th Series, XXI (June 1953): 14-30.

——. "The Reverend Mr. Joseph Morgan, An American Correspondent of the Royal Society, 1732-1739." *Proceedings of the American Philosophical Society,* VC (1951): 254-61.

Bila, Constantin. *La Croyance A La Magie Au XVIII^e Siecle En France.* Paris, Librairie J. Gamber, 1925.

Binger, Carl. *Revolutionary Doctor: Benjamin Rush, 1746-1813.* New York: W. W. Norton & Co., Inc., 1966.

Black, Robert C. III. *The Younger John Winthrop.* New York: Columbia University Press, 1966.

Blanton, Wyndham B. *Medicine in Virginia in the Eighteenth Century.* Richmond, Va.: Garrett & Massie, Incorporated, 1931.

Blau, Joseph Leon. *The Christian Interpretation of the Cabala in the Renaissance.* Port Washington, New York: Kennikat Press, 1965.

Bliss, William Root. *The Old Colony Town and Other Sketches.* Boston: Houghton, Mifflin Company, 1893.

Bolton, Ethel Stanwood and Coe, Eva Johnston. *American Samplers.* Boston: The Massachusetts Society of the Colonial Dames of America, 1921.

Bond, Richmond P. "Isaac Bickerstaff, Esq." *Restoration and Eighteenth Century Literature: Essays in Honor of Alan Dugald McKillop.* Ed. by Carrol Camden. Chicago: University of Chicago Press, 1963.

Boorstin, Daniel J. *The Lost World of Thomas Jefferson.* Boston: Beacon Press, 1960.

*Boston Herald,* February 6, 1919.

Bothell, Larry Lee. "Cloak and Gown: A Study of Religion and Learning in the Early Career of Samuel Johnson of Connecticut." Unpublished Ph.D dissertation, Princeton University, 1966.

Boyer, Paul and Stephen Nissenbaum. *Salem Possessed: The Social Origins of Witchcraft.* Cambridge: Harvard University Press, 1974.

Boyer, Paul S. "Borrowed Rhetoric: The Massachusetts Excise Controversy of 1754." *William and Mary Quarterly,* 3rd Series, XXI (July 1964): 328-51.

Bradley, Bert E., Jr. "The *Invento* of John Ward." *Speech Monographs,* XXVI (March 1959): 56-63.

——. "John Ward's Concept of *Dispositio.*" *Speech Monographs,* XXIV (November 1957): 258-63.

Brasch, Frederick E. "The Newtonian Epoch in the American Colonies (1680-1783)." *Proceedings of the American Antiquarian Society,* N.S., IL (October 1939): 314-32.

Brayton, Susan Stanton. "The Library of an Eighteenth-Century Gentleman of Rhode Island." *New England Quarterly,* VIII (June 1935): 277-83.

Bridenbaugh, Carl. "Dr. Thomas Bond's Essay on the Utility of Clinical Lectures." *Journal of the History of Medicine and Allied Sciences,* II (Winter 1947): 10-19.

Briggs, K. M. *The Anatomy of Puck: An Examination of Fairy Beliefs Among Shakespeare's Contemporaries and Successors.* London: Routledge and Kegan Paul, 1959.

Brinton, D. C. "Reminiscences of Pennsylvania Folk-Lore." *Journal of American Folk-Lore,* V (July-September 1892): 177-85.

*Bristol, Connecticut (In the Olden Times "New Cambridge").* Hartford, Conn.: City Printing Co., 1907.

Broderick, Francis L. "Pulpit, Physics, and Politics: The Curriculum of the College of New Jersey, 1746-1794." *William and Mary Quarterly,* 3rd Series, VI (January 1949): 42-68.

Brooks, Chandler McC., *et al. Humors, Hormones, and Neurosecretions.* State University of New York, 1962.

Brown, Elizabeth Gaspar. *British Statutes in American Law, 1776-1836.* Ann Arbor, Mich.: The University of Michigan Law School, 1964.

Browne, Ray B. "Superstitions Used as Propaganda in the American Revolution." *New York Folklore Quarterly,* XVII (Autumn 1961): 202-11.

Brumm, Ursula. *American Thought and Religious Typology.* New Brunswick, N.J.: Rutgers University Press, 1970.

Brunet, Pierre. *L'Introduction des Théories de Newton En France Au XVIIIᵉ Siècle.* Paris: Librairie Scientifique Albert Blanchard, 1931.

Buck, William J. *Local Sketches and Legends Pertaining to Bucks and Montgomery Counties, Pennsylvania.* Privately printed, 1887.

———. "Local Superstitions." *Collections of the Historical Society of Pennsylvania,* I (1853): 377-81.

———. "Local Superstitions." *History of Montgomery County, Pennsylvania.* Ed. by Theodore W. Bean. Philadelphia: Everts & Peck, 1884.

Bullock, Thomas K. "Schools and Schooling in Eighteenth Century Virginia." Unpublished Ph.E. dissertation, Duke University, 1961.

Bullough, Vern L. "An Early American Sex Manual, Or, Aristotle Who?" *Early American Literature,* VII (Winter 1973): 236-46.

Burke, John. *A Genealogical and Heraldic History of the Extinct and Dormant Baronetcies of England.* London: Scott, Webster, and Geary, 1838.

Bush, Douglas. *Science and English Poetry: A Historical Sketch, 1590–1950.* New York: Oxford University Press, 1950.

Butler, Caleb. *History of the Town of Groton.* Boston: Press of T. R. Marvin, 1848.

"By the Signs." *Foxfire,* I (Fall 1967): 14-23, 56-61.

Callow, James T. "Edward Taylor Obeys Saint Paul." *Early American Literature,* IV (no. 3): 89-96.

Camden, Carroll, Jr. "Elizabethan Astrological Medicine." *Annals of Medical History,* N.S., II (March 1930): 217-26.

Cappon, Lester J. and Duff, Stella F. *Virginia Gazette Index 1736-1780.* Williamsburg: The Institute of Early American History and Culture, 1950.

Carey, George G. "Folklore from the Printed Sources of Essex County, Massachusetts." *Southern Folklore Quarterly,* XXXII (March 1968): 17-43.

Carlson, C. Lennart. "Thomas Godfrey in England." *American Literature,* VII (1935-36): 302-9.

Carlson, Eric T. "Tarantism or Hysteria? An American Case of 1801." *Journal of the History of Medicine and Allied Sciences,* XXVI (July 1971): 293-302.

——— and Simpson, Meribeth M. "Models of the Nervous System in Eighteenth Century Psychiatry." *Bulletin of the History of Medicine,* XLIII (March-April 1969): 101-15.

Carnochan, W. B. "Witch-Hunting and Belief in 1751: The Case of Thomas Colley and Ruth Osburne." *Journal of Social History,* IV (Summer 1971): 389-403.

Cassirer, Ernst. *The Philosophy of the Enlightenment.* Trans. by Fritz C. A. Koelln and James P. Pettegrove. Boston: Beacon Press, 1965.

———. *The Platonic Renaissance in England.* Trans. by James P. Pettegrove. Austin, Tex.: University of Texas Press, 1953.

Chalker, John. *The English Georgic: A Study in the Development of a Form.* Baltimore: Johns Hopkins University Press, 1969.

Chiel, Arthur A. "Ezra Stiles—The Education of an 'Hebrician.' " *American Jewish Historical Quarterly,* LX (March 1971): 235-41.

Chinard, Gilbert. "A Landmark in American Intellectual History." *The Princeton University Library Chronicle,* XIV (Winter 1953): 55-71.

Clark, Michael D. "Jonathan Boucher: The Mirror of Reaction." *The Huntington Library Quarterly,* XXXIII (November 1969): 19-32.

Claudel, Calvin. "Tales From San Diego." *California Folklore Quarterly,* II (April 1943): 113-20.

Cohen, I. Bernard. "The Beginning of Chemical Instruction in America: A Brief Account of the Teaching of Chemistry at Harvard Prior to 1800." *Chymia,* III (1950): 17-44.

———. *Franklin and Newton: An Inquiry into Speculative Newtonian Experimental Science and Franklin's Work in Electricity as an Example Thereof.* Philadelphia: The American Philosophical Society, 1956.

———. *Some Early Tools of American Science: An Account of the Early Scientific Instrument and Mineralogical and Biological Collections in Harvard University.* New York: Russell & Russell, 1950.

Cohen, Hennig. *The South Carolina Gazette: 1732-1775.* Columbia, S.C.: University of South Carolina Press, 1953.

Cohn, Norman. *Europe's Inner Demons: An Enquiry Inspired by the Great Witch-Hunt.* New York: Basic Books, Inc., 1975.

C[okayne], G. E. *Complete Baronetage.* Exeter: William Pollard & Co., 1900-6.

Colbourn, H. Trevor. *The Lamp of Experience: Whig History and the Intellectual Origins of the American Revolution.* Chapel Hill: University of North Carolina Press, 1965.

Coleman, George P., ed. *The Flat Hat Club and the Phi Beta Kappa Society.* Richmond, Va.: The Dietz Printing Co., 1916.

Converse, Harriet Maxwell. *Myths and Legends of the New York State Iroquois.* New York State Museum Bulletin 125, New York State Museum, 1908.

Cook, Elizabeth Christine. *Literary Influences in Colonial Newspapers, 1704-1750.* Port Washington, N.Y.: Kennikat Press, Inc., 1966.

Copeman, W. S. C. *Doctors and Disease in Tudor Times.* London: Dawson's of Pall Mall, 1960.

Cothren, William. *History of Ancient Woodbury, Connecticut.* Waterbury, Conn.: Bronson Brothers, 1854.

Cowen, David L. "The Boston Editions of Nicholas Culpeper." *Journal of the History of Medicine and Allied Sciences,* II (April 1956): 156-65.

Craig, Hardin. *The Enchanted Glass.* New York: Oxford University Press, 1936.

Craven, Wesley Frank. *The Colonies in Transition, 1660-1713.* New York: Harper & Row, 1968.

Cremin, Lawrence A. *American Education: The Colonial Experience, 1607-1783.* New York: Harper & Row, 1970.

Cross, Arthur Lyon. *The Anglican Episcopate and the American Colonies.* Cambridge: Harvard University Press, 1924.

Cross, Tom Peete. "Witchcraft in North Carolina." *Studies in Philology,* XVI (July 1919): 217-87.

Curti, Merle. *Human Nature in American Historical Thought.* N.p.: University of Missouri Press, 1968.

Daniels, George H. *Science in American Society: A Social History.* New York: Alfred A. Knopf, 1971.

Darnton, Robert. "In Search of the Enlightenment: Recent Attempts to Create a Social History of Ideas." *Journal of Modern History,* XLIII (March 1971): 113-32.

———. *Mesmerism and the End of the Enlightenment in France.* Cambridge: Harvard University Press, 1968.

———. "Reading, Writing and Publishing in Eighteenth-Century France: A Case Study in the Sociology of Literature." *Daedalus,* C. (Winter 1971): 214-56.

Davidson, Gustav. *A Dictionary of Angels.* New York: The Free Prss, 1967.

Davis, Horace. "Dr. Benjamin Gott's Library." *New England Historical and Genealogical Register,* LVI (October 1902); 340-44.

Davis, Richard Beale. "America in George Sandys' 'Ovid.' " *William and Mary Quarterly,* 3rd Series, IV (July 1947): 297-304.

———. "The Colonial Virginia Satirist: Mid-Eighteenth Century Commentaries on Politics, Religion, and Society." *Transactions of the American Philosophical Society,* N.S., LVII, pt. 1 (1967).

———. "The Devil in Virginia in the Seventeenth Century." *Virginia Magazine of History and Biography,* LXV (April 1957): 131-49.

———. *George Sandys Poet-Adventurer: A Study in Anglo-American Culture in the Seventeenth Century.* London: The Bodley Head, 1955.

———. "The Intellectual Culture in the Colonial Chesapeake Bay Country." *Virginia Magazine of History and Biography,* LXXVIII (April 1970): 131-43.

———. "James Reid, Colonial Virginia Poet and Moral and Religious Essayist." *Virginia Magazine of History and Biography,* LXXIX (January 1971): 3-19.

Davis, Thomas M. "Edward Taylor's 'Valedictory Poems.' " *Early American Literature,* VII (Spring 1971): 38-63.

Demos, John. "Underlying Themes in the Witchcraft of Seventeenth-Century New England." *American Historical Review,* LXXV (June 1970): 1311-326.

De Santillana, Giorgio and Dechend, Hertha von. *Hamlet's Mill: An Essay on Myth & the Frame of Time.* Boston: Gambit, 1969.

Devore, Nicholas. *Encyclopedia of Astrology.* New York: Philosophical Library, 1947.

Dexter, Frederick Bowditch. *Biographical Sketches of the Graduates of Yale College.* Vols. I-V, New York: Henry Holt & Winston, 1896-1911. Vol. VI, New Haven: Yale University Press, 1912.

Dietheim, Oskar. "The Medical Teaching of Demonology in the 17th & 18th Centuries." *Journal of the History of Behavioral Sciences,* VI (January 1970): 3-15.

Dobie, J. Frank. *Coronado's Children: Tales of Lost Mines and Buried Treasures of the Southwest.* Dallas, Tex.: The Southwest Press, 1930.

Dobrée, Bonamy. *English Literature in the Early Eighteenth Century 1700-1740.* Oxford: Clarendon Press, 1959.

Dock, George. "The 'Primitive Physic' of Rev. John Wesley." *The Journal of the American Medical Association,* LXIV (February 1915): 629-38.

Dominy, Newton. *Genealogical History of the Dominy Family.* Dublin, Ohio: 1926.

Dorland, A. G. *The Royal Disallowance in Massachusetts.* Bulletin of the Departments of History and Political and Economic Science in Queens University, Kingston, Ontario, Canada, no. 22, January 1917.

Dorson, Richard M. *Jonathan Draws the Long Bow.* Cambridge: Harvard University Press, 1946.

Douglas, Mary, ed. *Witchcraft Confessions & Accusations.* Association of Social

Anthropologists Monograph no. 9. London: Tavistock Publications Ltd., 1970.

Drake, Frederick C. "Witchcraft in the American Colonies, 1647-62." *American Quarterly,* XX (Winter 1968): 694-725.

Drake, Milton. *Almanacs of the United States.* New York: The Scarecrow Press, Inc., 1962.

Drake, Samuel Adams. *A Book of New England Legends and Folk Lore.* Boston: Roberts Brothers, 1882.

Drinker, Cecil K. *Not So Long Ago.* New York: Oxford University Press, 1937.

Duncan, Edgar Hill. "The Natural History of Metals and Minerals in the Universe of Milton's *Paradise Lost.*" *Osiris,* XI (1954): 386-421.

Edgar, Walter B. "Some Popular Books in Colonial South Carolina." *The South Carolina Historical Magazine,* LXXII (July 1971): 174-78.

Eggleston, Edward. *The Transit of Civilization: From England to America in the Seventeenth Century.* Boston: Beacon Press, 1959.

Farwell, John W. "A Horoscope of Joseph Warren." *Transactions of the Colonial Society of Massachusetts,* XX (1917-19): 18-20.

Fiering, Norman S. "President Samuel Johnson and the Circle of Knowledge." *William and Mary Quarterly,* 3rd Series, XXVIII (April 1971): 199-236.

Fischer, David Hackett. *The Revolution of American Conservatism.* New York: Harper & Row, 1965.

Fogel, Edwin Miller. *Beliefs and Superstitions of the Pennsylvania Germans.* Philadelphia: American German Press, 1915.

Foster, F. Apthorp. "The Burning of Harvard Hall, 1764, and Its Consequences." *Transactions of the Colonial Society of Massachusetts,* XIV (1911-13): 2-43.

Foucault, Michel. *Madness and Civilization: A History of Insanity in the Age of Reason.* Trans. by Richard Howard. New York: Pantheon Books, 1965.

Fox, Cyrus T., ed. *Reading and Berks County[,] Pennsylvania: A History.* New York: Lewis Historical Publishing Company, Inc. 1925.

Fox, Dixon Ryan. *Ideas in Motion.* New York: D. Appleton-Century Company, 1935.

——. "The Old Farm." *New York History,* XIX (January 1938): 17-35.

Fox, Sanford J. *Science and Justice: The Massachusetts Witchcraft Trials.* Baltimore: Johns Hopkins University Press, 1968.

Frazer, James George. *The Golden Bough.* 3rd ed. New York: Macmillan Co., 1935.

Freeman, John F., comp. *A Guide to Manuscripts Relating to the American Indian in the Library of the American Philosophical Society.* Philadelphia: American Philosophical Society, 1966.

Frick, George Frederick and Stearns, Raymond Phineas. *Mark Catesby: The Colonial Audubon*. Urbana, Ill.: University of Illinois Press, 1961.

Friedman, Lee E. "Judah Monis, First Instructor in Hebrew at Harvard University." *Publications of the American Jewish Historical Society*, no. 22 (1914): 1-24.

Furnas, J. C. *The Americans: A Social History of the United States, 1587-1914*. New York: G. P. Putnam's Sons, 1969.

Furthey, J. Smith and Cope, Gilbert. *History of Chester County, Pennsylvania*. Philadelphia: Louis H. Everts, 1881.

Gardner, Emelyn Elizabeth. *Folklore from the Schoharie Hills New York*. Ann Arbor, Mich.: University of Michigan Press, 1937.

Gay, Peter. "The Enlightenment." *The Comparative Approach to American History*. Ed. by C. Van Woodward. New York: Basic Books, Inc., 1968.

———. *The Enlightenment: An Interpretation*. Vol. II: *The Science of Freedom*. New York: Alfred A. Knopf, 1969.

Gegenheimer, Albert Frank. "Thomas Godfrey: Protégé of William Smith." *Pennsylvania History*, IX (October 1942): 233-51 and X (January 1943): 26-43.

Gifford, Edward S. *The Evil Eye: Studies in the Folklore of Vision*. New York: Macmillan Company, 1958.

Gilbert, Edgar. *History of Salem, N.H.* Concord, N.H.: Rumford Printing Co., 1907.

Gillispie, Charles Coulston, ed. *Dictionary of Scientific Biography*. New York: Charles Scribner's Sons, 1970—.

———. *The Edge of Objectivity*. Princeton, N.J.: Princeton University Press, 1960.

Gitin, Louis Leonard. "Cadwallader Colden: As Scientist and Philosopher." *New York History*, XVI (April 1935): 169-77.

Goebel, Julius, Jr. *Law Enforcement in Colonial New York*. New York: The Commonwealth Fund, 1944.

Gohdes, Clarence. "Aspects of Idealism in Early New England." *The Philosophical Review*, XXXIX (November 1930): 537-55.

Gordon, Maurice Bear. *Æsculapius Comes to the Colonies*. Ventnor, N.J.: Ventnor Publishers, Inc., 1949.

Gorman, Mel. "Gassendi in America." *Isis*, LV (March 1965): 409-17.

[Gottesman, Rita Susswein, ed.]. *The Arts and Crafts in New York 1726-1776*. Collections of the New-York Historical Society for the Year 1936, vol. LXIX. New York: New-York Historical Society, 1938.

Grand-Carteret, John. *Les Almanachs Français*. Paris, 1896.

Graubard, Mark. *Astrology and Alchemy: Two Fossil Sciences*. New York: The Philosophical Library, 1953.

———. "Astrology's Demise and Its Bearing on the Decline and Death of Beliefs." *Osiris,* XIII (1958): 210-61.

———. "Some Contemporary Observations on Ancient Superstitions." *Journal of American Folklore,* LIX (January-March 1945): 124-33.

Greene, Donald. "Augustinianism & Empiricism: A Note on Eighteenth-Century English Intellectual History." *Eighteenth-Century Studies,* I (Fall 1967): 33-68.

Greene, John C. *The Death of Adam: Evolution and Its Impact on Western Thought.* Ames, Iowa: The Iowa University Press, 1959.

Greene, Robert A. "Henry More and Robert Boyle on the Spirit of Nature." *Journal of the History of Ideas,* XXIII (October-December, 1962): 451-74.

Greenleaf, W. H. *Order, Empiricism and Politics.* New York: published for the University of Hull by the Oxford University Press, 1964.

Greenough, Chester Noyes. "New England Almanacs 1766-1775 and the American Revolution." *Proceedings of the American Antiquarian Society,* VL (October 1935): 288-316.

Grimm, Jacob. *Teutonic Mythology.* Trans. from the 4th ed. by James Stephen Stallybrass. New York: Dover Publications, Inc., 1966.

Groce, George C. and Wallace, David H., ed. *The New-York Historical Society's Dictionary of Artists in America, 1564-1860.* New Haven: Yale University Press, 1957.

Guerlac, Henry. "Newton's Changing Reputation in the Eighteenth Century." *Carl Becker's Heavenly City Revisited.* Ed. by Raymond O. Rockwood. Ithaca, N.Y.: Cornell University Press, 1958.

Guerra, Francisco. *American Medical Bibliography 1639-1783.* New York: Lathrop C. Harper, Inc., 1962.

———. "Medical Almanacs of the American Colonial Period." *Journal of the History of Medicine and Allied Sciences,* XVI (July 1961): 234-55.

———. "Medical Literature in North America During the Colonial Period and the Revolutionary War." *Bulletin of the History of Medicine,* XXXV (March-April 1961): 149-55.

Gummere, Amelia Mott. *Witchraft and Quakerism.* Philadelphia: The Biddle Press, 1908.

Gummere, Richard N. *The American Colonial Mind & the Classical Tradition.* Cambridge: Harvard University Press, 1963.

———. *Seven Wise Men of Colonial America.* Cambridge: Harvard University Press, 1967.

Haddow, Anna. *Political Science in the American Colleges and Universities, 1636-1900.* New York: D. Appleton-Century Company, 1939.

Hagbert, Knut. *Carl Linnaeus.* Trans. by Alan Blair. New York: E. P. Dutton & Company, Inc., 1953.

Hall, A. Rupert. *The Scientific Revolution, 1500-1800.* 2nd ed. Boston: Beacon Press, 1966.

Hall, G. Stanley. "On the History of American College Textbooks and Teaching in Logic, Ethics, Psychology and Allied Subjects." *Proceedings of the American Antiquarian Society,* N.S., IX (April 1894): 137-74.

Hall, Michael G. "Renaissance Science in Puritan New England." *Aspects of the Renaissance: A Symposium.* Ed. by Archibald R. Lewis. Austin, Tex.: University of Texas Press, 1967.

Hampson, Norman. *A Cultural History of the Enlightenment.* New York: Pantheon Books, 1968.

Hansen, Chadwick. "The Metamorphosis of Tituba, or Why American Intellectuals can't Tell an Indian Witch from a Negro," *The New England Quarterly,* XLVII (March 1974): 3-12.

———. "Salem Witchcraft and De Forest's Witching Times." *Essex Institute Historical Collections,* CIV (April 1968): 89-108.

———. *Witchcraft at Salem.* New York: George Braziller, 1969.

Haraszti, Zoltán. *John Adams & the Prophets of Progress.* Cambridge: Harvard University Press, 1952.

Harris, F. L. "Charles Morton—Minister, Academy Master and Emigrant (1627-1698)." *Journal of the Royal Institute of Cornwall,* N.S., IV (1963): 326-52.

Harris, Jonathan. "De Witt Clinton as Naturalist." *The New-York Historical Society Quarterly,* LVI (October 1972): 265-84.

Harwood, Herbert Joseph. "Littleton." *History of Middlesex County, Massachusetts.* Compiled by D. Hamilton Hurd. Philadelphia: J. W. Lewis & Co., 1890.

Haywood, Charles. *A Bibliography of North American Folklore and Folksong.* 2nd ed. Revised. New York: Dover Publications, 1961.

Heimert, Alan Edward. "American Oratory: From the Great Awakening to the Election of Jefferson." Unpublished Ph.D dissertation, Harvard University, 1961.

———. *Religion and the American Mind from the Great Awakening to the Revolution.* Cambridge: Harvard University Press, 1966.

Henning, D. C. *Tales of the Blue Mountains.* Pottsville, Pa.: Daily Republican Book Rooms, 1911.

Henrioud, Marc. "Les Astrologues de Combremont-Le-Petit et Leur Almanachs (1697-1838)." *Revue Historique Vaudoise,* XXI (March 1913): 65-71; (July 1913): 211-23; (August 1913): 225-29; (September 1913): 257-65.

Hewitt, Bernard. *Theatre U.S.A. 1665-1957.* New York: McGraw-Hill Co., 1959.

Hill, Frank Pierce. *American Plays Printed 1714-1830: A Bibliographic Record.* Stanford, Calif.: Stanford University Press, 1934.

Hindle, Brooke. "Cadwallader Colden's Extensions of the Newtonian Principles." *William and Mary Quarterly,* 3rd Series, XIII (October 1956): 459-75.

———. *David Rittenhouse.* Princeton, N.J.: Princeton University Press, 1964.

———. *The Pursuit of Science in Revolutionary America 1735-1789.* Chapel Hill: University of North Carolina Press, 1956.

"The History of the Divining Rod; With the Adventures of an Old Rodsman." *The United States Magazine and Democratic Review,* XXVI (March 1850): 218-25, and (April 1850): 317-27.

Hocker, Edward W. "A Doctor of Colonial Germantown." *Germantown Historical Review,* II, no. 8.

Hoffman, W. J. "Folk-Lore of the Pennsylvania Germans." *Journal of American Folk-Lore,* I (July-September 1888): 125-35, and II (January-March 1889): 23-35.

Hofstadter, Richard. *The Development of Academic Freedom in the United States.* New York: Columbia University Press, 1955.

Hoke, N. C. "Folk-Customs and Folk-Belief in North Carolina." *Journal of American Folk-Lore,* V (April-June 1892): 113-20.

Hole, Christina. *Witchcraft in England.* London: Collier-Macmillan, Ltd., 1966.

Holmyard, E. J. *Alchemy.* Baltimore: Penguin Books, Inc., 1968.

Hornberger, Theodore. "Samuel Johnson of Yale and King's College: A Note on the Relationship of Science and Religion in Provincial America." *New England Quarterly,* VIII (September 1935): 378-97.

———. *Scientific Thought in the American Colleges, 1638-1800.* Austin, Tex.: University of Texas Press, 1945.

Hoskins, Michael A. " 'Mining All Within' Clarke's Notes to Rohault's *Traité de Physique.* " *The Thomist,* XXIV (January 1961): 353-63.

Howe, Ellic. *Astrology: A Recent History Including the Untold Story of Its Role in World War II.* New York: Walker and Company, 1967.

Howell, Wilbur Samuel. "The Declaration of Independence and Eighteenth-Century Logic." *William and Mary Quarterly,* 3rd Series, XXVIII (October 1961): 463-84.

———. *Eighteenth-Century British Logic and Rhetoric.* Princeton, N.J.: Princeton University Press, 1971.

———. *Logic and Rhetoric in England, 1500-1700.* New York: Russell & Russell, 1961.

Hudson, Roy Fred. "Rhetorical Invention in Colonial New England." *Speech Monographs,* XXV (August 1958): 215-21.

Hughes, Arthur. "Science in English Encyclopedias, 1704-1875." *Annals of Science,* VII (Dec. 28, 1951): 340-70, and VIII (Dec. 31, 1952): 323-67.

Hunter, William B. "The Seventeenth Century Doctrine of Plastic Nature." *Harvard Theological Review*, XLIII (July 1950): 197-213.

Huntley, Francis Carroll. "The Seaborne Trade of Virginia in Mid-Eighteenth Century: Port Hampton." *Virginia Magazine of History and Biography*, LIX (July 1951): 297-308.

Hurley, Gerard T. "Buried Treasure Tales in America." *Western Folklore*, X (July 1951): 197-216.

*Index to the Laws of New Hampshire Recorded in the Office of the Secretary of State, 1679-1883.* Manchester, N.H.: John B. Clarke, 1886.

Jackson, Stanley W. "Force and Kindred Notions in Eighteenth-Century Neurophysiology and Medical Psychology." *The Bulletin of the History of Medicine*, XLIV (September-October 1970): 397-410, and (November-December 1970): 539-54.

James, Eldon Revare. "A List of Legal Treatises Printed in the British Colonies and American States before 1801." *Harvard Legal Essays*. Cambridge: Harvard University Press, 1934.

Jantz, Harold S. "German Thought and Literature in New England, 1620-1820." *The Journal of English and Germanic Philology*, XLI (January 1942): 1-45.

Jeffrey, Lloyd N. "Snake Yarns of the West and Southwest." *Western Folklore*, XIV (October 1955): 246-58.

Jillson, Clark. *Green Leaves from Whitingham, Vermont.* Worcester, Mass.: privately printed, 1894.

Johnson, Clifton. *What They Say in New England: and Other American Folklore.* New York: Columbia University Press, 1963.

Johnson, Herbert Allan. "The Advent of Common Law in Colonial New York." *Law and Authority in Colonial America.* Ed. by George Allen Billias. Barre, Mass.: Barre Publishers, 1965.

Johnson, Thomas H. "Jonathan Edwards' Background of Reading." *Transactions of the Colonial Society of Massachusetts*, XXVIII (1930-33): 193-222.

Jones, Gordon W. "Medical and Scientific Books in Colonial Virginia." *Bulletin of the History of Medicine*, XL (March-April 1966): 146-57.

Jones, Howard Mumford. *Ideas in America.* Cambridge: Harvard University Press, 1944.

———. *O Strange New World.* New York: The Viking Press, 1964.

Jones, Pomroy, *Annals and Recollections of Oneida County.* Rome, N.Y.: privately printed, 1851.

Jones, W. R. "Abracadabra—Sorcery and Witchcraft in European Witchcraft." *History Teacher*, V (November, 1971): 26-36.

Jorgenson, Chester E. "The New Science in the Almanacs of Ames and Franklin." *New England Quarterly*, VIII (December, 1935): 555-61.

Josten, C. H. "Robert Fludd's Theory of Geomancy and His Experiments at Avignon in the Winter of 1601-1602." *Journal of the Warburg and Courtauld Institutes,* XXVII (1964): 327-35.

Kaledin, Arthur Daniel. "The Mind of John Leverett." Unpublished Ph.D dissertation, Harvard University, 1965.

Karst, Judith Ward-Steinman. "Newspaper Medicine: A Cultural Study of the Colonial South, 1730-1770." Unpublished Ph.D dissertation, Tulane University, 1971.

Katz, Edward and Paulson, Peter. "A Brief History of the Divining Rod in the United States." *Journal of the American Society for Psychical Research,* XLII (October 1948): 119-31, and XLIII (January 1949): 3-8.

Kerber, Linda K. *Federalism in Dissent: Images and Ideology in Jeffersonian America.* Ithaca, N.Y.: Cornell University Press, 1970.

Keifer, Monica. *American Children Through Their Books 1700-1835.* Philadelphia: University of Pennsylvania Press, 1948.

Kilgour, F. G. "Thomas Robie (1689-1729), Colonial Scientist and Physician." *Isis,* XXX (1939): 473-90.

King, Lester S. *The Medical World of the Eighteenth Century.* Chicago: University of Chicago Press, 1958.

Kinietz, Vernon. "Delaware Culture Chronology." *Prehistory Research Series,* III (April 1946-June 1960): 1-143.

Kittredge, George Lyman. "Cotton Mather's Scientific Communications to the Royal Society." *Proceedings of the American Antiquarian Society,* N.S., XXVI (1916): 18-57.

———. "Dr. Robert Child the Remonstrant." *Transactions of the Colonial Society of Massachusetts,* XXI (March 1919): 1-146.

———. "Letters of Samuel Lee and Samuel Sewall Relating to New England and the Indians." *Transactions of the Colonial Society of Massachusetts,* XIV (February 1912): 142-86.

———. *The Old Farmer and His Almanack.* New York: Benjamin Bloom, 1967.

———. *Witchcraft in Old and New England.* New York: Russell & Russell, 1956.

Klauber, Laurence M. *Rattlesnakes: Their Habits, Life Histories and Influences on Mankind.* Berkeley and Los Angeles: published for the Zoological Society of San Diego by the University of California Press, 1956.

Koch, Adrienne. *The Philosophy of Thomas Jefferson.* Gloucester, Mass.: Peter Smith, 1957.

Koch, Adrienne, ed. *The American Enlightenment.* New York: George Braziller, 1965.

Kocher, Paul H. *Science and Religion in Elizabethan England.* New York: Octagon Books, 1969.

Koyré, Alexander. *Newtonian Studies.* Cambridge: Harvard University Press, 1965.

Kraus, Michael. "America and European Medicine in the Eighteenth Century." *Bulletin of the History of Medicine,* VIII (May 1940): 679-95.

———. *The Atlantic Civilization—18th Century Origins.* Ithaca, N.Y.: Cornell University Press, 1966.

———. *Intercolonial Aspects of American Culture on the Eve of the American Revolution.* New York: Columbia University Press, 1928.

Kristeller, Paul Oskar. "The European Significance of Florentine Platonism." *Medieval and Renaissance Studies, 3.* Chapel Hill: University of North Carolina Press, 1968.

———. *Renaissance Thought: The Classic, Scholastic and Humanist Strains.* New York: Harper & Row, 1961.

Kuhn, Thomas S. *The Structure of Scientific Revolutions.* Chicago: University of Chicago Press, 1962.

Labaree, Leonard Woods. *Conservatism in Early American History.* New York: New York University Press, 1948.

Langdon, Carolyn S. "The Case of Lydia Gilbert (Witchcraft in Connecticut)." *The New England Galaxy,* V (Winter 1964): 14-23.

Lea, Henry Charles. *Materials Towards a History of Witchcraft.* New York: Thomas Yoseloff, 1957.

Leland, Charles G. *The Algonquin Legends of New England.* Boston: Houghton, Mifflin Company, 1884.

Lemay, J. A. Leo. "Richard Lewis and Augustan American Poetry." *Publications of the Modern Language Association of America,* LXXXIII (March 1968): 80-101.

Lévi-Strauss, Claude. *Structural Anthropology.* Trans. by Claire Jacobson & Brooke Grundfest. Garden City, N.Y.: Doubleday & Co., 1967.

Lewis, C. S. *The Discarded Image.* Cambridge: Cambridge University Press, 1964.

———. *A Preface to Paradise Lost.* London: Oxford University Press, 1961.

———. *Studies in Words.* Cambridge: Cambridge University Press, 1960.

Lewis, Lawrence, Jr. "The Courts of Pennsylvania in the Seventeenth Century." *Pennsylvania Magazine of History and Biography,* V (1881): 141-90.

Leyel, C. F., ed. *Culpeper's English Physician & Complete Herbal.* London: Herbert Joseph Limited, [1947].

Lichtenstein, Aharon. *Henry More: The Rational Theology of a Cambridge Platonist.* Cambridge: Harvard University Press, 1962.

Little, William. *The History of Warren.* Manchester, N.H.: William E. Moore, 1870.

Lokken, Roy N. The Social Thought of James Logan." *William and Mary Quarterly,* 3rd Series, XXVII (January 1970): 68-89.

Lough, John. *Essays on the Encyclopédie of Diderot and D'Alembert.* London: Oxford University Press, 1968.

Lovejoy, Arthur O. *Essays in the History of Ideas.* Baltimore: Johns Hopkins University Press, 1948.

———. *The Great Chain of Being.* New York: Harper & Row, 1960.

Lovely, N. W. "Notes on New England Almanacs." *New England Quarterly,* VIII (June 1935): 264-77.

Ludwig, Allan I. *Graven Images: New England Stonecarving and Its Symbols, 1650-1815.* Middletown, Conn.: Wesleyan University Press, 1966.

MacFarlane, Alan D. J. *Witchcraft in Tudor and Stuart England.* New York: Harper & Row, 1970.

McKeehan, Louis W. *Yale Science: The First Hundred Years, 1701-1801.* New York: Henry Schuman, 1947.

McLoughlin, William G. *Isaac Backus and the American Pietistic Tradition.* Boston: Little, Brown and Company, 1967.

———. *New England Dissent, 1630-1833: The Baptists and the Separation of Church and State.* Cambridge: Harvard University Press, 1971.

Malloch, Archibald. *Medical Interchange Between the British Isles and America Before 1801.* London: Royal College of Physicians, 1946.

Manuel, Frank E. *The Eighteenth Century Confronts the Gods.* Cambridge: Harvard University Press, 1959.

———. *Isaac Newton: Historian.* Cambridge: Harvard University Press, 1963.

*The Manuscripts of the Earl of Dartmouth.* Vol. II: *The American Papers.* In *Historical Manuscript Commission, Fourteenth Report, Appendix X.* London. Her Majesty's Stationary Office, 1895.

Marambaud, Pierre. "William Byrd of Westover: Cavalier, Diarist and Chronicler." *Virginia Magazine of History and Biography,* LXXVIII (April 1970): 144-83.

Marcus, Jacob Rader. *The Colonial American Jew, 1492-1776.* Detroit: Wayne State University Press, 1970.

———. *Early American Jewry.* Philadelphia: The Jewish Publication Society of America, 1953.

Martin, C. B. and Armstrong, D. M., eds. *Locke and Berkeley: A Collection of Critical Essays.* Garden City, New York: Doubleday & Company, Inc., 1968.

Martin, Edwin T. *Thomas Jefferson: Scientist.* New York: Henry Schuman, Inc., 1952.

Mason, George V. "The African Slave Trade in Colonial Times." *The American Historical Record and Repertory of Notes and Queries,* I (July 1872): 311-19.

Masterson, James R. "Colonial Rattlesnake Lore, 1714," *Zoologica*, XXIII (July 1938): 213-16.

———. "Traveler's Tales of Colonial Natural History," *Journal of American Folklore*, LIX (January-March 1946): 51-67 and (April-June 1946): 174-88.

May, Henry F. "The Problem of the American Enlightenment." *New Literary History*, I (Winter 1970): 201-14.

Mercier, Charles Arthur. *Astrology in Medicine*. London: Macmillan & Co., Limited, 1914.

Middlekauff, Robert. *Ancients and Axioms: Secondary Education in Eighteenth-Century New England*. New Haven: Yale University Press, 1963.

———. *The Mathers: Three Generations of Puritan Intellectuals, 1596-1728*. New York: Oxford University Press, 1971.

Midelfort, H. C. Erik. "Recent Witch Hunting Research or Where Do We Go From Here?" *Papers of the Bibliographical Society of America*, LXII (3rd Quarter, 1968): 373-420.

——. *Witch Hunting in Southwest Germany, 1562-1684: The Social and Intellectual Foundations*. Stanford, Calif.: Stanford University Press, 1972.

Miles, Wyndham. "Benjamin Rush, Chemist." *Chymia*, IV (1953): 37-77.

Milic, Louis T., ed. *The Modernity of the Eighteenth Century*. Studies in the Eighteenth Century, Vol. I. Cleveland: The Press of Case Western Reserve University, 1971.

Miller, Genevieve. "Medical Education in the American Colonies." *Journal of Medical Education*, XXXI (February 1956): 82-94.

———. "Medical Education in Colonial America." *Ciba Symposia*, VIII (January 1947): 502-32.

Miller, Perry. *Errand Into the Wilderness*. New York: Harper & Row, 1964.

———. *The New England Mind: From Colony to Province*. Boston: Beacon Press, 1961.

Miller, Ralph N. "Samuel Williams' 'History of Vermont.' " *New England Quarterly*, XXII (March 1949): 73-84.

Monter, E. William. "Inflation and Witchcraft: The Case of Jean Bodin." *Action and Conviction in Early Modern Europe*. Ed. by Theodore K. Rabb and Jerrold E. Seigel. Princeton, N.J.: Princeton University Press, 1969.

———. "Patterns of Witchcraft in the Jura." *Journal of Social History*, V (Fall 1971): 1-25.

———. "Witchcraft in Geneva, 1537-1662." *Journal of Modern History*, XLIII (June 1971): 179-204.

Moody, Edward C. *Handbook History of the Town of York*. Augusta, Maine: Kennebec Journal Company, [1914].

Mooney, James. "Myths of the Cherokee." Bureau of American Ethnology. *Nineteenth Annual Report* (1897-98), pt. I.

Moore. "Ezra Stiles' Studies in the Caballa." *Proceedings of the Massachusetts Historical Society,* LI (March 1918): 290-306.

Morgan, Edmund S. "Ezra Stiles: The Education of a Yale Man, 1742-1746." *Huntington Library Quarterly,* XVII (May 1954): 251-68.

———. *The Gentle Puritan: A Life of Ezra Stiles 1727-1795.* New Haven: Yale University Press, 1962.

Morison, Samuel Eliot. *Harvard College in the Seventeenth Century.* Cambridge: Harvard University Press, 1936.

———. *Three Centuries of Harvard, 1636-1936.* Cambridge: Harvard University Press, 1936.

Morrison, Leonard A. *The History of Windham in New Hampshire.* Boston: Cupples, Upham & Co., 1883.

Morton, Richard L. *Colonial Virginia.* Chapel Hill: published for the Virginia Historical Society by the University of North Carolina Press, 1960.

Mowet, Charles L. "That 'Odd Being' De Brahm." *Florida Historical Quarterly,* XX (April 1942): 323-45.

Nicolson, Majorie Hope. *The Breaking of the Circle: Studies in the Effect of the 'New Science' on Seventeenth-Century Poetry.* Revised ed. New York: Columbia University Press, 1965.

———. "The Early States of Cartesianism in England." *Studies in Philology,* XXVI (July 1929): 356-74.

Nietz, John. *Old Textbooks.* Pittsburgh: University of Pittsburgh Press, 1961.

Nisard, Charles. *Histoire de Livres Populaires.* 2nd ed. Paris: E. Dentu, 1864.

Oberholzer, Emil Jr. *Delinquent Saints.* New York: Columbia University Press, 1956.

O'Connor, John E. "William Paterson and the American Revolution, 1763-1787." Unpublished Ph.D. dissertation, City University of New York, 1974.

Oliver, Betty. "Grace Sherwood of Princess Anne: She Was a Witch, They Said." *North Carolina Folklore,* X (July 1962): 36-39.

Orcutt, Samuel. *A History of the Old Town of Stratford . . . Connecticut.* Fairfield County Historical Society, 1886.

Overfield, Richard A. "Science in the Virginia Gazette, 1736-1780." *The Emporia State Research Studies,* XVI (March 1968): 5-53.

Packard, Francis R. *History of Medicine in the United States.* New York: Paul B. Hoeber, Inc., 1931.

Parke, Francis Neal. *Witchcraft in Maryland.* N.p.: n.p., 1937.

Parkes, H. B. "New England in the Seventeen Thirties." *New England Quarterly,* III (June 1930): 397-419.

Parr, Johnstone. *Tamberlaine's Malady: And Other Essays On Astrology in Elizabethan Drama.* University, Alabama: University of Alabama Press, 1953.

Patrides, C. A. "Renaissance Thought on the Celestial Hierarchy: The Decline of a Tradition." *Journal of the History of Ideas,* XX (April 1959): 155-66.

———. "Renaissance Views on the 'Vnconfused Orders Angellick.' " *Journal of the History of Ideas,* XXIII (April-June 1962): 265-67.

Passim, Herbert and Bennett, John W. "Changing Agricultural Magic in Southern Illinois: A Systematic Analysis of Folk-Urban Transition." *The Study of Folklore.* Ed. by Alan Dundes. Englewood Cliffs, N.J.: Prentice-Hall, Inc., 1965.

Peel, Sidney. "Nicholas Culpeper, Soldier, Physician, Astrologer, and Politician." *Nineteenth Century,* XLIII (January-June 1898): 755-63.

Pennell, Francis, W. "Benjamin Smith Barton as Naturalist." *Proceedings of the American Philosophical Society,* LXXXVI (September 1942): 108-22.

Pitt, Arthur Stuart. "The Source, Significance, and Date of Franklin's 'An Arabian Tale.' " *Publications of the Modern Language Association of America,* LVII (May 1942): 155-68.

Pochmann, Henry A. *German Culture in America: Philosophical and Literary Influences, 1600-1900.* Madison, Wis.: University of Wisconsin Press, 1957.

Potter, David. *Debating in the Colonial Chartered Colleges: An Historical Survey, 1642 to 1900.* New York: Teachers College Press, Columbia University, 1944.

Poynter, F. N. L. *A Bibliography of Gervase Markham, 1568?-1637.* Oxford: The Oxford Bibliographical Society, 1962.

———. "Nicholas Culpeper and His Books." *Journal of the History of Medicine and Allied Sciences,* XVII (January 1962): 152-67.

Priestley, F. E. L. "Pope and the Great Chain of Being." *Essays in English Literature From the Renaissance to the Victorian Age Presented to A. S. P. Woodhouse.* Toronto: University of Toronto Press, 1964.

Pringle, James R. *History of the Town and City of Glouster, Cape Ann, Massachusetts.* Gloucester, Mass.: published by the author, 1892.

Prior, Moody E. "Joseph Glanvill, Witchcraft, and Seventeenth-Century Science." *Modern Philology,* XXX (November 1932): 167-93.

Quinn, Arthur Hobson. *A History of the America Drama From the Beginning to the Civil War.* New York: Harper & Brothers, 1923.

Raanes, Florence Eleanor. *The Celestial Hierarchy of the Pseudo-Dionysius and Its Influence Upon English Poetry of the Sixteenth and Seventeenth Centuries.* New York: New York University Press, 1957.

Rand, Benjamin. "Philosophical Instruction in Harvard University From 1636-1900." *Harvard Graduates' Magazine,* XXXVII (September 1928): 29-47.

Randolph, Vance. *Ozark Superstitions.* New York: Columbia University Press, 1947.

Rankin, Hugh F. *The Theater in Colonial America.* Chapel Hill: University of North Carolina Press, 1960.

"The Rattlesnake & Its Congerers." *Harper's New Monthly Magazine,* X (March 1855): 470-83

Reaske, Christopher R. "The Devil and Jonathan Edwards." *Journal of the History of Idea,* XXXIII (January-March 1972): 123-38.

Reinsch, Paul Samuel. "English Common Law in the Early American Colonies." *Bulletin of the University of Wisconsin,* II, no. 31.

Reynolds, John. *The Pioneer History of Illinois.* 2nd ed. Chicago: Fergus Printing Company, 1887.

Richardson, Lyon N. *A History of Early American Magazines 1741-1789.* New York: Thomas Nelson and Sons, 1931.

Riddell, William Renwick. "A Curious 'Witchcraft' Case." *American Institute of Criminal Law and Criminology Journal,* XIX (August 1928): 231-36.

———. "William Penn and Witchcraft." *American Institute of Criminal Law and Criminology Journal,* XIX (August 1928): 252-58.

———. "Witchcraft in Old New York." *American Institute of Criminal Law and Criminology Journal,* XIX (August 1928): 252-58.

Riley, I. Woodbridge. *American Philosophy: The Early Schools.* New York: Dodd, Mead & Co., 1907.

Ritterbush, Philip C. *Overtures to Biology: The Speculations of Eighteenth Century Naturalists.* New Haven: Yale University Press, 1964.

Robbins, Rossell Hope. *The Encyclopedia of Witchcraft and Demonology.* New York: Crown Publishers, Inc., 1959.

Rogers, Fred B. *The Healing Art: A History of the Medical Society of New Jersey.* Trenton, N.J.: The Medical Society of New Jersey. 1966.

Russell, Jeffrey Burton. *Witchcraft in the Middle Ages.* Ithaca, N.Y.: Cornell University Press, 1972.

Ryerson, Alice Judson. "Medical Advice on Child Rearing 1550-1900." Unpublished Ph.E. dissertation, Harvard University, 1960.

Sachse, Julius Friedrich. *The German Pietists of Provincial Pennsylvania, 1694-1708.* Philadelphia: privately printed, 1895.

Sailor, Danton B. "Cudworth and Descartes." *Journal of the History of Ideas,* XXIII (January-March 1962): 133-40.

St. Child, Julian R. "A South Carolina Physician, 1693-1697." *Journal of the History of Medicine and Allied Sciences.* XXVI (January 1971): 18-27.

Saintyves, P. [Emile Nourry]. *L'Astrologie Populaire: Etudiée Spécialement dans les Doctrines et les Traditions Relatives à L'Influence de la Lune.* Paris: Librairie Emile Nourry, 1937.

Sarton, George. "The Study of Early Scientific Textbooks." *Isis,* XXXVIII (February 1948): 137-48.

Saveson, J. E. "Differing Reactions to Descartes Among the Cambridge Platonists." *Journal of the History of Ideas,* XXI (December 1960): 560-67.

Schneider, Herbert W. *A History of American Philosophy.* New York: Columbia University Press, 1946.

Schneider, Wolfgang. *Lexikon Alchemistisch-Pharmazeutischer Symbole.* Weinheim/Bergstr.: Verlag Chemie. GmbH., 1962.

Schofield, Robert E. "John Wesley and Science in 18th Century England." *Isis,* XLIV (December 1953): 331-40.

———. *Mechanism and Materialism: British Natural Philosophy in the Age of Reason.* Princeton, N.J.: Princeton University Press, 1969.

Scholem, Gershom G. *Major Trends in Jewish Mysticism.* New York: Schocken Books, 1967.

———. *On the Kabbalah and Its Symbolism.* Trans. by Ralph Manheim. New York: Schocken Books, 1969.

Schwab, John C. "The Yale College Curriculum, 1701-1901." *Education Review,* XXII (June 1901): 1-17.

Scott, Arthur P. *Criminal Law in Colonial Virginia.* Chicago: University of Chicago Press, 1930.

Scott, William Berryman. "Development of American Palaeontology." *Proceedings of the American Philosophical Society,* LXVI (1927): 409-29.

Seligman, Kurt. *The History of Magic.* New York: Pantheon Books, 1948.

Semmes, Raphael. *Crime and Punishment in Early Maryland.* Baltimore: Johns Hopkins University Press, 1938.

Sensabaugh, George. *Milton in Early America.* Princeton, N.J.: Princeton University Press, 1964.

Seybolt, Robert F. "Student Libraries at Harvard, 1763-64." *Transactions of the Colonial Society of Massachusetts,* XXVIII (1930-33): 449-61.

Shackelton, Robert. "The Encyclopédie as an International Phenomenon." *Proceedings of the American Philosophical Society,* CXIV (Oct. 20, 1970): 389-94.

Shammas, Carole. "Cadwallader Colden and the Role of the King's Prerogative." *The New-York Historical Society Quarterly,* LIII (April 1969): 103-26.

Sheffield, William P. *An Address Delivered by William P. Sheffield Before the Rhode Island Historical Society in Providence, February 7, A.D., 1882.* Newport, Rh. I.: John P. Sanborn, 1883.

Sherman, Mandel and Henry, Thomas R. *Hollow Folks.* New York: Thomas Y. Crowell, [1933].

Shipton, Clifford K. "Literary Leaven in Provincial New England." *New England Quarterly,* IX (June 1936): 203-17.

———. "The New England Clergy of the 'Glacial Age.'" *Transactions of the Colonial Society of Massachusetts,* XXXII (1933-37): 24-54.

Shoemaker, Henry W. *The Origins and Language of Central Pennsylvania Witch-craft.* Reading, Pa.: Reading Eagle Press. 1927.

Shorr, Philip. *Science and Superstition in the Eighteenth Century.* New York: Columbia University Press, 1932.

Shryock, Richard H. "Eighteenth Century Medicine in America." *Proceedings of the American Antiquarian Society,* LIX (October 1949): 275-92.

———. "Empiricism Versus Rationalism in American Medicine, 1650-1950." *Proceedings of the American Antiquarian Society,* LXXIX (April 1969): 99-150.

———. *Medicine and Society in America, 1660-1860.* New York: New York University Press, 1960.

Sibley, Agnes Marie. *Alexander Pope's Prestige in America, 1725-1835.* New York: King's Crown Press, 1949.

Sibley, John Langdon. *A History of the Town of Union in the County of Lincoln, Maine.* Boston: Benjamin B. Mussey and Co., 1851.

———. and Shipton, Clifford K. *Sibley's Harvard Graduates.* Boston: Massachusetts Historical Society, 1873- .

Simpson, George Gaylord. "The Beginnings of Vertebrate Paleontology in North America." *Proceedings of the American Philosophical Society,* LXXXVI (Sept. 1942): 130-88.

Sloan, Douglas. *The Scottish Enlightenment and the American College Ideal.* [New York]: Teachers College Press, Columbia University, 1971.

Smallwood, William Martin and Smallwood, Mabel Sarah Coon. *Natural History and the American Mind.* New York: Columbia University Press, 1941.

Smart, George K. "Private Libraries in Colonial Virginia." *American Literature,* X (1938-39): 24-52.

Smith, Donald George. "Eighteenth Century American Preaching—A Historical Survey." Unpublished doctor of theology dissertation, Northern Baptist Theological Seminary, 1956.

Smith, Joseph H. "The Foundations of Law in Maryland: 1634-1715." *Law and Authority in Colonial America.* Ed. by George Allan Billias. Barre, Mass.: Barre Publishers, 1965.

Snow, Louis Franklin. *The College Curriculum in the United States.* Privately printed, 1907.

Speck, Frank G. "Reptile Lore of the Northern Indians." *Journal of American Folklore,* XXXVI (January-March 1923): 273-80.

Spiller, Robert E. *et al.* eds. *Literary History of the United States.* 3rd ed., revised. New York: Macmillan Co., 1966.

Stafford, John. "The Power of Sympathy." *Midcontinent American Studies Journal,* IX (Spring 1968): 52-57.

Stahl, William Harris. "Moon Madness." *Annals of Medical History,* N.S., IX (May 1937): 248-63.

Stahlman, William D. "Astrology in Colonial America: An Extended Query." *William and Mary Quarterly,* 3rd Series, XIII (October 1956): 551-63.

Stanford, Donald E. "The Great Bones of Claverack, New York, 1705." *New York History,* XL (January 1959): 47-61.

Starkey, Marion L. *The Devil in Massachusetts.* Garden City, N.Y.: Doubleday & Co., 1961.

Stearns, Raymond Phineas. *Science in the British Colonies of America.* Urbana, Ill.: University of Illinois Press, 1970.

Steiner, Bernard C. "Rev. Thomas Bray and His American Libraries." *American Historical Review,* II (October 1896): 59-75.

Stimson, Dorothy. *The Gradual Acceptance of the Copernican Theory of the Universe.* New York, 1917.

Stokes, Durward T. "Different Concepts of Government in the Sermons of Two Eighteenth Century Clergymen." *Historical Magazine of the Protestant Episcopal Church,* XL (March 1971): 81-94.

Stone, Lawrence. "The Disenchantment of the World." *New York Review of Books,* Dec. 2, 1971, pp. 77-25.

Stookey, Bryon. *A History of Colonial Medical Education in the Province of New York, With Its Subsequent Development (1767-1830).* Spingfield, Ill.: Charles C. Thomas, 1962.

Summers, Montague. *The Geography of Witchcraft.* New York: University Books, 1958.

Swanton, John R. "Religious Beliefs and Medical Practices of the Creek Indians." U.S. Bureau of American Ethnology. *Annual Report,* XLII (1924/25): 473-672.

Talbot, C. H. "A Mediaeval Physician's Vade Mecum." *Journal of the History of Medicine and Allied Sciences,* XVI (July 1961): 213-33.

Taylor, E. G. R. "Sir William Monson Consults the Stars." *Mariner's Mirror,* XIX (January 1933): 22-26.

Taylor, John M. *The Witchcraft Delusion in Colonial Connecticut, 1647-1697.* New York: The Grafton Press, 1908.

Testi, Gino. *Dizinario Di Alchimia e Di Chimica Antiquaria.* Rome: Casa Editrice Mediterranea, 1950.

Thomas, Keith. *Religion and the Decline of Magic.* New York: Charles Scribner's Sons, 1971.

Thomas, Daniel Lindsay and Lucy Blayney. *Kentucky Superstitions.* Princeton, N.J.: Princeton University Press, 1920.

Thompson, Stith. *Motif-Index of Folk-Literature.* Bloomington, Ind.: Indiana University Press, [1955-58].

———. *Tales of the North American Indian.* Bloomington, Ind.: Indiana University Press, 1966.

Thorndike, Lynn. *A History of Magic and Experimental Science.* New York: Macmillan, 1929-58.

———. "The True Place of Astrology in the History of Science." *Isis,* XLVI (September 1955): 273-78.

Tilley, Winthrop. "The Literature of Natural and Physical Science in the American Colonies from the Beginnings to 1765." Unpublished Ph.D. dissertation, Brown University, 1933.

Tillyard, E. M. W. *The Elizabethan World Picture.* New York: Random House, n.d.

Tolles, Frederick B. "James Logan, Quaker Humanist." *Pennsylvania Magazine of History and Biography,* LXXIX (October 1955): 415-38.

———. "A Literary Quaker: John Smith of Burlington and Philadelphia." *Pennsylvania Magazine of History and Biography,* LXV (July 1941): 300-33.

———. "Philadelphia's First Scientist: James Logan." *Isis,* XLVII (March 1956): 20-30.

Trachtenberg, Joshua. *Jewish Magic and Superstition: A Study in Folk Religion.* New York: Atheneum, 1974.

Trayser, Donald G. *Barnstable: Three Centuries of a Cape Cod Town.* Hyannis, Mass.: F. B. & F. P. Gross, 1939.

Tucker, Louis Leonard. *Puritan Protagonist: President Clap of Yale College.* Chapel Hill: University of North Carolina Press, 1962.

Turk, F. A. "Charles Morton: His Place in the Historical Development of British Science in the Seventeenth Century." *Journal of the Royal Institute of Cornwall,* N.S., IV (1963): 353-63.

Turnbull, G. H. "George Stirk; Philosopher by Fire." *Transactions of the Colonial Society of Massachusetts,* XXXVIII (1947-51): 219-51.

———. "Robert Child." *Transactions of the Colonial Society of Massachusetts,* XXXVIII (1947-51): 21-53.

Tyler, Moses Coit. *A History of American Literature.* New York: G. P. Putnam's Sons, 1881.

———. *A Literary History of the American Revolution.* New York: Barnes & Noble, 1941.

———. *Three Men of Letters.* New York: G. P. Putnam's Sons, 1895.

Upham, Charles W. *Salem Witchcraft.* New York: Frederick Ungar Publishing Co., 1966.

Van de Wetering, John E. "God, Science, and the Puritan Dilemma." *New England Quarterly,* XXXVIII (December 1965): 494-507.

Veith, Ilza. *Hysteria: The History of a Disease.* Chicago: University of Chicago Press, 1970.

Vernièr, P. "Au Aspect de L'irrationel au XVIIIème Siècle: Le Démonologie et Son Exploitation Littéraire." *Studies in Eighteenth Century Culture.* Vol. 2:

*Irrationalism in the Eighteenth Century.* Harold E. Pagliaro, ed. Cleveland: The Press of Case Western Reserve University, 1972.

Viatte, Auguste. *Les Sources Occultes du Romantisme: Illuminisme—Théosophie, 1770-1820.* Paris: Librairie Ancienne Honoré Champion, 1928.

Vogt, Evon Z. and Hyman, Ray. *Water Witching U.S.A.* Chicago: University of Chicago Press, 1959.

Walker, D. P. "Review of Julio Caro Baroja's *The World of the Witches.*" *New York Review of Books,* IV (June 15, 1965): 16.

———. *Spiritual and Demonic Magic: From Ficino to Campanella.* Leiden: E. J. Brill, 1958.

Walsh, James J. *The Education of the Founding Fathers of the Republic: Scholasticism in the Colonial Colleges.* New York: Fordham University Press, 1935.

Warch, Richard. *School of the Prophets: Yale College, 1701-1740.* New Haven: Yale University Press, 1973.

Warzée, A. "Récherches Bibliographiques sur les Almanachs Belges." *Bulletin du Bibliophile Belge,* VIII: 1-8, 97-113, 177-89, 265-85, 337-76, 425-65.

Watson, Helen R. "The Books They Left: Some 'Liberies' in Edgecomb County, 1733-1783." *The North Carolina Historical Review,* XLVIII (Summer 1971): 245-57.

Watson, John F. *Annals of Philadephia and Pennsylvania.* Privately printed, 1850.

Watts, Emily Stipes. "Jonathan Edwards and the Cambridge Platonists." Unpublished Ph.D. dissertation, University of Illinois, 1963.

Watts, George B. "Thomas Jefferson, The 'Encyclopédie' and the 'Encyclopédie méthodique.'" *French Review,* XXXVIII (January 1965): 318-25.

Weathers, Willie T. "Edward Taylor and the Cambridge Platonists." *American Literature,* XXVI (March 1954): 1-31.

Webb, Wheaton P. "Witches in Cooper County." *New York Folklore Quarterly,* I (February 1945): 5-20.

Weeks, Stephen B. "Libraries and Literature in North Carolina in the Eighteenth Century." *Annual Report of the American Historical Association for the Year 1895.* Washington, D.C.: GPO, 1896.

Wheeler, Joseph Towne. "Books Owned by Marylanders, 1700-1776." *Maryland Historical Magazine,* XXXV (December 1940): 337-53.

———. "Literary Culture in Eighteenth Century Maryland, 1700-1776: Summary of Findings." *Maryland Historical Magazine,* XXXVIII (September 1943): 273-76.

———. "Reading and Other Recreations of Marylanders, 1700-1776." *Maryland Historical Magazine,* XXXVIII (March 1943): 37-55, and (June 1943): 167-80.

———. "Reading Interests of Maryland Planters and Merchants, 1700–1776."

*Maryland Historical Magazine,* XXXVII (March 1942): 26-41, and (September 1942): 291-310.

————. "Reading Interests of the Professional Classes in Colonial Maryland, 1700–1776: The Clergy." *Maryland Historical Magazine,* XXXVI (June 1941): 184-201.

————. "Reading Interests of the Professional Classes in Colonial Maryland, 1700–1776: Lawyers." *Maryland Historical Magazine,* XXXVI (September 1941): 281-301.

White, Andrew Dickson. *A History of the Warfare of Science With Theology.* New York: Dover Publications, Inc., 1960.

White, Newman Ivey, general ed. *The Frank C. Brown Collection of North Carolina Folklore.* Durham, N.C.: Duke University Press, 1952-64.

Whittier, John Greenleaf. *Legends of New England (1831): A Facsimile Reproduction.* Gainesville, Fla.: Scholars Facsimiles & Reprints, 1965.

[Whittier, John Greenleaf]. *Moll Pitcher. A Poem.* Boston: Carter and Hendee, 1932.

————. *The Supernaturalism of New England.* London: Wiley and Putnam, 1847.

Wickersheimer, [Ernest]. "Figures Medico-Astrologiques Des IXe, Xe et XIe Siècles." *Janus* (1914): pp. 157-77.

————. "La Médicine Astrologique Dans Les Almanachs Populaires Du XXe Siecle." *Bulletin de la Société Francaise D'Histoire De La Médecine,* X (1911): 26-39.

Wild, John. *George Berkeley: A Study of His Life and Philosophy.* Cambridge: Harvard University Press, 1936.

Wilkinson, L. P. *The Georgics of Virgil.* Cambridge, Eng.: University Press, 1969.

Wilkinson, Ronald Sterne. "The Alchemical Library of John Winthrop, Jr. (1606-1676) and His Descendants in Colonial America." *Ambix,* XI (February 1963): 33-51, and XIII (October 1966): 139-86.

————. "George Starkey, Physician and Alchemist." *Ambix,* XI (October 1963): 121-52.

————. "New England's Last Alchemists." *Ambix,* X (October 1962): 128-38.

————. "The Problem of the Identity of Eirenaeus Philalethes." *Ambix,* XII (February 1964): 24-43.

*William and Mary College Quarterly Historical Magazine. (William and Mary Quarterly,* 1st Series).

Winsor, Justin, ed. *The Memorial History of Boston.* Boston: James R. Osgood, 1882.

Wish, Harvey. *Society and Thought in Early America.* New York: David McKay Co., Inc., 1950.

Wolf, Edwin, 2nd. "The Library of Ralph Assheton." *Papers of the Bibliographic Society of America,* LVIII (1964): 345-79.

Wright, Esmond, ed. *Benjamin Franklin: A Profile.* New York: Hill and Wang, 1970.

Wright, Louis B. *The First Gentlemen of Virginia.* San Marino, Calif.: The Huntington Library, 1940.

Wright, Thomas Goddard. *Literary Culture in Early New England, 1620-1730.* New York: Russell & Russell, 1966.

Yates, Francis A. *The Art of Memory.* Chicago: University of Chicago Press, 1966.

―――. *Giordano Bruno and the Hermetic Tradition.* Chicago: University of Chicago Press, 1964.

Young, Edward J. "Subjects for Master's Degree in Harvard College from 1655-1791." *Proceedings of the Massachusetts Historical Society,* XVIII (June 1880): 119-51.

# Index